AMERICAN FILM CRITICISM

AMERICAN FILM CRITICISM

CRITICISM

From the Beginnings to *Citizen Kane*

Reviews of Significant Films at the Time
They First Appeared

Edited by

STANLEY KAUFFMANN

with

BRUCE HENSTELL

GREENWOOD PRESS, PUBLISHERS
WESTPORT, CONNECTICUT

Library of Congress Cataloging in Publication Data

Kauffmann, Stanley, 1916-   comp.
    American film criticism, from the beginnings to
Citizen Kane.

    Reprint of the 1972 ed. published by Liveright,
New York.
    Bibliography: p.
    Includes index.
    1. Moving-pictures--Reviews. I. Henstell,
Bruce, joint comp. II. Title.
[PN1995.K293 1979]   791.43'7   78-31669
ISBN 0-313-21246-5

Published in 1972 by Liveright, New York

Reprinted with the permission of Stanley Kauffmann.

Reprinted in 1979 by Greenwood Press, Inc.
51 Riverside Avenue, Westport, CT. 06880

Printed in the United States of America

10 9 8 7 6 5 4 3 2 1

ACKNOWLEDGMENTS

Deep gratitude, from Bruce Henstell and myself, for help from: Anne Schlosser, Head Librarian, Charles K. Feldman Library, Center for Advanced Film Studies; Mildred Simpson and the staff of the Margaret Herrick Library, Academy of Motion Picture Arts and Sciences; Brooke Whiting, Special Collections, University of California at Los Angeles; Kaarina Flint, Reference and Inter-Library Loans Librarian of the same university; Charles Silver, Film Study Center, Museum of Modern Art in New York; Paul Myers and the staff of the Theater Collection, Library and Museum of the Performing Arts at Lincoln Center.

Thanks to Sam Melner, formerly of Liveright, for initial help; to Doug and Ruth Hollis, Dennis Sinclair, Richard Kahlenberg, Marvin Felheim, James R. Silke, and Robert Sklar.

Thanks to Frances Henstell.

And to Laura Kauffmann.

S.K.

Patterson Murphy, reprinted by permission of *Esquire Magazine,* © 1939 (renewed 1967) by Esquire, Inc.

Clifton Fadiman for permission to reprint "A Night at the Opera" by Clifton Fadiman.

Francis Fergusson for permission to reprint "City Lights" and "Le Million" by Francis Fergusson.

Articles originally published in *Exceptional Photoplays* and *The National Board of Review Magazine* are reprinted with permission of *Films in Review,* copyright 1920, 1921, 1923, 1925, 1927, 1930, 1931, 1932 by the National Board of Review of Motion Pictures, Inc.

The late Paul Goodman for permission to reprint "Faulty Cinematics of Hollywood" and "The Proustian Camera Eye."

B. H. Haggin for permission to reprint "Fantasia" by B. H. Haggin; copyright 1941 by *The Nation,* © 1949 by B. H. Haggin; reprinted by permission of the author.

Lewis Jacobs and Mrs. Elizabeth Goldman for permission to reprint "The Aframerican Cinema" by H. A. Potamkin.

Nannine Joseph and the Estate of Gilbert Seldes for permission to reprint "Dead End" by Gilbert Seldes.

Lincoln Kirstein for permission to reprint "Dancing in Films" by Lincoln Kirstein.

Pare Lorentz for permission to reprint "Blotto" and "Free and Easy" from *Judge;* Pare Lorentz and The Condé Nast Publications, Inc. for permission to reprint "I Am a Fugitive from a Chain Gang," "She Done Him Wrong," and "M" from *Vanity Fair.*

Dr. Edna O. Meyers for permission to reprint "Mr. Deeds Goes to Town" by Robert Stebbins (pseud. Sidney Meyers).

The Nation for permission to reprint articles originally published in that journal.

For articles originally published in *The New Republic,* acknowledgment is due to that journal and to: Bruce Bliven for permission to reprint "The Covered Wagon" by Bruce Bliven (copyright 1923 by *The New Republic*); Farrar, Straus & Giroux, Inc. for permission to reprint "The Gold Rush" by Edmund Wilson. A revised version of "The Gold Rush" appears in *The American Earthquake* by Edmund Wilson, copyright © 1958 by Edmund Wilson. Published by Octagon Books.

Lewis M. Isaacs, Jr., and the Estate of Stark Young for permission to reprint "The Circus" and "Greta Garbo" by Stark Young; Nannine Joseph and Signe Toksvig for permission to reprint "The Kid" by Francis Hackett; Nannine Joseph and the Estate of Kenneth Macgowan for permission to reprint "On the Screen" by Kenneth Macgowan (reprinted in *Beyond the Screen* by Kenneth Macgowan, copyright 1965 by the Estate of Kenneth

Macgowan); Nannine Joseph and the Estate of Gilbert Seldes for permission to reprint "The Cocoanuts" by Gilbert Seldes; Ruth Limmer for permission to reprint "Sunrise" by Louise Bogan; Temple University Press for permission to reprint "It Happened One Night," "The Informer," "Words and Music," "Modern Times," "Secret Agent," "The Philadelphia Story," "The Bank Dick" by Otis Ferguson. (Reprinted in *The Film Criticism of Otis Ferguson,* edited by Robert Wilson. © 1971 by Temple University. All rights reserved. Published 1971.)

Articles originally published in the *New York Post* are reprinted by permission of the *New York Post:* "The Three Musketeers" by P. F. Reniers, © 1921, New York Post Corporation; "Grand Illusion" by Archer Winsten, © 1938, New York Post Corporation.

Articles originally published in *The New York Times* are © 1922, 1934, 1935, 1937, 1938, 1939 by The New York Times Company. Reprinted by permission.

Acknowledgment is due to *The New Yorker* for "Ben Hur" by Ted Shane, reprinted by permission, copr. © 1926, 1954 The New Yorker Magazine, Inc.; "Little Caesar" by John Mosher, reprinted by permission, copr. © 1931, 1959 The New Yorker Magazine, Inc.; "Monkey Business" by John Mosher, reprinted by permission, copr. © 1931, 1959 The New Yorker Magazine, Inc.; "Scarface" by John Mosher, reprinted by permission, copr. © 1932, 1960 The New Yorker Magazine, Inc.; "Citizen Kane" by John Mosher, reprinted by permission, copr. © 1941, 1969 The New Yorker Magazine, Inc.

Partisan Review and the late Paul Goodman for permission to reprint "Chaplin Again, Again and Again" © 1940 by *Partisan Review.*

Norman Holmes Pearson, owner of the copyright, for permission to reprint "Passion of Joan of Arc" by H. D. (Hilda Doolittle).

Henry T. Rockwell for permission to reprint articles by Robert E. Sherwood originally published in *Life.*

Time for permission to reprint "Daybreak." Reprinted by permission from *Time,* The Weekly Newsmagazine; © Time Inc.

Articles originally published in *The New York Herald Tribune* are reprinted by permission of W. C. C. Publishing Company, Inc.: "The Torrent," "Anna Christie," "Little Caesar," "The Public Enemy," "Trouble In Paradise," "King Kong," "M," and "The Private Life of Henry VIII," by Richard Watts, Jr., copyright 1926, 1930, 1931, 1932, 1933, New York Herald Tribune, Inc.; "Mother," "Camille," "The Grapes of Wrath," by Howard Barnes, copyright 1934, 1937, 1940, New York Herald Tribune, Inc.

INTRODUCTION

I discovered film criticism some time in 1933. Up to then, although I had already been an avid filmgoer for some ten years, it had not occurred to me that films could be discussed in terms relative to those used by good critics of the theater or literature or music. Then one day in my college library I picked up a copy of *The Nation* and read a review by William Troy—I can't recall the title of the film—in which he compared a sequence in a new picture with a similar sequence in a previous one to show relations of style. I'm not sure that my jaw actually dropped, but that's the feeling I remember.

In a sense, this anthology dates from that day, but the more immediate impulse toward it began tugging at me in 1958. That was the year in which *Agee on Film* was published, a year that marks the beginning of change in general attitudes toward serious film criticism. Few posthumous recognitions have been better deserved than James Agee's, but a widespread inference from his book was: "Oh, so *that's* when serious American film criticism began—'way back in 1943." Before Agee, a presumable desert. Lately, some collections of individual critics and some historical studies that quote early reviews have helped to expose that fallacy, but misconceptions about the pre-Agee days, even among film professionals, can hardly be called dead. Memories of William Troy, strengthened by random researches into other past critics during the last ten years, have kept nagging at me. At last the confluence of that nagging with some other factors made this book possible.

A few quick clarifications. All the critics in this anthology are American, but they discuss both American and foreign films. Facing the fact that many of these writers are unknown today, I have arranged the book by film, not by critic. The plan was to trace a way through the early years of American criticism using memorable films as guideposts, rather than the names of unremembered critics or critics remembered otherwise.

The book begins, as the King of Hearts ordered, at the beginning, but it disobeys him and does not go on to the end. It stops. First, there was the matter of length. Second, I wanted to concentrate on the pre-Agee period. Third, I concluded with *Citizen Kane* because it came at the right time for the second purpose and because it is a peak that contrasts dramatically with the beginning.

This is not a history-by-anthology, nor a cross section of every kind of film writing that was being done in those decades. The aim, at its optimum, was to select important films and to find at least one important review about each, written at the time when the film was first shown in the United States. But this was only the ideal. Not all the films discussed in the book are deathless nor is all the criticism Parnassian. I have sometimes chosen a lesser film because a valuable review had been written about it, sometimes a "merely" interesting review because it dealt with an important film. But the aim was as described, and where the book deviates from it, I hope it supplies other satisfactions.

Some general critical articles are also included. In the earliest years, reviews worth reprinting hardly exist (for reasons given in my comments later), but there was a lot of interesting general writing at the time. In the latter sections, general articles are occasionally used for textural and supportive reasons. But the heavy emphasis is on reviews of specific films, American and foreign.

One way to use the book is as a reference work, to find what a contemporary critic said about a particular film when it was new. (More than one critic when the film is important enough and good reviews were available.) But the book's primary purpose is to show how film criticism developed in this country; how very quickly some of it became valuable; and how much that is valuable has been forgotten—or has not even been forgotten, is unknown.

To dispose of the obvious, I do not agree with all the views expressed, but I saw little point in harassing these writers with my arguments. My comments are intended only to supply information helpful to the appreciation of the reviews presented. I add only two comments here.

First, one can discern three groups of critics, distinguishable by date of birth, in the short, forty-five-year period covered. There are the critics who were adults when film was invented, those writing before 1910. Then there are the critics who were born about the same time as film and grew along with it. Third, there are the critics who came to consciousness when film was already a force in the cultural environment. Frank E. Woods has some of the tone of a Cortez; Gilbert Seldes insists that popularity does not necessarily mean inferiority; Harry Alan Potamkin neither discovers nor demonstrates, he acts on common assumptions.

But the assumptions were not all that common. That is my second point. When we read modern film criticism, or read earlier criticism today, it seems matter-of-course that films should be discussed seriously. This was certainly not always so. To be a serious film critic in the post-Agee age

is to be culturally apposite; earlier, there was something of cultural heroism in the act—in the United States, at least. Some critics had devotees
but nothing comparable to the present, and even some of the devotees
were patronizing. When W. H. Auden wrote his famous—I would say in-
famous—letter of praise about Agee to *The Nation* in 1944, he specified
that he did not care for movies and rarely saw them, and he deplored
Agee's subject as "rather unimportant." (The view persists, by implication;
when a selection of William Troy's literary essays was published posthu-
mously in 1967, neither of the eulogists who provided introductions saw
fit to mention that Troy had ever written a line of film criticism.) From
the changed context of our own time, we might remember that, in addition
to their other qualities, these earlier men and women had convictions that
required courage.

All of my comments precede the articles to which they refer and are in-
dented to distinguish them from the text. I have not used asterisks and footnotes in order to avoid clutter and to help maintain the feeling of reading
topical reviews. There are bibliographical notes pertaining to my comments,
but they are placed in the back of the book, for those who want them.

In almost all instances, I have used the title of the film discussed as the
title of the review, even if there was a different title on the piece when
published. I have done this for consistency and for the reader's ease in
locating reviews—and also because many magazine titles are not the author's, anyway. In a few cases where the author's title was essential to the
review, I have retained it. Titles of articles, as opposed to reviews, are un-
altered. Some reviews are excerpted from columns that also reviewed other
films, but no single review has been abridged. The only alterations have
been the deletion of the names of theaters or studios where they were
completely parenthetical, the correction of spelling and punctuation, and
the uniform usage of an author's name. It is always Robert E. Sherwood,
for instance, although some early columns were signed R. E. Sherwood.
If there is no biographical comment the first time a writer appears in the
book, it simply means I could find nothing about him.

Most of the research for reviews and articles was done by Bruce Henstell, who began with a plan I drew up. Luckily for the book, his expertise
and curiosity took him well beyond that plan. The result owes much to his
enthusiasm.

The selection and arrangement are mine, as are all comments and notes.

This book is only a sampler. I omitted at least an equal amount of material
that I have in hand, and the material in hand is only a fraction of what
I know exists—itself a small fraction of what must exist outside my knowl-

edge. There is no claim that reams of superlative film criticism lie buried in the files or that this anthology contains the best of everything that was written in the period. I do maintain that there are surprises and pleasures and rewards in the criticism of those first forty-five years and that this book is an introduction to them.

STANLEY KAUFFMANN

CONTENTS

Part Two
THE FEATURE FILM

Part Three
SOUND

Part One

THE BEGINNINGS

A superior number indicates a bibliographical note.
These notes begin on page 421.

The first theatrical exhibition of film in the United States took place in New York on April 23, 1896—coincidentally, Shakespeare's birthday—at Koster and Bial's Music Hall on Herald Square, the future site of Macy's department store. The following is a review of that show. The last paragraph indicates the relation of film to other matters on the bill, a relation that persisted for about four years.[1]

Edison had competitors in the manufacture of motion picture equipment, but he was the first to make theatrical use of the invention. Note that this first film was in color (for more on early color see p. 13) and that the screen figures were smaller than life-size.

EDISON'S VITASCOPE CHEERED

"Projecting Kinetescope" Exhibited for First Time at Koster & Bial's

The new thing at Koster and Bial's last night was Edison's vitascope, exhibited for the first time. The ingenious inventor's latest toy is a projection of his kinetescope figures, in stereopticon fashion, upon a white screen in a darkened hall. In the center of the balcony of the big music hall is a curious object, which looks from below like the double turret of a big monitor. In the front of each half of it are two oblong holes. The turret is neatly covered with the blue velvet brocade which is the favorite decorative material in this house. The white screen used on the stage is framed like a picture. The moving figures are about half life-size.

When the hall was darkened last night a buzzing and roaring were heard in the turret, and an unusually bright light fell upon the screen. Then came into view two precious blonde young persons of the variety stage, in pink and blue dresses, doing the umbrella dance with commendable celerity. Their motions were clearly defined. When they vanished, a view of an angry surf breaking on a sandy beach near a stone pier amazed the spectators. The waves tumbled in furiously, and the foam of the breakers flew high in the air. A burlesque boxing match between a tall, thin comedian and a short, fat one, a comic allegory called *The Monroe Doctrine,* an instant of motion in Hoyt's farce, *A Milk White Flag,* repeated over and over again, and a skirt dance by a tall blonde completed the views, which were all wonderfully real and singularly exhilarating. For the spectator's imagination filled the atmosphere with electricity, as sparks crackled around the swiftly moving, lifelike figures.

So enthusiastic was the appreciation of the crowd long before this extraordinary exhibition was finished that vociferous cheering was heard. There were loud calls for Mr. Edison, but he made no response.

The vitascope is only one feature of an excellent bill at Koster and Bial's, in which, of course, the admirable art of the London monologue man, [Albert] Chevalier, is a notable item. There are persons who admire and understand stage art who do not go to the music halls. For their sake it is well to say that to hear and see Chevalier in such selections as "The Nipper's Lullaby," "My Old Dutch," and "The Old Kent Road" amply atones for any irritation an over-sensitive mind may receive from, say, Miss Florrie West's expression of her opinion of Eliza, and her juvenile confidences as to the information on delicate subjects imparted to her by Johnny Jones. People whose minds are not oversensitive find Miss West intensely amusing. But everybody likes Chevalier, though it is doubtful if the perfect naturalness and delicate finish of his impersonations are generally appreciated. He is not "sensational."

The New York Times, April 24, 1896

In the next decade film activity bubbled and boiled, but there was little that could be called film criticism. Almost all the writing about motion pictures, plentiful as it was, merely described them, or discussed them in social or economic or scientific terms.

During the earliest days, just before and just after the turn of the century, films were fragments—scenic views, newsreel items, brief comic bits—not much more than demonstrations of the invention. In 1903, a full seven years after the first theatrical exhibition at Koster and Bial's, Edwin S. Porter, production head of the Edison Studio in New York, made the first complete American film drama, *The Life of an American Fireman,* which ran eight minutes. It was a success. Porter then made a film of *Uncle Tom's Cabin,* which ran twelve minutes, and still in that same crucial year of 1903 he made *The Great Train Robbery,* which ran ten minutes and was even more successful.

Porter's ideas prompted quick imitation by the Lubin company of Philadelphia. Their catalogue quotes a review of the Lubin train robbery film. Like most reviews of the day, it was largely a synopsis.

THE GREAT TRAIN ROBBERY
What *The Philadelphia Inquirer* of June 26th, 1904 has to say about Lubin's Great Picture

The Great Train Robbery has proved a "thriller" in nearly all the larger cities of the United States. They have been a source of wonder as to how photographs of such a drama could have been taken in the Rocky Mountains.

The picture play begins with a view in the lonesome telegraph station, in which an operator, receiving train orders, is overcome, bound hand and foot, gagged, and left unconscious on the floor by the desperadoes; proceeds with the capture of the train, murder of the fireman, killing of the express messenger, blowing open of the safe, holdup of passengers, and shooting of one who attempts to escape; and winds up with a horseback ride through the mountains with bags of booty, a wild, weird dance in a log cabin, pursuit by the sheriff's posse, and death of all the robbers.

There is a great amount of shooting. The smoke of the pistols is plainly seen, and men drop dead right and left, but no sound is heard. Nevertheless, while witnessing the exhibition women put their fingers in their ears to shut out the noise of the firing.

The fireman attacks his assailants, with six shooters in his face, while his only weapon is the shovel, and he fails to brain his man by a narrow margin.

After one of the robbers gets him down and beats his brains out with a lump of coal, his body is picked up and thrown off the tender.

The desperadoes are a tough-looking lot. The horses look like some of Colonel Cody's bronchos. They dash through the Orange Mountains with the surefootedness of burros. The men are good riders. In the pursuit by the sheriff one is shot in the back as he dashes madly downhill, and the way in which he tumbles from his horse and strikes the ground leaves the spectators wondering if he is not a dummy, for it does not seem possible that a man could take such a fall and live.

The motion picture business boomed. Theatrical journals like *The New York Dramatic Mirror* started film departments. Film trade journals were founded. The first, begun in 1906, was *Views and Film Index,* followed in 1907 by *The Moving Picture World* and *Moving Picture News.*

Films were still being made in no more than one reel, and ran about twelve minutes or less. There were several on any one bill, and bills were changed frequently. Reviews, where they existed, were short and not deep; the pictures themselves were short and did not stay around long. Most reviews were still plot synopses with a few comments—especially in trade journals for the guidance of exhibitors.

This trade review, of an obscure film, is interesting for several reasons. First, it shows that the Civil War, which had been a reality for many yet living, became a film subject quite early. Second, it shows, in its last sentence, how brief most reviews were and, in its first sentence, that film criticism had already developed its own temporal perspective. The phrase "in a long time" in 1908!

Also, it shows that the film medium was developing its own inner, temporal sense. The point that the reviewer objects to, the distention of a dramatic moment, was evidently accomplished by intercutting. The invention of this device has sometimes been attributed to D. W. Griffith, who was in fact finishing his first film as this review was being published.

Actors were not then identified by producers. The studios were afraid that if actors' names became famous, they would want bigger salaries. Moreover, in this first decade, some actors, recruited from the theater, were afraid that screen identification would hurt their stage careers.

THE BLUE AND THE GREY

No film that has been issued by any company in a long time can be classed with *The Blue and the Grey* for consistent dramatic force, moving heart interest, and clearly told story. Not for a single moment is the spectator in doubt as to the import of the thrilling situations and action. The manner, also, in which it is played, costumed, and staged, if we may be permitted such a term, is beyond praise. The scenes move rapidly and straight to the point, but not too rapidly for the purpose of the story. Briefly, the plot hinges on the love of a young Northern officer in the Civil War for a Virginia girl, the daughter of a Confederate general. The young man is carried wounded to her home and nursed back to life. While there, it is made to appear by circumstances that he has assisted in the escape through Union lines of the girl's brother, a bearer of rebel dispatches, from Gen.

Lee. The Union officer is tried, convicted, and sentenced to be shot. The girl appeals to Gen. Grant in vain and then rides to Washington and begs a pardon from President Lincoln, securing which, she hastens back in time to save her lover's life. In only one point does the construction of the story appear faulty and that is when the young officer has been stood up to be shot and the command of "fire" is about to be given, the scene is shifted to Washington, where the girl pleads with President Lincoln. The spectator is thus asked to imagine the firing squad suspending the fatal discharge while the girl rides from Washington to the Union camp. It would have been better if the Washington scene had been inserted somewhat earlier. The impersonation of Lee is very good, but those of Grant and Lincoln are hardly mature enough, although they are readily recognized. Photographically, the film is a little blurred at times, but these are all minor defects and *The Blue and the Grey,* although it might be called hackneyed on the stage, is such a notable step in advance in dramatic film production that it fully warrants this extended review.

The New York Dramatic Mirror, June 20, 1908

On June 18, 1908 D. W. Griffith, a thirty-three-year-old actor and playwright, began to direct films for the American Mutoscope and Biograph Company, afterward the Biograph Company, whose studios were at 11 East 14th St., New York City; and began to realize and refine film language. Griffith worked for Biograph until October 1913, during which time he made about 450 films, the vast majority of them in one reel.[2]

Here is a review of his first film, nothing more than a synopsis but included here because, unknowingly, it is a milestone in world cultural history.

THE ADVENTURES OF DOLLIE

One of the most remarkable cases of child-stealing is depicted in this Biograph picture, showing the thwarting by a kind Providence of the attempt to kidnap for revenge a pretty little girl by a gypsy. On the lawn of a country residence we find the little family, comprising father, mother, and little Dollie, their daughter. In front of the grounds there flows a picturesque stream, to which the mother and little one go to watch the boys fishing. There has come into the neighborhood a band of those peripatetic nomads of the Zingani type, whose ostensible occupation is selling baskets and reed ware, but their real motive is pillage. While the mother and child are seated on the wall beside the stream, one of these gypsies approaches and offers for sale several baskets. A refusal raises his ire, and he seizes the woman's purse and is about to make off with it when the husband, hearing her cries of alarm, rushes down to her aid, and with a heavy snakewhip lashes the gypsy unmercifully, leaving great welts upon his swarthy body, at the same time arousing the venom of his black heart. The gypsy leaves the scene vowing vengeance, and the little family go back to the lawn, where the father amuses little Dollie with a game of battledore and shuttlecock. During the game the mother calls papa to the house for an instant. This is the gypsy's chance, for he has been hiding in the bushes all the while. He seizes the child and carries her to his camp, where he gags and conceals her in a water-cask. A search of the gypsy's effects by the distracted father proves fruitless, and the gypsy with the aid of his wife gathers up his traps into his wagon, placing the cask containing the child on the back. Down the road they go at breakneck speed, and as they ford a stream the cask falls off the wagon into the water and is carried away by the current. Next we see the cask floating down the stream toward a waterfall, over which it goes; then through the seething spray of the rapids, and on, on, until it finally enters the quiet cove of the first scene, where it is brought ashore by the fisher boys. Hearing strange sounds emitted from the barrel, the boys call for the bereft father, who is still searching for the lost one. Breaking the head from the barrel, the amazed and happy parents now fold in their arms their loved one, who is not much worse off for her marvelous experience. Length, 713 feet.

The Moving Picture World, July 18, 1908

A paradox occurred. Criticism of specific pictures remained in the long-synopsis-and-brief-comment form, at the same time that, especially in film trade journals, articles addressed large critical-esthetic problems. Evidently this was because of the difficulty in criticizing brief items that flitted by rapidly in the theaters; it was much easier to discuss the phenomenon as a whole.

Thus at a surprisingly early date comes an essay, one among many published then, treating film esthetics with a penetration that might have been expected only after more than the twelve-years' life of the medium—and that life made up only of very brief works.

Note the continuing comparison with foreign films, a theme that began with the beginning of American criticism, recurred constantly, and, explicitly or implicitly, has not stopped.

THE MOVING PICTURE DRAMA AND THE ACTED DRAMA
Some Points of Comparison as to Technique

ROLLIN SUMMERS

That the moving picture drama is an art, is a proposition as yet not well recognized by the public at large. That it has a genuine technique, largely in common with the acted drama yet in part peculiar to itself, is a proposition which seems not to be well recognized within the moving picture field itself. It is important to the development of the moving picture that these two propositions be established. It is not likely, however, that the public at large will recognize the first proposition until the producers begin to take the second proposition more seriously.

THE PRESENTATION OF THE CAST AND PLOT

No serious discussion should be required to make it plain that in most of the fundamental principles the technique of the moving picture play is identical with that of the acted drama. For example, the principle of unity of action, i.e., the presentation of a single consistent story without irrelevant matters, is equally a requirement of both types of play. If a film is unscientific in this respect it may still have interest at points of its progress, yet its final complete impression will be bad.

Similarly, the moving picture requires as strictly as does the acted drama that adequate motivation be presented for the actions of the characters. It should take as serious and as clearly expressed a quarrel to separate two moving picture lovers as it does to estrange two lovers of the real stage.

Again, the demands of "action" in the acted drama are that there shall be an element of doubt and suspense in every moment of the play. The requirement is the same in the play to be presented through moving pictures.

The acted drama must explain itself. Its story must be unfolded bit by bit, without explanation, from a prologue or lecture. The moving picture play should be similarly constructed. In the acted drama, to establish the identity and the interrelations of the characters is of prime importance. It is equally important in the moving picture. (A recent film showed a large preliminary picture of each of the characters with the name underneath. This is a helpful device and probably is as justifiable as the publication of the "cast of characters" in a program.)

These propositions as to the similarity of the two types might be indefinitely continued and would all seem obvious enough, yet nothing is more common than to see them disregarded. The impression seems to prevail that much more carelessness will be overlooked in a moving picture play than in one of the actual stage. Quite the contrary is the case. The public is more helpless to express itself in the case of the moving picture, but the wise manager can note effects, and the reputation of a given producer for bad or for effective pictures is thereby established. To the extent that these two types of play are alike, their respective techniques are equally strict. The authors and experts employed by the producer should be primarily familiar with the technique of the acted drama. They may then add to a firm foundation their knowledge of the special opportunities and requirements of motion photography.

When perfection is accomplished in those points of moving picture technique which are identical with the principles of the acted drama, it still remains to recognize the particular technique of the moving picture drama itself. Every art has its peculiar advantages and disadvantages growing out of the particular medium in which it expresses itself. It is the limitations and advantages of its particular means of expression that give rise to its own particular technique. An observation of the limitations and advantages of motion photography will suggest the particular technical laws of the moving picture play.

THE IMPORTANCE OF PANTOMIME

The most apparent limitation of the moving picture is its powerlessness to use dialogue. A primary means of expression is thus eliminated and only pantomime remains. This fact causes an immediate distinction between the plot of the drama proper and that of the moving picture. In every acted drama there are facts supposed to have happened before the rise of the curtain. These facts furnish the motives of one or more of the characters and add a certain amount of complication to the story. They are made known to the audience incidentally at one time or another and always by means of dialogue. In the moving picture, the plot must be complete without such facts. This seems obvious enough, yet it is the attempt to introduce past events and relationships into a moving picture that frequently leaves an entire scene worse than obscure and meaningless. All necessary facts in a moving picture play must be visibly presented. The heroine cannot tell the story of her life in a moving picture—yet this is exactly the sort of thing that some pictures attempt to do.

It is a corollary to the above principle that events which in the acted drama are supposed to take place off-stage or between acts must be actually presented in the moving picture play.

A much more serious difficulty than the inability to present previous or off-stage events is the moving picture's inability to express the precise mental states of the characters. *"I go, but I will return,"* says the villain of the melodrama, and a shudder of apprehension for the heroine's safety seizes the audience. *"I go"* is an idea that the moving picture villain may express by actually going, but the fate-laden line, *"I will return,"* is impossible to him. He may shake his fist, but that is all.

The principle to be deduced from this is that the plot of the moving picture drama should avoid the necessity of presenting precise trends of thought. The elemental emotions, love, hatred, jealousy, despair, any of these may be effectively presented by the moving picture, but the Ibsen plots are not proper moving picture material.

To the limitation of lack of dialogue, however, there is this possible exception, that where the action of the moving picture shows that a letter or written message has been received the message may be thrown as a large picture on the canvas. This is, of course, pure device. The more artistic way being to avoid it. On the other hand, in the acted drama it is frequently necessary to look at the program to find such facts as "Ten years elapse," "The interior of Duke B.'s castle," etc. It seems equally justifiable to use the device of the printed message, and if it is presented in such sequence that curiosity is aroused as to its contents it will probably be received by the audience without substantial loss of illusion. Printed explanations thrown on the screen before scenes are not at all similar in principle and are entirely crude and unjustifiable. They destroy the suspense and interest by outlining the scope of the scene in advance.

ADVANTAGE OF SCENIC CHANGES

What the moving picture play loses in lack of dialogue it to a large extent makes up in certain great advantages which it has over all acted drama. The unlimited number of scenes which may be shown is the most striking of these advantages.

A large percentage of acted plays seem to have been fairly contorted out of all semblance to truth in order to get the action to take place in one or two localities for each act. It is often utterly ridiculous to see how all the principal characters show up first here and then there without any adequate excuse except that the author needs them. In the moving picture play, on the contrary, the principal characters, having been once well identified, may be separated and the scene may shift from one to the other and back again. If the sequence of the scenes is well contrived there is a decided gain in the quality of the action and a perfected illusion of reality in the method.

The danger to be avoided in such change of scenes is that of giving episodic or substantially unimportant facts a scene for themselves. This would undoubtedly over-emphasize them and cause disproportion just as it would in acted drama. For the presentation of events that actually carry forward the plot, however, there seems to be no technical limit on the number of scenes.

The discussion of the possible number of scenes suggests the advantages of the moving picture play as to selection of scenes. The moving picture play has the whole world for its stage. Lately some of the producers have discovered that it pays to travel many miles to get impressive scenery. The possibilities of the moving picture in this respect are, however, not yet fully realized. A recent French picture showed an actual lighthouse on the cliffs with the big breakers rolling in. The setting was there in this case and it lacked only a beautiful story to make the picture a poem in photography. A genuine story of the sea would have been a well-received blessing to thousands of inland audiences. The actual plot, however, was a dirty little French intrigue, thus actually letting the play spoil the scenery. The moving picture producer has a rare chance to get "atmosphere" into his stories and to heighten illusion by the use of proper scenery.

WELL-TRAINED ACTORS A NECESSITY

Perhaps the most important feature of the technique of moving pictures concerns the manner in which they are acted rather than the details of their authorship. From the proposition that the moving picture cannot rely upon dialogue it follows that it must develop the art of pantomime to the highest point.

This proposition is apparently not fully appreciated by many producers. A demonstration of this may be seen by comparing a good French dramatic subject with a first-class American film. The French seem natural adepts at pantomime. An arch of the eyebrows, a shrug of the shoulders, a gesture of the hands, all these are aids in expression to them. The American relies in his daily life more entirely upon his words, and the American actor is likewise comparatively dependent on them. The result is that, other things being equal, the French dramatic film will noticeably surpass the American product. The possibilities of pure gesture should be an interesting investigation. Moving picture actors should study their parts with reference to bringing out every possible point by legitimate pantomime. If this is done with artistic seriousness it will improve many films such as heretofore have been entirely lifeless and mechanical on one hand or have been orgies of gesticulation upon the other.

The last paragraphs suggested the further technical point that where shades of emotion are to be expressed the pictures as a rule should be at close range. The moving picture may present figures greater than life size without loss of illusion, and if an emotional climax is well worked up, the power of good pictures to convey these phases of emotion by the facial expression of the actors is greater than that of the actual stage.

It is probably not worth while to try to formulate into terms all the details of the technique of the moving picture drama. Mechanical invention may vary its precise needs at any time. On the other hand, it must not be overlooked that it has a technique which is worth close observation and which must be followed if even approximate perfection is to be gained.

The Moving Picture World, September 19, 1908

The anonymous author of this article is another of the first serious American film critics. His piece is astonishing at this early date both for the complexity of film experience on which it draws and for the intricacy of analysis.

Note his use of the phrase "long or complicated story" and remember that we are still in a world of ten- to twelve-minute films.

Note, too, the reference to color. Both color and sound were conceptually present from the beginning of film and were repeatedly employed in different methods. Neither element was an afterthought that came into being sometime later. Color came into general use almost a decade after sound, but, like sound, the idea of color had been there all along, waiting the right technological means of entry.

Pathécolor was one of the first processes to have a trade name and consisted of hand-painting the film.[3]

EARMARKS OF MAKERS

The confirmed visitor to moving picture theaters learns in time to recognize almost at sight the product of different film manufacturers, by certain peculiarities independent of the trade-marks that now accompany all films. Some of these distinguishing characteristics are impossible to describe, being more in the nature of vague, general impressions than anything else; but there are other differences that are conspicuous and easily pointed out —infallible earmarks of the particular studios from which the pictures come. It may be the faces of the actors, the scenic backgrounds, the style of acting, the quality or peculiarities of the photography, or it may be the picture story itself and the manner in which it is constructed or handled that gives the information, but whatever it is, there is something about each manufacturer's films that distinguish them from the films of others. It will be interesting to inquire into these differences of style and at the same time discuss the good and bad points of each maker.

First, let us classify the film product of the world as American and foreign. It is easy to recognize the imported dramatic or comedy pictures by a number of clear marks of difference. Most foreign pictures come from France and Italy, and if they are outdoor scenes we know them by the architecture of the buildings, by the costumes worn, or by the national characteristics of face and figure of the actors. We will also note that the French and Italian performers are more adept than any other nationality in talking with their hands, their shoulders, their bodies, and their facial expressions. In this the French are rather better than the Italian, but both are better than the American, who in turn are so far ahead of the English as to be almost out of sight. Indeed, the English are easily the poorest pantomimists for moving pictures on the face of the globe. French and Italian pictures also rarely tell a long or complicated story. They are apt to consist of some simple episode or amusing situation worked out in the action with a nicety of detail that pictures from other countries seldom approach. Frequently, to American eyes, these episodes appear trivial and the comic situations silly and childish, but the excellence of the acting very often makes up for these objections. French comedy is superior to the Italian, but Italian makers exhibit generally a first-class ability to turn out pathetic or tragic pictures. Photographically, foreign films rank high. They are clear and sharp in outline, and one seldom sees in them the spots or imperfections noted so often in American pictures, due, it is said, to difference in atmospheric conditions between Europe and America. On this point the writer was informed by an official of the American Vitagraph Company that the atmosphere in America, being dryer than in Europe, fine particles of dust settle on American films in the making, and these dust particles, being magnified on the curtain, appear as serious imperfections. However, this defect may be remedied in time, and, in fact, the French Pathé Company claims to have found the remedy and to be making practical use of it in its American studio, where films for the American trade are printed from negatives imported from its foreign studios. Before leaving the subject of foreign films, it should be noted that colored, spectacular pictures, usually telling magic or fairy stories, and sometimes religious allegories, are almost invariably French, coming either from the studios of Pathé Frères, Méliès, or Gaumont. Suggestive or immoral pictures are no longer brought over from the other side—at least they are never shown in public, as the foreign makers long ago discovered that the American exhibitors would not accept them. Indeed, so careful have foreign producers become in this respect that they frequently go to the other extreme, and one rarely sees, even where stage dances are being represented, female performers displaying the lower limbs in tights above the knees.

While American dramatic or comedy pictures as a rule are not so good in pantomime as the French and Italian, they are very much superior in plot and in the literary merit of the stories they tell. Of course, trash is too often produced on both sides of the ocean, but American trash generally has more novelty of idea than foreign trash. Some American manufacturers also will spend on elaborate scenic effects more money for a single picture than would ever be dreamed of in Europe for a dozen ordinary productions. In fact, nearly all American films are superior to the usual European output in this respect, and they appear to be improving constantly along this line, as they are in constructive and photographic qualities and in the acting ability displayed. However, in the last-named particular the American still has much to learn from the foreigner. Take one instance to illustrate. When a foreign picture (not English) shows a farmer or peasant, the character appears to be real and genuine, not the work of an actor at all. Costume and action are faithful to the part represented. On this side, on the other hand, the actor, speaking generally, cannot conceal himself and his theatrical training. If he is a farmer he is too often a stage farmer, with the inevitable wisp of whiskers on the chin. Nevertheless, speaking still in a general way, American picture actors, as they become better trained in the art, are showing constant improvement all along the line, and American picture plot, construction, and stage direction are growing better and better with each successive month and year. In the end *The Mirror* has no hesitation in predicting American films will lead the world in all essential qualities, as they do now in the important particulars already referred to.

Let us now examine briefly some of the peculiarities, faults, and merits of individual manufacturers, advanced not in an overcritical sense, nor as an infallible verdict, but for what it is worth, as the conscientious opinion of a single observer.

Pathé Frères will be considered first because this firm is not only the largest producer of moving picture films in Europe, but is the chief one of the world. What has already been said of French pictures as a class may be said in particular of this firm's output—only more so. Most Pathé actors have been long in the same employ and are readily recognized by the spectator. Like many dramatic stock players, they have become favorites with habitual patrons, and their appearance in a picture is usually hailed with delight. Pathé pictures are famous for their good photographic quality, superior pantomime, ingenious trick effects, beautiful colored results, and the clear, lucid manner of telling a picture story. The characters in a Pathé picture are usually of heroic size, more attention being paid to making the story plain to the spectator than to beauty of scenery, although outdoor scenes are often selected with a view to artistic prospect. One fault sometimes present is shallowness of plot and story, especially in comedy pictures. Another fault is the cheap and worn-out stock scenery often used for interiors. A few good scene painters might be profitably added to the Pathé employees.

Gaumont pictures are very similar to Pathé in general appearance, at first glance, but they do not display as much acting ability and they show careless haste in production, not often to be noted in the Pathé work.

Méliès pictures usually run to the trick and spectacular style, with an occasional effort at comedy. Photographic quality of Méliès films is invariably good, but the comedy has not often been of a character to find appreciation among American patrons of picture houses.

Urban-Eclipse films are manufactured in both England and France. Those done by English actors are awkward and bungling, but the travel pictures and views of events are usually well done.

The Radios, Italian films, are especially strong in photography and are usually darker in tone than is the product of houses named above. Pathetic dramatic subjects are frequently well done by this company, and travel views are of a high quality, but the comedy production is seldom of much account.

The Rossi films, another Italian product, are similar in character to Radios, but not so carefully prepared.

Lux, French pictures, resemble Gaumont in quality and character.

Great Northern films manufactured in Copenhagen are distinguished by clearness and perfection of photographic quality. The acting is not as spirited as the French, but it is invariably appropriate and conscientious. Scenery backgrounds are often specially beautiful.

Italian "Cines" productions are among the best of the Italian output. Photographic quality is always excellent, and the subjects are usually well handled.

Eclair is a new French maker of films, and from what has been seen of them on this side they give promise of gaining a very high reputation. They appear to resemble Pathé films in quality and general appearance.

American pictures are, of course, the best known on this side, next to the productions of Pathé Frères, with which moving pictures patrons the world over are familiar. American films which most nearly resemble Pathé in style of treatment are the pictures of the American Mutoscope and Biograph Company. These motion pictures are distinguished, like the Pathé, by their heroic size, enabling the actors to convey the ideas intended with utmost clearness. Subjects produced by the Biograph Company are almost invariably of a superior character, whether melodramatic, tragic, or comic, and the acting and stage management are always able and skillful. Scenic backgrounds out of doors are usually well selected, but painted interiors are not marked by novelty or artistic excellence. On the contrary, they are usually rather meager. An excellent company of stock actors is employed, and their faces are familiar favorites with moving picture patrons.

Edison pictures are noted for elaborate scenic productions and the artistic beauty of the scenes, whether natural or painted interiors, but these results are sometimes secured at the expense of clearness in telling a picture story. Important action taking place in artistic shadow or at a distance which permits of a beautiful and extended view may, and usually does, weaken the dramatic effect. This criticism is not always true of Edison pictures, as there are frequent occasions when art has been attained without loss of lucidity. Edison subjects are nearly always of striking character with novel effects.

The American Vitagraph Company produces a greater number of subjects than any other American film, and while its comedy and dramatic work is not always distinguished by the most elaborate detail in scenic results, Vitagraph scenery is by no means inadequate. Indeed, in special cases the Vitagraph Company produces exceedingly expensive sets for important scenes, and it must be noted that an effort is always made to have scenery accurate and consistent. This is especially true of clever historical stories, for which this company is famous. Its comedy also is usually good and is marked by vivacity and frequently by rich humor. Vitagraph actors are a trained body of players, many of them favorites with spectators. The scenes are taken to a certain extent, like Biograph, at short range, although the figures are not so heroic in size. Occasionally weak and ineffective subjects are noted, but not often, considering the large output. We must not dismiss this company without mention of its occasional pictures of important events, which are always excellent and decidedly welcome.

The Kalem Company has not been in operation as long as the other New York producers, but it is showing marked improvement in its work. Obscurity in telling a story was formerly observed in the dramatic work of this company, but this tendency has lately been largely overcome. Like the other American producers, the Kalem Company is clearly moved by constant endeavor to improve and elevate the character of its work, as witness the recent elaborate religious spectacles, *Jerusalem in the Days of Christ* and *David and Goliath,* mentioned favorably in a recent number of *The Mirror.*

The Selig Polyscope Company, of Chicago, is the one other American firm that rivals the Edison Company in large and striking scenic effects. Indeed, the Selig studio settings are on a larger scale, if anything, than the Edison, and it is the only company that has gone to the Rocky Mountains for the magnificent natural backgrounds to be found there better than anywhere else in the world. But all too frequently beauty of perspective has been accompanied by obscurity of dramatic action. The spectator remarks, "How pretty! How realistic!" but he doesn't follow the story, and it is a question if more is not lost than gained by such a policy. It must be noted also that Selig picture stories are sometimes constructed without due regard to lucid narrative. However, the Selig Company is entitled to the highest praise for its ambitious and painstaking efforts in the direction of moving picture perfection.

The Essanay Film Manufacturing Company, of Chicago, has gained a wide popularity for clever comedy subjects, admirably acted and constructed. Recently this company has been producing a number of melodramatic stories with fair success, and it has just made a notable production of a high class drama with a star actor in the cast, but its comedy work will be best remembered by moving picture patrons, who will hope that the "comics" are not to be abandoned. Essanay pictures are always photographically good and clearly obvious to the spectators, although there are times when inconsistencies creep in.

The Lubin Pictures, manufactured in Philadelphia, are among the earlier American productions, and consist of comedy, drama, and travel subjects. Of the three styles, the last named are the most meritorious, although not frequently enough produced. In comedy and drama there is much spirit displayed in the acting, but too often the stories are feeble or ragged and not handled with the best dramatic effect. The photography, however, is usually excellent.

The New York Dramatic Mirror, November 14, 1908

Made in November 1908, five months after he became a director, *The Song of the Shirt*—derived from Thomas Hood's poem—was D. W. Griffith's thirty-eighth picture. The review reflects three of his continuing characteristics: his literary coloring, his extraordinary ability with actors, and his concerns with social problems.

The "young woman" was Florence Lawrence who played in

more than forty Biograph films for Griffith and, long before her name was known to the public, was famous as "the Biograph Girl." [4]

THE SONG OF THE SHIRT

We can recall no picture of recent months so impressive in conveying a deep meaning and so artistic in the manner of its handling as this one. Not only has the sentiment that Hood sought to teach been comprehended by the producers, but also the beauty of the poet's lines, in a measure, has been approximated by the picture language employed. In order to do this the producers have incorporated in the subject a simple and intensely pathetic story, that of a poor working girl slaving at her sewing machine to earn a bare existence for herself and her dying sister. But she labors in vain. The work is declared unsatisfactory by the unfeeling factory employer, the girl returns to her hovel to find the invalid close to death, while the employer is enjoying in high living the wealth wrung from the sweat and lifeblood of the white slaves in his employ. The effectiveness of the story is enhanced by the insertion in the film of appropriate lines from the poem, of which the following is not the least impressive: "Stitch-stitch-stitch! In poverty, hunger and dirt, Sewing at once with a double thread A shroud as well as a shirt." The acting of the Biograph players is in strong harmony with the sentiment of the story—powerful without over-acting. This is especially true of the young woman who was cast for the part of the poor shirt sewer.

The New York Dramatic Mirror, November 28, 1908

An anonymous critic begins a career. His first review gives us an idea of a contemporary film theater and program. *Mrs. Jones Entertains,* with Florence Lawrence, was D. W. Griffith's forty-first film and evidently revealed an exceptional eye for composition.

WEEKLY COMMENTS ON THE SHOWS

BY OUR OWN CRITIC

"Write just what you think of them in your own words," was the editor's final order as he detailed me to criticize the programs and the conduct of the moving picture shows.

My first visit was to the Fourteenth Street Theater, Fourteenth Street near Sixth Avenue, New York. The entertainment at this house is bright and popular, but I think crying babies should be denied admittance and I object to the industry of a chewing gum boy in marketing his goods whilst the show is actually in progress. A small orchestra would enhance the attractions of the place, and the highly colored song slides to which a Mr. Driscoll sang a soulful ballad do not impress one as being artistic. The announcement slides were crude and tawdry and could easily be replaced by something more finished and artistic.

The films subjects ran too much toward the obscure and the lugubrious. A French subject, *Tit for Tat,* illustrated workmen playing practical jokes on one another, but the story was the reverse of obvious to the audience (and me) and it passed without a hand. *For Baby's Sake,* another French subject, told that to comfort a dying child, a poor workman went out and stole a doll, only to find upon his return that the little one had died and that he himself had been pursued as a thief. Excellent conception and photography could not redeem the subject from gloom, and again I thought Mr. Rosenquest, the manager, was not happy in his choice. There was humor of a caustic kind in *A Wonderful Discovery.* This showed a party of savants exulting over the discovery, the nature of which was not clear, although it looked like a big camera on a tripod. Anyhow, it enabled you to see things that were happening elsewhere: A desk robbery; policemen at card-play; and, finally, the secretly married daughter of the discoverer visiting her husband. A clever but cynical picture. There was a masterly Gaumont relating how a baby girl was washed on shore from a shipwreck. She was adopted by an old sailor; whose son, also a sailor, falls in love with her. So does the captain of his ship. The course of true love goes somewhat awry, for the girl sticks to the captain and finally the disappointed sailor commits suicide by throwing himself off the rocks and dies a ghastly death as the waves sing his requiem. Quite a great cinematographic achievement, but what a dismal ending, to be sure, Messrs. Gaumont.

Fortunately there was some much-needed comic relief in *Mrs. Jones Entertains,* a fine humorous triumph for the Biograph Company. I have never laughed so heartily at a film in my life, nor have I seen a better piece of photography. And how neatly and effectively the Biograph subjects are framed as they appear on the screen! Well, dear little Mrs. Jones once gave a tea party to her temperance friends, at which Mr. Jones unfortunately got intoxicated. So his presence was objected to when the ladies met again. As luck would have it the waiter who was to serve the repast could not come, and so Jones, poor fellow, consented to disguise himself and act as waiter to his own wife's guests. These prim and virtuous ladies duly arrived; the meal was served and all proceeded happily until Jones, who received the dishes from a pert maid in the kitchen, was seized by a desire to try an experiment before the meal was finished. Discovering a bottle which appeared to contain a spirituous liquid, he poured some into each of the guests' cups. The effect of the experiment was soon apparent. The ladies got more communicative toward each; they warmed and melted; they clamored for more "tea"; they got quite boisterous and just slightly indecorous, and finally so abusive and intoxicated that Mrs. Jones had to clear them off, and then husband and wife were reconciled, presumably with a promise on his part to behave himself in future.

Now this, it is true, is broad farce, but it was never allowed to fall into coarseness, suggestiveness, or indecency, and the audience at the Fourteenth Street Theater were genuinely amused by it: all of them, men, women, and children. That fact should give the managers of moving picture theaters an infallible guide to the kind of entertainment which pays best at these places. It must be bright, clean, wholesome, amusing. Most emphatically my fellow visitors the other night—people obviously of good social position—were not on the *qui vive* for the unclean or the salacious; and they did not get it, thank goodness!

The Fourteenth Street Theater is a well conducted moving picture house, and if Manager Rosenquest will bring it up to date in respect of the small details treated of in this notice, he will please his patrons and swell his bank balance.

The Moving Picture World, January 9, 1909

The growing impact and the potentialities of the medium are celebrated in the following, which was reprinted from the *Chicago Tribune* (February 8, 1909) by *The Moving Picture World.* Frederick Starr of The University of Chicago was an eminent anthropologist who wrote books on American Indians, Japanese aborigines, and Mexican Indians.

THE WORLD BEFORE YOUR EYES

FREDERICK STARR

I have seen Niagara thunder over her gorge in the noblest frenzy ever beheld by man—I have watched a Queensland river under the white light of an Australasian moon go whirling and swirling through strange islands lurking with bandicoot and kangaroo—I have watched an English railroad train draw into a station, take on its passengers, and then chug away with its stubby little engine through the Yorkshire Dells, past old Norman Abbeys silhouetted against the skyline, while a cluster of century-aged cottages loomed up in the valley below, through which a yokel drove his flocks of Southdowns—I have been to the Orient and gazed at the water-sellers and beggars and dervishes—I have beheld fat old rajahs with the price of a thousand lives bejeweled in their monster turbans, and the price of a thousand deaths sewn in their royal nightshirts as they indolently swayed in golden howdahs, borne upon the backs of grunting elephants—I saw a runaway horse play battledore and shuttlecock with the citizens and traffic of a little Italian village, whose streets had not known so much commotion since the sailing of Columbus—I know how the Chinaman lives, and I have been through the homes of the Japanese—I have marveled at the daring of Alpine tobogganists and admired the wonderful skill of Norwegian ski jumpers—I have seen armies upon the battlefield and their return in triumph—I have looked upon weird dances and outlandish frolics in every quarter of the globe, and I didn't have to leave Chicago for a moment.

No books have taught me all these wonderful things—no lecturer has pictured them—I simply dropped into a moving picture theater at various moments of leisure, and at the total cost for all the visits of perhaps two performances of a foolish musical show, I have learned more than a traveler could see at the cost of thousands of dollars and years of journey.

Neither you nor I fully realize what the moving picture has meant to us, and what it is going to mean. As children we used to dream of a journey on a magician's carpet to the legendary lands, but we can rub our own eyes now and witness more tremendous miracles than Aladdin could have by rubbing his fairy lamp. But we're so matter-of-fact that we never think of it that way. We're living at a mile-a-second gait in the swiftest epoch of the world's progress—in the age of incredibilities come true. We fly through the air—chat with our friends in Paris by squirting a little spark from a pole on one shore of the Atlantic to another pole on the other side, and so we take as a matter of course that which our great-grandfathers would have declared a miracle.

The talking machine has canned the great voices and master melodies of our time, but the moving-picture machine has done more—it is making for us volumes of history and action—it is not only the greatest impulse of entertainment but the mightiest force of instruction. We do not analyze the fact that when we read of an English wreck we at once see an English train before us, or when we learn of a battle that an altogether different panorama is visualized than our former erroneous impression of a hand-to-hand conflict—we are familiar with the geography of Europe—we are well acquainted with how the Frenchman dresses, in what sort of a home he lives, and from what sort of a shop he buys his meat and greens.

We take so much for granted—we are so thoroughly spoiled by our multiple luxuries—that we do not bestow more than a passing thought upon our advantages, because the moving picture machine is an advantage —a tremendous, vital force of culture as well as amusement. An economy, not only of money but of experiences—it brings the world to us—it delivers the universe to our theater seat. The moving picture is not a makeshift for the playhouse—its dignity is greater—its importance far beyond the puny function of comedy and tragedy. It is a clean entertainment, lecture, and amusement all rolled in one—in its highest effort it stands above literature—in its less ambitious phase it ranks above the tawdry show house. It teaches nothing harmful, and it usually teaches much that is helpful.

Today the moving picture industry is developed to a high degree of perfection in America and in Europe. Millions of dollars are invested in the production of moving picture films—entire companies of trained and practiced actors are carried to every interesting spot on the continent and carefully drilled to enact pantomimes which will concentrate within the space of a few minutes the most entertaining and instructive incidents of the world. A new type of dramatist has arisen—men who search through the literature of the ages and construct tableaux in action which will render vividly the entire contents of famous works of the drama, of the novel and of history.

The moving picture is not a makeshift, but the highest type of entertainment in the history of the world. It stands for a better Americanism because it is attracting millions of the masses to an uplifting institution, drawing them to an improving as well as an amusing feature of city life. Its value cannot be measured now, but another generation will benefit more largely through its influence than we of today can possibly realize.

The Moving Picture World, February 20, 1909

Nothing could be so popular so quickly without stirring the censorious. Censorship was the first major issue in American film writing and has remained a painfully hardy perennial. This editorial appeals for reason in those who, quite rightly, sensed that the film was socially disturbing, who were frightened and fought back with the handiest weapon, conventional moralism.

The last sentence of the editorial is particularly striking in its thirteen-year-old self-confidence.

THE PRESS AND THE MOVING PICTURE

"The Fourth Estate," as Edmund Burke called the press, is one of the greatest powers for good or evil in the world. And it must be free, for through it and in it, a people vindicates its right of freedom and of thought. But that power and that freedom must be exercised with wisdom and moderation or public opinion is likely to be misled and the cause of good government injured.

We have observed with regret for some time that many important sections of the American press, either through ignorance or some interested motive, assume toward the moving picture an attitude that can only be described as condemnatory, unfavorable, and unfair, which is all the more to be wondered at having regard to the fact that this form of entertainment is now firmly established in the favor of millions of Americans—as much so as the theater, the concert, instrumental music, and the like. The moving picture, in fact, is now part of the national life and should be treated as such.

But the American press seems blind to the potent truth that the moving picture is an accepted institution of the people. They still affect to treat it as a novelty, an interloper, a curiosity. If this is not inexcusable ignorance then it is downright stupidity, and the sooner more intelligent writers are employed the better for the newspapers' reputation for common sense, which at present is not so high as it might be. An unfailing source of misrepresentation in the press is an accident or a fire at a moving picture theater. Ten to one a wrongful cause is assigned, or the facts are exaggerated. Rarely does the film catch afire; more often than not the trouble or accident has nothing whatever to do with the projection apparatus and its accessories. The alarmist press, however, seldom takes the trouble to ascertain the facts. Cold fact, you see, is not sensational and does not make for effective scare lines. If the newspapers confined themselves to facts many of them would have to go out of business.

The unsafety or unsanitary conditions of moving picture theaters are legitimate subjects for newspaper discussion, but how often are they handled with knowledge and discretion? Seldom. No, they are too frequently denounced on insufficient evidence. Then as to the alleged obscenity or unsuitability of the pictures shown; the dreadful behavior of the people in Nickelodeons—the "immorality," the "vice," and all the rest of the wild farrago of abominations that take place, nine-tenths of all this we unhesitatingly declare to exist in the imaginations of the reporters, and the Pharisaical clergy whose utterances they print,—these, and *these alone.* Such things unquestionably obtrude themselves here and there—they exist, Gentlemen of the Press and the Pulpit, *everywhere* on this earth—but not more so in the moving picture field than in any other. We protest against the Nickelodeon being saddled with all the sins of the community.

Throughout the whole of the United States of America there is an earnest desire to uplift the moving picture; to make it clean, bright, dramatically and photographically beautiful; something that shall delight the eyes and stimulate the minds of millions and millions of people who find in moving pictures a satisfying form of entertainment and relaxation.

We bespeak the cooperation of the American press to that good end. Have done with foolish sensations; exaggerations; falsehoods; loose writing and not disinterested attacks, brothers. Encouragement not depreciation is needed. Criticize if you will, but criticize justly, impartially, and above all with knowledge. Then you will have the consolation of feeling that you are encouraging and not retarding the progress of a form of entertainment, the possibilities of which are only just being revealed. For the moving picture will last just as long as the newspaper, and in any competition for the popular suffrage would outlast it.

The Moving Picture World, March 20, 1909

"The Spectator" was a pseudonym used by Frank E. Woods, an advertising salesman for *The New York Dramatic Mirror,* who persuaded his journal to run film reviews and then to give him a column. Woods wrote his weekly column until 1912, during which time he also sold screen stories to Biograph. He then joined Griffith and moved to California with him. According to Mrs. Griffith, he grew so wealthy within ten years of his start in films that he came to "own" a town near Barstow, which he named Lenwood.[5] He became the head of Griffith's scenario department and subsequently held the same post for Lasky Studios.[6]

Lewis Jacobs says that Woods soon was known as "the film's major critic," that "from the outset Frank Woods impressed the movie makers: they read his column steadily, respected his opinions, and often acted upon his advice."[7] M. O. Lounsbury says of his writings: "What started as an apology for the film manufacturers became the earliest exploration into a number of important esthetic and social issues concerning the motion picture.'[8]

This is Frank Woods's first column.

The Patents Company he refers to was a group formed in 1909 of seven domestic and two French companies and an American distributor, who, strictly speaking, had legal control of patented machines and processes. The members were sometimes called Licensed companies. But the exploding cultural situation could not endure such a monopoly. Opposition groups of Independents were formed, and the "outlaw" companies finally busted the trust—*de jure* in 1917, *de facto* in 1914.[9]

"SPECTATOR'S" COMMENTS

Motion pictures are at last gaining recognition as an institution of immense value to mankind. People who formerly spoke lightly of them are commencing to perceive their great possibilities as an educational as well as an entertainment factor. Some are terribly distressed lest the character of pictures shall injure the young and ignorant mind, and they desire to "regulate" the supply; others would like to see them done away with altogether; still others are fearful that the fault-finders and enemies may hamper or do the business irreparable harm. In the opinion of the Spectator none of these fears are warranted. The motion picture is already an engine of human progress too great and powerful to be long or appreciably affected by regulators, enemies, or promoters. It will continue to move forward of its own force, and those who seek to absolutely direct its course can have about as much influence on it as a child would have damming Niagara with a toy shovel. As it is developing it is a new form of combined literature and art. It is a new and universal language in which the artist, the actor, the author of fiction, the historian, the traveler, the philosopher, and the theologian may convey ideas and information to his fellow men. Naturally enough, the first efforts in addressing the public in the new picture language are crude and unpolished, but he must be blind who cannot perceive the constant advancement that is being made in character of subject and elegance of style. This advancement was bound to come with experience, and is bound to continue as actors and authors of greater ability are attracted to its use. Like the printing press, it has opened up a vast opportunity for the dissemination of human thought, and, like the printing press, it can only move onward and upward.

~

The Spectator does not desire to be understood as condemning whatever efforts are being made to uplift the business, to eliminate undesirable pictures and improve conditions of exhibitions. Let the volunteer regulators go to all the trouble they care to along that line. They are showing a very worthy interest in the direction of advancement, but they should not deceive themselves and imagine they are accomplishing any very wonderful results. All that they can do to "reform" the pictures is bound to come about in any event. Picture literature, like printed literature, will reform itself where reformation is needed. It may be retarded or accelerated to a certain degree, but it cannot be prevented.

~

In the long run the public is the censor and the regulator, speaking, of course, of the public in a free country. The newspaper or the magazine that comes nearest to giving the public what it wants is the publication that gains the largest circulation. The play that best pleases the people is the play that scores the greatest success. Thus we have competition and a constant striving for improvement. Motion pictures are no exception. The picture producers who strive to improve and succeed are the ones that will last the longest and accomplish the most. The public is constantly wanting something better on the stage and in the press, and so it will be on the picture curtain.

~

It is fortunate for immediate picture progress that the Patents Company organization of American manufacturers and importers is along a liberal line, insofar as competition is concerned. While the patented mechanical devices are controlled by one company, the production of pictures comes from ten companies, each one realizing that its business can be increased only by improvement in character and quality of subjects. To this friendly rivalry we owe the artistic Pathé Films d'Art, the Vitagraph Napoleon pictures, with others to follow of the same character, the remarkably strong and ably acted Biograph dramatic and comedy subjects, and the ambitious and enterprising Selig feature films. The other allied manufacturers cannot afford to remain behind in this contest, and there is good ground for believing that they will not remain behind. They are all showing improvement, and we may confidently expect them to do work just as notable as that quoted above within a very short time. Indeed, there is every reason why every licensed manufacturer should make it a point to produce great feature subjects at every opportunity. As a certain manufacturer remarked to the Spectator recently, such a course followed up by all the Patents Company producers would solve the Independent question in very short order, unless the Independents should succeed in making the same sort of progress, and even then the entire motion picture business would have been elevated and improved to an amazing extent, which, after all, is the condition most to be desired and the condition that must eventually prevail.

~

How can motion pictures be best improved? There would appear to be only one reply to this question, outside of the mechanical end, which may be trusted to take care of itself. When a magazine or a newspaper company sets out to increase the circulation of its publications it employs first more able writers. When a theatrical producer gains permanent success he does it through better dramatists and better actors. The motion picture producer can only improve by the same policy, and he will be compelled to improve by that policy or eventually lag behind and go out of business. The story or "suggestion," as the producer erroneously calls the scenario of his comedy or dramatic subject, is the foundation on which he must work. With a good and clever plot and able actors he may do much. With a flat or feeble story he must fail, no matter how capable his acting, directing, and scene painting force may be. On the stage it has long been recognized that the "play's the thing." So it must be in the motion pictures —"the story's the thing."

~

The part played by *The Dramatic Mirror* in motion picture advancement in America must not be overlooked. As the Spectator has argued above, the great advancement that is taking place was bound to come and is bound to continue, but certain influences may retard or accelerate, and no influence from any source has been more potent for good in more ways than one than that of *The Mirror*. More than two years ago, before any theaters of considerable size had gone over to pictures, *The Mirror* recognized the invasion that must take place and advised managers of regular theaters to get into the game. The advice was repeated from time to time, and it was not long before theater after theater of the standard type were turning permanently to the picture policy. No doubt much of this tendency would have developed without *The Mirror*'s influence, but it will be conceded that it would hardly have taken place so rapidly. The result has been that a more intelligent and enterprising class of managers has been drafted into the moving picture business, and to the same degree a more intelligent class of spectators has been attracted to the exhibitions. Likewise *The Mirror* has had undoubted influence, through its impartial film reviews, in elevating the artistic quality and character of motion picture subjects. It was the first paper in the world to review motion pictures seriously, systematically, and with sufficient intelligence to win the respect of the manufacturers themselves. By this policy of review *The Mirror*, from its commanding position, was able to do what no other amusement publication was in a position to accomplish—place motion picture publication on the higher plane of literature and art.

The New York Dramatic Mirror, May 1, 1909

"SPECTATOR'S" COMMENTS

It has been demonstrated in the Comments a number of times that motion picture acting is progressing upward in America as well as in France, and that good acting is appreciated at its true value by all classes of patrons, the uncultured included. No individual is so dense as not to recognize, even though unconsciously, the difference between people who do things like real human beings and those who act after the fashion of the lurid melodrama stage. The fact that the classes that made up the audiences of popular price theaters used to accept mock heroics and applaud them is beside the question. It does not indicate that they would not have applauded good acting to a greater degree had they ever had the opportunity. The moment that motion picture dramas were offered to them showing natural surroundings instead of painted scenes the popular price public deserted the melodrama theater and put it out of business. And they did not necessarily come to the pictures because they liked the cheap theatrical style of acting formerly deemed essential, but more probably because they saw in the pictures scenes that more nearly represented nature and real life. Having never seen anything but bad acting, they possibly supposed that no actor could do anything else, and they accepted him as one of the necessary evils. When, however, certain venturesome individuals in the motion picture business timidly commenced to introduce a little art into their dramatic and comedy pantomime, the effect was astonishing. The uncultured were quick to applaud, though they may not have known why. At the same time the cultured, who had hitherto looked on the motion picture drama as a joke, which it was to a large degree, began to sit up and take notice. The result is that today the makers of pictures generally concede that good acting is worth to them all the extra money they must pay to get it.

~

In the recent Spring number of *The Mirror* Mr. Dyer, of the Edison Company, is quoted in an interview as saying that the quality of picture pantomime is improving quite as rapidly as the public is prepared to receive it. He then referred to an experience the Edison Company had in offering high class music in phonograph records, showing that the American public is not yet educated up to a high standard of art in music and much prefers the so-called popular music. From this he argued that the same thing is true of motion pictures and that the evolution toward a higher grade of art must be gradual in both instances. While Mr. Dyer's reasoning is sound his conclusions in this instance are apt to be misleading. The American masses may not be yet educated to appreciate operatic music, but that does not argue that they prefer their simpler popular airs trashy rather than well composed. The history of popular music proves quite the contrary. It is so, too, in literature as well as the arts. Themes that are simple, direct, and elementary may be in greatest demand, but excellence of style and execution is sure to receive public approval.

~

Pantomimic literature as seen in motion pictures is proving the truth of this last assertion every day. A simple story, no matter how melodramatic in plot, is all the better if it be well constructed and naturally acted. The masses may prefer corned beef and cabbage as a diet, but it must not be tainted or half cooked. And this leads up to a matter which the writer desires to call to the attention of certain picture producers whose names need not be mentioned here. While all are showing more or less desire to improve the style of acting, some of them—nearly all, in fact—too often permit inconsistencies and anachronisms to creep into their film stories. A perusal of the film reviews in *The Mirror* from week to week will reveal scores of these, and there are doubtless others that have gone unmentioned. Such errors could all be avoided if the manufacturers would employ qualified and educated persons who could occupy positions analogous to editors and proofreaders in a publication office, and give them authority to make corrections, holding them strictly responsible for all errors that may occur. Some of the manufacturers are doing this to a greater or less degree, and their superior product is proving the value of the practice. Motion picture making is a publication business and should be conducted from start to finish with the same intelligent care that is customary in the making of magazines and newspapers.

The New York Dramatic Mirror, June 19, 1909

Mary Pickford began in films with a bit part in Griffith's *Her First Biscuits*. The next day she played the female lead for him in *The Violin Maker of Cremona*—without billing, of course.[10]

THE VIOLIN MAKER OF CREMONA

One grows so used to praising Biograph productions that it becomes difficult, at times, to find new words and phrases in which to describe the excellence of a film. In this subject the Biograph Company has repeated its previous best work in all respects and has left the reviewer no room for criticizing. The story is coherently arranged and intensely interesting, while the acting is almost perfect as to each character. The photography is particularly artistic—the closing scene in which the light is made to fade away on the figure of the sorrowful youth who has made the supreme sacrifice being art in its highest sense. Two young violin makers are in love with the same girl, the belle of Cremona. A prize is offered by the guild for the best violin, and to this prize is added by her father the hand of his daughter. One of the young lovers is conceded to be the best of all in ability to fashion a violin, but he is not the favorite of the girl, being a cripple. When he learns that the girl cannot love him, he secretly changes violins with the other lover so that the prize shall go to him. But the rival, in his great love for the girl, has also thought of secretly exchanging the violins, and he carries out his plan, with the result they are returned to their original cases, and the cripple is awarded the prize and the girl. Not to be balked in his magnanimous sacrifice, he latter smashes his winning instrument and resigns the girl to the one she loves.

The New York Dramatic Mirror, June 19, 1909

A week after *The Violin Maker of Cremona,* which was shot in two days, Mary Pickford played one of the children in *The Lonely Villa,* also directed by Griffith. Both pictures were released so close together that they were reviewed in the same issue of the *Dramatic Mirror.*

These unsigned reviews may have been written by Frank Woods, whose "Spectator" columns appeared in the same journal. Woods had also begun to write screen stories for Griffith, which adds piquancy to his criticism, if it is his, of Griffith's use of "alternate scenes" or intercutting. Woods's right hand evidently kept well away from his left.

THE LONELY VILLA

Possibly to show us that they have not forgotten how to do thrilling melodrama with intense interest, held in suspense till the final curtain, the Biograph producers have given us in this film a picture that will no doubt prove more popular than it deserves. For although the story is badly constructed, we are not inflicted with the grotesque style of acting that formerly distinguished this class of picture pantomime. The people move like real human beings, and theatrical posing is entirely wanting. The story is therefore as effective as it is possible to make it, considering that fact that it is not without serious flaws. Robbers lure a suburban citizen from his home by a fake message supposed to be from the man's mother, stating that she has started on an earlier train and for him to meet her at the depot at 10:30. The man appears not to have been suspicious of the note, although the impossibility of any one successfully forging a person's handwriting on a pad of paper while out in the shrubbery of a garden at night is quite obvious, not to mention the inconsistency of a note, not a telegram, being delivered personally by a stranger, although the note states that the mother had already taken the train and is on her way. However, the gentleman sets out in his automobile, which conveniently breaks down, and he telephones his wife that he will be detained. He then learns, as we have already seen by the pictures, that the robbers have broken into the house. In alternate scenes we see the robbers laboriously breaking down one door after another as the wife and children bar the way with locks and light furniture, while the husband is making frantic efforts to secure a vehicle to come to the rescue. In a gypsy wagon, after a furious drive, he arrives with two policemen just as the burglars have reached the safe. In real life burglars could have smashed through all the obstacles with which this trio were confronted in one-tenth the time, and it would appear that this fact should have been recognized. The interval of time necessary to bring the rescuing party on the scene might better have been filled in by the burglars working over the safe, while holding the wife and children as helpless captives looking on.

The New York Dramatic Mirror, June 19, 1909

The Films d'Art company was formed in France in 1907 to elevate the lowly, parvenu screen. This company produced potted versions of famous plays with famous actors, who were billed. As Arthur Knight says, "People who would never have dreamed of going to the nickelodeons to see a cowboy picture, a tear-stained melodrama, or a slapstick comedy, somehow felt that movies must be all right if they showed you the classics." [11]

LA TOSCA

This is probably the most notable of the Films d'Art series thus far presented by the Pathé company of distinguished French players. The subtle finesse and artistic finish with which it is acted must be seen to be appreciated. In every scene and in every movement we see evidence of the most painstaking care and foresight. The result is a polished work of art, almost flawless throughout. It is worthy of the respectful study of all motion picture players and producers. It is said that the adaptation was arranged by Sardou himself. The part of Floria Tosca is admirably played by Madame Cécile Sorel of the Académie Française, but the Scarpia of Le Bargy and the Mario of Alexander are the most powerful representations in the pantomime.

The New York Dramatic Mirror, June 19, 1909

For centuries the theater had been considered the popular art, the art that appealed to the largest numbers of people and that needed to do so in order to survive. Suddenly another art had appeared that made the size of the theater audience relatively minuscule. Because of its wide availability and low price, the film attracted an immense audience, proportionately less educated than the theater audience had been. This raised questions of appropriate subject matter that, in various ways, are still being debated.

Of Woods's two examples of unlikely film material, Browning and Ibsen, one was (unwittingly?) ironic. In August 1909 Griffith had made a screen version of *Pippa Passes,* which possibly Woods knew about when he wrote this. When it was released in October of that year, *The New York Times* said: *"Pippa Passes* is being given in the nickelodeons, and Browning is being presented to the average motion picture audience, which has received it with applause and is asking for more." [12]

Ibsen's *Ghosts* was filmed in 1915, unsuccessfully. [13]

"SPECTATOR'S" COMMENTS

In the progress upward of motion pictures a question frequently raised is this: Are not picture producers in danger of getting over the heads of their patrons? In discussing this matter all depends on what is meant by it. Some producers who apparently held to the idea that sensational melodrama was the thing most wanted by motion picture spectators and that melodrama could only be expressed in picture pantomime by the furiously athletic style of acting, have argued that repose and subtle finesse must be wasted when presented to the average public as found in picture theaters. The old idea was that because the pictures are moving pictures all the characters must be on the jump. Arms must wave, bodies squirm and writhe, and legs keep in constant action. "They told me," said an actor in describing his experience to the writer, "that in running I must always lift my knees high. I was to be a sort of a high-stepper, like a fancy carriage horse." But this happened two or three years ago, and ideas of producers have changed. It is now pretty well recognized among the most successful film makers that people do not think with their arms and legs in real life, and that a story in which none of the characters do any thinking must be a poor sort of story for any class of public to enjoy. It has been found that even the most intense melodramatic situations may be best expressed by making the characters do things as human beings in real life would do them. As was pointed out in this paper many months ago, the motion picture drama or comedy gets its chief charm of illusion from the fact that scenes are represented as taking place, not on a stage behind footlights, but amidst actual surroundings. All the more reason, therefore, why stagy acting in pictures only tends to destroy the illusion of reality. The better and more real the work of the players, the closer they come to approximating actual life and therefore the more convincing the picture. So it may be safely answered to the question propounded at the opening of this paragraph that picture producers cannot get beyond the intelligence of their public so far as the quality of the acting and stage management is concerned.

~

But there is another view of the matter, and it is worthy of the careful attention of all producers. While the picture language in which a story is told cannot be too polished and clear, the story itself may be too deep for the average public appreciation, just as the stage drama may aim too high or certain classes of literature may be too elevated for popular understanding. It is obvious that picture translations of Browning or adaptations from Ibsen would find small welcome in picture theaters.

~

It is not, however, intended to insinuate that manufacturers are showing a tendency to go too far in the "high-brow" direction, but experience already shows that there must be a limit, although the exact boundary line will be difficult to fix. The recent Pathé production, *The Wild Ass's Skin,* from Balzac, approached very closely to the doubtful point in this respect, but Edison's *Coward,* from Maupassant, was clearly obvious even to the least intelligent, and held spectators spellbound. The Biograph pictures, which were really the pioneers in the direction of higher work in America, cannot be said to go over the heads of the public. Usually the theme has been simple and direct, and it is only in the novelty of idea, subtlety of acting, and the fine coloring of the pantomime that this company has pointed the higher way. There is no rival manufacturer that does not cheerfully give the Biograph producers full credit for this service they have done to motion pictures, and, indeed, this same feeling of goodwill of all the affiliated manufacturers toward the successful efforts of each other is one of the marked and most pleasing features of the situation, so far, at least, as the Licensed companies are concerned. This is as it should be, for the welfare of each is the welfare of all. . . .*

The New York Dramatic Mirror, September 11, 1909

The subject of subject matter was debated in regard to national origin as well as quality. This article shows how high the degree of foreign influence was in these early days, although it also indicates the quick popularity of Westerns.

Maude Adams was famous for her performances in plays by J. M. Barrie. The Irving is Henry Irving, both of whose sons were also actors who visited America.

WHAT IS AN AMERICAN SUBJECT?

We should be glad to receive answers from our exhibiting readers to this question. We think that if they would express their views freely and openly on the subject in our columns the manufacturers would derive many useful hints. Much has been said and written the last twelve months on the desirability of providing American film subjects for American moving picture audiences. It has been urged against the imported film that it usually has the drawback of not dealing with a subject suitable for an American audience. The urgent necessity of American subjects made by American labor has been predicated, and the poor importer as well as the European manufacturer has therefore been, to some extent, prejudiced in the eyes of the American exhibitor.

Examining the parallel of the ordinary or talking stage it is surprising to

* "Spectator" columns consist of separate paragraphs or groups of paragraphs, and not all the topics are of present interest. Where paragraphs have been omitted from the columns reprinted here, this is indicated by ellipsis at the end. No part of any one paragraph or connected sequence has been dropped. s.k.

see how very few American subjects hold the stage for any length of time in New York City. If we go to the recently opened New Theater we see that most of the works presented are by foreign authors. At this moment America's leading actress, Miss Maude Adams, is playing in a comedy by a Scottish author. Irving's son has brought a European piece with him. Mr. Frohman's most recent success is *Arsene Lupin,* a French subject. So it goes pretty well down the list of recent metropolitan successes. Both opera houses put on French and Italian music. Why is this? Dare we reply because there is a dearth of suitable American subjects?

Let us look at the moving picture field. Out of about forty films commented upon in the last number of *The Moving Picture World,* exactly one-half are foreign subjects and were made abroad. Of those that were made in this country, not more than ten are of American themes, that is, themes "racy of the soil" and distinctly American in characterization, scenery, and surroundings. The other subjects were such as might have been made in Europe. In the licensed releases for the week ending January 15, out of about thirty-one pictures, eleven are foreign subjects; of the remaining twenty only six are clearly American. The remainder are, if we may so put it, of a nondescript kind.

It will be seen from this, that the American subject, even after a year's plugging away, does not seem to have secured a predominant part in the film program of the moving picture theaters of the United States. It is permissible to inquire whether this is because the makers are unable to keep up the supply of purely American subjects, or because the tastes of the public are many and varied and have to be catered for accordingly? We incline to the latter view. There seems to be amongst exhibitors, among whom we have made the inquiry, a strong and increasing demand for Indian and Western subjects, and here probably we get the most satisfactory answer to our own question. Indian and Western subjects may fairly be considered American, because they deal with the aboriginal or original life of the pioneers of the country. When you come to the comedy subject, the dramatic subject, the purely humorous subject, the American aspect of things is not perhaps so obvious as it might be.

We have examined this little question at some length, in order, first of all, to see what is meant by the common generalization expressed in the phrase "American subjects," and also for the purpose of starting the theme for discussion so as to learn the views of our exhibiting readers. It would be a good thing if our exhibiting readers would write us and give us an idea of the class of subject which their audiences like, which are the most popular and understood—what, in fact, the audience prefers. It will possibly be found that if exclusively American-made subjects were presented in the moving picture theaters of the United States the audiences would clamor for more variety, so that we should be brought round to the same condition of things as prevails at the present time.

The Moving Picture World, January 22, 1910

Film criticism, in any meaningful sense, was only about two years old, yet it, in itself, had already become a subject of criticism—and, as we shall see, a continuing subject.

"SPECTATOR'S" COMMENTS

A gentleman interested in the moving picture business recently advanced the argument to the writer that criticism by the press in the free manner that plays are reviewed is not entirely justified in the case of films, because they are articles of manufacture. This view, while not generally held by film manufacturers, may have occurred to some of them, and it may be as well to dispose of it.

~

It is not as articles of manufacture that films are criticized—at least insofar as *The Mirror* is concerned. If films were sold like shoes or even photographs they could be properly considered merchandise, and they are in fact so considered by this paper up to the time they are offered for public exhibition and entertainment. They are then on the same footing as any other act, play, or amusement for which public patronage is solicited. The critical review of public amusements and entertainments has become an established right of the press on the broad principle that it is for the public good. People engaged in entertaining the public are quasipublic servants, and their actions and offerings are legitimate matters for public discussion. To contend that motion pictures should not be judged on the same basis as other varieties of public entertainment is to deny them the very consideration which *The Mirror* was the first paper to seriously accord them—treatment as art and dramatic productions instead of mere articles of merchandise.

~

That motion pictures have profited by the policy of criticism there can be no reasonable doubt. They have improved since criticism was inaugurated as they had never improved before, and the improvement has been most marked in the one country where criticism prevails. It all constitutes only another evidence in favor of the freedom of the press and the influence of publicity on the progress of mankind. It goes without saying, of course, that the kind of criticism referred to is the kind that is strictly impartial as well as fearless, and this is the kind that *The Mirror* endeavors to give.

~

"But," remarks a friend, "while you may be right as to the value of impartial newspaper criticism of public amusements for the benefit of the public, which is asked to pay its money at the box-office, does this apply to the amusement or trade papers, which are not largely read by the general public?"

Why not, so far, at least, as the amusement papers are involved? *The Mirror,* at any rate, is published not alone for managers and the profession but also for that great element of the public which desires authoritative information regarding amusement affairs, and it numbers among its readers many thousands in all parts of the country who come legitimately within the description, "the show-going public." Coming more directly to the matter of motion picture exhibitors who have become *Mirror* readers since the inauguration of this department, are they not the direct representatives of the general public as well as a part of the public themselves? If there be good reason why the ordinary newspaper reader has a right to the expert opinion of the newspaper reviewer, by what argument is the motion picture exhibitor denied the same advantage? He is equally helpless with the public in his opportunity to examine the goods he is buying before he pays his money. His very business existence depends on the manner in which he can please his patrons, and it would be a strange sort of discrimination that would deny him the opportunity of profiting by the printed opinions of the reviewers in whom he has confidence.

~

Nor would it be desirable from the manufacturer's point of view for serious and impartial picture reviews to be abandoned. To what extent their producing forces have been spurred on to greater endeavor and more painstaking care to avoid ground for criticism or to merit praise, only the manufacturers themselves know. Certainly it has not been inconsiderable, and the question may well be asked, if honest reviews were to be discontinued how long would it be before actors and all concerned would fall into the former slipshod habit of arguing that defects would never be noticed? There would still be the verdict of the public to strive for, but with no voice to speak for the public the verdict would be lost in obscurity before it could reach the responsible producers.

The New York Dramatic Mirror, November 27, 1909

"SPECTATOR'S" COMMENTS

It is the opinion of the Spectator that every individual connected with the production or exhibition of motion pictures should consider carefully the thought presented last week in this column, viz: that the strange power of attraction possessed by motion pictures lies in the semblance of reality which the pictures convey; that by means of this impression of reality the motion picture exerts on the minds of the spectators an influence akin to hypnotism or magnetism by visual suggestion; that this sort of limited hypnotic influence is capable of more powerful exertion through the medium of motion pictures than is possible in any sort of stage production or in printed fact or fiction, and that it is therefore the part of wisdom to cultivate absolute realism in every department of the motion picture art. Artificial drama and artificial comedy appear to have no attraction for the public mind when displayed in motion pictures, no matter how satisfactory they may be on the stage or in printed literature.

~

There has often been wonder expressed by theatrical players engaged in picture work why their stage comedy and dramatic tricks fall down in the silent drama. They wonder, too, why the public will tolerate on the stage suggestive and plainly indelicate actions and words when the same thing presented in pictures comes as a shock. There need be no wonder about it. It is all explained by the mental attitude of the average spectator in witnessing motion pictures. He is looking at what his mind accepts as reality, and risqué things for instance which may be safely done in a musical comedy on the stage would never be tolerated in one's parlor, and hence the public is properly shocked. The psychology of motion pictures as understood above by the Spectator may not have been very clearly expressed or it may be voted by the unthoughtful as all bosh, not worth bothering about, but eventually, let it be here predicted, something along this line of reasoning will be generally accepted as fact, and those picture producers who most intelligently steer their course by the compass of such reasoning will be found to be the undisputed leaders in this growing field of art and literature.

~

Realism being the chief end of motion picture acting and directing, just as probability is the thing most to be desired in framing the orignal story, we may now turn to some of the details. The most conspicuous offense committed by motion picture producers and players against this quality of reality is the tendency that nearly all of them have at times to play to the front, thus betraying unconsciously that they know they are being pictured, and giving the impression to the spectators that they are going through their parts before an audience which is not seen in the picture but which appears to be located in front of the scene. The arrangement of interiors almost invariably accentuates this impression. The chairs almost always face the camera, sometimes reminding one of a minstrel first part. The actor almost always sits at a table sideways, so that he can show his full face front. Sometimes he will seat himself with his back squarely to the table located behind his chair while he faces the camera trying to eat, write, or talk by occasionally twisting his neck and body into unnatural positions. Two people conversing will deliberately walk down front and instead of facing each other as in real life will face the camera, turning only occasionally to look at the person addressed. An entire room full of people may be seen facing front—we see nothing but a sea of white faces with never a back or side view.

~

Many actors and directors will contend that it is necessary to get the facial expressions over to the spectators and that this continual and monotonous facing front is therefore unavoidable. How weak this contention is must be apparent after a moment's thought. When the movement or attitude of the player is obviously unnatural in turning his face toward the camera he betrays by the act the fact that he is acting—that there is someone in front unseen by the spectators to whom the actor is addressing himself. Immediately the sense of reality is destroyed and the hypnotic illusion that has taken possession of the spectator's mind, holding him by the power of visual suggestion, is gone. It is as if a hypnotist were to snap his fingers in the face of his subject and say, "Right!" The motion picture spectator does not realize and analyze this shock, but he experiences it, and the subtle charm of the picture action is weakened. It therefore follows, and this writer advances it as fundamental, that no player should face the front except when his movements and attitudes may be made to appear to consistently permit it. Be natural above all things, and it will be found that the face may be presented to the front quite frequently enough for all real purposes of perfect expression.

~

There are other ways to convey expressions than by making faces to the front. Side views should be just as expressive when the situations call for them. Even the back may be eloquent if the actor knows his business. Indeed, the player who can only express his emotions by contortions of the face is no real picture player at all, and he should get out of the profession. The Spectator has dwelt on this point rather strongly, because, in his opinion, it is one of the defects that is apparent to a greater or lesser degree in the work of every picture producer at the present time. Not one of them is wholly free from it, however much they may think they are. . . .

The New York Dramatic Mirror, May 14, 1910

"SPECTATOR'S" COMMENTS

Probably the most marked change that has taken place in the style of picture acting in the last year or two has been in the matter of tempo. In the old days the pictures were literally "moving" pictures, and lively moving at that. Everything had to be on the jump. The more action that could be crowded into each foot of film the more perfect the picture was supposed to be. Some of this manner of picture acting still survives, usually when an old-timer does the acting or directing, but, generally speaking, it has given place to more deliberation. People in the pictures now move about somewhat after the style of human beings, instead of jumping jacks. For all of which let us give due thanks to the special divinity that rules over motion picture affairs.

~

One producing company, the Biograph, was a pioneer among American producers in this reform, and its films have long been distinguished by deliberation and repose, to such an extent that at one time it was a matter of much comment and criticism on the part of those who looked on the innovation as little short of sacrilege. Indeed, it may now be told as a matter worthy of record that the Biograph's first experiments along this line were undertaken with no little hesitation and fearsome doubt. Those having the responsibility for the change felt that they were treading on thin ice. So deeply rooted was the notion that speed was the thing that the experimenters were fearful that their attempts to introduce real acting into the films would be met with derisive laughter. Possibly to their astonishment the change at once met with the approval of the public. The people who paid their money to look at the pictures applauded the new idea (new in American pictures), and from that moment the habit commenced to grow, and has kept on growing ever since.

~

There is good reason why the public approves of slow acting without itself knowing or realizing the reason why. The spectator who is reading the story by the action of the picture is better able to understand the things that are going on when the acting is properly timed. The slow, impressive, and deliberate speaker is always more effective as an orator than the rapid-fire talker. Even the successful actor or popular singer is obliged to make himself understood, and the actor employs both speech and acting. The same rule applies to picture acting, with this difference, that in the pictures the action alone must tell the story; there are no spoken words to aid in conveying the idea. The public is not rapid in comprehension, as a general rule. We have only to remember how slow many people often are to see the point of an obvious joke when it is told to them from the stage to understand the truth of this statement. It is not strange, therefore, that spectators generally prefer deliberation in picture acting.

~

How far can and should this matter of deliberation and repose be carried in motion picture work? Again we find the answer in the one rule: Be natural. Let there be as much deliberation as the character of the action will naturally permit. Any more deliberation is ridiculous; any less is tempting failure. It is the mark of the good director to know just how far he can go in this direction. Some of them—one in particular that this writer has in mind —very often go to the limit in seeking for effective deliberation, but the one referred to seldom if ever goes too far, although to some people there may be times when he appears to do so. But excessive deliberation is not a matter that can be safely handled by novices or by those who are not sure of their ability to master the situation. It requires rare skill and delicacy of feeling to avoid overstepping the limit and to get just the proper degree of deliberation for the most impressive effect. Unless perfectly sure of himself, the average actor and director would do well to steer his craft by the signal light already pointed out: Be natural. Small boats should sail close to shore. . . .

The New York Dramatic Mirror, June 4, 1910

Says Lewis Jacobs: "Too much credit for the improvement of the movie art cannot be given the trade-paper critics of this period, especially Stephen Bush, Louis Reeves Harrison, Epes Sargent, and Frank Woods." [14] Woods, as noted, was the "Spectator." Here is Harrison; examples of the others' work follow. Harrison later wrote a book called *Screencraft*.

Credits were still not given on most films. Harrison did not know that he was here praising Mary Pickford in another Griffith film, one that was made during the Griffith company's first California sojourn.[15]

Sir William Osler, referred to near the end, was an internationally famous Canadian physician.

RAMONA

LOUIS REEVES HARRISON

I secured one of a few unsold box-seats, pushed through a crowd back of the rail, and sat down. A mediocre variety act was in progress on the stage; so much the better—the auditorium was lighted, and I could study the people. Every orchestra and balcony seat was occupied, and the deep standing room was packed to the limit. The audience was a quiet one, was rather above than below the average in quality, and it was largely composed of men. The men were of all classes and conditions, they were uniformly earnest-looking, most of them seemed to be business men, who had possibly left the absorbing occupation of trying to do others as they might reasonably expect to be done, in order to rest an hour or two and recuperate from brain fag. The theater was a popular one, usually well attended, but, on this occasion, early in the afternoon, the attendance was unusually large. The occasion was that of a special release, the release of a great picture play, a play greater than its announced theme.

The wrongs of the American Indian are not present wrongs; he was once an interesting type, especially in Cooper's novels, but to those who knew him as he was and those who know him as he is, the red savage is not associated with pictures of injured innocence, but what's the odds! Story writers naturally affiliate with hazy historical conditions from an ingrained dislike of conforming to facts.

No matter about the ostensible theme. How about the play?

When the vaudeville act ended, not a man left the place. The lights were turned down, a title was shown on the screen, there was intense silence, the breathless expectancy which usually precedes an important stage presentation. Advance interest was clearly indicated.

The producers were known. They were strongly entrenched in public confidence. They were known to be in earnest, striving to attain the best possible results, never pandering to the baser elements of society nor catering to perverted instincts. They were not in the habit of trifling with serious patrons of picture shows nor of jollying the noisy and unthinking element. They were known to be conscientious producers, who regarded their business seriously, who strove to maintain a high average of quality. They had not committed the error of setting the theater-going public down as being the scum of the community, and, in consequence, their bare announcement of a special feature was enough to draw a crowd, including many who ordinarily stay away from exhibitions of motion pictures. If it is within the province of honest criticism to discover what merits appreciation and encouragement, the lesson is right here, a concrete lesson, easily comprehended by those who really have the exhibitor's interest at heart.

The play was *Ramona*.

Wherein was it great?

The idea of the white man's injustice to the Indian did not reach out into the sympathies of the audience at all, but it seemed as though the playwright or director, or possibly both, had consciously or unconsciously emphasized a bigger, broader, and finer theme, the great force responsible for our origin, the one which has inspired poets of all ages, but recently discovered by scientists as the most effective cause in the evolution of man.

Natural selection!

The story of Ramona as told on the screen is as dear as it is old. It is that of an impassioned girl who breaks through the exactions of a superior but rigorous and unsympathetic environment to follow the natural dictates of her heart. She loves and marries a weaker character simply because he responds to an ideal set up in the shrine of her affections, and, womanlike, when she is dominated by the most powerful of human emotions, she is bent on self-sacrifice. She takes up the heavier burden and carries it with superior strength. White men despoil the husband, they acquire a habit still in operation regardless of race, the habit of not allowing conscience to handicap business. The husband submits like a weakling. He deplores his fate instead of making a manly effort to accomplish something for the sake of the sweet creature who has given him all a woman has to give. He loses his head, winds up in miserable collapse, and is removed from the face of the earth in the cold-blooded way that nature eliminates the unfit.

The part is effective as an offset and is admirably acted.

But the woman?

Having sacrificed every material interest for the man's sake, having shared and sweetened his humble lot, having brought into the world one of God's own little creatures, only to bury it in heart-breaking sorrow, she follows her weary way with unwavering courage to the bitter end, to the final excess of devotion at her husband's funeral pyre. This splendid character is the pivotal one and is portrayed with an intelligent grasp of fine detail which gives exquisite finish and charm to the play.

Here is where personality comes in.

With no audience to kindle enthusiasm and stimulate esthetic effort, it would seem as though the characters must depend wholly on academic postures, gesticulation and facial expression, but those who sit in front know better.

What is it that goes over into the hearts of thousands who attend picture plays?

What is it that reaches out and gets a grip on human hearts at business, political, or social gatherings?

What else is it but the genial glow, the thrilling magnetism, of an exuberant and interesting personality?

Here is where woman's personality comes in.

No one ever looks twice at a man's picture. As a mere thing of beauty, he is usually unmanly; as a creature of forceful character, he is usually unlovely. We look to woman for what beautifies existence, and, as interest in picture plays is stimulated by what is seen, it becomes centered on the heroine of the story. To suit the role, she must be lovable. Thoughtful appreciation of what is required by the role and good taste in things feminine count, but, when she delights the eye and stirs the irresponsible pulses of responsible men with a dazzling array of potent womanly attributes, she wins because she represents the ideal creatures of our heartaches and dreams. *She* goes over. Any man who does not think so should send for Doctor Osler.

Ramona, as played, is a powerful drama of natural love. It is set amid scenes of surpassing beauty, so sympathetically chosen as to lend the whole play a pure spirit of poesy; scene and dramatic art are so harmoniously blended that the picture play is a veritable poem. The producers have advanced a step in the evolution of a new art and blazed the way for additional, greater achievement.

The Moving Picture World, June 4, 1910

In the following Harrison apparently uses the term "art director" not as it is used today but to mean the director of the art—or, simply, the director.

HOW TO IMPROVE THE BUSINESS

LOUIS REEVES HARRISON

The men who have money invested in the production of moving pictures are not blind to the advantages of turning out high-class reels because the present benefits are large and the future gain from superiority of production will be two or three times that of today. It is especially favorable to present success that photoplays should so interest the intelligent class throughout the country as to bring in the desirable patronage of those who have the means and leisure to go every day to the picture exhibitions. A high state of prosperity for the exhibitor will be reached whenever the average quality of the pictures shown rises to a point of merit that will command the patronage of those who now regard the picture shows as a childish and decidedly inferior form of entertainment. Splendid plays, of enduring interest, would enable the exhibitor of the present day to charge more for desirable seats, would fill his house at better rates, and would tend to elevate the quality of the average audience without decreasing its numbers. It is true that many exhibitors are catering to the lowest class only. They imagine that all human nature is on their level, but it is equally true that those pictures which appeal to the most enlightened members of moving-picture audiences are at the same time more satisfactory to the people who occasionally spend five or ten cents for a couple of hours of amusement.

Why not give the exhibitors the finest motion pictures that money can procure? Because of the greater cost?

That is certainly a short-sighted policy. If a producer's present sale is limited to fifty or one hundred reels of each subject, the poor ones will go to the junk pile in the future, while those strongly popular to-day will be like the most enjoyable music rolls for self-playing pianos—they will be in large demand for private and family use. This means thousands of dollars additional profit in an untouched market. Every strong play helps all concerned, strengthening the hold of moving pictures on the public, pleasing people in general, advancing the interests of the exhibitor, and giving every department of the business a dignity which no part of it now enjoys. Every such play means ten thousand dollars or more supplementary profit to the far-sighted manufacturer, so that a few hundreds of dollars additional expenditure necessary for improved quality seems trivial indeed.

How and where can that added outlay be most profitably and beneficially placed in the manufacture of picture reels?

Where are the weak spots in production?

The initial weakness is due to the fact that an enormous number of amateurs, who would like to see their ideas set forth in print or on the screen, who have not taken sufficient pains to prepare themselves for dramatic work of any kind, pour in a misleading flood of scenarios containing occasional ideas, but so badly presented as to need reconstruction at the hands of an overworked director or some one individual employed for the purpose. The result is a monotony of production, a feeble sameness of idea, where vigor and variety are needed. The cowboy chases the Indian, the sheriff pursues the villain, the hero embraces the heroine at the end, or the pianist plays the wedding march at the foreseen conclusion until the steady patron grows sick and weary of motion pictures as a form of entertainment. Brilliant professional writers, whose stories command from fifty to five hundred dollars in current periodicals, are given no inducements to write picture scenarios, or they would otherwise contribute to this much desired end.

Another weak spot is the lack of a competent "art director."

I realize perfectly that these little plays must be popular to succeed. When I refer to high quality, I do not mean anything technical or abstruse. When I speak of an "art director," I do not mean a man of such exalted ideas that he will attempt to lift the pictural drama above the comprehension of the common people. I mean that the regular stage manager should be put in charge of the actors; this will give him enough to do. He is obliged to place them and move them in a very limited scope, to concentrate his mind upon an infinite number of details in the swift performance of each scene, and his natural activities are on the stage. Picture plays, like those on the stage, are the result of composite activity in which the author, the director, and the actor participate, but the picure play's appeal is purely visual. There must be a man of imagination to mentally portray the various scenes in advance, just as the author does, and he should have enough artistic sensibility to be aware of what goes wrong in the rehearsed presentation. I saw a "thriller" the other day representing the forecastle of a vessel in a storm on the rocks. A dipper-full, then a bucket full of water dashed over the bow barely wet a portion of the deck. Then a hose was kept spraying in one place. Then came a scene sub-titled "The Calm After the Storm." In nature, there is a higher sea running after than during mid-storm, but we were treated to the spectacle of a man hanging to a log in a mill-pond. Grass was visible in the left corner and a little kid-critic near me said: "Hully gee, see dem weeds!" There was no thrill. The performance was ambitious but in parts so inept that it broke the spell. A competent art overseer would not have let that scene spoil the rest of the reel. If it disgusted the kid-critic, there can be small wonder why others regard such productions as childish and unworthy of the money spent on them. No concern engaged in turning out examples of the pictural art can enjoy the favor of the people long if those engaged to turn out reels are deficient in appreciation of art. "Art is an instrument of thought the knowledge of which is to be acquired in order to be applied."

Get original plays, modern or historical, conveying an idea or picturing truly some interesting phase of human life, put them on with intelligence and good taste. That is the sum of my idea. If I am wrong, I am always open to conviction.

The Moving Picture World, December 24, 1910

The more things change . . .

VIOLENCE AND BLOODSHED

LOUIS REEVES HARRISON

There is nothing new about public hostility to the introduction of scenes of violence in plays. For a long time the French theater—when it laid down the law for Continental Europe—permitted no killing in the sight of the audience, one peculiar exception being suicide. A character could kill himself in a tragedy, by poison or steel, but was not allowed to kill any other character in the play—not so you could see it.

The English were more bloodthirsty.

Voltaire rejoiced in an English theater when he saw Brutus harangue the mob with a bloody knife in his hand over the body of the murdered dictator. Early tragedy in England was given to shedding blood on a grand scale. The rude audiences especially enjoyed the feast, the more there was of it, the stronger they thought the play, while no such representation was tolerated in France. The audience learned of what had happened from an eye-witness.

Just how far art should follow nature is a delicate question. To my way of thinking the struggle is an essential part of the play; there are pathetic and telling situations tamed, if not lost, where tragedy is implied instead of actually seen. On the other hand, I am disgusted with any deliberate attempt to awaken bestial desire, or feed blood to the coarser element of an audience by working up to a brutal scene for the mere sake of its brutality. Accounts of suicides, hangings, and stabbings which are given a prominence in the daily press are often of no advantage to the community, and it is just as well to eliminate them from moving pictures altogether, unless intelligent censorship can be exercised. The accumulation of abhorrent incidents given in Indian and cowboy plays under the pretense of picturing actual life is so repulsive in its low savagery, so beastly and unsavory, that it might be just as well to cut out such plays indiscriminately. When these plays are filled with murder, rapine, torture, and false sentiment, they are not only inartistic, but are ineffective save with the few low-brows who like them, and, besides, are turning millions away from the little theaters. They are repellant to the cultivated, and even cease in the course of time to stimulate the jaded appetites of the unwashed. No necessity exists for any such representations; they are not pictures of life; rarely have they the faintest pretense to historical accuracy; supposed thrillers they are, but they excite more derision and disgust. I have seen decent people before a theater entrance turn away at the sight of a poster announcing one of these dramas of blood and nastiness, and many refuse to go inside of a picture show because of them.

It is quite another thing if tragedy comes in the natural course of a story as a matter of poetic justice when it tends to elevate the struggle or the characters presented, where the effect is ennobling instead of degrading, or where there is a profound lesson involved.

Why should not art be natural?

It is true that all things in nature may not be fit for representation on the stage, but no reason exists why art should directly oppose nature. Where there is a valuable idea to be conveyed the audience is unwilling to accept mere resemblances. If there is suffering involved, such as we all feel in the eternal struggle, the suffering must be shown; it excites our compassion and may lead to greater tenderness in our views. In our secret hearts we all like to see life depicted on the stage as it really is, and rebel against conventions and traditions as we do against a picture given purely for the sake of its sickening horrors. Let us have what is true, what is going on; existence of today as we all recognize it; hold up the shame to ridicule; lay bare the grafting of politicians and other unclean birds of prey; extol the nobility and the value of splendid efforts, and tell again the same old, sweet story of love as often as possible. We all enjoy a play taken from any old era, when it's good, but we enjoy it most when it reflects our own times; we like it best when its scenes, and manners, and characters, and morals are of today. If, in the natural course of things, the story involves a death struggle, that is all right if the tragic feature is an incident in a design, not a designed incident.

It is all right for the dramatist to see the immoral as well as the moral side of life; he can be fully aware of the worst characteristics and basest motives of those around him, and it may be to the advantage of what he writes; he can even be influenced by the same forces as those operating against human betterment, but he must have a strain of lofty aspiration if he would appeal to the highest as well as the lowest elements in the average audience. Let his purpose be high, the incident is excused.

Let no playwright be worried about the "happy ending." Such a termination is an anomaly, if not an impropriety, if the trend of human weakness and the impelling forces of nature point straight to a tragic finale. We know where neglected disease leads, and bad habit is disease. The transforming power of evil habit not only furnishes an abundance of dramatic material, but gives the audience a theme to study and can be made to point a lesson with a tragic ending. The drama has often found its finest expression in tragedy, consistent and true to nature, yet moral. The moral nature of Macbeth had become a horrible wreck before his overthrow and death.

The latter was expected and deserved. The tragedy was the natural sequence to his crimes, and poetic justice was exemplified.

The man, whether he be playwright or producer, who says that our people want to see in picture plays certain things that are vitiating such plays, is in ignorance of what is going on around him. The whole country is aroused on the question of race betterment, and is deeply and unselfishly interested in making the lives of those who are to follow us finer and more beautiful than our own. We do not desire to stimulate what is low in our children, but to train them to exercise self-control, to let their minds dominate their animal natures. We hope to make them better than we are; millions of parents are giving the best part of their lives to that noble end. Moving pictures are now a factor in this evolution, and the best we can do —we who are interested in the business—is to treat the public with the same sort of decency and respect that we hope to receive.

The Moving Picture World, April 22, 1911

The following editorial highlights the conditions and tactical problems of film criticism at that time.

The Fall of Troy was an import, "perhaps the first important revelation to America of the glories of the Italian film." [16] It was also one of the multiple-reel foreign films whose impact here showed that the American public was ready for something more than the short domestic product. *The Tale of Two Cities* —this was already the second film version—had, in its leading roles, Maurice Costello, destined to be one of John Barrymore's fathers-in-law, and Florence Turner, the "Vitagraph Girl." Also in the cast was the relatively new Norma Talmadge.

Alan Dale was then the influential drama critic of the Hearst newspapers. Those who think that the power of drama critics is a modern phenomenon may be interested in this comment on Dale: "When he takes pen in hand, the playhouses throughout the land tremble upon their foundations and the faces of actor folk burn white with fear." [17]

FILM CRITICISM IN THE LAY PRESS

In certain quarters, exhibitors of moving pictures are suggesting that the newspapers should send their dramatic critics to the picture houses, the same as they are now sent to the houses playing regular drama. We had thought that matter over many times before. Sometimes the idea looked good to us, and then at other times it did not.

Eventually we expect to see the lay press take up the work of criticizing the films and in that way relieve us of a very monotonous and thankless job. This will come at a time when the average photoplay has reached a height which will compel the recognition by newspapers of the work of motion picture dramatists. At present, newspaper criticism of films in the locality where the film is being shown will be of very little value to the exhibitor who is asking for the innovation. The film criticism in that case would naturally come a day after the picture had been seen and had gone on its way, which would be of very little value to anybody. Local comment, moreover, is not compatible with the change-daily and first-run idea. Neither is it a good idea when one thinks of some of the films that are being produced nowadays, because some untrammeled dramatic critic might turn into very humorous reading the serious efforts of some misfit producer. That this is true is already demonstrated, for we have before us now as we write this, a criticism which makes a burlesque of a dramatic film. The criticism appeared in the Albany, N. Y., *Evening Journal*. It is filled with mock heroics, and altogether the critic seems to have had a very hilarious time writing it.

When the films are uniformly better and finally attract the attention of the metropolitan press, those great newspapers with a subscription list near the million mark may do something in the line of criticism that will be of service. Large metropolitan dailies cover a great deal of ground in their immediate vicinity, and often as far as five hundred miles from where they are printed, but to a very limited extent. The metropolitan daily critic will be of no great benefit to the community until pictures are good enough to be kept on the boards for a week. Such pictures as *The Fall of Troy* and *The Tale of Two Cities,* which are masterpieces in their line, are already attracting the attention of the press in many cities, where in many cases the film is booked for a long run or a return engagement.

Perhaps the film critic of a metropolitan paper will never be able to work as much havoc in the picture trade as he has done before in the theatrical line. By his edict the dramatic critic has done, or undone in the past, many productions costing thousands of dollars. This he will not be able to do with the film play. If the critic comes out in the morning edition with a scathing comment and manages to show why and wherefore the film is not worthy, the said film, if it be below the advertising, can be put into the "can" and another substituted for it much easier than a whole production of theatrical people can be disbanded and scenery sent to the storehouse and another production substituted in its place.

The lay critic will have to adopt a new plan of attack in going after the picture drama, because the film is more elusive than the road company. The film critic's powers will be, so far as the exhibitor is concerned, limited to his own locality. What Alan Dale has to say about a moving picture in New York will make very little difference to the exhibitor in San Francisco. One thing is certain, that some of the manufacturers of inferior plays will be told the truth in very unsparing terms. It will do them very little good to become peevish and whine when anybody tells the truth about some of their faulty films. There are some manufacturers who have received a good notice occasionally for something that they have done. It is surprising to note how some of them can "kid" themselves into believing that they are turning out uniformly high-class stuff simply on the strength of one or two flattering press notices at some time or another.

There must still be an authoritative paper that goes everywhere, in order that the exhibitor may know what is coming to him, and that paper we expect will be, as it has been in the past, the *Moving Picture World.* We shall be glad when the day arrives when we can copy directly what the *New York World* critic says, or the *Times* or the *Herald,* and pass it on to our readers in States far away. It will not only be cheaper for us, but what a relief it will be from the whining of the man who cannot stand the truth.

The Moving Picture World, May 20, 1911

Sargent was a scenario writer who also wrote articles about scenario-writing, which helps to explain his difference with Harrison (see p. 45) on the director's importance.

THE EARMARK ON THE FILM

EPES WINTHROP SARGENT

Nothing more to the point has been said about the sameness of photoplays than was printed in a recent issue of *The Moving Picture World* in a letter from an old exhibitor to the new manufacturer, in which he alluded to the marks by which certain of the directors leave their imprints upon most of the stories produced by them. But little more was said than to give a hint, but the subject might have been extended almost to the number of directors in the business.

The matter was treated lightly, but it is pregnant with suggestion and the earmark of the director is the real answer to the questions as to the sameness of the films.

A magazine represents the work of perhaps a score of authors. Most editors, certainly all successful ones, seek to retain as much of the individuality of the writer as is possible. The stories may have been selected because they conformed to certain editorial requirements; indeed, a magazine without an established editorial policy could not last long, but so long as the stories meet the broad requirements of that policy they are let alone and the necessary editing is done with a view to retaining as much of the personality of the author as possible.

In the studio the reverse is the case. A story may be edited with due care and be turned over to the director with the individuality of the author, but the director will have none of it. He protests that the story will never do, that he must fix it up—and he does, precisely as he has "fixed up" every story he has made in the past six months.

The original idea in advertising for scenarios from outside authors was to get away from the sameness of the pictures the studio director was making. It was planned that the story writers and other outsiders should give variety to the product, but this end is not gained if the stories in their final development still represent the producer rather than the author.

The trouble appears to be that in most studios there is no one to direct the director. He is regarded with undue respect by his employers, and they defer to him in most things. The attitude is a relic of the days when the photoplay was yet young and when a director who could direct meant something more than mere profit. More than one company has been given its first uplift by a director who could make good pictures, and even when the field broadened until there were plenty of able directors, the superstition that it was bad luck to cross a director still obtained and still does obtain in many studios. The director is not human who will not avail himself of this position to do precisely as he thinks best, even though his ideas of best are the exploitation of his personal beliefs as opposed to dramatic rule, common sense, and the change in the fashion of films.

Hundreds of plays are spoiled each year because directors are permitted without restraint to make a picture precisely as they please, owing to the belief that a director must not be interfered with. Any original bit in a script that does not harmonize with the producer's own ideas of originality is rewritten to conform to the hard and fast rule, and then the cry is raised that there is no use getting outside scripts because there is no originality among authors. There never will be so long as there is a double check against originality in the form of an editor and a producer each of whom is determined that things shall be done thus and so. The producer has the last word and his personality is the more strongly dominant, but the script often comes to the director already half spoiled because the editor himself has some pet theories.

Those familiar with the conditions in any studio can tell almost invariably which director made a certain story simply through the earmarks on the film. The ingenious bit on which the author spent a couple of hours may be done to death in ten lines—and upon the flattened wreck is raised another of the same old stories with all the earmarks of the producer, and the manufacturer wonders why his stuff seems so same, but doesn't dare ask the producer lest he be offended.

Audiences are less thoughtful of the absent producer's feelings, and now and then when two photoplays from the same production get on the same program, the marked similarity brings forth comment that is far from appreciative. The successful, the continuously successful, photoplay maker is the man who will insist that every member of his staff devote his endeavor to preserving the originality of the writer, whose editor merely edits for technical faults, whose director directs the script given him, and whose players do not know more than the author, editor, and director combined. Such things may come to pass some day. May that day be soon.

The Moving Picture World, August 26, 1911

Part Two

THE FEATURE FILM

In addition to his critical writing, W. Stephen Bush was an early lecturer about—and with—films. Hence his partiality to lectures expressed in this article and on p. 63.

DO LONGER FILMS MAKE BETTER SHOW?

W. STEPHEN BUSH

Within the last six months the production of subjects consisting of two or more reels has shown a marked increase. The most notable of them, Dante's *Inferno* and Torquato Tasso's *Jerusalem Delivered,* the former in five and the latter in four reels, have been produced in Europe and marketed in this country independently of any organization of film makers. The success of these two features has greatly stimulated a trend toward releases of greater length among American manufacturers, who had begun to give the possibilities of longer films their earnest attention. As a result releases of greater length have become numerous in both the Licensed and Independent camps. There is every reason to believe that this tendency toward feature films of greater length will continue and that the growing number of such films will bring about some important changes in the business of exhibiting moving pictures. Some of these feature films have been offered as regular releases, the various reels constituting the same subject being given to the exhibitor two or more days apart. The disadvantages of such an arrangement were too obvious, however, to continue very long, and of late all reels treating the same subject have been released at the same time and placed in the hands of the exhibitor as special releases. It is upon the theory and practice of a simultaneous release of all one-subject reels that these remarks are based.

I think the day when patrons counted the number of pictures and judged the show by quantity rather than by quality has passed never to return. That kind of patronage was never of the most desirable kind. In the course of the development of the moving picture it has been replaced by audiences of a decidedly higher grade and better average. Quality is to-day the test much more than quantity. This has been proved again and again in practice. Two good reels, maintaining a high average, will always win out against a greater quantity of junk. The argument then, that the higher quality will bring the better results, seems indisputably sound.

Viewed from this standpoint of plain logic the feature film ought to be the best guarantee of financial as well as artistic success. The notion so prevalent among the ignorant, that art cannot be served without sacrifice of profit, is fatally wrong. Art in moving pictures pays in dollars and cents, which plain fact is respectfully commended to every person connected with this great industry.

The feature film of greater length must be built upon quality, it must breathe quality in every inch, or it is doomed before it is fairly born. It is a most significant fact that of all feature films so far released by either domestic or foreign makers, every one comes up to the test of superior quality. Only people of brains, who understand a story and know how to tell it with effect, are capable of producing such films. No feature film, of which we have any knowledge, has been produced from any original scenario. The time for such productions will come, sooner perhaps that we believe, but it is best that, at present, literature and history shall furnish the materials for the feature film exclusively.

It is the masterpiece of the ages that especially invites filming, and the reason for it is very plain. An epic that has pleased and charmed many generations is most likely to stand the test of cinematographic reproduction. A work of fiction that has moved millions of men and women and children to happy laughter and healthy sorrow will not lose its charm on the screen of a moving picture theater. After all, the word "classic" has some meaning. It implies the approval of the best people in the most enlightened times. The merits of a classic subject are nonetheless certain because known and appreciated by comparatively few men. It is the business of the moving picture to make them known to all. Because the feature film, as we have seen it so far, has measured up to this great mission of inviting the masses to enjoy the treasures of literature with the favored few, it has found such a profound and instantaneous response wherever it has been shown.

Do practical men agree with this? For an answer we need not confine ourselves to this country, where the proof of success is so manifest to view. In England and in continental Europe the exhibitors have risen to their opportunities. From various parts of England managers have, according to interviews in a British trade journal, expressed themselves thus: "If the quality of long films is maintained as in *Zigomar,* short films will eventually become a drug on the market." "These long films enthral one ten times more than short ones, they are so absorbing, that I simply forget all the troubles of my business day." "I believe long films are the future standby of the picture palace." "Of course the public wish for long films or why should I secure the coming long 'uns."

There is no danger that these feature films will become too numerous. Their production requires an extra outlay of money, an unusual amount of skill and experience, often they demand a high degree of scholarship in addition to a thorough knowledge of the silent stage and its peculiar needs. Even the exhibitor with a small seating capacity, with a three-reel show, will find the occasional showing of a feature film a profitable venture. A two-reel production will invariably tell the story more satisfactorily than a one-reel effort and the two-reel production ought not to embarrass any exhibitor. To the exhibitor with a large seating capacity the feature film of greater length offers unusual opportunities. It places in his hands a weapon with which he can successfully encounter almost any theatrical opposition.

What the feature film, however, demands absolutely is proper presentation. It will not be slighted. If it is run with undue speed its charm and power will invariably suffer. Music, effects, and lecture are indispensable adjuncts. Effects for a feature film can be carefully prepared and rehearsed, having due regard to consistency and psychological moments. There is time, too, for the arranging of a special musical program, which should not be entrusted to any but a competent and experienced player. A lecture will relieve that natural tension and impatience which a long, dumb show is bound to cause and will make the story plainer and the enjoyment of the patrons keener.

Nothing could be more suitable to vary the daily program than an occasional feature film. The only difficulty the exhibitor, who is prepared to give such a film proper presentation, must encounter is the securing of a date far enough advanced to allow of effective advertising.

The question of the feature film in more than one reel is the vital one, affecting every branch of the industry, but more especially the exhibitor. It would seem, therefore, that exhibitors ought to be heard from freely and fully. It is hoped that these remarks will give rise to a useful discussion of so important a subject. *The Moving Picture World* is the proper forum of such a discussion, and the hospitality of its columns is heartily extended to all who have a word to offer on the situation as it stands today and as it will probably develop in the future.

The Moving Picture World, October 28, 1911

The move to longer films was inevitable. A confluence of forces brought it about. First, foreign films of more than one or two reels were having success that showed the public appetite for longer work. Second, the Independent companies, eager to do things differently from the Licensed companies, opted for the longer films that the Licensed companies had resisted. Third, there was a growing impulse in film artists themselves to burst the twelve-minute bond. Griffith made a few two-reel films toward the end of his Biograph days and, in mutiny against his employers, made one four-reel film, *Judith of Bethulia*. This outraged the executives, who saw no reason for tampering with a successful formula; so, in order to grow, Griffith left Biograph. (Which soon sank.) [1]

From the viewpoint of criticism, this general move to the feature film was absolutely crucial. Now there was not only more substantial work to write about, it *had* to be written about. The repertorial function of criticism was needed as longer films played longer engagements in any one place; and the evaluative functions had greater play.

Before the change-over was quite accomplished, the long films were still the foreign films. *Homer's Odyssey* was precisely what Stephen Bush had asked for in the previous selection: a "masterpiece of the ages" in multiple-reel form. This was not the first or the last Italian film to make a strong impression in this era. The influence of one foreign country often dominates at one time. Before the First War, it was Italy; in the twenties, as we shall see, it was Germany; in the thirties, it was France.

HOMER'S ODYSSEY

W. STEPHEN BUSH

The filming in three reels of a number of episodes taken from the Odyssey of Homer marks a new epoch in the history of the motion picture as a factor in education. To make my meaning clear, I wish to emphasize once more that I do not use the expression "educational" in its narrowest sense; in other words, I do not speak of A-B-C books, primers, slates, lead pencils, chalk, and blackboard. Every film that broadens the mind, stimulates the faculties, and awakens an admiration for what is beautiful may in the best and widest sense of the word be termed educational. If the work of the Milano Films Company should only please readers and students of Homer, if its superb art were entirely lost upon the masses, I could say but little for the genuine educational value of these reels. Unless these reels shall please, delight, entertain, and instruct the average moving picture audience, they fail in the highest mission and destiny of the cinematographic, *i.e.,* to bring the great treasures of art and literature within the reach of the general public. Here is the crucial test: Have the makers of the film transferred the spirit of the poem, its indescribably charming and fascinating atmosphere, its sweetness, its power, its heroic size, its winning simplicity from the cold black type to the moving strips of celluloid? The answer is "Yes." They have indeed done all of this, and have performed their task in a manner which leaves the critic silent in admiration.

It is but just to say in connection with the subject that the Milano Films Company and their American sponsors owe no little debt of gratitude to the small group of ambitious and resourceful American manufacturers who have within the past five or six years labored without ceasing for the uplift of the motion picture. They have paved the way for the success of such a picture as this. In improving the quality of the American-made film they have improved the taste of the moving picture patrons and have slowly but surely attracted the best classes of the population to attendance at the moving picture entertainment. Utterly discarding the cheap melodrama and the vulgar farce, which at one time threatened to overwhelm the picture, they went for the sources of their inspiration to history, to sacred and classic literature, to clean and popular fiction, steadily growing with the greatness of their tasks. The names they used to conjure with were immortal names, from Shakespeare and Molière to the great dramatists, novelists, and poets of more modern days. Were it not for their labors, such a production as this release of the Milano Films Company might have small reason to expect a welcome at the hands of the average exhibitor.

With a full appreciation of the labors of these few American film-makers I have no hesitation in saying that their best efforts have been eclipsed by this Milano production. To find a standard of comparison I will have to take the *Inferno* of Dante, made by the same manufacturers. In both productions I find the same painstaking care in the elaboration of details, the same ability to understand and make visible in pictures the spirit of the poems. The Milano Films Company brings to the aid of the director or directors the suggestions of scholars, of painters, of sculptors, of historians. No scene is presented that does not show these pleasing proofs of artistic skill and thoroughness. Every inch of film proclaims the fact that different masters of their crafts are doing their best. I am convinced that every human being looking at these reels is bound to feel from the very first scene the subtle influence of the genius of Homer. Let it be remembered that Homer sang his heroic ballads to a primitive people who knew nothing of libraries and of all the aids of modern education and who had to be moved chiefly by the beauty of form. In this respect the masses of the people have undergone little change; they are still enchanted by the beauty of form. With the possible exception of vaudeville performers on the cheap circuits, no man or woman can stand in the aisles of a Gothic cathedral without feeling a deep, yet pleasing thrill; no man or woman can hear the strains of Mozart's music without perceiving, however vaguely, some of its spell over the heart; nobody can look at a great painting without at least a slight stirring of the nobler nature. It is much the same with a first reading of Homer. The spectator at an exhibition of these reels will have an even keener experience than the reader of the poem. Am I paying too high a tribute to this production? Consider that the *Odyssey,* after more than twenty-five centuries, is still revered and cherished as the greatest of poems; remember how generation after generation has held fast to this precious heritage; bear in mind that it is even at this day the basis of every academic course, and no tribute here can be more than as a drop of water in a mighty ocean.

The story of the *Odyssey* is simplicity itself. Ulysses, the King of Ithaca, a small island in the Ionian Sea, having helped to conquer Troy, sets out on his homeward journey. He meets with many misfortunes and adventures, at last reaches his native land and wreaks his vengeance on the men who in his absence had cruelly harassed his wife and eaten up his substance. He is recognized by his wife, and the two are reunited. Less than a hundred words tell the tale. "The "plot" of the story was old before Homer was born. The unsurpassed merit of the great epic lies in the characterization of its hero, Ulysses, and in the description of the incidents of the long and troubled journey. To understand and to feel fully what is meant by the genius of Homer you must see the pictures.

It has seemed strange to me that the makers of the films contented themselves with the production of three reels. They have chosen the parts of the poem which presented the most difficulties, and seemed to enjoy the work just because it made unheard-of demands on the filmer's art. The adventure of Ulysses and his companions in the cave of Polyphemus, the giant, seemed, next to the picturing of the Sirens, the hardest to render in moving pictures. The skill the producers have shown in two scenes is beyond the power of praise. The scenery and settings of the feast of the Phæacians are a delight to the eye and marvelously true in respect to Greek customs, manners, religious rites, the appointment of the household, as they existed in the Homeric age. The adventure on the Island of Helios and the fearful passage through the narrows between Scylla and Charybdis are based on famous classic paintings and have now the element of motion added to their art. The Milano Company has created a true Ulysses even to the fine physical proportions, a hero in the ancient sense of the word. He commands both admiration and sympathy from the first. The acting of Ulysses makes the character perfect from the standpoint of the reader of Homer. There is not a false move throughout the three thousand feet of film, every look, every gesture measures up to the Homeric conception. Telemachus, the son of Ulysses, is another perfect creation of Milano art. Even the semblance of son to father, so often mentioned in the poem, is there. Penelope is well rendered, and so are the minor characters—Laertes, the old swineherd Eumaeus, Antinous, the chief of the suitors, Alcinous and Arete, the king and queen of the Phæacians and their lovely daughter, the "white-armed Nausicaa." Even in this minute detail the film makers have adhered to the letter of the poem. The element of the supernatural has been cleverly treated by the makers. A modern audience is all too easily surfeited with an overdisplay of supernatural forces, and yet it would be impossible to portray the adventures of Ulysses without showing in some way the intervention of the gods. The Milano Company wisely confined themselves to the introduction of Pallas Athene (Minerva), always an impressive figure and not without the attributes of loveliness. Music and effects will suggest themselves to every intelligent exhibitor, and a lecture would of course greatly heighten the effect of the reels on any audience, whether cultured or otherwise.

Few people will content themselves with one view of these pictures. As with a favorite book we want to renew the acquaintance as often as we can. The eternal message of Homer, the message of youth and happiness, is much like the "eternal feminine"—"it draws us on."

There is much proof in these pictures that the motion picture is both a fine and an useful art.

The Moving Picture World, March 16, 1912

The success of *Quo Vadis?* was a decisive factor, if one was still needed, in shifting American film-making to the long feature. For one reason, its great length—two hours—justified an admission charge of $1.50 in its first engagements, as against the otherwise prevailing fifteen cents.[2]

Enrico Guazzoni, the director, is credited with influencing Griffith, Lubitsch, and Hollywood spectacles in general through this and similar films.[3] (Rodin called *Quo Vadis?* a masterpiece.[4]) Gustavo Serena continued to act in Italian films until the 1960s. Amleto Novelli was one of the most famous actors of the Italian silent film.

QUO VADIS?

JAMES S. MC QUADE

Some time ago, when reviewing *Pharaoh, King of Egypt,* by Cines, I made the assertion that when the Societa Italiana Cines attempted to do a big thing it was always done well. In the case of *Quo Vadis?* the assertion is altogether too tame, and even to say that the production is "superbly well done" falls short of the mark. But the mere use of superlatives is inadequate to do justice to any great work; there must be careful analysis and a keen study of the component elements, as well as a nice appreciation of what constitutes their harmonious arrangement and treatment in the synthetic whole.

Surely one of the most vital and indispensable requisites in the production of such a subject as *Quo Vadis?* is that of atmosphere, by which, in this case, for the lack of a better term, is meant the subtle power of translating the beholder into the midst of old Rome when the early Christians were looked upon as members of a pernicious secret society, when the last of the Caesars and his favorites drained to the dregs the cups of the revelling and cruelty, and when arenic spectacles included fights to the death of gladiators and the devouring of men, women, and children by ravenous beasts.

The *Quo Vadis?* of Cines does more; it gives us a view of Rome, burning, one of the most impressive spectacles ever pictured. Nowhere else could this have been done with equal fidelity; for the style of architecture has changed but slightly, though the narrow, tortuous streets of the old city have been replaced by broader, straighter avenues and the buildings made more substantial, while those in charge of the selection of the sections in front of the camera were perfectly familiar with the appearance of the old. Where else could the hiding places of the early Christians have been pictured so realistically? The catacombs and the other underground retreats of the new sect in Rome would have been imperfectly reproduced had the pictures been made in any other country. And where else could the vast amphitheater, with its perfect outlines and faithful observance of the minutest details, have been secured? One is actually impressed, as he looks at the flying chariots in the arena, the clash of the gladiators, the shimmer of the white garments of the vestal virgins, on a section of the amphitheater immediately to the right of that occupied by Nero and his court and patrician followers, the huddled-up crowd of devoted Christians calmly, or affrightedly, awaiting death in the arena, and the rush of the hungry lions on their prey, one, I say, is actually impressed, for the moment, that he has forced his way back through the past, for a period of some nineteen hundred years, and is gazing into the face of Nero with its imperious and cruel lines.

Are there yet other examples needed to accentuate the omnipresence of atmosphere throughout this photodrama? If there be, come with me to the last banquet of Petronius, the Arbiter, the Canon, of Court taste at the time, who, after drinking his last drink, crashes the costly and exquisitely fashioned myrrhine bowl on the floor so that Nero may not possess it, and then smilingly bleeds to death. View also the banquets at the Imperial Palace and on the Pond of Agrippa. There you have extravagant expenditures on costly wines and rare delicacies; lavish display of dress and ornament and furnishings, with flash of wit and show of fair beauty, intermixed with beguiling coquetry and shameless debauchery.

And atmosphere is accompanied by fine dramatic construction and treatment. Interest becomes more tense as the photodrama proceeds, with climax succeeding climax—each outrivalling its immediate predecessor— until the scene showing the great amphitheater is reached and eclipses all of them. The photodrama follows closely the story by Henryk Sienkiewicz, but I am of the opinion that the scenes in the Imperial Gardens, showing the Christians being burned alive as human torches, might better have been omitted for the sake of dramatic effect. The only scenes which can follow that in the arena acceptably and effectively are the flight and death of Nero.

It is, perhaps, necessary to note here, in view of the tremendous impression which a presentation of *Quo Vadis?* creates, that the story by Sienkiewicz does not conform strictly to historical facts in certain places. The photodrama conveys the impression that Nero gave orders to fire Rome. Most of the writers since Tacitus have conveyed the same impression, but the best scholars are agreed that the fire occurred by chance. The fire broke out at night near the Great Circus at the base of the Palatine and Caelian hills, raging for six days, when it seemed to have spent its fury, then suddenly broke out again on the north side of the city and continued for three days more. Nero was at Antium, thirty-five miles away. "His own palace and all its treasures were lapped up by the flames. He opened the Campius Martius by the river side and all the public buildings on it to harbor the homeless. He built shelters in his own garden to house them. He hurried up stores from Ostia and the neighboring towns to feed them, and fixed the cost of corn at one-half the prevailing market price. Though conspirators sought his life, he roamed the city all night alone as his noble palace flared away to ruin. His efforts at succor and his careless exposure of his person were, however, quite useless to restore his reputation, and the ruined denounced him as the author of the conflagration. Men whispered that he had been seen on the tower of Maecenas, on the Esquiline height, clad in habit of the stage gazing down on the lurid inferno beneath, revelling at sight of the beauty of the flames while chanting in wild glee the song of Illium's (Troy's) capture. To ascribe the fire to its real cause, chance, would never appease the mob of Rome." But Nero supported gladly the charge against the Christians and indulged with fiendish cruelty in their massacre.

A striking feature of the production, and one that cannot fail to please the eye of the most critical, is the care bestowed on detail. One fails to find, even in a great mob scene, a single instance where something better than that which happens could be suggested. Watch the crowds dashing frantically through the burning streets, the streams of humanity sometimes rushing in opposite directions. Is it not panic conceived fully to the letter? Or take the patrician throng in the great banquet scene, in the Imperial Palace, after the Empress Poppaea has retired, her exit being the signal for still greater license and more delirious revelling. Or again refer to the death scene of Petronius at his last banquet. What amazing painstaking has been taken in their rehearsal as in all the other big scenes of the photodrama! And the almost interminable array of costumes, interior furnishings and properties! What a labor these must have cost the archeologist! Indeed the perfection of detail makes one wonder while he sings its praises.

The photography and technique of this eight-reel photodrama are in full keeping with its other excellent features. In several cases one is treated to scenes with extraordinarily beautiful light effects. Take, for example, the scene in the underground room where Lygia is nursing Vinitius back to health, after she has saved his life from the wrath of Ursus. Could there be finer depth and definition in moving pictures than are shown there, or greater softness? Another example is the scene showing the baptism of Vinitius by the Apostle Peter, where we have shadows photographed, yet every person and object in the room are clearly and softly defined.

And now the acting. What a splendid assemblage of histrionic talent! Or should I more happily say photodramatic talent? G. Serena as Petronius is undoubtedly our favorite among the leading parts. A. Mastripietri as Chilo commands attention next for forceful, artistic character acting. But it is really like splitting hairs to praise any one of the principals at the expense of the others in the cast. A. Novelli as Vinitius, C. Moltini as Tigellinus, Miss L. Giunchi as Lygia, C. Cattaneo as Nero, Mrs. O. Brandini as Poppaea, J. Gizzi as the Apostle Peter, L. Lupi as Aulus Platius, Mrs. A. Cattaneo as Eunice, and B. Castellani as Ursus are other bright stars in the firmament of this extraordinary production.

The Moving Picture World, May 17, 1913

From the very beginning, some commentators had foreseen that the film was going to be an instrument of social revolution, whatever its subject matter. "Mass culture" was an unknown term, but the film became a prime mover of that phenomenon, a particularly apt twentieth-century means of fulfilling twentieth-century impulses. As Frederick Starr pointed out (p. 21), on the minimal informational level the film allowed the poorest people to "see" the world, which had previously been the global province of the well-to-do. In imaginative and quasimythological effect, it was to prove omnipotent. Politically, there was hope that the film would also fulfill the ideals of American democracy, a task that Whitman, some forty years before, had thought literature might perform.[5]

THE TRIUMPH OF THE GALLERY

W. STEPHEN BUSH

One of many causes of the present popularity and the glorious future of the motion picture is to be found in the fact that it has practically abolished the numerous and envious distinctions of price and class in all the playhouses where it holds exclusive sway. It has brought the gallery as close to the "footlights" as the orchestra and the first balcony. It has wiped out forever the odium and ridicule that has from time immemorial been cast upon the gallery, where the poor and lowly were tolerantly permitted to delight their senses and feed their minds. From the "gens infima," "the lowest kind" of the Colosseum, to the "groundlings" of Shakespeare, the great masses were admitted grudgingly, for the theater was considered an expensive luxury and a fashion of intellectual sport which depended mainly upon the patronage of the wealthy and the noble. This constant appeal to the so-called higher classes has left its distinct traces on very much of the world's best literature. It accounts, for instance, for the distinctly antidemocratic vein in Shakespeare. Dramatic art in those days often languished or prospered as royalty frowned or smiled.

Nor were these sharp distinctions of class unknown to the later generations. In many theaters there are even at this day separate and less pretentious entrances to the gallery or second balcony, and while the distinctions may in some instances have been due to architectural necessity, it is a modern echo of the old belief that the poor must be herded and segregated in all fashionable places of amusement.

The motion picture has emancipated the gallery. I might say the gallery is having its revenge on the boxes and loges, but there is no question of revenge. The facts merely show that no single factor in our modern civilization has done more to emphasize the brotherhood of man than the motion picture. No single factor has done more to create that sympathetic understanding between individuals and nations which is really an asset of the whole race and which does more for the preservation of peace among the nations than The Hague Tribunal or the Peace Society.

Much of the hostility against the motion picture abroad is due to its enlightening and leveling influence. In autocratic countries like Russia and in the old feudal kingdoms like Prussia the ruling classes bitterly oppose the growth of the motion picture theater. In Austria, which disputes with Spain the distinction of being the most backward country in Europe, motion picture theaters are subjected to the most annoying regulations and their number is arbitrarily restricted by the authorities.

In our own country whatever hostility there has been is rapidly dying out, and, of course, it never had its origin in any consicous opposition to human progress and enlightenment. We are still prone to look upon all pleasure with a degree of suspicion, but have not been slow to recognize the great mission of the motion picture entertainment, and prejudice is constantly disappearing. We are keenly responsive to every improvement in the motion picture entertainment, as witness the vast throngs that have besieged the Regent Theater in this city [New York], where all may get a glimpse of the coming art of motion picture presentation.

What has been the effect of emancipating and ennobling the gallery? I think the effect has been the best possible. The motion picture, like a great public institution, is now committed to the care of the public. This means another triumph of American democracy. It means that the people of the country stand guard over the welfare of the motion picture. Just as the beautiful lawns and the pretty flowers of a public park are today protected from vandalism, not so much by the policeman's club as by the enlightened sentiment of the public, even so the motion picture is protected against the vandalism of men who for the sake of getting a few dollars in a great hurry are willing to bring disgrace and degradation upon the motion picture. The public will not tolerate obscene and criminal pictures. No need to invoke the undemocratic and un-American idea of censorship; the public are capable of protecting their own favorite amusement. The gallery and the orchestra and the balcony have been merged in one great audience, which is none other than the whole people without distinction of class.

It has been said that the character of our amusements is deteriorating. This statement does not apply to the motion picture. The motion picture is a sort of people's forum, and the men that go to the show with their wives and children are quite willing to speak out if anything comes upon the screen that calls for unfavorable comment.

It is, alas, possible at all times to debauch the public taste, but it is much harder to debauch the taste of the many than the taste of the few. We believe in all sincerity that the motion picture has a corrective and enlightening effect upon the speaking stage. We regard it as a bulwark against the abuses from which the speaking stage has been suffering lately, such as an overproduction of sex problems and "immorality" plays. To paraphrase a famous saying: "You can corrupt the taste of some of the people all of the time and you can corrupt the taste of all the people some of the time, but you cannot corrupt the taste of all of the people all of the time"—not, in any event, in these days of the triumphant gallery.

It is but a tribute to history to say that in modern days the morale of the play has improved with the importance of the gallery and with the democratizing of the stage entertainment. The nearer the art has been brought to the masses, the cleaner has it become in the course of the centuries. You cannot find any period in the history of the English-speaking races which in the tone of its public entertainments compares favorably with the present. This desire to keep the stage clean and to raise the tone of all public amusements will grow with the growth of the motion picture. The whilom despised gallery will lead where it was wont to follow. This is no longer the gallery of old, but the representative American audience. The motion picture has educated the old gallery out of existence. What little remains of the old-fashioned gallery is a negligible quantity and growing less day by day.

From all over the country we hear theatrical managers bewail the loss of the gallery, and we know that in many theaters the galleries have actually been out of use for years. It is true that the motion picture theater has absorbed most of them, but it has done more than merely absorb them. It has refined them, and today the gallery mingles before the screen on even terms with the occupants of boxes and loges.

No other lesson can be drawn from the foregoing than a great lesson of responsibility for the exhibitor, the producer, and indeed every one associated with the industry. The public will be the final arbiter in all cases, but we can do much by working in harmony with the best public sentiment at all times.

The Moving Picture World, December 13, 1913

One important result of the Licensed-Independent struggle was the billing of actors, directors, and others involved in the making of films. The Independents began it to draw audiences from the (uncredited) Licensed films by identifying public favorites. Relatively soon, credits were common practice.

So we get a review of an American film with director and actors identified. Mack Sennett, says Theodore Huff, "is rightly called the father of American film comedy." He had acted in comedies for Griffith from 1908 to 1912, had begun directing in 1911, and was the head of the Keystone studio, in Glendale, California, by 1912. Within a year, as this review shows, his reputation was established.[6] (*Zuzu* was in two reels; comedy was the type of film most reluctant to expand.)

Mabel Normand was a fixture in Sennett's work and life until her premature death in 1930. Ford Sterling was Sennett's first male star, had a salary tiff and left to form his own company in 1914, and returned in 1915.[7]

ZUZU THE BAND LEADER

GEORGE BLAISDELL

It seems to be the mission in life of Mack Sennett to make not only the unskillful but also the skillful laugh. If there be those who fail to see the humor of the situations he builds for us, surely they are few in number. Mr. Sennett has done much to add to the gaiety of nations, particularly this one. That he is a master of farce comedy or, phrasing it differently, of burlesquing melodrama, there can be no question. His peculiar talent of imparting to others the comedy spirit was finely illustrated in the most amusing Keystone release of *Children*. In this picture there are a thousand feet of almost steady fun. Scant basis for it there may be, but everybody laughs at it just the same. When a man can highly entertain for a full reel with child actors we expect much from him in a two-reel subject played by adults. That *Zuzu the Band Leader* will in a measure disappoint the average house, we are inclined to believe. This remark applies to the first half of this farce comedy, which also is lacking in the spontaneity of its humor. The introduction is long-drawn-out. Much could be cut from the alternating views of the antic-performing bandmaster and the maid Mable (the spelling is the screen's), who is so openly smitten with him in utter disregard of the proximity and size of her ferociously-mustached companion Caesar.

Ford Sterling plays Zuzu. Into the interpretation of his part surely he puts all the extra-gingered animation for which he is noted. In his gymnastics he outdoes the wildest efforts of the longest-haired Latin that ever crossed the ocean at the head of a royal musical aggregation. Miss Normand, as Mable, is as nimble as always, time and again risking a session with a bonesetter. Mr. Haggerty is Caesar, he of the striped sweater and skin-tight trousers who essays on various occasions and in divers ways to exterminate the band leader whose efforts to avoid him and escape him are exceeded in strenuosity only by his unavailing and futile attempts to indicate to the lovesick girl that her affection is unreciprocated.

At the opening we see the idolized Zuzu in the center of his most industrious musicians. The bandstand is the roof of a single-story jewelry establishment. In front of him are hundreds of idolizers, among them Mable, who is accompanied by Caesar. The latter, we are told, is "peeved." That his irritation is not insubstantially founded we may easily judge from the condition of the spellbound, cross-eyed Mable as Zuzu leads his hardworking crew in a soulful interpretation of "The Chicken's Dream." It is a moving picture. We see the Dream, plainly. It is even possible the sophisticated may discover the Chicken—a whole brood, in fact, ranging in experience more or less plainly indicated from the squab to the uncertain stage.

Mable is fickle—being a woman, of course, that is her prerogative. While clandestinely attempting to pour her love into the ear of Zuzu even as she tries to jam down his throat the battered relic of a bouquet, she is adding fuel to the fires of jealousy raging in the bosom of Caesar. To this guntoting bearer of martial visage and ancient name she cooingly suggests that she just knows he does not love her—the only way he can prove to the contrary is by killing Zuzu. History repeats itself. Caesar falls.

We will not follow the many incidents of the pursuit of the shorter by the longer jumpingjack. The two tear through crowds of idolizers and across a skating rink floor, followed always by the stumbling Mable. The end comes when Caesar and Zuzu are caught in an exploding powderhouse. We see the two going up, up, headfirst, and then coming down, down, also headfirst into a tall, soft tree, the flight followed by the eyes of the terror-stricken Mable.

Zuzu the Band Leader will go over.

The Moving Picture World, December 13, 1913

THE ART OF CRITICISM

LOUIS REEVES HARRISON

What is the first and most important requisite of a photodrama to be classed as a masterpiece?

A. That it shall contain a vital meaning.

That being a general answer, what specific use is made of the words "vital meaning"?

A. Soul must speak to soul on a subject of deep interest to those receiving the message.

Are there subjects of universal interest?

A. Many.

What, for instance?

A. The purpose of existence; the significance of what we are doing; our own artificial creations, such as religion, law, and society, for human betterment, and what pertains to *their* betterment; the efficiency and reward of effort; harmonizing achievement with improvement; in what sense ideas rule the world——

The highest and brightest ideas?

A. Only when they can be so presented as to permeate the great mass and shape the thought of society in general. Many that have *not* ruled the world through literature and the drama may become universally effective through screen portrayal.

How about war as a subject?

A. Its pictured horrors should argue for peace.

Do they not excite the military spirit?

A. The spirit of struggle for supremacy is as old as the human race; it furnishes abundant material for the drama; its visualization, if truthful, must draw attention to war's misery and woe, and to its appalling waste of vital energy.

How should tragedy operate?

A. As a tonic.

And intense drama?

A. To quicken sympathy.

How about high comedy?

A. To entertain and encourage.

And farce?

A. To brighten dull moments.

Should each have a message?

A. To be a masterpiece.

Is a message essential in photodrama?

A. Not even life. But there must be power or beauty in the inanimate portrayal. One or the other of these is often satisfying to the eye in what both nature and art have to offer, even though it be soulless, but, unless they are pregnant with suggestion, their chief importance lies in their relation to a theme. This enters upon the domain of "treatment."

Granting the importance of a vital meaning, what is a prime requisite of treatment?

A. Critical instinct.

Above imagination?

A. It may go astray. Imagination is common to nearly all, whereas the critical instinct of a true artist is so rare that it alone advances creative work beyond mediocrity. Imagination may be illusion—criticism is the natural child of cultivation and thought. All artistic treatment of a subject implies the critical faculty.

It molds the form?

A. When unaided by creative imagination, hence so many lifeless photodramas of artistic form, all body and no soul. The finest treatment requires a faculty critically creative or creatively critical, such as is possessed by genius. The sum of intellect plus character in a man is untrammeled in its expression, because its standard is itself.

Then genius is rare?

A. It is abundant enough, but it needs careful nourishment to attain full growth. It thrives on opportunity well removed from drudgery.

What does masterly treatment involve?

A. In a general way, preparation that clarifies while exciting curiosity, exposition that is tense yet delicately suggestive of the end in view, characterization that quickens interest in the outcome, an unobtrusive undercurrent of logic that does not drift into unimportant or inconsistent details, and a conclusion satisfying to common intelligence and sympathy, all contributing to make effective the author's aim.

Do most photodramas hit where they aim?

A. Most photodramas are arrows shot in the air. In the absence of sharp competition, producers have been satisfied to make a chance hit now and then, especially with visualizations of what has been done in other arts.

To what may their failure be ascribed?

A. Lack of good critics, for actors and directors must have the critical faculty to exhibit a work of art in a form different from that of its first presentation. They try to reproduce exactly, not grasping the essential principle that the art of screen portrayal is not merely imitative, and one result is usually a loss of what animated the original. An author who has a story to tell selects among several possible arrangements such construction as *seems* best suited to his purpose, though he may never be entirely satisfied with what he has done. There is, therefore, nothing particularly sacred about the way he presents his subject matter. If he possessed creative and critical instinct in high degree, he would be first to appreciate the necessity of tremendous changes to meet the requirements of a different art. In the matter of adaptation, it is better to approximate an author's meaning rather than his method.

Will original stories supersede adaptations?

A. That is reasonable to expect in due time. There are men and women of character plus intellect who have weathered storms of passion, who grasp the meaning of the present from the past, who perceive the farcical side of our antiquated codes, who could advance ideas of our future social state or charmingly mirror this or that phase of life's infinite variety, who might struggle in vain with technics of literature and the stage, yet be able to give their thoughts vivid expression on the screen. Some producers seeking popularity and profit by superior work are already encouraging talent wherever they find it.

What is the future of criticism?

A. Undetermined. A good critic must be able to collect evidence of power successfully exercised and use it to guide this new art out of a labyrinth of mediocrity. Such men will be hard to find as long as production is more sincerely commercial than artistic. Improvement is bound to come in the course of keen competition, but there is a present need of clearer vision. Men are blind on one side who do not see that this art of thought communication, the only one besides printing discovered in two thousand years, must have something worth while to communicate.

The Moving Picture World, January 31, 1914

The Squaw Man was in six reels. It was Cecil B. DeMille's first film, codirected with Oscar Apfel, who, says Kenneth Macgowan, "taught DeMille the techniques of directing and editing." [8]

THE SQUAW MAN

LOUIS REEVES HARRISON

One of the best visualizations of a stage play ever shown on the screen, *The Squaw Man,* was a source of surprise and delight to me, and to the able critic at my side during the private exhibition, from beginning to end.

Credit must, however, be given almost entirely to the direction and interpretation, the direction in this case embracing both form and treatment of an almost flawless production. To the lucid arrangement and delicate appreciation of dramatic values, to unwavering logic and consistency, to the pains taken in those tiny details which make action realistic, to the pervading sense of beauty, and to highly intelligent interpretation, quickening interest in the outcome, must be ascribed the charm this feature is bound to exert.

I have not seen Oscar Apfel's name made prominent in connection with this winner, but I recognize his handiwork without difficulty. Cecil DeMille, I am told, put his heart and soul into making *The Squaw Man* an unqualified success, but his unbounded enthusiasm could only act as a support to the unhampered skill and decided native ability of the active director. First honors must go to the gentleman whose discriminating judgment cleared the path of this notable production of a thousand thorny errors. Dustin Farnum's unobtrusive and masterly characterization ranks next in value—he was largely responsible for the "surprise and delight" already mentioned—for he has certainly grasped the essential principles of screen interpretation. His performance is so manly, so apparently devoid of stale artifice, that I could only regret that he was not representing a typical American.

The general theme, that of frenzied self-sacrifice on the part of a blameless man for the sake of a villain who happens to be a member of the same family, "for the family honor," whereby he blasts his own career, has been very popular with lady novelists since Ouida used it, and variations of it have been seen on both stage and screen until it has become almost as familiar as "Mary had a little——" but it is time that it should be shelved, along with a lot of overdone expedients. Nothing in the photodrama is less conducive to progress in the new art than this old billposter theme. But it is all the more creditable to the producers that they have presented with exquisite charm what is no longer considered to be within the bounds of common sense. The truth is that they have depended upon a rattling good story of adventure, running with unbroken unity, sustained by a character of magnetic personality, through perils at sea and on shore.

To begin at the beginning, Jim Wyngate, with whom we are better acquainted as Dustin Farnum, agrees to be the scapegoat for his relative, the Earl of Kerhill, who has embezzled the funds of Wyngate's regiment, and, as soon as Jim is disentangled from a lot of other officers that our affections may be fastened upon him, he leaves England in a trading schooner, and the real fun begins. He has been followed by a detective. Every small boy in the audience and a large portion of the big ones will begin to sit up and take notice when Jim gets busy with that detective. Jim is every inch an athlete, and he does not mince matters as they do in stage struggles. He succeeds in making a fool of the spy at the end of a game fight and soon after performs greater feats, when the ship catches fire. The fire scenes aboard ship are made plausible by using an actual vessel, sailing in the open, and there is a delightful fidelity to legitimate requirements not ordinarily seen in the escape of crew and passengers in the boats.

Jim is picked up by an American vessel, landed in New York, and gradually drifts from the lurid White Way to ranch life in the far west, accompanied by "Big Bill," whom he has saved from the deft "touch" of a tango artiste. They arrive at a railroad station that is a veritable gem of its kind—we look through the combination bar and station, where cowboys assemble at train time, to the track on which actual trains are passing. Some of the high scenes occur in this room, and the view of cars running without gives them an unusual atmosphere of realism. Jim gets into difficulties there with Cash Hawkins, and the latter is shot dead in the station by an Indian girl, a veritable one, and a remarkably fine actress, when he attempts to murder Jim in cold blood.

It is not altogether a pleasing spectacle to see white women impersonating Indian squaws, and they are seldom, if ever, successful at it; on the other hand, Indian girls who can awaken and hold sympathy for their roles are few and far between, but Princess Redwing performs her part with exquisite fidelity and great depth of feeling. The play's highest merit is the opportunity it affords this accomplished actress. The love of this child of the forest for the splendid specimen of manhood injected into her dull career forms the most touching and beautiful part of the story, and it was probably the essence of interest in Royle's stage version. So artless, so appealing to the protective instincts of true manhood, so self-abnegating is that love, that it is bound to make heartstrings throb in the audience.

It is quite probable that both Royle and DeMille, when they come to study this characterization from the viewpoint of spectators, will realize that the art of producing moving pictures is to be measured by its own canons alone. Both may perceive that this new method of thought transmission has a grander scope than the boxed-in stage presentation once they are enfolded in the charm of its method of telling a story. Its directness, the lack of intervening utterance, its very silence, all contribute to a fascination long proven to exist, not only for the mixed audience, but for those familiar with superior examples of the older arts. When these gentlemen come to us, as they surely will, with the finest products of their creative talent, unhampered by what they have learned in a totally different medium of expression, with a cause that is compelling, it will be with quickened fondness, for what can give such free release to their forces.

Note the characterization in action of the Indian maid when the man she loves goes snow blind, when she follows the trail of his horse until she finds it where he was thrown, and thereafter trails his steps to the sulphurous crevice into which he has fallen. Note the impression made by witnessing her patient courage and native resource in the almost insurmountable task of rescue, the comparison suggested of her sturdy and simple devotion to the dependent and resourceless man hunter of civilized society, the lady who affects to steer the boat while man does the rowing, who relies on sex attraction rather than sex qualification. The physical superiority and mental alertness of the woman enjoying fewer advantages could never be so forcibly presented in the related narrative as in the pictured story.

Note the compelling beauty and nobility of actual scenery as compared to stage affectations. The complex impression produced is powerful enough to make one subscribe to the view expressed by a great creative critic, "Art's first appeal is neither to the intellect nor to the emotions, but purely to the artistic temperament that guides civilized man back to nature for relief." The same critic said, "I hold that no work of art can be tried otherwise than by laws deduced from itself; whether or not it be consistent with itself is the question." Note the Indian maid "fighting it out alone in the foothills, only nature looking on," the distance tragically mellowed by a setting sun—how fascinated we become by this visible world of form and color, not only because its delicate beauty is so appropriate to a communion of a human soul with the spirit of the Great Invisible, but because of its imaginative insight and poetic aim!

This one scene might well have been the last, discovering, as it does, the finest sentiment of the story, the tortured appeal of a human heart—"will we ever come to our own?" Sickened with pursuit of the unattainable, how often have each of us secretly communed with something we only vaguely recognize as a power that makes all our boasted ones pitiful. Such occasional glimpses may be less intelligible than those more commonplace, but they belong to life in its artistic entirety, enter a sphere of deep feeling, stir the nobility too often dormant within us, rouse our better selves. The touches of great beauty contain a secret of success known only to screen presentation—they cause us to to surrender ourselves more completely to the story that is being told and to love this new art for its own sake.

The Moving Picture World, February 28, 1914

Hanford C. Judson also wrote verse, and published a book called *Songs toward the Sunlight.*

THE PERILS OF PAULINE

HANFORD C. JUDSON

The motion picture serial has come to stay. Serial novels have long held a commanding position in the magazines; but one of the most popular of these has concluded that they are no longer popular and is offering a complete novel with short stories. No one will deny that this, from the reader's standpoint, is a wise move; for the serial in the magazine, especially the monthly, was, except in cases of "three decker" novels, only a business expedient to induce an even, dependable distribution. But, quite on the other hand, the requirements of an evening's entertainment in a motion picture theater that accents the mechanical difficulties of presenting long stories would have made the serial picture imperative. The modern spectator wants variety and won't stand being wearied. The serial picture is so vivid and the impression it leaves on one is so clear-cut that the period of waiting between installments is rather a pleasant experience than otherwise. This is going to work out distinctly for the good of the business; for the serial that isn't vivid and doesn't leave an impression deep enough to last over the gap, is going to be the sharpest kind of frost. The serial that doesn't "get over" had better not have been made. By the same token, the serial picture that does get over with a real punch is going to be a great money-maker. *The Perils of Pauline* seems, on this account, to this reviewer, an ideal offering for the exhibitor.

There are several things that contribute to its excellence as a show. There are big prizes offered to spectators clever enough to solve certain mysteries that come up in the progress of its story, and we may add at once that these mysterious things are not, so far, in connection with the plot and we feel sure that they will not hamper the interest in the story at all. But even better than the $25,000 in prizes that are offered is the good quality of the entertainment. Only the first installment, the first three reels, has as yet been shown to us. We know nothing of the rest of the picture; but are sure that this part is good and when it closes we are, in our hearts, certain that Pauline, charmingly portrayed by Pearl White, is in real danger from the much trusted but very villainous secretary (Paul Panzer) of her foster father, now dead. By the old man's will, the precious secretary will inherit, "if anything happens" to the heiress.

Miss White hasn't had so good a chance in a long while to show her art, and she plays this picture's ingenuous heroine with the truly wonderful naturalness that she has so surely at her command. Perhaps she doesn't always hit square in the center of the effect she desires; but she does it so often that she continually commands the heart-interest of the audience.

Mr. Panzer, in the villain's part, finds it his duty to intensify this. His work on the audience is, of course, through the heroine, and in the playing that he is doing and will do, he stirs an antisympathy that is every bit as worthy of praise; for the audience takes it with the left hand, so to speak, and affectionately hands it back to the heroine with its right. Crane Wilbur, as the hero, has little chance in this beginning portion. The character is still colorless and we can hardly as yet criticize the player. The picture's weakest point is in its relief. The "comedy" gaucherie of the outdoors man, a sort of gardener, but too much of a fool to tend a garden, is weak and not less so is the "fall" of the butler who is running out to the gate to help the gardener bring in the mummy box that comes to the house shortly before the heroine's foster father dies. The old man is drawn very well. He has now passed away and will not appear again—at least we presume so. The mummy, who comes to life while the old man dreams, is graceful and pleasing. There is also a very fair "tough" character in the story. All the characters, except Miss White, are guilty, now and then, of over-registering their points.

The mechanical work is meritorious, and we wish we could say that the photography, the prints, are perfectly clear and serviceable. That the thickness of the photographs in some of the scenes fails to hinder our comprehension of the story, speaks well for the simplicity and clearness of the script. At the opening of the double exposure scene in which the mummy comes to life, an awkward jump is noticeable; but the unsubstantial figure flits about the room in the best possible way and goes back to her mummy case again in so perfect a closing of the double exposure that the eye can detect no manipulation at all; it is done as naturally as dream.

The story has a story within a story; for Pauline is a budding writer and has got one of her novelettes accepted and printed by the *Cosmopolitan Magazine* and the old man, her foster father, reads it to us (in pictures) without wearying us at all. She doesn't want to get married to the hero for a year; she wants to see life first so that she can write things worthwhile. In the old man's will, her part of the fortune is left in charge of the secretary until she gets married. As the picture's first installment ends, it is clearly to her interest to elope with almost anyone; but what she really does do is left undecided as yet till the next of the series.

The Moving Picture World, April 4, 1914

Cabiria was another spectacle, twice the length of *Quo Vadis?*, and was another success from Italy. The director was Giovanni Pastrone, who had codirected *The Fall of Troy*. Pastrone made his last film in 1919, although he lived until 1959. Amleto Novelli of *Quo Vadis?* was in *Cabiria.*

This film marked the first time that an author of d'Annunzio's stature had written directly for the screen. Vachel Lindsay did not quite share Bush's enthusiasm for the result. "But," said Lindsay, "the mistakes of *Cabiria* are those of the pioneer work of genius. It has in it twenty great productions." [9]

Note the phrase "greatest classics" in the final paragraph— another example of how the vocabulary of film criticism shot up at least as quickly as the art itself.

CABIRIA

W. STEPHEN BUSH

This is the day of the new masters. We are witnessing a new style in dramatic kinematography. Within the last four weeks there have been splendid manifestations of a new art on the screen. The skill and the inspiration of the director, the skill and the patient striving of the cameraman, a deep and conscientious study of screen possibilities, a new school of actors who have fathomed the mysteries of unspoken language—all these elements working toward the harmony of the whole have in part been responsible for the new school, which is opening the eyes of the world. I have not mentioned the keystone of the success of the new art in this hasty enumeration. The keystone is the story written for the screen and for the screen alone. The freest adaptation imposes restraints on the producer. In the novel we are confronted by the problem of what to leave out and what to leave in, in the adaptation of the speaking stage we are still in the bonds of tradition. How different is the free untrammelled flight of the Muse of the Screen. She conquers every obstacle which is insurmountable to pen or stage.

In *Cabiria* a genius furnishes the theme—Gabriele d'Annunzio. He wrote the story directly for the screen. Nobly does the screen respond to every touch of the gifted hand. D'Annunzio is a very wizard of description. In this film-drama his thoughts and images stand forth as vividly as the summer landscape in a prolonged flash of lightning. The tremendous moral of the play, the keenly dramatic and the broadly humorous, the historic facts— are all absorbed in an incredibly short time. Of course the spectacular features help—with all due respect to its classic predecessors I must confess that in the portrayal of the spectacular this film creates new records. The torrent of fiery flakes, the mouth of the volcano a veritable furnace of the Inferno, spewing forth unceasing sheets of fire, the rush of the fugitives lit up by a ruddy glow which half conceals and half reveals, the temple of Moloch with its worshippers and its fearful rites, the hero of Carthage passing over the Alps, the siege of Carthage, the burning of the ships which the aged Archimedes fought with the power of the sun, all these and a hundred other marvels of the spectacular make this feature pre-eminent among the spectacular successes in all the history of spectacles. It is true that the classic theme always carries the spectacular element best, and this advantage the producer has pressed to the limit.

It would be a grave mistake, however, to emphasize the spectacular in this film above the dramatic. The spectacular is all the more impressive because an artistic masterhand has subordinated it to the dramatic and poetic moments of the play.

Cabiria is the name of the child whose strange salvation after cruel perils forms the skeleton of the story. The plot takes us to the days when the dominion of Rome was threatened by the growing power of Carthage. To this day the site of Carthage has remained more or less of a mystery. We know that the plough of the Roman conqueror passed over the site of the fated city, but no mortal even in our day knows where the site is. Carthage magnificiently situated on the northern coast of Africa was sending her ships and her soldiers into every part of the world, her trade and the martial spirit of her people made her a conquering nation. At last she threw the gauntlet down and challenged Rome. Rome in later years achieved a magnificence never equalled in the chronicles of man, but at no time in her career was she as rugged, as noble and as brave as in the third century before the Christian era, when the hordes of Carthage set their foot on her sacred soil. In the midst of this struggle between two nations and two civilizations the little girl Cabiria was born in Italy of noble parents. The city in which her parents lived was overwhelmed by a fearful eruption of a volcano, and when the wretched survivors looked about themselves even as Nature seemed at last to have tired of her anger, little Cabiria could not be found. She was believed to have perished in the general destruction. Such, however, was not the case. She and others were captured in their flight—Phoenician pirates brought them into the slave market at Carthage. She was with her nurse, and the man who bought Cabiria also took the little girl's faithful nurse Croessa. The sweetness and purity of the child attracted the notice of the High Priest of Moloch, the horrible idol to whom little children were sacrificed. He places little Cabiria with the children in the temple where they are being prepared for sacrifice. In spite of all the protests of Croessa little Cabiria is selected as a victim for the next day of sacrifice. Croessa in despair looks about for means of rescuing the little child. Fulvius, a Roman patrician, and his slave, a huge black named Maciste, are wandering about the outer temple when Croessa begs them to save Cabiria, giving the Roman a charm which she promises will never let him perish.

Just as in the midst of the worshippers in the temple little Cabiria is offered to Moloch the monster that glows and shines and devours, Fulvius and Maciste defy the priests by seizing the child in the moment of its supremest peril. They flee, and the black slave escaping offers the child to the queen into whose protection Cabiria is now commended. She grows up to be a beautiful young woman. In the meantime the arms of Carthage have suffered defeat after defeat, the noble Scipio has risen up to grapple with the armies of Carthage, and the mighty Hannibal, the hero and the hope of Carthage, perishes. The priests, seeking to divine the cause of the anger of the gods, discover that a victim has been hidden from Moloch, hence the impending destruction of Carthage and her people. Cabiria is found and her sacrifice demanded by the priests. How Cabiria is saved again and finally reunited to her parents and joined in wedlock to Fulvius who has dared so much for her is the theme of the last part.

I have only mentioned the more prominent parts of the story, which has many episodes too numerous for detailed recital here. I must at least allude to the tragicomic part of Maciste and the wine-merchant in whose shop so many of the strange adventures of the knight and his servant took pace.

Summing up, it may well be said that *Cabiria* ranks in the very first flight of the masterpieces of kinematographic art. Nor must I omit a tribute to Italy, the country which has given us all our greatest classics in films. Those of us who remember the Italia Company's first ambitious effort, *The Fall of Troy,* will be in a good position of judging of the giant's strides with which the art is approaching its summit. *The Fall of Troy* was considered a new departure in 1910; four years later it is eclipsed by *Cabiria.* Who knows what the next four years may bring?

The Moving Picture World, May 23, 1914

The cast to whom Harrison refers in the following, which was printed above the review, included Charles Chaplin, Mabel Normand, Mack Swain, and Phyllis Allen. Chaplin's first film was released on February 2, 1914. This one, made nine months later, was his thirty-first; it was the fourteenth that he had both written and directed. Most of his 1914 films were in one reel, although this one and several previous ones were two-reelers.

"Max" was Max Linder, a popular and accomplished French star of silent comedies.

HIS TRYSTING PLACE

LOUIS REEVES HARRISON

Who they are cast for is lost in the shuffle. And it really does not make the slightest difference. We begin to laugh within a few seconds after the farce begins and we keep it up until there is really need of tragedy relief. Critics get the frozen face from trying to discover merit where it is most successfully hidden. In the average screen portrayal, they are eternally anxious to find something really praiseworthy that they may not have to compromise with their own consciences, and this is a sad business in other respects. The average picture has about the same effect on me as an after-dinner speech—both are usually inadequate expressions of a desire to make an impression—but I began to snicker as soon as Chaplin started his antics in Scene 1, Act 1, and the two reels slipped away before I realized it, though I will find it no easy matter to tell you what I was laughing at. Who cares?

Productions of obvious merit need no publicity. They take care of themselves whatever critics, either favorable or carping, may say. Their commercial value lies in their inherent apposition of good structure, better treatment, and the best of acting. The comic spirit is entirely too deep and subtle for me to define. It defies analysis. The human aspect is certainly dominant. It is funniest when it is rich in defects of character. The incongruity of Chaplin's portrayals, his extreme seriousness, his sober attention to trivialities, his constant errors and as constant resentment of what happens to him, all this has to be seen to be enjoyed. He merely sits down in the kitchen to read the war news, while Mabel tries to tend baby on the kitchen table and make bread at the same time. He leans back and puts one foot on the stove, upsetting the boiling kettle, when a flame leaps up and burns his leg, then trouble begins. There is no end of it. One aggravating triviality leads to another, until we are plunged into the complications of a well-devised screen story.

There might as well be no end to it. No fatigue results from two reels—no fatigue for the spectator. Chaplin must be an acrobat to stand the strain. Mabel helps materially in all the amusing scenes that follow, and she exhibits the endurance of a trained athlete in her strenuous role. "Max" was never funnier than Chaplin, and no attractive comedienne I recall could survive the activities of smiling Mabel and still smile. Great team!

While learned gentlemen are discussing Oedipus and attempting to explain the extremely simple plot of Shakespeare's *Comedy of Errors,* the
reduplication of a coincidence, we are having more than one veritable
Comedy of Errors in real life, before our very eyes, so why go so far a-
field? The Keystone comedies are delightfully realistic. They are of today.
They are not revived skeletons in tawdry costumes. They depict weaknesses
which any mixed audience is quick to recognize and enjoy. What they are
about is of minor consequence. They start us laughing and keep us laughing, with no other purpose than that of chasing away dull care, and their
charm seems to lie in their utter unaffectedness. They do not strain for
effects nor pretend to be funny, but to all appearances, simply happen to
be amusing phases of everyday life.

The Moving Picture World, October 31, 1914

Chaplin's very next picture, released five days later, was his
first feature—in six reels. It was directed by Mack Sennett.

TILLIE'S PUNCTURED ROMANCE

GEORGE BLAISDELL

When Mack Sennett was in the East a couple of months ago he confided
to a friend that in the making of his six-reel comedy in which Marie
Dressler was starred he had given all that he had. After viewing *Tillie's
Punctured Romance* we are bound to say he had a lot to give. At the time
the Keystone producer was here he was in doubt as to what the title of the
comedy would be. When he intimated to a party of film men that he was
thnking of *She Was More Sinned Against Than Necessary,* there was
hearty acclaim. The advisability of incorporating "Tillie" in the title, that
the star of the piece by reason of previous associations might be more
clearly identified, turned the scale.

Marie Dressler breaks into the story at the first jump. She is in the scene
every minute right to the finish. She fits into the Keystone style of work as
to the manner born. She kicks and is kicked, she falls and gets up or is
laboriously picked up; sober or unsober she is inimitable. Trouble follows
in her ample wake; if at any moment there seems an insufficiency of dis-
turbance she beats a strategic retreat and takes a fresh stranglehold on
everything and everybody and starts something new. That she survives her
strenuous experience is remarkable; it is a tribute to her vitality as well as

her agility. In fact, it is inexplicable that these boneless but never spineless Keystone players live to play another day.

Charles Chaplin plays opposite Miss Dressler. In apposition with the famous woman of the legitimate comedy stage, the screen player suffers not a whit by comparison. The two constitute a rare team of funmakers—the sort of combination that not only tempts but impels an ordinary fallible reviewer to indulge in extravagant language. Chaplin outdoes Chaplin; that's all there is to it. His marvelous right-footed skid—and it seems to make no difference whether he have under him rough highway or parlor floor—is just as funny in the last reel as it is in the first. Chaplin's serious face is seldom crossed by a smile. With perfect confidence he leaves laughter to others; and well he may.

Mabel Normand is the third principal in the large cast. She has the role of the unsuccessful rival for Charlie's hand; that is, she is unsuccessful for a short but exceedingly lively period ending in the harried and bedraggled Tillie resigning her claim to the fickle bridegroom. Miss Normand sustains in her own mirthful way the quieter role—always speaking comparatively, of course—that falls to her. Charles Bennett is the millionaire uncle who is not killed by the fall down the snow-covered mountainside and whose return to the scene of Tillie's rampage is the climax as it is also the dramatic catastrophe of his sole heiress's flight in high society. We also recognized Mr. Bennett in two minor characters.

The picture is finely staged. The interiors of the mansion wherein Tillie and her husband entertain society are elaborate and luxurious. The bit in the snow above the clouds makes an impressive contrast with the sunshine-flooded vegetation of the lower country. The photography throughout is of a high order.

There is no use talking about situations. In *Tillie's Punctured Romance* there are nothing but situations. There's a story, of course, and it is sufficient. It shows how Tillie is wooed by Charlie and is given the mitten in favor of Mabel. When Charlie reads that through the death of the uncle Tillie is heir to three millions, he encompasses a hasty marriage before Tillie gets the news. Of course, it afterward develops uncle is not dead, but very, very much alive. Tillie, however, is pretty near dead by the time she has removed from her expansive chest several matters that weigh heavily upon it. Before the battle is over the Keystone "cops" have the riot of their tempestuous, catlike lives, an automobile takes a plunge into the Pacific— the only calm element in the show—and Tillie, after several tedious lifts and sudden immersions is finally landed on the pier. Mabel falls in the arms of Tillie. Charlie is "jugged."

Mack Sennett has done well.

The Moving Picture World, November 14, 1914

The issue of *The Moving Picture World* that carried the following review also ran a news story about the opening of the film at the Liberty Theater, New York City, on March 3, 1915, that said: "The dramatic critics of all the New York daily papers attended the premiere and in almost every instance the picture was reported at length and in glowing terms." This notifies us that there were as yet no specialized film critics on those papers and that all the dramatic critics attended only important films.

The Battle, to which Bush refers, was a one-reel Civil War film that Griffith had made at Biograph in 1911 and that Vachel Lindsay, too, thought a "work of art." [10]

One editor has noted that Bush misquotes a subtitle of the scene between Stoneman and the mulatto, which should read: "The great leader's weakness that is to blight a nation." [11]

Griffith, who had strained for years at the limits of short films, had now made the longest American film to date.

THE BIRTH OF A NATION

W. STEPHEN BUSH

The two outstanding features of Griffith's remarkable production, *The Birth of a Nation,* are its controversial spirit (especially obvious in the titles), and the splendor and magnificence of its spectacles. Based in the main on *The Clansman,* it breathes the spirit of that well-known book. *The Clansman* was a special plea for the South in the forum of history. The screen-adaptation has made the plea far more passionate and I might say partisan than the book or the play. It is impossible to give the reader a good idea of this production without sketching at least briefly the views and sentiments expressed and sharply emphasized and reiterated by the distinguished author. The very introduction tells us that the South never had a fair record made of its trials in the Reconstruction Period. We are told both in pictures and in titles that African slaves were brought to this country by Northern traders who sold them to the South. Puritan divines blessed the traffic, but when slave trading was no longer profitable to the North the "traders of the seventeenth century became the abolitionists of the nineteenth century."

We next see a typical Northern congregation assembled to hear a sermon. About the platform from which the preacher addresses his audience stands a group of colored children. The preacher takes a young colored boy and passes with him through the congregation. A motherly looking old lady stretches out her arms in sympathy toward the child of the black race, but immediately repulses him with every manifestation of disgust caused by the odor which we must assume the boy carries around with him. Much is then said in titles about "state sovereignty," and we are reminded of what we read in school of Southern statesmen like Calhoun and Toombs and Northern statesmen like Vallandigham.

Mr. Griffith then unfolds a picture of conditions in the South before the Civil War, showing both in titles and pictures that the slaves had easy hours, plenty of time for recreation, comfortable quarters, and kind masters. Here a strange and puzzling character is introduced in the person of a man said "to have risen to great prominence in the House of Representatives in 1860." This man, who plays a very prominent part all through the production, is called "Austin Stoneman." The titles make it plain that this is a fictitious name. Stoneman has a daughter who is never allowed to enter his library. The reason for this must be found in the illicit relations between Stoneman and a mulatto woman. The latter is "insulted" by Charles Sumner. She works herself into a fury of passion. Stoneman enters to find her with part of her upper body exposed. The scene ends with Stoneman kissing the mulatto and with this title: "Thus the fatal weakness of one man blights the nation." The man called Stoneman bears a striking facial and physical resemblance to the man who succeeded Lincoln in the presidential chair. The description of him in the titles forbids the belief that he is identical with President Andrew Johnson. He is an altogether mystical and apocryphal personage whose identity remains veiled to the very end.

It would be difficult to overpraise the spectacular part of these reels. Mr. Griffith has given us a sample of what he can do in staging military spectacles in his wonderful picture of *The Battle*, released in the summer of 1911. Here he surpasses himself. The march of Sherman from Atlanta to the sea made the audience gasp with wonder and admiration. Nothing more impressive has ever been seen on the screen, and I have to refer to *Cabiria* for a standard of comparison. Nor are the war spectacles the only impressive spectacular features. Two of the most wonderful pictures ever seen on the screen are Lincoln signing the first call for volunteers and the surrender of Lee to Grant at Appomatox. It may be said in passing that a finer impersonation of Lincoln has never been witnessed on any screen or on any stage. The audience was deeply stirred by the inspired portrayal of Lincoln, and when it became known that the artist who had given the portrayal was present the audience gave him an impromptu ovation between the first and second part. He lived up to the best of Lincoln traditions both in appearance and in action. The assassination of the martyred president is shown in full detail on the screen. It was a task full of difficulties, and one misstep might have proved fatal. The great tragedy is "acted o'er" in the most irreproachable and touching manner.

It must be mentioned too that Mr. Griffith has again shown himself a master in creating and prolonging suspense to the agonizing point. His favorite method of chasing pursued and pursuer through one room after another is still effective and always has the desired effect on the audience. When speaking of the spectacular features of *The Birth of a Nation,* I must not forget his treatment of the Ku Klux Klan. The weird and mystical garb of these defenders of "Aryan race supremacy" has given the director splendid opportunities which he utilized to the fullest. When these "crusaders of the South" are seen mounted on superb horses, dashing furiously through field and forest and river to rescue innocent maidens from brutal assault or to punish "wicked Africans," the audience never fails to respond, but applauds while the spectacle lasts.

It is scarcely necessary to say that the photography is exceptionally fine in a production to which Griffith lends his name. He shows a good deal of his renowned skill in working "close-ups," creating many tense and thrilling situations.

The acting is such as might have been expected with a director of the type and power of Griffith. He has the art of bending his instruments to his uses. They work in strictest obedience to his orders and as a result the Griffith idea is always transferred to the screen with a negligible loss of power and directness. Mr. Walthall's performance was particularly fine. This gifted artist invariably succeeds in merging his personality into his part. He might at times have shown a little trace of the grime and the hardship of soldiering. It seemed somewhat improbable that a soldier could look so trim and spick and span after what "the little Colonel" passed through. The parts of Stoneman and Silas Lynch were well taken care of, the old "southron" was a piece of very clever character acting. Not enough praise can be given to the settings, both exterior and interior. Mr. Griffith is justly famous for his ability in these things.

The audience which saw the play at the private exhibition in the Liberty Theater was a most friendly one. It was significant that on more than one occasion during the showing of the films there were hisses mingled with the applause. These hisses were not, of course, directed against the artistic quality of the film. They were evoked by the undisguised appeal to race prejudices. The tendency of the second part is to inflame race hatred. The Negroes are shown as horrible brutes, given over to beastly excesses, defiant and criminal in their attitude toward the whites and lusting after white women. Some of the details are plainly morbid and repulsive. The film having roused the disgust and hatred of the white against the black to the highest pitch, suggests as a remedy of the racial question the transportation of the Negroes to Liberia, which Mr. Griffith assures us was Lincoln's idea.

Whatever fault might be found with the argumentative spirit found in both the titles and the pictures there can be no question that the appeal to the imagination will carry the picture a good way toward popular success. In the South of course where memories of Reconstruction horrors are still vivid, the picture will have an immense vogue. It is altogether probable that its many fine points will outweigh its disadvantages in every other section of the country.

The Moving Picture World, March 13, 1915

Now that films were longer and more substantial, now that the audience was not only widening but deepening, newspapers and general magazines had to consider regular reviewing of the medium. Well-established serious journals like *The Nation* began to comment on films. For *The New Republic,* founded a year before *The Birth of a Nation* appeared, comment on such a film as this had already become almost mandatory.[12]

Francis Hackett, an editor of the new journal, was Irish-born, a critic, historian, and biographer.

THE BIRTH OF A NATION

FRANCIS HACKETT

If history bore no relation to life, this motion picture drama could well be reviewed and applauded as a spectacle. As a spectacle it is stupendous. It lasts three hours, represents a staggering investment of time and money, reproduces entire battle scenes and complex historic events, amazes even when it wearies by its attempt to encompass the Civil War. But since history does bear on social behavior, *The Birth of a Nation* cannot be reviewed simply as a spectacle. It is more than a spectacle. It is an interpretation, the Rev. Thomas Dixon's interpretation, of the relations of the North and South and their bearing on the Negro.

Were the Rev. Thomas Dixon a representative white Southerner, no one could criticize him for giving his own version of the Civil War and the Reconstruction period that followed. If he possessed the typical Southern attitude, the paternalistic, it would be futile to read a lecture on it. Seen from afar, such an attitude might be deemed reactionary, but at any rate it is usually genial and humane and protective, and because it has experience back of it, it has to be met with some respect. But the attitude which Mr. Dixon possesses and the one for which he forges corroboration in history is a perversion due largely to his personal temperament. So far as I can judge from this film, as well as from my recollection of Mr. Dixon's books, his is the sort of disposition that foments a great deal of the trouble in civilization. Sometimes in the clinical laboratory the doctors are reputed to perform an operation on a dog so that he loses the power to restrain certain motor activities. If he is started running in a cage, the legend goes, he keeps on running incessantly, and nothing can stop him but to hit him on the head with a club. There is a quality about everything Mr. Dixon has done that reminds me of this abnormal dog. At a remote period of his existence it is possible that he possessed a rudimentary faculty of self-analysis. But before that faculty developed he crystallized in his prejudices, and forever it was stunted. Since that time, whenever he has been stimulated by any of the ordinary emotions, by religion or by patriotism or by sex, he has responded with a frantic intensity. Energetic by nature, the forces that impel him are doubly violent because of this lack of inhibition. Aware as a clergyman that such violence is excessive, he has learned in all his melodramas to give them a highly moral twang. If one of his heroes is about to do something peculiarly loathsome, Mr. Dixon thrusts a crucifix in his hand and has him roll his eyes to heaven. In this way the very basest impulses are given the sanction of godliness, and Mr. Dixon preserves his own respect and the respect of such people as go by the label and not by the rot-gut they consume.

In *The Birth of a Nation* Mr. Dixon protests sanctimoniously that his drama "is not meant to reflect in any way on any race or people of to-day." And then he proceeds to give to the Negro a kind of malignity that is really a revelation of his own malignity.

Passing over the initial gibe at the Negro's smell, we early come to a negrophile senator whose mistress is a mulatto. As conceived by Mr. Dixon and as acted in the film, this mulatto is not only a minister to the senator's lust but a woman of inordinate passion, pride, and savagery. Gloating as she does over the promise of "Negro equality," she is soon partnered by a male mulatto of similar brute characteristics. Having established this triple alliance between the "uncrowned king," his diabolic colored mistress, and his diabolic colored ally, Mr. Dixon shows the revolting processes by which the white South is crushed "under the heel of the black South." "Sowing the wind," he calls it. On the one hand we have "the poor bruised heart" of the white South, on the other "the new citizens inflamed by the growing sense of power." We see Negroes shoving white men off the sidewalk, Negroes quitting work to dance, Negroes beating a crippled old white patriarch, Negroes slinging up "faithful colored servants" and flogging them till they drop, Negro courtesans guzzling champagne with the would-be head of the Black Empire, Negroes "drunk with wine and power," Negroes mocking their white master in chains, Negroes "crazy with joy" and terrorizing all the whites in South Carolina. We see the blacks flaunting placards demanding "equal marriage." We see the black leader demanding a "forced marriage" with an imprisoned and gagged white girl. And we see continually in the background the white Southerner in "agony of soul over the degradation and ruin of his people."

Encouraged by the black leader, we see Gus the renegade hover about another young white girl's home. To hoochy-coochy music we see the long pursuit of the innocent white girl by this lust-maddened Negro, and we see her fling herself to death from a precipice, carrying her honor through "the opal gates of death."

Having painted this insanely apprehensive picture of an unbridled, bestial, horrible race, relieved only by a few touches of low comedy, "the grim reaping begins." We see the operations of the Ku Klux Klan, "the organization that saved the South from the anarchy of black rule." We see Federals and Confederates uniting in a Holy War "in defense of their Aryan birthright," whatever that is. We see the Negroes driven back, beaten, killed. The drama winds up with a suggestion of "Lincoln's solution" —back to Liberia—and then, if you please, with a film representing Jesus Christ in "the halls of brotherly love."

My objection to this drama is based partly on the tendency of the pictures but mainly on the animus of the printed lines I have quoted. The effect of these lines, reinforced by adroit quotations from Woodrow Wilson and repeated assurances of impartiality and goodwill, is to arouse in the audience a strong sense of the evil possibilities of the Negro and the extreme propriety and godliness of the Ku Klux Klan. So strong is this impression that the audience invariably applauds the refusal of the white hero to shake hands with a Negro, and under the circumstances it cannot be blamed. Mr. Dixon has identified the Negro with cruelty, superstition, insolence, and lust.

We know what a yellow journalist is. He is not yellow because he reports crimes of violence. He is yellow because he distorts them. In the region of history the Rev. Thomas Dixon corresponds to the yellow journalist. He is a clergyman, but he is a yellow clergyman. He is yellow because he recklessly distorts Negro crimes, gives them a disproportionate place in life, and colors them dishonestly to inflame the ignorant and the credulous. And he is especially yellow, and quite disgustingly and contemptibly yellow, because his perversions are cunningly calculated to flatter the white man and provoke hatred and contempt for the Negro.

Whatever happened during Reconstruction, this film is aggressively vicious and defamatory. It is spiritual assassination. It degrades the censors that passed it and the white race that endures it.

The New Republic, March 20, 1915

Henry MacMahon wrote *The History of the French Pictorial Service in America* and novelized two of Jeanie MacPherson's screenplays for Cecil B. DeMille, *The King of Kings* and *The Ten Commandments.*

THE BIRTH OF A NATION

HENRY MAC MAHON

The lack of adequate interpretation and criticism must astonish the Martian or other visitor coming to these shores and noting the predominant position rapidly being taken in the amusement world by the motion pictures. The cinema is a Topsy "dat jes' growed." There are no canons of the art, no rules of criticism, no intelligent body of opinion, and no agreement on anything except that D. W. Griffith as a producer is the "best ever" and his film *The Birth of a Nation* is by far the greatest motion picture work yet put forward.

My especial interest being in that film, I have taken pains to collate the expressions concerning it by such "old-line" critical leaders as Metcalfe, Eaton, and Hackett. Not one offers any comprehensive analysis of the new art. Not one offers any constructive suggestion as to the future. Walter Prichard Eaton, writing in *The Boston Transcript,* March 13, is singularly obtuse to the possibilities of the new art.

"The assumption," he says, "that we can go back to what amounts to sign language at this stage of civilization is one of the most touchingly naïve examples of motion-picture makers' credulity."

How about the "sign language" of pure music? The "sign language" of sculpture? The "sign language" of painting? Mr. Eaton's choice of a sneer at the motion picture art seems singularly unfortunate. For the function of all art is to touch the emotions ideally, and it matters not whether the "signs" or media are words or tones or carvings or pigments or mere facial and bodily attitudes and expressions.

No one seems to have sensed the fact that the new art is symbolistic. Mr. Eaton ridicules the throw-back and the simultaneous action, while Mr. Metcalfe in *Life* objects to "the constant shifting of scenes, the intrusion of things that are not essential, the prolongation and repetition of the same actions." With all due respect to these eminent thinkers, the fact must be stated that they are talking in terms of their old art the "indoor drama." The technique of the motion picture is closer kin to music; the frequent recurrence of parallel themes is both agreeable and necessary, and the "constant shifting of scenes," instead of being a blemish, is the very virtue of this new dramatic-musical-photographic form, which is best characterized as "art by lightning flash."

Every little series of pictures, continuing from four to fifteen seconds, symbolizes a sentiment, a passion, or an emotion. Each successive series, similar yet different, carries the emotion to the next higher power, till at last, when both of the parallel emotions have attained the *nth* power, so to speak, they meet in the final shock of victory and defeat.

A series of pictures *has* to be swiftly moving. The picturemaker *has* to use the rapier of suggestion rather than the bludgeon of logic. The environment often counts for more than the act. The fiction of the "removed fourth wall" of the staged drama is gone forever, and the position of the motion picture spectator is that of one who looks out of doors from an open window upon the whole of Life spread as on a panorama, seeing swiftly, understanding swiftly, because the eye is so much swifter and more understanding than the ear.

Suggestions for the improvement of a new artistic vehicle are always welcome. Mr. Eaton, in his *Transcript* article, complains of "amateur kodakery." Alas! there is too much of that everywhere. But so there is likewise too much of amateur English and amateur drama. There is ugly sculpture and badly botched painting; discordant, unharmonious music; and (whisper it in the presence of the High Priest of the Older Art!) "legitimate" staging galore that grossly offends both eye and ear. Where in the Older Art is there the selective reverence for beauty that is exhibited in the making of a great film? For example, *The Birth of a Nation,* wherein Mr. Griffith took 140,000 feet of pictures to cull out 12,000 feet (less than one-tenth) for public use. Would David Belasco build and rebuild ten times as many stage scenes as he wanted?

My point is that the efforts at criticism are neither truly analytical nor constructive. They do not lead anywhere, nor show the direction the next great step forward will take. Often they belittle the New Art or deliberately ignore its finest phases. Thus we are told by one prominent New York reviewer that youth, beauty, and facial expressiveness are the sole requisites of a great motion picture actress—in other words, it's not art at all but merely a trick imparted to a bright girl by a clever director. I wonder if that reviewer ever studied the career and achievements of Mae Marsh? If he had, he would have found genius in the film as well as in his Old Art.

In general, the most learned critics of the pictures seem to be as far behind the art-form they are criticizing as the Edinburgh Reviewers were hopelessly to the rear of Wordsworth, Shelley, Keats, Coleridge, and Byron, whom they vainly attempted to extinguish whilst upholding the time-worn art of Dryden and Pope. There are honorable exceptions, however. Let me quote from two of them. James Shelley Hamilton in the current *Everybody's* says:

"All people who call movies a cheap and inferior substitute for the spoken play base their opinion on pictures that are made in imitation of the spoken play. Griffith . . . saw that the story must be told wholly by action, that the introduction of long, explanatory subtitles was just as awkward a method of construction as it would be in a spoken play if each character were to advance to the footlights and explain to the audience who he was and how he came to be there. He saw that past action had to be presented visually, and that often it had to be recalled to the audience to give point to the present action; so he invented the 'flash-back,' which is a view of a past or distant scene, inserted almost as an illustration is inserted in a story. To give emphasis to a particular character, a face, or an important bit of stage property, he invented the 'close-up,' . . . He introduced, too, the device of simultaneous action, the method by which the last part of *The Birth of a Nation* is made so exciting. . . . All of Griffith's pictures have excelled in some particular respect, and they have all been different. But Griffith is not the only man who is doing things in motion pictures. Directors who make artistic productions are multiplying rapidly."

Last, as to the position and future of the film art, let us hear from the *New York Independent* reviewer, Dr. E. E. Slosson, whose technical insight is entirely and rightly unswayed by the fact that he is a bitter opponent of *The Birth of a Nation* on social grounds:

"The film play, compared with its rival, the stage play, has certain serious defects, notably the absence of sound and color. But on the other hand it has certain compensating qualities of its own, and producers are very wisely laying more stress on these instead of imitating what the stage can always do better. For instance, the film playwright can use all outdoors for his background instead of a painted and rumpled backdrop. He can change the scene oftener than the Elizabethan dramatist. He can dip into the future or the past as though he were in Wells's Time Machine. He can use literally an army of supernumeraries in place of a dozen attendants with spears. He can reveal the mind of his characters in two ways, neither of them possible on the stage, first by bringing the actor so close that the spectator can read his facial expression, and second, by visualizing his memories or imaginings. He can, if he so desires, wreck a train, burn a house, sink a ship, or blow up a fort, since he does not have to repeat the expense every night. It is natural that the new art should tend to run to excess in those things which it can do best. The film artist is so tickled at the idea that he can portray motion that he is apt to put in too much motion. . . . But these are the inevitable extravagances of youth and are already being eliminated in the best of the feature films. The motion picture has established itself, and in some form or other will become a permanent part of the intellectual and esthetic life of the nation."

The New York Times, June 6, 1915

Thomas H. Ince was the one American director of the period comparable with Griffith. He soon gave up directing for producing, devised advanced and intelligent production methods, and died in Hollywood, in 1924, at the age of forty-two (see p. 151).

Before 1917 film-makers of differing views were trying to influence attitudes toward the war in still-neutral America. In 1915 J. Stuart Blackton made the "preparedness" polemic, *The Battle Cry of Peace,* with Norma Talmadge. In 1916 Herbert Brenon made the pacifist *War Brides* with Alla Nazimova. Ince's film, also pacifist, was not hugely successful "because America was at war within ten months of its opening." [13]

The Ford expedition was a "peace ship" chartered by Henry Ford that went to Scandinavia in 1915 in a quest for neutral mediation to end the war.

CIVILIZATION

Civilization, Thomas H. Ince's effort to rival D. W. Griffith with a photo spectacle of the scale and scope of *The Birth of a Nation,* was displayed in New York for the first time last evening at the Criterion Theater. It is an excellently elaborate photo pageant on the physical horrors of war, a big motion picture marked by lavishness in production and beauty in photography.

Civilization attempts to serve the pacifists as *The Battle Cry of Peace* tried to serve the cause of preparedness. Its argument is elementary, a leaf out of the pacifists' primer, a projection on the screen of something of that state of mind that was most in evidence in this neighborhood at the time the Ford expedition set forth from these shores. Its program describes it as a direct appeal to the "mothers of men."

The hero of *Civilization* is the submarine commander who, secretly wearing the purple cross of the Mothers of Men Society, refuses to torpedo a defenseless passenger vessel. In the mutiny that follows the submarine is sunk. He is drowned, and his spirit goes to an inferno inspired by Doré. There the Christ comes to him, receives him as a redeemed soul, returns among men in the discarded body of the dead man, and there takes the warlike king on such a review of war's horrors as to make him cry for peace. The king then heeds the pleas of the Mothers of Men, and the last picture shows the soldiers returning jubilant to their peasant homes.

In the earlier part of this photoplay there are many stirring battle scenes, and the whole episode of the submarine and the sinking of another *Lusitania is* extraordinarily graphic—so graphic, indeed, that at this point in the unfolding of the spectacle last evening Billie Burke fainted.

Civilization was displayed last evening with a full orchestra in full blast, with off-stage singing, both solo and choral, and with a preliminary corporeal pantomime of the sort employed in *Ramona,* and always of doubtful value in the screen world. A large audience, full of notables, saw and applauded the picture at its first showing, and at the end called for Mr. Ince, who was led on by Al Woods, his associate in the New York display of the film. Mr. Ince spoke his acknowledgments with a modesty and brevity in striking contrast with the fulsome Ince-adulation which makes the program such painful reading. He has projected a philosophy of war on a par with *War Brides,* an entertainment on an artistic level with *Ben Hur,* a dramatic photo spectacle that falls somewhat short of *The Birth of a Nation.*

The New York Times, June 3, 1916

Heywood Broun was a literary and dramatic critic on newspapers for some years, then went on to a longer and more celebrated career as a socially progressive reporter and columnist. In passing, Broun refers here to Carrie Nation, the renowned anti-alcoholist, Robert Fulton Cutting, a social reformer and one-time president of Cooper Union, Maurice McLaughlin, an outstanding tennis player of the day, Augustus Thomas, the popular playwright who later wrote *The Copperhead,* and Richard Harding Davis, a colorful war correspondent who subsequently wrote romantic novels and plays.

INTOLERANCE

HEYWOOD BROUN

David W. Griffith is an immature philosopher, a wrongheaded sociologist, a hazy theologian, a flamboyant historian, but a great movie man. As a picture *Intolerance* is quite the most marvelous thing which has been put on the screen, but as a theory of life it is trite without being true. Mr. Griffith ought to know that "laissez faire" is the battle cry of a lost cause and that "mild wines and beer" is a slogan which no longer thrills. It is a pity that a man with this producer's power should go out of his way to attack such a useful institution, for instance, as the juvenile court; and whatever the defects of organized charity it no way merits the abuse heaped upon it by *Intolerance*.

As a matter of fact, the scheme of Griffith is not logical. The piece is called "a sun play of the ages," which doesn't mean anything at all, but in the course of the picture it is made clear that the author believes the fall of Babylon, the Crucifixion, the Huguenot massacre, and social reform of today were all animated by the same spirit, which is that of persecution or intolerance. In other words, Mr. Griffith would have us believe that Catherine de Medici was a former incarnation of Carrie Nation and that Cyrus was the spiritual ancestor of Robert Fulton Cutting. The philosophy of *Intolerance* really doesn't make any difference and will not detract from anybody's enjoyment of the picture, but it merits consideration since the producer evidently sets great store by it.

Griffith's history is more entertaining than his philosophy. It is as vivid as Macaulay and about as accurate. The master of the screen seems to have discovered history in his maturity. As such it is not a dull memory of school study, but something fresh and alive; something to get excited about, like Maurice McLaughlin or the Giants or Theodore Roosevelt.

Griffith is tickled to death to learn that there was once a town called Babylon full of folk who loved and laughed and fought, with never a thought that they were ancients. He thrills to the poet's "When I was a king in Babylon and you were a slapstick slave" and puts slave, slapstick, and king into the picture.

It may be remembered that Augustus Thomas once discovered science late in life and manifested symptoms of enthusiasm similar to those which Griffith is now showing.

Paris of the late sixteenth century and Palestine at the time of Christ interest Griffith greatly, but Babylon is more to him than California to a native son. While it may be true that Babylon has fallen, Griffith has caught it on the first bounce. Up go the walls again and the great temples and the mighty gates and the palaces.

A great reconstructor is Griffith. We haven't a doubt that he could put Humpty Dumpty together again. But then the king with all his horses and men never mustered such an army as Griffith has mobilized to capture Babylon. One view in particular gives the impression of thousands upon thousands of men marching. From the effect the producer has gained it might be the never-ending gray army which Richard Harding Davis saw flowing through Brussels. The battle before, on, and over the walls is quite the finest achievement of moving picture art. It is a wall wide enough for two chariots to drive abreast of each other, and they do. Great towers topple and flame, and the air is dark with spears and arrows.

Griffith is sometimes too literal in his slaughter. Upon at least one occasion he permits a warrior to start a sword slash on one side of an opponent's neck and finish on the other. Of course, we don't doubt that it was a property head which rolled off, and yet we mourned its loss.

Not only is Babylon the most impressive pictorial portion of the Griffith film, but it is the scene of the best of the four stories. As a matter of fact, there are only three stories, and that of the French period is slightly developed. Not a great deal of time is spent in Palestine, where occasional glimpses are furnished of the life of Christ. These pictures are beautiful, and personally we did not feel any spirit of irreverence manifest. The stories on which the greatest amount of attention is lavished relate the love of a slave girl of Babylon for Belshazzar and of a modern American boy for an American girl. Of course, the story of our day has largely to do with white slavery. The modern story is vivified by the extraordinary acting of Mae Marsh. To our mind it sets a top watermark of film performance. Robert Herron is good as the boy. Next best is Constance Talmadge as the Mountain Girl of the Babylonian story.

Babylon and New York go pretty well together. There is a parallelism in these two stories which holds the interest. Thus, for an instant we see an automobile racing to save the boy from the electric chair while in the next the girl is galloping along the Euphrates in her chariot to save Belshazzar. Strangely enough, the sudden switch from Cyrus to Sing Sing to Babylon and back to the Bowery does not work against the suspense of either story, but heightens it. In the end the boy is saved but, much to his chagrin, Griffith is obliged to sacrifice his beloved Babylon.

It should be remarked that the genius of this film director does not lie only in the handling of mass effects. Indeed, much of the effectiveness of his pictures lies in the manner he will drop a big effect to hammer home an interesting detail. In all the technical aspects of screen photography the picture is remarkable. To our mind, it is much more absorbing than *The*

Birth of a Nation, but we feel that Gritffih can go further when he devotes himself entirely to production and calls upon somebody else for a story worthy of his directing talents.

The New York Tribune, September 7, 1916

George Soule was an editor of *The New Republic* who wrote usually on economics.

INTOLERANCE

GEORGE SOULE

"Yes, they actually cut a man's head off. You see the sword slice through, and the trunk stands there for a minute, and falls. I can't imagine how it's done."

"Really!"

"That's in the siege of Babylon. It's the most enormous thing I ever saw. Walls at least seventy-five feet high with chariots driving around on the top. And you ought to see the men fall off. Even if they had nets at the bottom, I don't see how they could keep from getting hurt."

It was the account of such wonders that attracted me to *Intolerance.* The theater flaunted a Babylonian warrior and program-maiden in the lobby. Bearded, manheaded lions, with the right fore-leg nobly in advance, concealed the walls. I opened the program. "D. W. Griffith presents the Colossal Spectacle *Intolerance,* A Sun Play of the Ages." Then two full pages of cast in small type, ending with: "Assyrian, Persian, Median, Roman, and French soldiers, militiamen, mill workers, Babylonian dancers, Persians, Ethiopians, East Indians, Numidians, Eunuchs, Roman mobs, people of Jerusalem, Pharisees, Scribes, Publicans, members of the Sanhedrin, ladies in waiting and courtiers at the Court of Charles IX, attendants at the wedding feast of Cana, denizens of the streets of Paris, knights, Huguenots and Guisards, handmaidens of the Babylonian temples, Priests of Bel, Nergel, and Ishtar, convicts, camp followers, nobles, and subjects of Babylonia."

I looked on the next page for the account of the menagerie and sideshows. These were not mentioned, but I can assure the timorous that there are leopards fearlessly caressed, camels, possibly elephants—I have really lost track of some of the gigantic features—and any number of fine horses. There is a professional strong-man—Elmo Lincoln, "The Mighty Man of

Valor," he who lops off the head—and there are a number of babies who smile obligingly at the camera and share the applause with the big things. Audiences always applaud movie babies, just as they always applaud pink scenery.

I had asked my friend whether there was a plot. "Oh, yes," he had replied, "four of them; but I don't remember them very well." Now I understood. "There are four separate stories," reads the program, "each with its own set of characters. Following the introduction of each period there are subsequent interruptions as the different stories develop along similar lines, switching from one to the other as the mind might do while contemplating such a theme." Of course—four rings. You had no sooner found that you were expected to dislike three reforming ladies in a Middle-western city than you were switched over to Babylon and the temple of Bel, watching a flaming idol. This magically dissolved to the streets of Jerusalem, with a bedizened Mary Magdalen in a luxurious litter. Before you really had time to get a good look at her she changed to Catherine de Medici registering hate of the Huguenots. Of course I couldn't swear that this was the actual sequence, but it will do for illustration. And when the various plots thickened, they thickened at cross-purposes, like an indigestible rarebit made by a novice who puts in the beer, the cheese, the eggs, and everything else at the same time. The result was indescribably orgiastic to a frugal imagination. Mr. Griffith might really stick a little closer to his prototype by running his four stories simultaneously on different screens. This would at least give the weak-minded a chance to concentrate.

I do not intend to imply that Mr. Griffith's ingenuity has not improved on Mr. Barnum's. He has discovered another great amusement of the American public, and has exploited it—the moral lesson. An easy generalization—that intolerance is the only sin which keeps earth from being paradise—is richly suggestive. To prove the theme he maintains that Babylon fell before Cyrus on account of the intolerance of the Priest of Bel; he portrays the Christian tragedy of Palestine as the result of religious hatred; he tells the old story of the massacre of St. Bartholomew's Eve; and he shows the activity of an imaginary modern charitable foundation whose chief function seems to be sequestrating babies from unfortunate but deserving mothers. All this would appear dangerous to sensibilities. But it is safe to assume that nobody now takes sides between Bel and Ishtar, and in the other stories Mr. Griffith has hedged. He is careful to placate the Jews; he matches the intolerance of Catherine with the intolerance of the Huguenots; and he explains that his charitable foundation is not representative. All the many individual vices and crimes which form part of his story are traced somewhat obscurely to a vast impersonal Intolerance. The result is comfortable in the extreme. Everybody in the audience can hate his enemy for being intolerant. Everybody can assume that he is never intolerant himself. And everybody can feel such an excess of generous virtue that he can stare without a qualm at the many gorgeous pictures of vice which Mr. Griffith strews before him. In the end the theme is doubly valuable because it makes possible a magnificent flight of angels.

The spectacle's the thing, of course; but only a bill-poster would do it justice. Imagine everything Mr. Griffith might say about it, and still words would fail. Probably the archeology is correct to the smallest jewel. Probably more people are on the screen at a given moment than in any other production. There are battles and sudden death, strange ancient engines of war, chariot races, dancing maidens, exotic feasts, scenes in the court of Charles, etc., etc. It ends by the traditional race between locomotive and motor car. Occasionally there flashed a really well-composed picture in lovely brown tones. Authorities without number are cited for the sources of the setting. As to the modern story, says the program, "citations can be had from Woodrow Wilson, Ralph Waldo Emerson, John Stewart Mill (sic), Frank P. Walsh, Longfellow, Rousseau, Dr. Charles F. Aked, John Koren, and others." But even the spectacle is circused. The accuracy and the beauty appear to have been employed merely in order to be advertised. The film hurries by so rapidly that nobody has time to evoke any real pleasure from these things. An added sense of the stupendous is the only result.

People who still speak of the movies as a possible form of drama will have to exclude such a film as *Intolerance* from their calculations. The surprising, the enormous, the daring, the sumptuous, in a terrific mêlée of attack on the sensations, eject one from the theater with the memory of no human emotion except visual amazement and wonder as to how it was done. The attempt is not to stimulate the imagination, but to gorge the senses. Even this attempt is unsuccessful, because the illusion is not played for honestly; one is astounded at the tricks, the expense, the machinery of production, more often than one is absorbed by their result. One might enjoy a quarter of it, stretched out to the full time. But as it is, one prefers Messrs. Barnum and Bailey.

The New Republic, September 30, 1916

Among the astonishments of Charlie Chaplin's swift rise to immense international fame is the speed with which he was taken seriously. Some other stars had large followings, but none became so quickly the subject of serious discussion. Much of this was due of course to his quality; some of it was due to opportune timing. He came along just as cultural attitudes toward the film began to change. The article by Mrs. Fiske referred to below appeared in *Harper's Weekly* for May 6, 1916, little more than two years after his film debut.[14] Additionally remarkable is the fact that it was written by Minnie Maddern Fiske, one of the great actresses of the American stage, who hailed a performer in a previously disregarded medium.

O'Higgins was a well-known playwright who became a screenwriter.

CHARLIE CHAPLIN'S ART

HARVEY O'HIGGINS

There died last winter, in New York, a notable artist who was comparatively unknown because he had the ill-luck to miss his right artistic medium. He was a circus clown—"Slivers" of the delectable "baseball game." He should have been "Frank Oakley of the movies." He was condemned to pantomime because of a voice that was inadequate to public utterance, but he was a comedian of surprising imagination, a serious observer, a real student of comic effects, and inherently pathetic even at his funniest.

Charles Chaplin has come into the kingdom that poor Slivers missed. He wears, as Slivers did, a grotesque costume. He has the same gift for clowning—an ability to translate any natural gesture into caricature without the slightest apparent exaggeration—a gift that seems inherent in his body as grace is so often in the body of beauty. Slivers used to say: "Put a real clown in the middle of a three-ring circus, with nothin' to work with but a shoelace, an' he'll make the whole tent laugh." Slivers did it by virtue of a penetrating imagination. He would see the shoelace as anything from an angleworm to a string of spaghetti, and see it and relate himself to it so convincingly that he made you see it as he did. Chaplin performs the same miracle with a walking-stick. He will see it—outrageously—as a toothpick, but he will use it exactly as you see toothpicks used at a lunch counter, looking at you with an air of sad repletion, with a glazed eye from which all intelligence has withdrawn, inwardly, to brood over the internal satisfaction of digestive process—absurdly, but with unimpeachable realism. Or, he is a clerk in a pawnshop, and a man brings in an alarm clock to pledge it. Chaplin has to decide how much it is worth. He sees it first as a patient to be examined diagnostically. He taps it, percusses it, puts his ear to its chest, listens to its heartbeat with a stethoscope, and, while he listens, fixes a thoughtful medical eye on space, looking inscrutably wise and professionally self-confident. He begins to operate on it—with a can-opener. And immediately the round tin clock becomes a round tin can whose contents are under suspicion. He cuts around the circular top of the can, bends back the flap of tin with a kitchen thumb gingerly, scrutinizes the contents gingerly, and then, gingerly approaching his nose to it, sniffs with the melancholy expression of an experienced housekeeper who believes the worst of the packing-houses. The imagination is accurate. The acting is restrained and naturalistic. The result is a scream.

And do not believe that such acting is a matter of crude and simple means. It is as subtle in its naturalism as the shades of intonation in a really tragic speech. In one of Chaplin's films, another actor, disguised as Chaplin, walked into the picture and was received by the audience with a preliminary titter of welcome. He went through a number of typical Chaplin antics with a drinking fountain that squirted water in his face. There was half-hearted laughter. He was not funny. He moved through a succession of comic "stunts" unsuccessfully before it dawned on me that this was not Chaplin at all. When Chaplin followed in, and repeated the exact passages that had failed, the laughter was enormous. It was the difference between a man acting a comic scene and a man living it, and the difference was apparent in a thousand niceties of carriage and gesture and expression of face. In this hairbreadth of difference lies the triumph of Chaplin's art. Expressed in salary, it is the difference between a few dollars a day and a half-million a year. In reputation, it is the difference between the obscurity of the still unknown comedians who competed with Chaplin in the early films and the success of the most famous clown in the world—for Chaplin is as preëminent a favorite in Paris, for instance, as he is here. It is the difference between a genuine artist and an artificial one.

That difference goes very deep. Slivers used to say: "It's imitatin' life—that's what does it. You can't get it by muggin' "—making faces—"it has to be real to you. Why, in that baseball game——" and he would describe how he had built up his elaborate caricature of a catcher from innumerable observations, holding his glove between his knees instead of dropping it on the ground—when he paused to put on his chest-pad—because So-and-So always did it that way, and snatching off his mask with just *this* gesture because it was the way he had seen another catcher do *that*. And he would say: "You know, it's hard work—that turn. You have to keep in mind where all the players are, on the field and on the bases, all the time. It keeps you watchin'." He was as serious about it as a Russian realist. And, as a result, you would see the baseball fans at the circus wiping the tears of helpless laughter from one eye at a time so as not to lose sight of him for an instant.

The curious thing is that none of the clowns who worked with Slivers in the circus learned the lesson from him. They imitated his "make-up." They stole his "business." But they never reached his secret. And on the films, to-day, as on the stage, you will find all the would-be comedians "mugging" diligently, trying to "put over comedy" with consciously comic gesture and intonation, saying to the audience tacitly, "I'm funny—laugh at me," and concluding that the audience is "a bunch of bone-heads" because they do not laugh. The author gives the stage comedians amusing lines, and Chaplin has no lines. Elaborately humorous plots are invented for the spoken drama, and Chaplin's plots are so simple that the popular legend credits him with improvising them as he goes along. He is on a stage where the slapstick, the "knockabout," the gutta-percha hammer and the "rough-house" are accepted as the necessary ingredients of comedy, and these things fight against the finer qualities of his art, yet he overcomes them. In his burlesque of Carmen he commits suicide with a collapsible dagger, and the moment of his death is as tragic as any of Bernhardt's. His work has become more and more delicate and finished as the medium of its reproduction has improved to admit of delicate and finished work. There is no doubt, as Mrs. Fiske has said, that he is a great artist. And he is a great lesson and encouragement to anyone who loves an art or practices it, for he is an example of how the best can be the most successful, and of how a real talent can triumph over the most appalling limitations put upon its expression, and of how the popular eye can recognize such a talent without the aid of the pundits of culture and even in spite of their anathemas.

The New Republic, February 3, 1917

Kenneth Macgowan began writing film criticism in 1916 and worked for several newspapers and journals. In 1923 he joined Eugene O'Neill and Robert Edmond Jones at the Provincetown Playhouse in New York; later he became a Broadway producer. In the early 1930s he went to Hollywood where he produced fifty films; subsequently he became chairman of the Theater Arts Department at UCLA. His posthumous book *Behind the Screen* (1965) contains further comment on *The Monster of Fate,* an early version of *The Golem* mentioned below.[15] Hugo Münsterberg was a Harvard psychologist who wrote one book on film, an estimable one.[16]

ON THE SCREEN

KENNETH MACGOWAN

Two things I find that give the movies a promise of art. Both are imponderable. One is light, the creation of an expressive atmosphere. The other is sequence, the assembling of innumerable pictorial impressions in an order which not alone tells a story but reinforces it with a mental, almost a subconscious, gathering of details. It is manner, not matter, that makes a day of even the most routine of weekly "features" in some degree profitable. The stories may be no better than the traffic of stage and popular magazine. The technique of camera and scenario brings keen pleasure and keener promise into ten hours of such habitual screen-gazing as has been my biweekly duty as "photoplay editor" of a daily newspaper.

The first impression of the theatergoer at the movies used to be that, amid scores of flat, almost footlighted, scenes, the camera showed every now and then a lighting effect such as the American theater had never risked and probably could not achieve. Generally it was the illuminating of an interior from a single point, as, for instance, a lantern or a candle. Thousands of striking lights and shadows filled the scene. They created an atmosphere of vivid life. Faces became more expressive, more beautiful or more hideous. Of course, it was not often that the action of a film gave excuse for this effect; only once in Morosco's *Peer Gynt,* for example, in the cabin scene, was the director who exploited this effect able to use it. But presently a producer, Cecil DeMille, and his art director, Wilfred Buckland, began to try something of the kind on almost all interior scenes. Instead of utilizing the filtered sunlight of open-air studios, or the even glare of banks of Cooper Hewitts from top and sides, they threw their illumination in a great strong sheet from one or at the most two angles. The result was the brilliant "Lasky lighting" that the "movie fan" began to note in Farrar's *Carmen.*

Beginning at first as an "effect" on the level with prints in sepia, it has developed in the Lasky company's productions into something that heightens atmosphere. In Mary Pickford's film, *A Romance of the Red Woods,* the variations in this lighting within a single room are most interesting. Under a small, single source of light, the walls of the cabin and the faces of the actors are filled with staring shadows to match the terror of the episode enacted. Under ordinary clear studio lighting, the same scene takes on the cold grayness of the morning that follows. When comparative peace and security reign again, the cabin is warmed into mellow evening lamplight by the use of two or three brilliant sources of illumination.

Still further refinements of this matter of lighting come to me in this day at the movies. In the Thomas H. Ince production, *Chicken Casey,* as in virtually all his films, the possibilities of half illumination have been wonderfully realized by his art director, Robert Brunton. Light becomes atmosphere instead of illumination. Coming naturally from some window, lamp, or doorway, it illumines the center of the picture and the people standing there, with a glow that in intensity, in volume, or in variety of sources has some quality expressive of the emotion of the scene. Moreover, it illumines only the human figures and the things with which they are concerned. Behind them is a great, solid, realistic room, far more complete in every detail than any stage setting yet absolutely unobtrusive. In the ordinary screen production it is lit up within an inch of its life. Care is taken to make us see the sculptured reality of its every molding, each sure-enough wrinkle of its hangings. The result, of course, is that we don't see the drama. The tawdry human figures jump about and distract us; that is all. In an Ince production all that massive detail fades into the dimness of shadow corners. We know reality is there, rich reality, but we have something more important in hand. It is the human drama that Ince is presenting. He centers our attention on the one thing we need to understand, the people and the things they do and feel. There is something of Rembrandt in the Ince method.

Another type of production tries to do the same thing by a trick of the camera. It is well represented by *The Americano,* a film made by another and now departed element of the Triangle Film Corporation, the Fine Arts Studio, once dominated by Griffith. Here we watch the actors, too, and nothing but the actors. In a clear and mellow light, we see a man at his desk; behind him the details of his office fade into the shadows of the theater outside the screen. Out of the shadows steps Douglas Fairbanks, and into the spot of light where we have been watching the older man. The same general effect of concentration of acting and atmosphere is gained in almost all the other interior scenes of the film.

But it is gained, as you may observe, by hardly any genuine use of light. The margins of the picture outside the central portion given to the figures are masked in by an iris which makes a vignette of the center. As the background is always of dark wood or canvas, the effect is almost the same as in the Ince method; for the edge of the iris fades into the dark hue of the setting. The usefulness and necessity of a dark background are easily apparent by comparison with pictures where this iris effect is used in out-of-doors scenes, as in *The Barrier.* There the edge of the iris cuts sharply across the light sky or landscape. And the instant that line is visible, you not only become aware of the trick, but grow camera-conscious. The mood of belief is lost; you are thinking of the director and the actors and the camera and all the make-believe, instead of feeling the story as a reality.

Aside from the fact that the Fine Arts method is a trick that keen observation can penetrate, it lacks pictorial virtues which the Ince enjoys. By the Ince method, the light is not only concentrated on the actors' figures; it may be composed in designs other than the rough circle of the iris. In the club scene from *Chicken Casey,* for instance, the light strikes across a group of men in evening dress from a tall window, throwing shadows that suggest in the angle and the lines of the panes the height and magnificence of the room. In the dramatist's library, the daylight is shaped and tempered by simple but handsome hangings at the windows. It enters his bedroom by both window and door, accomplishing the necessary job of illumination yet suggesting too the more Spartan arrangement of the room and the proximity of the library, from which the action flows.

Naturally, other directors have learned these tricks, and some use them extremely well. There is Alan Dwan, for instance, a keen-minded student of the screen since the early days. In *Panthea* he builds up amazingly effective prisons with nothing but inky shadows, and constructs a palatial dining room out of a great space of floor and table and a very large chandelier above. He knows how to control his light even in exteriors where he must depend on the sun. For this Russian photoplay he has built up Vermeer-like walls and shadowed commons that are full of the quality of Russian historical painters. His opening scene is as genuine a work of art as any composition by Steichen. Out of the darkness of the theater comes a gray room, with three patches of photographic color. One is a small window high at the left. Under its light a young woman is just distinguishable above the corner of a grand piano. To the left is the door of a dimly lighted passage in which stands her old teacher. Then the camera picks out for us other features of this room, composed with the simplicity and dignity that reside in the piano itself. They are three men sitting apart from one another in the half light, listening. Music and the occasion—a private recital before connoisseurs—are the very breath of the scene.

But what is all this atmosphere alone? True, it is nothing unless it is spent on stories by a method that makes of them something filled with the completeness of life as our minds roam over it. And that the American movie has learned to do. It is our contribution. We have gone by experiment, by trial and error, by instinct, straight to the intricate, sub-mental nature of the photoplay which Münsterberg recognized in his valuable analytical volume. We throw on the screen in half a minute a dozen aspects, great and small, immediate and remote, obvious and inferential, actual and reminiscent, of the thing that is to be told.

It is a quality which resides first in the scenario and which the director must realize as he works. Alan Dwan, who makes his own scenarios, uses thoroughgoing, Griffithian technique with sure effect in *Panthea.* He gathers that music room into our vision with undeniable sureness. He gives us Russia through a dozen small touches, crisp "flash-backs," intimate and pungent "close-ups." When he gets to the swiftest part of his story, he drives us through it unerringly and irresistibly by following physical actions to the minutest details. When, for instance, the police raid a dwelling, he shows not only the approach, the groups on both sides of the door, the violence of the entry, and the scattering of the dwellers, but as the police charge upstairs after the hero, he smashes it home to us with a sudden flash of feet pounding the steps. Again he uses that same "close-up" expedient—and with an even greater, because characterizing, effect—when, after the officer has shot the hero, he kicks him over with his spurred boot to make sure he is harmless. Dwan catches in his "close-up" of the kicking boot not only the beastliness of the act, but a curve in the boot itself and in the direction of the blow which is amazingly characteristic of the hard, perky, Prussian-like little officer. Such a detail serves no purpose in the tale. Eliminate it and every necessary step of the action would be there. But, when not dwelt on at such lengths as to seem to have a plot importance which it lacks, such a means builds up conviction and atmosphere to an astounding degree. It is things of this sort—intuitions of writer and director—which will give photoplays some of the quality of observation and character that make literature.

Occasionally these technical means of light and of sequence and observation get themselves used in an episode that grows big with imagination. Such a moment occurs in the last photoplay of this blissful day, *The Monster of Fate*. It is a German film which, though using the Ince type of lighting with fine effect throughout, realizes the possibilities of the true movie technique only at rare moments when the story calls imperatively for this American-made device. One of these is unforgettable. The Monster is an old stone figure which comes to life when a scroll of magic has been inserted in a sort of hollow button on his chest. After many centuries of solitude in an abandoned well, the stone figure comes into the possession of an antiquarian who possesses also the secret of the scroll. He brings the stone giant to life and uses him for various picturesque purposes, including the guarding of a daughter who prefers to frisk with a young nobleman. The woman arouses the curiosity of the Monster, and ultimately a sort of passion, and when she escapes from the house, he follows her. Then comes the discovery of the world, still more wonderful than the finding of passion. The giant lumbers across the square of the German village staring at its Gothic buildings. He reaches a brook and with a grin of amazed pleasure wades and splashes across. On the other side he finds a flowering bush. He takes a blossom in his great hand. Staring at it, he brings it close enough to his nose accidentally to smell the odor. Another of life's simplest and grandest things is caught on the broad, elementally stupid countenance of the creature. All, of course, in varied "long-shots" and "close-ups."

And now the best and most perfect moment, as we, and the camera, follow the Monster across country. We climb a slight rise of ground to a wooded crest. Out of that wood we stare, through a Fine Arts circle of shadowed boughs, toward a cathedral city raising its spires to God. Suddenly, up from the foreground, rears the bulk of the Monster. His head is turned to gaze at the sight which, if it has arrested us, must strike him dumb. We watch with an amazingly personal interest. The body rises higher and higher, the head tilts back, the shoulders lift, the arms spread from the sides in a gesture of astounded wonder which encircles our vision of the miraculous city. Light and shadow, composition, selection and arrangement of pictures, drive home that miracle-laden pilgrimage of the Monster as few arts could do. Through them it realizes every quality of the imagination that word or paint can summon. It is the foreshadowing of such things in even the most commonplace of pictures that makes the routine of the movies in some degree a glorious venture.

The New Republic, September 15, 1917

This editorial was unsigned, but its basic idea—the mass media's disregard of the diversity of the audience—is one that occurs subsequently in the writings of Gilbert Seldes, who joined *The Dial* in 1920 and was an editor until 1923. For more on Seldes see p. 221.

EDITORIAL

When a new art has completely outgrown criticism, the critics' job of catching up is comparable to that of pruning a jungle. Thankless and hopeless as it may be to begin at this late date to frame special standards for the movies, it does seem that the producers and the public generally might be willing to apply here certain old axioms developed in other fields. The first of these axioms is perhaps this: that sincerity is a virtue. By reason of the vastness of his chosen audience the movie producer can deal only in motives that most men have in common. The theme that makes the widest human appeal is that of sex relationship—particularly if this relationship happens to be somewhat risqué. The variations that may be played upon this theme are, in America, very definitely limited by the tradition that sex may appear in public only when garbed with respectability. Nowhere does

this tradition have such force as in the middle-class conscience, still powerful in the cities, and dominant in the small towns that have the movies for
their only amusement. The man who stages plays for a limited audience may
choose between the indecency of burlesque and the frankness of Ibsen; not
so the movie man, whose films are destined to flicker before all eyes. Sex
he must have to get great audiences—respectability, to keep them. To meet
the situation, there has been developed a hypocrisy without parallel in art.
People who would not think of countenancing a frankly vulgar musical
show may see in the movies pictures of surprising indecency spiced with
moral phrases and grouped under some such allegorical title as Purity or
Virtue; or triangle plays that inevitably wind up with what passes for a
great moral triumph for the innocent party, who wishes the dark pair all
(of their sort of) happiness. Whoever will face the situation frankly will
confess that we have far less to fear from honest nastiness than from this
kind of lip-licking sophistry. Certainly the movies will receive more consideration as an art when the movie people accept variety in their audiences
and do not attempt, by blending goodness and badness, to appeal all at
once to everybody in the United States.

The Dial, July 12, 1919

Exceptional Photoplays had recently been founded by the
National Board of Review, which had been founded in 1909,
thus was a further sign of the recognition of the need for serious
comment. The magazine contained signed articles and unsigned
reviews prepared by a committee. The chairman was Alfred
B. Kuttner who wrote on film for *The Nation* and *The New Republic* and was a well-known translator from the German.

The last line refers to a film that Griffith had made the previous year.

WAY DOWN EAST

It was almost a foregone conclusion that *Way Down East* would make an
exceptional picture. Its long life and nationwide popularity on the stage had
already stamped it as an unusual play. As a rule melodramas have a short
lease of life and are easily forgotten. When one of them succeeds in maintaining itself in the national repertory for a great number of years, it is safe
to assume that the human appeal of the characters or a touch of real poetry
in the story rises above the conventional effects at which melodrama usually

aims. A play of this kind is sure to attract the producer of pictures because melodrama is undoubtedly the favorite art form of the screen. Mr. Griffith has a sure instinct for such things.

The story of *Way Down East* is too familiar to need complete retelling. It is, in its way, a classic of American rural life and is almost as widely known as *The Old Homestead* or *Uncle Tom's Cabin*. There is a real and unaffected poignancy about the betrayal of a young and ignorant girl by a sophisticated seducer which can easily be brought home to vast audiences. Here the moving picture has the advantage over the play. For photoplay art has resources which permit it to soften the crassness of melodrama and to disguise its shopworn qualities. The silent drama leaves our imagination more free, and the girl's misery, which is none the less real for being one of the oldest stories in the world, can still be brought to us with artistic freshness.

Mr. Griffith has gone to work with his usual lavishness. He tells his story against a panorama of country life and manners full of much delightful detail, and thus adds an element of spectacle to what would otherwise have been indeed a "simple tale." Anna Moore's visit to her rich relatives is translated into a gorgeous fashion show and the simple farm of Squire Bartlett is turned into somewhat of a show place. Mr. Griffith favors large gestures to reach his screen public.

The climax of the picture is furnished by Anna's blind flight into the snowstorm. Here Mr. Griffith has let himself loose, and the result, to judge from the applause which greets this scene, justifies the method. But the scene becomes very long and the suspense threatens to lose itself as the spectator begins to doubt the possibility of David's ice-jumping feats. They are certainly enough to make poor Eliza of *Uncle Tom's Cabin* fame turn over in her grave, and any real country folk who know something about ice jams will probably realize that they are being told a pretty tall story. But, as Mercutio said, "it will serve," and there is no doubt of its being a head-line thriller. It is possibly the most spectacular thing, giving at moments a sense of real terror, that has ever been photographed for a dramatic picture.

Mr. Griffith could be depended upon for bringing out the full pathos of Anna's tragedy. His genius for this sort of thing has always been great. And, as usual, he has had the advantage of Miss Lillian Gish's unlimited cooperation. It is a truly astonishing thing about this young artist that one can always say that her latest work is her best. One wonders how high she can still climb on the ladder of superb screen acting. Or perhaps it is a question of how far Mr. Griffith and Miss Gish could go together, for it is often impossible to tell in their work where direction ends and interpretation begins. The rest of Mr. Griffith's cast is, as usual, well balanced, and shows some fine individual work.

Here and there, however, Mr. Griffith has lowered his artistic standard. Some of his comedy scenes, the country dances and the village store episodes, are carelessly done, as if taken in haste, and are not properly joined to the rest of the story. And the scene where Anna gives birth to her child throws the emphasis on the physical side to a degree which is decidedly in questionable taste. It is a pity that in this case the acting of Miss Gish is forced beyond the line of expression into sheer distortion. Nor can anything be said for the colored tintings which Mr. Griffith has introduced here and there into his landscapes. All the delicacy and mellowness which has so distinguished his landscape work in the past is lost by this fatal pink intrusion.

As for the scenes during the function in the home of Anna's city relatives, in which colored foreground portraits of Anna are introduced in contrast to the black and white backgrounds of the longer shots, one hardly knows what to think. To some the idea will appear as an artistic blunder. Others will forgive the incongruity on the theory that Mr. Griffith was endeavoring to create the color impression of a very gaudy and sumptuous social affair. At least one of these colored portraits—that which reveals Miss Gish in tones of blue and silver—is quite beautiful and satisfactory in itself. Perhaps here Mr. Griffith is on the track of an impressionism which has tremendously effective possibilities.

There is one thing, in addition, which may be pointed out. With all the various life and movement of *Way Down East,* there is sometimes a carelessness in the cutting and matching of scenes which certainly interferes with the illusion. There is no reason why a character should rise from a chair in a close-up view and in the succeeding long shot, which is supposed to be part of a continuous action, should appear rising from the chair again.

Yet there cannot be any doubt of the general effectiveness of the picture. Mr. Griffith cannot touch any story without putting his stamp upon it. His version of *Way Down East* will travel far and long. When it has travelled long enough he may perhaps again find courage to try his hand at another *Broken Blossoms.*

Exceptional Photoplays, December 1920

Robert E. Sherwood, later famous as dramatist and screenwriter, was film critic of *Life* from 1920 to 1928. This *Life* was the humorous weekly whose name was afterward sold to the pictorial newsmagazine. The speed of film's rise is illustrated once again by the fact that Sherwood had been born in the month that the first theatrical picture show was held at Koster and Bial's Music Hall.

Rudolph Valentino had been playing screen roles of varying size since 1914, but this was the vehicle that made him an international romantic idol.

F. P. A. was Franklin P. Adams who, under his initials, conducted a famous column, *The Conning Tower,* that appeared in several New York newspapers from 1913 to 1941.

George Creel had been the head of President Wilson's wartime Committee on Public Information, charged with convincing the American people that the war would make the world safe for democracy and would end war.

THE FOUR HORSEMEN OF THE APOCALYPSE

ROBERT E. SHERWOOD

In a hundred years there will be no one left in the world who can give a first-hand account of the great war—no one who can say, "I was there; I saw it as it was"—and people will have to get their knowledge of it from the books and plays that it inspired. The vast maelstrom of words which has flowed since the machine guns and the typewriters first started clicking in 1914 will remain, in greater or lesser degree, throughout all time, and by them will we and our actions be measured.

It is quite important, therefore, that we get the record straight, and make sure that nothing goes down to posterity which will mislead future generations into believing that this age of ours was anything to brag about. Imagine the history which some H. G. Wells of the thirtieth century would write concerning the world war, basing his conclusions on such books as *From Baseball to Boches,* such plays as *Mother's Liberty Bond,* or such songs as "Hello, General Pershing, Is My Daddie Safe To-night?" It might be entertaining reading, but hardly instructive.

Rather let us hope that this future Wells will depend upon the books of Philip Gibbs and Henri Barbusse, and the poems of Rupert Brooke, Alan Seeger, and John MacRae. And if, after reading these, he is still doubtful of the fact that war is essentially a false, hideous mistake, then let him go to see the production of *The Four Horsemen of the Apocalypse,* and be convinced. It took us a long time to get around to that statement, but the picture is well worth the trip.

Blasco Ibanez wrote the novel, and achieved widespread fame thereby. There are many, including the present reviewer, who believe that this fame was not altogether deserved. In fact, we must confess that we belong to that society (recently organized by F. P. A.) of "Those-who-started-but-did-not-finish *The Four Horsemen of the Apocalypse.*"

The motion picture adaptation, however, succeeded in holding our undivided attention more consistently than any dramatic production since the day when, at the age of seven, we broke down at a performance of *Uncle Tom's Cabin* and were carried out in a sinking condition.

The great strength and vigorous appeal with which *The Four Horsemen of the Apocalypse* has been endowed is largely due to the superb direction of Rex Ingram, who produced it. His was a truly Herculean task, and he has done it so well that his name must now be placed at the top of his profession.

June Mathis did the work of adapting the story, and her scenario is coherent, and strongly constructed on logical lines, with a fine sense for dramatic values. At no time does the action drop or the suspense weaken, except for a few moments near the end when a crowd of frolicsome dough-boys and Salvation Army lassies are dragged in just to give the orchestra a chance to blare out "Over There."

The cast is uniformly good, and selected with such great care that every part—Spanish, Indian, French, and German—is played by a character who is actually true to type. In the leading rôle is a newcomer to the screen, Rudolph Valentino, who has a decided edge—both in ability and appearance—over all the stock movie heroes, from Richard Barthelmess down. He tangoes, makes love, and fights with equal grace. Both he and Alice Terry, who plays opposite him, will be stars in their own right before long.

It is impossible to detail the work of the others in the large cast, but more than passing mention should be made of Joseph Swickard, Pomeroy Cannon, Nigel de Brulier, John Sainpolis, Stuart Holmes, Wallace Beery, and Beatrice Dominguez.

The pictures themselves are at all times striking, and occasionally beautiful—for Ingram has evidently studied closely the art of composition, and almost any one scene, taken at random from the nine reels, would be worthy of praise for its pictorial qualities alone.

The four horsemen—Conquest, War, Pestilence and Death—are convincingly frightful figures, and the fleeting pictures of them galloping through the clouds in a stormy sky are decidedly impressive. Usually, when movie directors attempt to introduce an allegorical note, the result is little more than laughable.

Comparisons are necessarily odious, but we cannot help looking back over the brief history of the cinema and trying to find something that can be compared with *The Four Horsemen of the Apocalypse*. The films which first come to mind are *The Birth of a Nation, Intolerance, Hearts of the World,* and *Joan the Woman;* but the grandiose posturings of David Wark Griffith and Cecil B. DeMille appear pale and artificial in the light of this new production, made by a company which has never been rated very high. Nor does the legitimate stage itself come out entirely unscathed in the test of comparison, for this mere movie easily surpasses the noisy claptrap which passes off as art in the box office of the Belasco Theater.

It is our belief that the film will not be an unqualified success in the United States, where the entire war now resolves itself into terms of Liberty Loan Drives and George Creel. But in France, *The Four Horsemen of the Apocalypse* will be hailed as a great dramatic achievement; one which deserves—more than any other picture play that the war inspired—to be handed down to generations yet unborn, that they may see the horror and the futility of the whole bloody mess. Ingram has recorded the martyrdom of France as no writer could have done.

Praise is difficult to compose, for it is always easier to be harsh than it is to be ecstatic. The reviewer's task would be much simpler if every movie was of the caliber of *Man-Woman-Marriage*, for instance. Nevertheless, we have told our story, and we shall stick to it.

The Four Horsemen of the Apocalypse is a living, breathing answer to those who still refuse to take motion pictures seriously. Its production lifts the silent drama to an artistic plane that it has never touched before.

Life, March 24, 1921

Chaplin had appeared in a six-reel film directed by Mack Sennett, *Tillie's Punctured Romance* (see p. 84). Since leaving Sennett and the Keystone studio in early 1915, he had written and directed and played in thirty-three films, the longest of which was four reels—*Carmen* (1916). Now Chaplin made his first six-reel feature on his own.

THE KID

The most outstanding figure in our moving picture world is an Englishman who seems to have found this country entirely congenial and who has never used his leisure moments to dash off a book to tell the world what he thinks of America. Instead, he has put much sweat and labor into giving us a criticism of life. To do this he has relied upon a trick mustache, a small bamboo cane, a tilted derby, a pair of enormously large, flat shoes, and a pair of the most ominously threatening yet never quite descending pair of trousers in which mortal man has ever dared to walk forth. These have been, so to speak, his artistic resources, and with them he can bring tears or laughter to the largest audience in the world with less apparent effort than any other actor on the screen.

Charles Chaplin's method is what is commonly called "slapstick." The term is used in disparagement. In many quarters Chaplin is considered very lowbrow, very vulgar, very unesthetic. The endless beatings which he gives and takes, his tumbles and recoveries, his waddling walk, are not accepted in the upper circles. That is, they are not officially accepted, for it is very curious how surreptitious many people are about what they really enjoy in a picture. They will often roar their heads off and then turn up their noses. They say it is nothing but "slapstick," and that seems to anger them enormously.

You would think that slapstick had been invented in the movies. It happens, however, that slapstick has been used to entertain mankind ever since monkeys started to throw cocoanuts at each other. The classics are full of it. The *Don Quixote* of Cervantes contains more slapstick than all the movie comedies thus far made. The comedies of Aristophanes are so full of the frankest kind of slapstick that only scholars of the chastest reputation are allowed to read them in the original. Suppose you were to put Falstaff and the Merry Wives of Windsor into a movie. Would you cut out the slapstick? Goethe would laugh at you. Think of the tricks he made Doctor Faust play. Yet these antics are often cause for disproval in the movies.

The plain fact of the matter is that it is quite absurd to criticize an artistic method if the effect is genuine. Laughter is achieved by incongruities and distortions. On the screen this must be done in terms of action. If you can upset the bumptious hero by making him slip on a banana peel or ruffle a false sublimity by tickling it with a feather, you are producing valid satire. Pity often lurks in the ludicrous just as much as in the pathetic. Watch Chaplin closely and you will find that, when he wishes, he can be a master of irony.

Something of this revolt against the dishonor of slapstick must have been in his mind when he made *The Kid*. He is telling the story of a foundling who is taken in by an itinerant mender of window panes and is reared to young boyhood. He does not alter his method, though he refines it. There is still lots of rough-and-tumble. But there is also more feeling, and more understanding of childhood, than in a hundred *Little Lord Fauntleroys*. Slapstick triumphs over sentimentality.

The mother deposits the child in an empty limousine with the hope that the rich owner will adopt it. But the car is stolen and the thieves throw the child on a heap of refuse where Charlie finds it.

Charlie becomes a parent. He becomes both parents. He sits upon the edge of the bed and cuts diapers out of an old bedsheet and folds them with the gravity of the All Mother. Meanwhile baby hangs suspended from the ceiling by four strings and a bag and drinks his milk contentedly from the spout of an inverted coffee pot which swings in the air nearby.

The child has grown into a boy of five. Very few children grow into such irrestistible boys or such marvelous actors as little Jack Coogan, who in the picture is known as John. John goes into partnership with his father. He precedes him down the street and breaks the windows which his father afterwards mends. Except for occasional encounters with the minions of the law, the partnership works famously.

Meanwhile the plot begins to thicken. John's mother has become a rich stage celebrity and indulges her maternal instinct in an unpretentious way by playing Lady Bountiful to the children of the slums. John and she have already met and have just naturally taken a shine to each other. But with the sudden illness of John, the villain enters. Charlie confesses to the doctor that he is John's father only by force of circumstances, with the result that the orphan asylum authorities are called. With them Charlie has a battle royal, is defeated but recovers John at the very gates of the asylum.

But meanwhile John's mother has found out that he is her son. He is again snatched away from Charlie, who wanders about in search of him until he falls asleep from exhaustion. He dreams that he is in Heaven, where he finds John and all the rest of the inhabitants of the neighborhood. On awakening he is led to the house where John and his mother have been happily united.

Such a picture cannot be retold in words. It is a miniature epic of childhood in the comic manner in terms of the screen. There is infinite humor and swift pathos and subtle satire. Consider the beginning of the child's career. His mother deposits him in a limousine but he immediately lands in an ash can; very undignified, very incongruous, but is it not just like the chance we take of being born with that silver spoon in our mouth? Luckily we do not know enough to care at the time and, if we did, is it so sure that we would all choose the silver spoon? John certainly had more fun with Charlie Chaplin as his father than he could possible have had with any duke.

Or take the Chaplin vision of Heaven. (To be sure the sub-title labels it "Fairyland"!) A slum street suddenly festooned and garlanded and all the people wearing white wings tacked on to their otherwise unchanged clothing. They have not changed at all in any other respect, except that they can fly about ludicrously on invisible wires: a cross between a cabaret and a children's ball. The people fight and envy just as before, and a policeman with wings has to enforce brotherly love with his pistol! What an ingenious travesty on our easy beatitudes!

The episode of the fight with the orphan asylum officials, exaggerated as it is, presents an excellent burlesque on institutionalism and illustrates the difference between individual and machine care for children.

Chaplin's main concern in *The Kid* is to give us a picture of childhood and fatherhood and to show us how boy and man get along in this world of ours. That kid and his father love each other, and it is the charm of their relation against egotism and unconcern of the rest of the world which makes the picture so fascinating. That is, after all, a simple matter for everybody to understand, and it is simply and beautifully handled. There is no doting, no slobbering over the child, no attempt to achieve cuteness for its own sake. It would have been a sweet and sentimental ending, for instance, to have the mother marry the fosterfather after she had providentially discovered that his oddly surreptitious window mending had disguised a stained-window artist. We do not know what he did. Perhaps he just went back to his job. Or perhaps the kid's mother fitted him out with a regular window pane shop. But whatever he did we may be sure that John visited him frequently and that they had happy reunions.

An astonishing picture, true to the common stuff of human attributes. A picture that a makes a very deep scratch in the possibilities of the screen. Millions will enjoy it, and many of those who have stood aloof will have to admit, if only to themselves, the supreme genius of the new Ariel who walks among mortals in the most incongruous shoes that an immortal ever wore.

Exceptional Photoplays, January/February 1921

THE KID

FRANCIS HACKETT

The best motion pictures, I hear, are written with the scissors. The scissors, at any rate, have a great deal to do with the triumph of Charles Chaplin in (and with) *The Kid*. It is a movie stripped to its emotional essentials. The result is form, in which practically all American movies are just as much lacking as are our industrial architecture, display advertising, public cooking, and private conversation. In certain American institutions one does find form. Women's public meetings usually have it. The better sort of women's hats have it. So do certain kinds of house interiors and New England domestic architecture and those expositions of chamber music, baseball, and tennis which have never failed of appreciation here. But the movies are usually like the Sunday newspapers, Golden Oak furniture, Yonkers carpets, the snubnosed and stub-toed Ford car. The moviemakers have simply wallowed in the license extended by American incompetence and indulgence, knowing that a people which puts its hotels in the noise-area and its hotel kitchens in the dust-area will be content to have its movies as loud and as insanitary as its life. It has remained for Charlie Chaplin to scout this indulgence, to adopt a standard absolutely and relatively high, and to be rewarded by the gratitude of millions. For millions of harassed and dissatisfied movie-patrons are finding joy in the integrity of *The Kid*.

This integrity is to be enjoyed least of all in the anecdote itself. It is a silly enough story of a woman who is reunited with the child she deserted after a separation of some time and considerable space. A woman might conceivably abandon her baby in this fashion. There must be a score of abandoned babies for every few hundred abandoned women. But to fail to trace the baby at the time and yet to run into the growing child some years later—years gilded with success and yet yearning with heartache—is almost Shakespearean in its absurdity. Still, an excellent bean may be grown on the humblest of beanpoles, and that is the case with *The Kid*. Chaplin knows that the story of his adopted waif is a joke between the experienced movie-patron and himself. The merchantable maternal instinct and the sure-fire lost che-ild and the beautiful Lady Bountiful and the glad reunion—he glides over them with a touch like a light-beam. What he has to play with is his own gorgeous predicament as the victim of a maternal problem. He has himself to present in the role of a Madonna. It is this preposterousness, with its possibilities of bathos and vulgarity, which he brings successfully through.

He does it as only a superb interpreter could. He realizes that when he, the authentic splay-footed cane-twirling comedian, inherits the baby, he must steer his course clean away from farce in the direction of sentiment, but must keep enough comedy to correct the least hint of sentimentality. It gives him just the chance that his fine creativeness demands. With a boldness that no other comedian could attempt, he exhibits himself feeding and providing for the baby. This boldness, which he pushes far enough to earn laughter and not so far as to exploit it, he immediately banks up against his first exhibition of real feeling. And his exhibition of feeling is preserved from excess or unreality by a resourcefulness in by-play which is beautifully right. He makes a contrast between The Kid's deportment, so sternly inculcated, and his own dilapidation, which never fails to give amusement; and he carries that dilapidation to extraordinary lengths. But just as he seems to have violated taste by projecting the dirty sole of his bare foot out of bed, his head is slipped through a hole in his bedspread—converting it into so comical a dressing-gown that the very invasion of good taste is turned to grotesque account. This is only one of twenty tricks that he wins in his sly game with (or against) his audience. He plays on his audience with an audacity that conquers prig and groundling in the same instant, and gives both of them a chance to be amused and moved.

Chaplin's relations to his audience may once have been deferential. Now he is an artist who uses his medium as he wills. When he opens the sewer-trap and debates whether to slip the baby into it, he gains the credence which is only won by complete expressiveness. And his audience accepts his sincerity in this role of foster father with precisely the shade of amusement that he artfully conveys. To dominate photography with a personality is in itself marvelous. It is all the more marvelous when one remembers that Chaplin is not a projection of the average but a variation, a sport. This violates in every detail the Philistinism which seems to be the motion picture religion.

Without the Coogan boy it couldn't be done. It is dreadful to think of such a perfection as this child pushing out of his treble exquisiteness into something perhaps theatrical and overstimulated and unstable. But in his present manifestation, under the hand of Chaplin, he is as expressively and imaginatively natural as if he himself had Chaplin's genius. His eyes speak, and they say not only direct and eloquent things but things indirect, troubled, complicated. And not only do his eyes speak, but so do the turn of his head, his entrances and exits, his place on a lonely doorstep or on a curb. No child that I have ever seen on the stage created so full a part before. Most of the children one sees are limited to one or two postures. They appear but do not represent. This "Kid" represents, and with a lovely mobile countenance, a countenance that is at once quite childlike and deep as an Italian masterpiece.

The dream of Heaven I thought highly amusing. What amused me was its limitedness, its meagerness. It was like a simple man's version of the Big Change, made up from the few properties with which a simple man would be likely to be acquainted. The lack of inventiveness seemed to me to be its best point. Others tell me that it was a failure of inventiveness. Mayhap. But after suffering the success of movie-inventiveness so many times, with the whole apparatus of the factory employed to turn out some sort of slick statement or other, I rejoice over this bit of thin and faltering fantasy. And I venture to believe that it represents exactly what Chaplin intended. It was the simplified Heaven of the antic sprite whom Chaplin has created and whose inner whimsicality is here so amusingly indulged.

Chaplin's lightness of touch is shown not merely in the pictures, with the sporting elimination of unnecessary detail and the occasional note of mocking sophistication. It is shown technically in the admirable insistence that the pantomime must tell the story without any particular help from the desiccated medium of words. To read titles is to impede the flow of feeling rather then to aid it. It is to distract the pictorial mind. By cutting out as many titles as possible Charles Chaplin and his company keep close to the visual, and the visual in their case is frequently the beautiful, because of the effort that has been made to represent by hieroglyphic, to eliminate and simplify. Nothing could be better than the way *The Kid* is launched: the mother's plain clothing, her Salvation Army bonnet, her listless walk, and her short brooding in that open-air cathedral of broken humanity, the city park. The quickening of pace when she sees the wealthy motor, just before it is stolen (with her baby in it), tells everything that a world of newspaper-readers needs to know. And the discovery of the baby, its awkward removal, its abandonment in the meanest of lanes until it falls into the surprised hands of the little hobo—this is also sufficiently pointed by the expert action of the company Chaplin has wisely chosen. His wisdom, his sincerity, his integrity, all exhibited in this film, should go some way to revolutionize motion picture production in this country. From an industry *The Kid* raises production to an art. An art it should be, in spite of the long-suffering public.

The New Republic, March 30, 1921

Hardly had the war with Germany ended than the German films began to come over, and to be welcomed. *Passion,* originally entitled *Madame Dubarry,* was directed by Ernst Lubitsch and starred Pola Negri. *The Cabinet of Dr. Caligari* had been made in the same year as *Passion,* 1919, but reached the United States some six months later, imported by Samuel Goldwyn.

THE CABINET OF DR. CALIGARI

ROBERT E. SHERWOOD

We are told that, what with Bolshevism and Anarchy and all that sort of thing, it is usually safest and wisest to err on the side of conservatism. Anything suggesting revolution and change should be viewed with the conventional alarm.

In spite of which, we could not help viewing *The Cabinet of Dr. Caligari* —which represents artistic radicalism in its most rabid form—with intense satisfaction. For, after sitting through miles and miles of films of the old school, we were ready to extend a hearty welcome to anything which attempted to be different.

The Cabinet of Dr. Caligari comes from Germany, being the first big production to follow in the wake of the enormously successful *Passion.* The story concerns the fiendish activities of one Dr. Sonnow, the head of a lunatic asylum, who masters the secrets of somnambulism. Under the name of Dr. Caligari, he operates a side show at a county fair, using his trained somnambulist, Cesare, as Exhibit A. At night, when the fair has closed up, Cesare is sent forth by the overwhelming will of his master to murder certain persons who have been a source of annoyance to Dr. Caligari during the course of the day.

That is a bare and inadequate outline of the idea, but we cannot enlarge upon it without giving away the ingenious trick which provides the whole motif of the story. It is a distinctly Poe-esque conception, and it is treated in a remarkable manner. The scenes are all represented by means of futurist art—it is not Cubism or Vorticism, but rather Post-Impressionism—so that the picture has the quality of a weird, horrible nightmare. Streets, buildings and trees are crazily crooked and grotesque—and yet terribly real.

Werner Krauss, as Dr. Caligari, proves to be an extraordinarily skillful pantomimist, and Conrad Veidt is imposing and terrifying as Cesare. These two characters, in their actions and their make-up, fit in perfectly with the backgrounds; but most of the other players are discordantly normal in appearance, and do much to spoil the illusion. The picture suffers greatly by inexpert editing and cutting, presumably the fault of those who adapted it for American audiences.

We can think of no native producer (with the possible exception of Maurice Tourneur) who could do anything like this; nor should we care to see them make the attempt. But there are a few stories which deserve treatment in this strange medium ("The Fall of the House of Usher," for example), and if we must go to Germany to get them, by all means let us continue to do so.

Life, April 28, 1921

THE CABINET OF DR. CALIGARI

The Cabinet of Dr. Caligari is a revelation and a challenge. It is a revelation of what the motion picture is capable of as a form of artistic expression. It challenges the public to appreciate it and challenges the producer to learn from it. The revelation is there for all to see. If the appreciation fails, the motion picture itself, and all that it has promised, is in danger of failing.

In *The Cabinet of Dr. Caligari* the motion picture for the first time stands forth in its integrity as a work of art. It is one of the paradoxes of art that it is at the same time an abstraction and something tangible in terms of our bodily senses. It is form and idea.

The story of Doctor Caligari is a fantasy of terror told with the virtuosity of a Poe, in terms of the screen. Its emotions appeal directly to a universal audience. Even if stripped to its barest outline it would still compel our attention, for it deals with the fascinating problem of one person's supernatural control over another person. But it acquires the irresistible quality of all true art because it is told with such complete mastery of medium that its terror becomes an esthetic delight. We find that we have shared the experiences of a madman without suspecting that he is mad; we have been transported into that sphere where man creates his own imaginative realities of life which constantly overwhelm without ever completely satisfying him.

Specifically, there is an evidence in this picture, for the first time in America, at least, of something of the point of view of the "Dadaist" to whom everything in the world is equally important—a sort of reflection in the world of plastic representation of the conceptions of relativity which are agitating mathematicians and astronomers. Thus, the picture stands in the current of living thought. It becomes a motion picture with an underlying significance that is worthy of serious discussion. The picture itself questions, makes sanity relative as insanity is relative—and constitutes a valuable offset to the American tendency to oversureness of intellectual values. Moreover, it is related through its use of form and decoration to the modern art movements of the Continent.

The plot is a simple one. It concerns itself with the strange happenings in a fantastic town of problematic reality, where a Fair is being held. To this Fair comes a Dr. Caligari with his cabinet in which he keeps a wonderful sleeping puppet named Cesare, whom Caligari alone can awaken to somnambulistic speech and action. Soon after Dr. Caligari sets up his attraction at the Fair and Cesare has been made to perform, strange murders begin to occur in the town. Suspicion points to Caligari. And now is perpetrated the crowning outrage—the abduction of a beautiful girl on the very night her lover, who has already numbered a student friend among those murdered, is keeping watch over Dr. Caligari. The authorities are called and arrive at the Fair only to find Caligari sitting beside the cabinet in which is seen the form of the sleeping Cesare. But investigating further they find that the real Cesare, who, acting somnambulistically at the hypnotic direction of his master, has been the direct cause of the crimes, has been replaced by a dummy. Dr. Caligari, seeing that his ruse has been discovered, makes good his escape and is pursued up a bleak and tortuous hill and over an eery bridge, beyond which he enters through the gates of an insane asylum. Within this asylum a denouement takes place as uncanny as any that ever unravelled a tale of nightmare mystery.

The impact of this picture upon the spectator is overpowering. The expressionistic treatment of the background loses its bizarre quality almost at once; it is justified by its appropriateness. The story unfolds swiftly, with an astonishing economy of description. It does not wait for you; it compels you to follow. It baffles you without leaving you at a loss; you try in vain to outguess it. The titles do not usurp the cinematographic function; when they occur they appear merely as footnotes. The actors appear anonymously; their excellence is sufficient introduction. Everything is sacrificed to the potency of imaged action.

The picture is not a story told; it is a story moved. Everything is moving and fluid. The background enters into the action. Its bizarre, cubistic design suggests grotesqueness and distortion. These reflect both the character of the story and the mental state of the people in it. The leaning, top-heavy houses and the crooked, winding, cul-de-sac streets seem to crush and overwhelm; they suggest lurking danger and reflect the growing dread of the characters. The effect is sustained throughout. The design on the floor of the insane asylum suggests mental confusion. The girl's bedroom, with its fleecy draperies and lofty Gothic lines, suggests the very spirit of sleep.

The whole picture is expressive of the eloquence of pure action. The murders are swift, relentless stabs of motion. When the somnambulist breaks into the girl's room he does not merely break the window. He utterly destroys it with a single movement of his hand. He becomes the spirit of destruction. When he carries the girl out of the room he takes the whole room with him. He gathers up an interior and turns it inside out. He projects us out of the room with him. When he staggers under the burden of the girl, his weariness comes over us like sudden torture. The picture is a continual rush of movement. We feel emotion rising from motion as an immediate experience. That is the quintessence of cinematographic art.

The Cabinet of Dr. Caligari owes its pre-eminence to the perfect fusion of its elements. It has a plot which would remain effective under almost any treatment because it is one which stands on its own merit as a folk narrative, besides possessing essentially cinematographic qualities. It is told to us on the screen against a novel background which is a contribution to the art of the moving picture in itself. The photography is a masterly piece of experimentation, and the direction is of a quality whose virtuosity shines through its apparent unobtrusiveness. All this is crowned by superb acting. We know of nothing in this country that can approach either the impersonation of Dr. Caligari, which is a triumph of the art of pantomime, or that of Cesare, the somnambulist. The latter is a puppet for the imagination of an artist to play with. A figure that alternatively rouses our pity and inspires us with dread. The actor who plays it seems superhumanly tall, with thin, shrunken legs that suggest the emaciation of the somnambulist's life-in-death, and eyes grotesquely enlarged whose "leaden lids" take an eternity to open. His movements in the scene where he approaches the house of the girl are a lesson in the art of stalking. He literally winds his way through the tortuous passages and appears at the window with a sharp and sudden surprise of a genie rising mysteriously out of the earth.

The girl Jane is acted with admirable restraint. She is pictorially beautiful. She suggests the woman with a few short strokes of action, and carries the complete story of her love in a few flashes of her face. The scene where she learns of the death of her lover is one of the finest bits in the picture. The sharp movement of shrinking from the teller is full of sudden horror and alarm. The eloquence of grief flashes over her face like a swift transformation. The thing is done without titles in less than a dozen feet of film, showing again that where a part is conceived in terms of motion, captions become artistic impertinences.

In *The Cabinet of Dr. Caligari* the motion picture has proved its kinship with the other arts. Its popularity ought to be assured. It comes to us at a critical period of our motion picture industry when the public is jaded by many inferior domestic pictures and our producers themselves are still at a loss as to how to get out of their rut. It should give the public a new standard and imbue the producers with the courage to live up to it. Its release has all the aura of a great advent. Is it too much to assume that the American public can appreciate the best when it is given a chance to see it?

Exceptional Photoplays, March 1921

Besides his newspaper criticism, P. F. Reniers also wrote on film for numerous magazines and was coauthor of a book on West Virginia.

THE THREE MUSKETEERS

P. F. RENIERS

With Douglas Fairbanks as d'Artagnan, Alexandre Dumas's immortal historical romance has come to the American screen after much blowing of trumpets. They have, as they say, "interpreted" it, of course, but there is no gainsaying the fact that they have made of it a stirring, compact, dramatic, and beautiful piece of work.

Some important points of the book have been winked at, others have been elided, which was to be expected. M. Bonancieux is no longer the husband of Constance, seamstress to the Queen, but, quite properly, her uncle, and the romance of Constance and d'Artagnan is further "purified" by ignoring the fact that she was his mistress. And, for purposes of a cinema ending (which Dumas could not possibly have foreseen and prepared), she does not die in his arms, poisoned by the rapacious Lady de Winter, but is united to him by Richelieu, turned *deus ex machina* for the purpose. Of the siege of La Rochelle, of Mme. de Chevreuse, of the murder of Buckingham there is nothing, and it is in these cases quite as well. There are limitations to length and complication, and the demands for pruning have been seen to nobly. This interpretation by Edward Knoblock and Mr. Fairbanks is one of which they may well be proud, for the adventuresome spirit of the tale and the color and movement of the time have achieved a splendid pictorial setting at their hands.

Those who find that Mr. Fairbanks's Paris of 1626 looks too new and tidy, somewhat as though it were "made in America," will have some cause for their point of view. Care has been taken to vary the stonework in the multiplicity of sets; architecture has been faithfully copied, and an attempt at antiquing is noticeable, but still the perfect illusion has escaped their efforts. But for one who might note these things (a carping one, perhaps) a hundred will be carried away by the rush of action, the amazing dexterity of Mr. Fairbanks, the ever-engrossing story of intrigue that coils itself about the tiring rooms of Anne of Austria, and that streches its serpentine length from Paris to the London of Charles I.

Fred Niblo directed, and in more than one way he has accomplished a film that can stand by itself imaginatively and pictorially. By the movement of the scheming Richelieu's hand he characterizes him, by the substitution of action for words he gives incidents and events a graphic significance, and in more than several instances gets scenic effects that both startle and satisfy. Still, and with all due credit to Mr. Niblo, it is Mr. Fairbanks's invention and tireless energy both as director and chief actor that hold the stage. As in *The Mark of Zorro,* his duelling scenes are spectacular feats, and one loses the consciousness that they are safely prearranged in the hero's interests by reason of their agility and humor, and because of the anxiety this precious make-believe engenders for a hero so adept at winning his way to the affections. But Mr. Fairbanks flashes through brawls and dangers and court assemblies with the dashing assurance of a good American salesman, and one does not care whether his line is hair tonic or acrobatic romance. One buys, and willingly.

The costumes are excellent and the people that move in them, albeit most of them betray a modernity of feature (and something of the Latin expressiveness), are good. In the cases of Nigel de Brulier, Willis Robards, Lon Poff, Adolphe Menjou, Boyd Irwin, Eugene Pallette, and Thomas Holding, they are excellent. Of the women, Marguerite De La Motte as

Constance Bonancieux, and Barbara La Marr as Lady de Winter, are the best, through they are not altogether satisfactory. Mary MacLaren emphasizes the pathetic and negative qualities of the Queen.

Joseph Plunkett of the Strand Theater has given the film a beautiful and simple presentation, and Edward Knoblock has furnished a prologue in verse.

The New York Evening Post, August 29, 1921

The American actor E. H. Sothern was best known for his partnership in Shakespearean repertory with his wife, Julia Marlowe. The English actor Lewis Waller, apart from his talents, was a notable matinée idol.

THE THREE MUSKETEERS

ROBERT E. SHERWOOD

When Alexandre Dumas sat down at his desk, smoothed his hair back, chewed the end of his quill pen, and said to himself, "Well, I guess I might as well write a book called *The Three Musketeers,"* he doubtless had but one object in view: to provide a suitable story for Douglas Fairbanks to act in the movies.

Dumas did his work well, and he deserves all the credit that he will get from the millions of people who are destined to see *The Three Musketeers* on innumerable screens throughout the world.

It is so thoroughly satisfying a performance on the part of all concerned that your correspondent, whose laudatory equipment has become rusted through long disuse, finds it difficult to say anything that is anywhere near adequate. Mr. Fairbanks as D'Artagnan can best be described in the dashing Gascon's own word, "marvelous." Never has a famous character from a famous novel found finer treatment in motion pictures. D'Artagnan lives in Fairbanks. Fairbanks lives in D'Artagnan. Not only is the physical grace and superb poise there—but also the intense inner fire, the animation of spirit that was so vital a part of Dumas's magnificent hero.

Mr. Fairbanks performs a great number of his athletic stunts, with some excellent swordplay thrown in for the occasion; but, more than that, he acts D'Artagnan with a degree of skill that can be compared favorably with the performances that Sothern and Lewis Waller gave of this role in the stage version of *The Three Musketeers.* Without recourse to many close-ups, he manages to develop a considerable variety of expression, ranging from the familiar Fairbanks smile to a slightly impudent grimace that is remarkably reminiscent of Charlie Chaplin.

As for the rest of the production, *The Three Musketeers* is well worthy of its story and its star. Nigel de Brulier lends a quiet forcefulness to the role of Richelieu, and Marguerite De La Motte is a pretty and spirited heroine. The costumes and settings are excellent, and the scenes well staged.

In apportioning the praise for the success of *The Three Musketeers,* one is inclined to overlook the fact that a considerable share of the credit belongs to Edward Knoblock, who adapted the story, and who has made an intelligent if free translation of Dumas.

All things considered, *The Three Musketeers* is the superior of any of the German pictures that have been brought to this country. It takes rank with *The Four Horsemen of the Apocalypse* and *The Kid* as one of the great achievements of the movies.

Life, September 22, 1921

Erich von Stroheim started in films in 1914 as an extra, worked as extra and actor and assistant with Griffith, and began directing in 1918. Of *Foolish Wives* Jean Renoir has said that, early in his career, he saw it twelve times. "It changed things. . . . After *Foolish Wives* I began to look." [17]

The figure of 320 reels is an obvious error. The highest estimate of the original is thirty-two reels, cut to fourteen reels for release. The version now generally available runs eighty-five minutes.

The wealthy American called Andrew J. Hughes in this review is actually called Howard Hughes in the film (!). He was played by two actors because, when the picture was nearly finished, the original actor, George Christians, died of a heart attack. Robert Edeson was engaged to finish the role and was photographed from the back.

FOOLISH WIVES

Erich von Stroheim's *Foolish Wives,* which has been on the way for more than a year and is said to be one of the most costly motion pictures ever made, finally arrived at the Central Theater last night. More than is the

case with most other photoplays attributed to an individual, this production is the work of Mr. von Stroheim, for he not only wrote and directed
it, but is by far the most conspicuous figure in its cast. So to him, therefore, must go the bulk of whatever approval and disapproval the picture
wins. And, from different people, with varying ideas—and powers of
endurance—he is likely to receive much of both.

Foolish Wives, first of all, but not most importantly, is an expensive
picture. It is said to have cost exactly $1,103,736.38, and although a good
deal of this cost was probably due to delays and other misfortunes that
beset the production of the film, no inconsiderable sum was actually spent
in the things that show on the screen, especially the settings. The action
takes place in Monte Carlo, and Mr. von Stroheim seems to have reproduced the chief city of Monaco on the coast of California. The settings
cannot be even mentioned in detail. But they are as rich and splendid as
one who thinks of Monte Carlo can imagine, though in some instances, it
must be confessed, photographic effects that might have been obtained
with them have been missed, principally because of faulty lighting. This
is not generally true. Many of the photographs are strikingly effective. It
is only that some are not.

However, splendid settings never made a dramatic photoplay, and *Foolish
Wives* could have been made with much less architecture without losing
its essential dramatic quality. It does possess this quality, in many separate
scenes and in frequent sequences of scenes, because, most importantly, it
is largely composed of dynamic, expressive motion pictures. He has a keen
sense of the dramatic and a pictorial point of view, and the result is that
Foolish Wives teems with scenes that mean something, that throw light
on character and action, that strike the spectator fairly between the eyes
and make him sit up and read pictures. This is the chief value of the film.

The picture is thus vitalized through Mr. von Stroheim's own cinematographic skill, and through the acting of himself and the others in the
cast. His role is that of a human beast of prey, an unbelievably contemptible
animal whose vocation and avocation is preying on women—without
scruple and indiscriminately. He takes their money and their honor, whether
they are serving maids, half-witted girls, or the wives of men in high station. And Mr. von Stroheim makes this character most repellently realistic.
All of the polish of such a villain, all of the cruelty, all of the cowardice,
are portrayed in his finished, fiendish acting.

Posing as a Russian count, he works with two accomplices, a pair of
women who pose as countesses, his cousins, played by Maude George and
Mae Busch in his own style of sharp emphasis, only now and then becoming too exaggerated. Miss Dupont has the role of the principal "foolish
wife" and, without giving it any particular individuality, makes it suf-

ficiently clear to serve the purposes of the story. Her husband, who is a special envoy of the United States to the Principality of Monaco, is programmed as Rudolph Christians, although it is reported that, when Mr. Christians died during the production of the picture, Robert Edeson was drafted for the part. If both do appear in different scenes of the photoplay as presented, any attempt to identify them separately would become a guessing contest.

The character, Andrew J. Hughes, is consistently presented, and is, as presented by Mr. Christians or Mr. Edeson or both, an adequately forceful figure. Dale Fuller, as a maid and one of the victims of the bogus count, does telling work, as does also Cesare Gravina as the father of a half-witted girl whom the beast destroys. It is through this father's vengeance that the monster finally meets a horrible end. The wife of the American envoy narrowly escapes him.

From all of which you may gather the main idea of the story. It is not pleasant. In many places it is decidedly repulsive. It is what is generally called "continental," and as such is exceedingly well done.

But whether you like that kind of a story is a question and whether you like it for fourteen reels of film, or three hours and a half on a stretch, with only five minutes' intermission, is another question. Surely, no matter how well done the picture is, and no matter how absorbing the story may be, the film is too long. It achieves its effects by its illuminating details, but it is too detailed to hold the attention for so long. You don't read a book written on such a subject as *Foolish Wives,* in its style, for three hours and a half at a sitting. You couldn't. And it is wearying to sit through the film. Yet it was cut from 320 reels!

As the picture approaches its end it stirs the interest with an exciting fire scene, which comes as if to show that Mr. von Stroheim can be spectacular, too. It is as good as anything of its kind yet seen on the screen, except that the flames sometimes appear white and sometimes red, with disconcerting effect.

The New York Times, January 12, 1922

Dream Street had been drawn, like *Broken Blossoms,* from the London Limehouse stories of Thomas Burke. Griffith experimented with the addition of sound to parts of it during its New York run.[18] *All for a Woman* was the American title of *Danton* with Emil Jannings. *Passion,* as noted earlier, was a Lubitsch film about Madame Dubarry.

ORPHANS OF THE STORM

ROBERT E. SHERWOOD

After his disastrous jaunt down *Dream Street,* David W. Griffith returns to his own in *Orphans of the Storm.* In many ways, it is the best thing that he has ever done, and that, it need hardly be explained, is saying a great deal.

There is a definite Griffith tradition in the movies, and *Orphans of the Storm* lives up to this tradition in every respect. It contains the usual elements of pure, unsullied love as contrasted with base, degenerate passion, the usual suspense that is promoted by obvious but none the less efficacious tricks, the usual amount of strife, the usual railing against intolerance and oppression, the usual beauty, the usual note of sordid tragedy, and, above all, the usual Ku Klux Klan climax. All these elements are to be found in every Griffith picture, from *The Birth of a Nation* to *Way Down East.*

Pictorially and dramatically, *Orphans of the Storm* is better than any of them. There is scarcely a scene or an effect in the entire production that is not beautiful to look upon, and there is scarcely a moment that is not charged with intense dramatic power.

A large part of this is due to the acting. The ever-reliable Misses Gish are the storm-tossed heroines of the piece and they are both superb, as is Joseph Schildkraut as the Chevalier de Vaudrey. Monte Blue, Sidney Herbert and Frank Puglia also contribute skilful characterizations.

Because the scenes of *Orphans of the Storm* are laid in the period of the French Revolution, definite comparison may be made between the methods of Griffith and those of the Germans who produced *Passion* and *All for a Woman.* Save for the details of the mob scenes, Griffith shows a marked margin of superiority. His photography is immeasurably better, and his players, while they lack the unquenchable fire of such as Pola Negri, are more evenly capable than the German casts. Monte Blue, in the role of Danton has it over Emil Jannings, as Mr. Khayyam said, like a tent.

Life, February 2, 1922

Buster Keaton began his screen career in 1917 and, after an eleventh-month interruption for military service in the First War, kept going and growing. *The Paleface* was a two-reel picture; he had not yet made features.

Keaton is considered today to be an artist of Chaplin's stature, yet, as we have seen, Chaplin was taken quite seriously from the start, and Keaton was not. Keaton was successful and got warmly reviewed, but nothing was written about him during his early career that compared with the analyses, encomiums, even poetry that were heaped on Chaplin. Gilbert Seldes, writing two years after this in *The Seven Lively Arts,* still was not "sure" about Keaton.[19]

There are at least two possible speculations on this difference. First, in Chaplin's private life, he was much interested in intellectual matters and associated with intellectuals; Keaton was not and did not. So Chaplin became a pet of writers of all kinds. Second, the Tramp, Chaplin's character, was an outsider usually destined to stay outside, unsuccessful in jobs, usually in trouble with the police, vaguely anarchic. Keaton's character was usually a conformist whose troubles arose from trying to stay inside or else an outsider who quite genuinely wanted to get in. The Chaplin character was possibly more appealing, even flattering, to the intellectual's self-view.

Chaplin's praise was certainly merited, and few would wish it had been less or had come later; but we can also wish that Keaton's had been more and sooner. Sherwood was one of the early few who, most of the time, saw Keaton's quality.

THE PALEFACE

ROBERT E. SHERWOOD

It is strange that the silent drama should have reached its highest level in the comic field. Here, and here alone, it is pre-eminent. Nothing that is being produced in literature or in the drama is as funny as a good Chaplin, Lloyd, or Keaton comedy. The efforts of these three young men approximate art more closely than anything else that the movies have offered.

They are slapstick, they are crude, they are indelicate, to be sure; but so was Aristophanes, so was Rabelais, so was Shakespeare. How many humorists who have outlived their own generations have been otherwise?

In *The Paleface,* Buster Keaton is captured by a tribe of Indians who have a grudge against the white men because some oil promoters have attempted to steal their lands. Buster is sentenced to death, but the fact that he wears an asbestos union suit saves him from considerable embarrassment when the Indians try to burn him at the stake. He is then made chief of the tribe, and he proceeds to outwit the oil sharks and save the reservation.

The Paleface is a veritable epic.

Life, June 1, 1922

Robert Flaherty was an Arctic explorer for mineral deposits who lived with Eskimos and shot some amateur, badly made film about them. Several years later he went back, financed by the fur merchants Revillon Frères, and made this first full-length documentary, or film of fact, which has had a huge influence on the field since then.[20]

Frances Taylor Patterson was an instructor in scenario writing at Columbia University.[21]

Sir Arne's Treasure was directed by Mauritz Stiller. For further comment on Stiller, see p. 171.

NANOOK OF THE NORTH

FRANCES TAYLOR PATTERSON

In a day of emotional and artistic deliquescence on the screen, a picture with the fresh strength and pictorial promise of *Nanook of the North* is in the nature of Revelation. It may be said to be the first photoplay of the natural school of cinematography. Here are natural scenery, natural actors, the unembellished *conte* of a portion of life in Ungava. The "stars" are the native Eskimos. The "extras" are the polar bear, the seals, and the walrus that wander about the ice country. The "sets" are the frozen fastnesses of the North. For drama there is the struggle of Nanook, the hunter, to wrest sustenance from barren wastes of snow. For the note of heroism there is the seemingly hopeless battle he wages against the elements. There is no conventional plot fabric. There are no fictionized situations. Yet the picture is dramatic in the highest sense of the word. There is suspense in the huntsman's combat with his quarry. The outcome is as sustained as it is doubtful. There is vicarious satisfaction for the spectator in his final triumph. The film is a story of a people transcribed through the experiences of the hunter Nanook. The photoplay may be said to have its analogue in contemporary literature in *Maria Chapdelaine*. As Louis Hémon has set down in memorable words the simple tradition of Lake Saint John and Peribonka, so Robert Flaherty has set down in memorable pictures the primitive gropings of these Eskimos of the far North toward the light of science and civilization.

But all this, it may be argued, is not entirely new in the history of the screen. There have already been filmed exquisite scenics. The camera has long ago imprisoned bits of beauty in distant corners of the earth. It has brought home to us glimpses of strange peoples and strange customs. There have been Martin Johnson's *Cannibals of the South Sea Islands*, Vandenburgh's *Pigmies of Central Africa*, Burton Holmes's Travelogues, Bruce's *Wilderness Tales*. But *Nanook of the North* is different from all these. It has, as I have said, a strikingly dramatic quality. And in addition it has a continuity which these forerunners lack. There is unity—there is singleness of impression in *Nanook*. The film marks a transition from the so-called educational film and the formal photoplay. It bridges a lacuna which has long cried aloud to be bridged. The narrative unwinds absorbingly. It flows smoothly and naturally to completion.

Anthropologically the Eskimos are a remarkable people. Their minds are singularly keen and alert. Certainly it is amazing to see the vast amount of scientific information these unlettered huntsmen have acquired through empirical methods. The building of the igloo—a feat which can be accomplished in the short space of an hour—is at a glance akin to wizardry, but in reality shows a mastery of the laws of equilibrium and gravitation. A knowledge of light, of reflection and refraction, is exhibited by Nanook's method of fitting a window into the igloo. Naturally enough the light of Heaven cannot penetrate the opaque snow blocks which form the walls of the hut. So, from a neighboring stream, Nanook cuts a clear square of ice. This he fits into the top of the igloo. Still the light through the "glass" is dim. Nanook intensifies it, however, by placing a great block of white snow vertically above the window, thus reflecting light into the inner recesses. The constant problem of these people is to outwit nature. They must use the cunning of their eyes and their hands to convert animal life into the coin of the realm—food and fuel. The process makes them uncannily inventive. Out of apparent nothingness they create the necessities of life and a few luxuries. Light and heat they gain from soaking moss—the only vegetation which survives the bitter cold of that country—in walrus oil. This they burn on the outer rim of a stone vessel hollowed shallowly. The moss is the wick, of course, and forms a ring of flame on the edge of the vessel instead of burning in the center as our wicks do. Knives, harpoons, sea gaffs they make from the ivories of the walrus tusks. Metal is unknown to them. Boats are fashioned from skins and ribbed with odd bits of driftwood. Nanook's wife has a complete sewing kit, needles of sharp ivory, thread from the sinews of animals. With these she makes trousers of bearskin and coats of reindeer fur.

But although the picture is full of information which steals into the mental content of the spectator ere he is aware, the greatest appeal of *Nanook of the North* is its pictorial beauty. Harbors locked fast to the sea. Icefloes moving with solemn force. Imperishable snow "five thousand summers old." Low banks of clouds with "the copper ball of the sun a mockery in the sky." Impenetrable silences. Infinite solitude. The picture has managed even to imprison the elemental force of wind and cold. In this sense the picture is creative art: it projects and sustains a mood. In another sense it is reproductive art in that it captures natural beauty. With the exception perhaps of the Swedish picture, *Sir Arne's Treasure,* which utilizes the splendor of a Scandinavian winter, there has never been a more graphic presentation of hibernating nature. If for no other reason than the portrayal of the snowstorm, the film must rank as a thing of beauty. The composition is masterly. The director felt that the things which best epitomize the spirit of loneliness and desolation in the North are the howling of the dog teams, the eerie lament of the wind, and the swirling of blown snows. Yet these are sound impressions. All three nevertheless had to be caught within the picture if the regional atmosphere of grim infinitude was to be created. This Mr. Flaherty managed admirably to do by a graphic representation almost equivalent to literary onomatopeia. Instead of having a word, he had a picture represent sound. The result is winter visualized. The picture calls up Grieg's music and the Aurora Borealis.

We have said that the film marks the beginning of the naturalistic school of cinematography. Yet all this naturalness has been achieved through the purely artificial means of the camera. And it is precisely here that the picture manages to turn craftmanship into artistry. The director has used his mechanical device to gain the highest quotient of dramatic efficiency. The camera is subordinated to, and in fact almost eliminated from, the final effect. It is an invisible magician. There is no internal evidence that a camera was used. The story is the story of the Eskimos. Therefore, with the single exception of the white trader at the lonely trading post, not a white man obtrudes himself upon their territory.

That the picture exists at all is due to the possession of remarkable qualities by the director, who is a fellow of the Royal Geographical Society, an engineer by profession, and an explorer by preference. To produce such a picture required skill of no mean order. There was need for thorough photographic knowledge to record the thin blue light of the North, that "unwarming light which only seemed where'er it fell, to make the coldness visible." There was need for an artist's eye to select the stretches of white wastelands and to compose them into cinematic beauty. There was need for persevering patience to secure any sort of photographic effects in the short spaces of northern sunlight which is not kindly to actinic processes at best. The obstacles offered by nature to the taking of her own picture in some of her fiercest manifestations were almost insuperable.

One other thing about *Nanook of the North.* It is composed and expressed in terms of the motion picture. We are excessively weary of adaptations from the other arts, the art of the stage and the art of the printed word. Here at last begins our native screen language, as original in concept as *The Cabinet of Dr. Caligari,* yet as natural as that is fantastic. It reproduces actual beauty as *Caligari* reproduces expressionistic beauty.

The New Republic, August 9, 1922

Harold Lloyd broke into films in 1913 after a lot of odd jobs and some acting experience. Now, as Chaplin had done and Keaton was soon to do, he launched his own feature-length career. It's possible to quibble about that statement. Lloyd had already made *A Sailor-Made Man* in four reels. But he later referred to this as a "semifeature" and to *Grandma's Boy,* in five reels, as "our first feature-length picture." 22

GRANDMA'S BOY

When the pictures were young it was decreed that the more evident comedies should be not more than one or two reels in length, and except in the case of a handful of favorites the custom has been followed down to the present. It is a canon of the craft, and generally a wise one, that comedy should be more fleeting than those sturdier dramas of the great outdoors. And so, when a comedian emerges from the ranks of the two-reelers and makes bold to try the five-reel form, it is a turning point in his artistic career.

It was Harold Lloyd who came forth at the Strand Theater yesterday in his first full-length comedy. As a matter of fact, it is something of a compromise in the matter of length—it runs a bit less than an hour. It is a variously authored entertainment entitled *Grandma's Boy*—amusing nearly always and hilarious a good part of the time. It carries its hero through a series of familiar adventures, but they are tricked out, as Mr. Chaplin tricks out his comedies, with enough amusing incident to provide good entertainment.

The comedian is on familiar ground all the way, and it is only in the matter of length that he is breaking into new territory. In style, of course, he is a blend of certain features of the Messrs. Chaplin and Fairbanks. He cannot reveal those fine nuances of meaning that Mr. Chaplin is master of, nor has he all of Mr. Fairbank's athletic virtuosity. But he has a share of the qualities of each, and a dash of his own personality to complete the mixture.

Grandma's Boy is the story of a boy who won't fight back. It is reasonably certain, as soon as the bully looms on the scene, that Lloyd will clean up the film with him in the final reel, but this merely adds to the enjoyment of the scene. The story is a purely farcical episode dealing with a hunt for a desperado, with the timid Lloyd, greatly to the atonishment of everyone but the audience, capturing him single-handed in the end.

Grandma's Boy contains a generous amount of amusement and even a dash of excitement.

The New York Times, September 4, 1922

ROBIN HOOD

A story-book picture is *Robin Hood,* as gorgeous and glamorous a thing in innumerable scenes as the screen has yet shown. It is a splendid example of the one type of serious photoplay that has any future in a land where the fear of the censor works more efficiently than the fear of God, and it is hard to see how in many respects the future can improve on this particular example. It is romance—the romance of chivalry—in all the lovely trappings the heart can desire, and thrilling entertainment for the whole family group, from oldest to youngest.

Naturally no one wants realism in a tale of the merry men of Sherwood Forest—and no one gets it in this picture. The realest looking things in it are the stones of the magnificent castles and the noble trees. The knights and fair ladies are what we would like our ideal knights and ladies to have been, moving beautifully through a story in which we know the wicked prince will be fittingly punished after the last exciting fight. The manners of the twelfth century are merely hinted at in the king's method of tackling his food, which has more the effect of proving Richard a jovial monarch than of being a bit of historical accuracy. Even the Crusade looks like a jolly pleasure jaunt.

The picture is sharply divided into two parts of which the first is by far the better. In it Richard the Lion-Hearted prepares to march off to the Holy Land, and a bit of love-story is started between the Earl of Huntingdon and the Lady Marian to provide a reason for the Earl to return and be Robin Hood in the second part.

This part of the picture, reaching its high spots in a tournament and in the marching away of the crusaders, has extraordinary beauty and suggestiveness. The tournament is especially well done. There is one instance when a charging knight seems to make the whole age of chivalry come to life before our eyes—come to a far lovelier life than it probably ever had in fact. It is the old England of Scott and boyhood dreams.

In the second part the Earl of Huntingdon becomes Robin Hood and Douglas Fairbanks becomes Doug. Old England gets a thorough jazzing, and though it remains entertaining the glamorous atmosphere is gone. The outlaws of Sherwood Forest smack more of comic opera than of the merry greenwood, and Fairbanks himself has developed a little tripping movement at the end of his stunts that is reminiscent of a vaudeville acrobat when he pauses for a hearty round of applause. Perhaps it was impossible to resist the temptation to give the thing a whirlwind finish that would be faster and more furious than anything ever done before, but it is too bad, considering the tremendous advance the first part of the picture makes over anything Fairbanks has done before, that he did not take the trouble to make his own characterization at least as good as his Zorro. If he had done that, his acting might have equalled his production.

Wallace Beery is a genial and likeable king, and Sam De Grasse a sinister prince—two picturesque and effective pieces of acting. Enid Bennett is the fair Lady Marian—a rather insipid one, but pictorially satisfactory. Willard Louis as Friar Tuck, with his waddle and his swashbuckling, helps materially to keep the second part of the picture on a comic plane, and Alan Hale, while hardly the Little John of the legend, is a convincing personage whenever he has the opportunity to bring the character to the fore, particularly in the episode where he rescues Huntingdon from the prison in which Prince John has had him confined. The rest of the cast capably assist in lending the proper tone to the picture.

It is hard to tell to what extent the director, Allan Dwan, was responsible for the merit of a production into the making of which the talents and technical knowledge of many people have patiently gone. Whatever his share of the work was, he is entitled to due credit for having transferred an elaborate scenario from paper to the scenic background provided for its unfoldment on the screen.

To Arthur Edison must go a large share of the praise. It would appear that without the brand of photography he supplied much of the scenic grandeur and the tonal effects of the picture would never have been achieved.

Exceptional Photoplays, January 1923

THE FIRST PERSON SINGULAR

ROBERT E. SHERWOOD

Impersonal criticism is going out of style almost as rapidly as tweed sport clothes for misses and Eskimo Pie. The writer who never injects himself into his reviews of other people's works is becoming almost extinct. Nowadays, the critic refers to himself, baldly, as "Me." What is more, he announces his likes and dislikes, just as though he were entitled to prejudices of his own.

Therefore, before I go any further, I might as well come right out and state my position as regards the cinematographic art. Not that any one has asked me to do so, or has indicated an intention to attach any importance to my views. I cannot say, in advance, that "a number of readers have written in to ask me what I think of the movies," because that would be a violation of the truth, in its strictest sense.

However . . . In the first place, I like the movies. I should go to the movies, even if I were not paid to do so. For the self-conscious high-brows who know nothing about motion pictures, and dismiss them with a sneer, I have no respect whatever. When they discuss this subject, contemptuously or patronizingly, they are talking through their official hats. One does not judge literature in terms of Elinor Glyn, or the drama in terms of Avery Hopwood, or art in terms of cover designs on the *Smart Set.*

Of all the different types of movies, the comedies appeal to me most. Charlie Chaplin is the greatest genius that the cinema has developed— possibly the only real genius. Harold Lloyd and Buster Keaton are not far behind him. I like Mack Sennett's comedies, particularly when they involve Mabel Normand, Ben Turpin, and Phyllis Haver, but I have small admiration for Mr. Sennett when he goes in for heart interest. I am very fond of animated cartoons, particularly *Felix the Cat* and *Mutt and Jeff.*

I hate society dramas, especially those produced by Cecil B. DeMille. This may be a false prejudice, but it is not a personal one. I think that William DeMille is an infinitely greater director than his brother, although I am aware that his pictures do not make money.

I also hate mother-love dramas, because they constitute an insult to the sanctity of mother love. There is one exception to this—*Humoresque.*

Douglas Fairbanks and Mary Pickford are two great artists. They have both taken the trouble to study the movies, and their knowledge of this subject is plainly perceptible in their works.

I think that Rudolph Valentino is a fine actor, but that Ramon Navarro is a finer one. Richard Barthelmess is altogether admirable. Charles Ray is an off-and-on performer. He has not always been wise in the conduct of his own affairs, and some of his pictures have suffered in consequence. The same may be said of William S. Hart.

I love Jackie Coogan. I respect Thomas Meighan.

Lillian Gish, Leatrice Joy, Priscilla Dean, Pola Negri, and Alice Terry are all excellent actresses, but I have never been able to summon up much enthusiasm for Gloria Swanson.

I admire Douglas MacLean, Nazimova, Wallace Beery, George Fawcett, Lewis Stone, Helene Chadwick, William Norris, Madge Bellamy, Theodore Roberts, Enid Bennett, the Moore brothers, Richard Dix, the Talmadge sisters, Lois Wilson, Conway Tearle, Vera Stedman, Tom Mix, Betty Compson, Will Rogers, Henry B. Walthall, Virginia Valli, Clyde Cook, and Strongheart, the police dog.

Of the directors, Rex Ingram is undoubtedly my favorite, although D. W. Griffith must still be called the greatest. Allan Dwan has done one remarkable picture, as have Henry King and Robert Flaherty. Frank Lloyd has done two.

I like the Christie Comedies that William Beaudine has directed, and I think that Rupert Hughes has turned the corner and is now going straight. Marshall Neilan has shown tremendous promise, but has never quite fulfilled it. I believe that he understands motion pictures better than any of them.

Robert Vignola deserves untold credit, if only because of the miracle that he has performed with Marion Davies.

In all the movies that I have seen, these episodes stand out most clearly in my regrettably fallible memory:—

The picture of Lincoln and the old mother in *The Birth of a Nation;* the boy who shouted "Vive la France!" as he faced a firing squad in *The Four Horsemen of the Apocalypse;* the expression on the face of Tol'able David's mother when she realized that her son had delivered the mail; the little cripple in *The Miracle Man* casting away his crutches; the girl, in *The Cabinet of Dr. Caligari,* as she awoke and gazed into the countenance of Cesare, the somnambulist; the death of King Louis in *When Knighthood Was in Flower;* the cats in *Grandma's Boy;* Pola Negri's shrug in *Gypsy Blood;* Charlie Chaplin's meditation by the manhole in *The Kid.*

These were all great moments. The awful moments will have to be published in book form.

Life, November 22, 1922

SAFETY LAST

ROBERT E. SHERWOOD

. . . Harold Lloyd wastes no time in *Safety Last*. He plants his thrill crop at the start of the picture, and he reaps a rich harvest before the story has faded to a close.

Safety Last is a mechanical effort which lacks the usual spontaneity and buoyancy of a Harold Lloyd comedy. Nevertheless, it is marvelously ingenious. It is brimming with tricks that are calculated to tickle the ribs and chill the spine at one and the same instant.

The big moment of the film is provided when Lloyd performs a "human fly" stunt up the wall of a building. He has engaged a substitute, a professional at this hazardous work, to do the job for him—but the substitute fails to come through. So Lloyd goes up the sheer wall himself, hand over hand. When he reaches the clock on the eighth story, he clutches feverishly at the minute hand. But the face of the clock falls off, and he is left suspended precariously at a dizzy height above the street. The audience tries to laugh, but only succeeds in gurgling. Again, when he is perched on a narrow ledge, feeling comparatively safe for the minute, an impertinent mouse appears and runs up his leg. The audience is then reduced to a maudlin state of gibbering hysteria.

Safety Last is a terrifying affair. It is recommended only to those who possess the stoutest hearts and the least sensitive nerves.

Life, April 19, 1923

Bruce Bliven was an editor of *The New Republic* and a prolific social commentator.

THE COVERED WAGON

BRUCE BLIVEN

How to begin a review of a remarkable motion picture, without making it seem too remarkable? I might adduce the fact that I paid $7 for three seats (to a ticket speculator) and did not regret it . . . but no; probably the best opening is the Careful Summary, like this:

In this film, *The Covered Wagon,* it seems to me that the motion picture finds the field for which it is best adapted. It has done this before, of course, but not often: four or five times in the decade which comprises its history as an art. *The Covered Wagon* is not so fine an artistic achievement as *The Birth of a Nation* or *Broken Blossoms,* but it does show, better than almost any other film ever made, what sort of theme and treatment are best fitted to the powers and limitations of the screen. Whether the happy result in this case is the result of intelligent intention or just accident doesn't particularly matter as far as I am concerned.

The Covered Wagon's story fits the motion picture because it is an epic: the epic of Westward, Ho! across the plains in the roaring forties. Before our eyes a great wagon train assembles on the west bank of the Mizzoury river, opposite where Kansas City stands today. We travel with this train all the way to the Pacific slope: out along the slow, heartbreaking trail to Oregon, which was the homesteader's bright fixed star in 1848 before the Gold Rush. Our wagons bump behind the snail-like crawling oxen across uncounted miles of prairie; we have a heartbreaking struggle, and lose some of our cattle in crossing the terrible flood waters of the Platte. A few of us, faint hearts, give up and turn our oxen's faces toward the East— back to Pennsylvany and safety from Injuns and prairie fire, cyclone and water-starvation; but most of us press on—a great, slow, sure migration of people who have half a continent to loot and know it, and bend willing shoulders to the task.

Over and over, in this picture, you stand at the head of the long line of prairie schooners, temporarily halted, dwindling off toward the horizon. A bugle sounds: a leader on horseback makes a semaphore of himself, and slowly the whole great train lumbers forward in its dust. The twenty-foot whips crack above the oxen; the women and babies peer out from the puckered canvas doorway, the lads on their ponies gallop ahead. You get an irresistible feeling of the movement of a whole population toward the sunset; of scores and scores of similar trains pouring through every gap in the Alleghenies, moving across the Mississippi basin, sometimes down along the Santa Fe trail in the south, sometimes with Pike's Peak for a lodestar, or through Wyoming toward Oregon.

These people took with them into the West the Puritan civilization of New England; whether you like it or not, the land is marked with it today. Their sacred implement was the plow, their dominant passion was to fence and dig. Mercilessly they drove out the Indian as he in turn had once driven out a previous Aztec people. No one who has pondered the meaning of the frontier in the development of American institutions, or who has, like the writer, lived through a prairie boyhood long enough to have seen the last members of the Great Trek jolting westward, always westward, in the rutted roads between fenced fields, can fail to feel a clutch at the heart as the prairie schooners go bobbing and struggling up and down the long slow slopes.

What I am praising, you note, is the theme of the picture, rather than its execution. Yet the latter is excellent, not only for what it does but for movie temptations resisted. For instance:

The handsome hero, suffering repeated attempts at murder by the villain, always catches him at it, always lets him go. Whereupon the hero's back-woods Faithful Friend (magnificently played by Ernest Torrence) de-nounces him roundly as a careless fool, a dolt, an idiot; and finally, to the audience's unbounded delight kills that villain—when he isn't looking. You wouldn't, to paraphrase the useful Mr. Kipling, find that in a mere movie.

Point two: most of the males, including a twelve-year-old hellion who is all boy, chaw tobacker; and they chaw it in the unlovely, juice-dripping style of real life.

Point three: The highly virtuous back-woodsman and his truly noble chum, the scout, arrive at a trading post. Thereupon, to the undoubted anguish of the troglodytes on the Pennsylvania Board of Censors, they proceed to get good and drunk. (Incidently, I defy you, I defy you not to hold your breath when these two rip-roaring drunken old scoundrels pro-ceed, à la William Tell, to shoot tin cups off each other's head at fifty yards.)

Point four: An old lady dies en route, and is buried on the lone prairie. It is easy to see how a director with less passion for historical fact than James Cruze would have done this bit: the lonely little white cross in the illimitable gray waste, etc. Iris out on cross silhouetted against sunset; cut to closeup of coyote's head, howling. Not so Mr. Cruze. It is explained that the Indians who lurk behind every big wagon train waiting for strays and stragglers had just as lief loot a grave as not. Therefore ashes are scattered over the leveled top of this one and the entire wagon train runs over it.

Point five: There are some exquisite scenes showing the pioneers, halted for the night, seated about their campfires. Leaping flames, flickering lights on the canvas wagon tops in the background, and the high wide heavens of the West overhead; a lovely piece—and right in the middle of the fore-ground, the prairie mothers in hideous rocking chairs, temporarily ap-propriated from the wagons' cargo. A bit of sheer ugliness which (for me, at least) synthesizes into a whole possessing the beauty of the truth.

Not all of the film lives up to these high marks, of course. We have a hero who, having been dismissed from the army for cattle-stealing, submits to a tongue-lashing from his lady love and never even tries to tell her that he took the cattle only to keep his troop from starving to death in the desert. We have, again, the heroine herself, under no sort of compulsion from her doddering parents, about to marry a villain whom she does not love—an act without a shadow of a reason unless we are to infer a congenital preference in the buxom miss for the worst of marriages as against the best of spinsterhoods. Finally, it annoyed me to see this heroine, in the midst of grime and sweat and dust, always unutterably clean, as immaculate in snowy linen collar and cuffs as a Lucille mannequin, standing out against the crowd like a bar of soap in a coal bin.

These are minutiae, however, and perhaps hardly fair to mention. As a whole this motion picture must certainly rank among the four or five best ever produced, and as a wholly admirable attempt at the task to which the powers of the camera best lend themselves—the recording of an epic story, where the struggle is all on the surface, and with man's first and last enemy, Mother Earth herself.

The New Republic, April 25, 1923

Clayton Hamilton was an eminent academic drama critic and the author of several books on playwriting.

THE COVERED WAGON

CLAYTON HAMILTON

The great dramas of the world, like *Othello* or *Oedipus the King,* do not offer such excellent material for motion pictures as the great epics, such as *The Odyssey, The Aeneid, or Jerusalem Delivered.* The drama focuses attention on the tiny problem of whether or not a certain individual is to have his way and get what he desires; but the epic deals with the larger problem of whether or not thousands and thousands of people, linked together by allegiance to a communal ideal, shall achieve an undertaking which is of permanent importance to all subsequent mankind.

The adjective "great" is used very sparingly by the present commentator; but it may honestly be said that *The Covered Wagon* is a great picture, because it is conceived and executed in the epic mood. It does not try to do what has been done, or might be done, much better on the speaking stage; but it exhibits a communal struggle and narrates a civilizing undertaking so vast that it could not adequately be summarized within the limitations of the traditional theater. We are interested only slightly in the semi-close-up scenes between the hero and the heroine, and we do not care particularly whether or not they marry each other at the end of the story and live happily ever after; but we do care, and care tremendously, whether or not the hundreds of prairie schooners piloted by dauntless pioneers, which started boldly westward in 1848 from the little settlement which has subsequently grown to be Kansas City, shall achieve the communal quest of arriving safely in distant Oregon and shall accomplish the great civilizing task which Theodore Roosevelt once dubbed, with one of his enlightened phrases, as "the winning of the West." Individuals count for little in this epic narrative; it is the long, long train of covered wagons that evermore remains the hero of the story. We see this wagon-train trekking over illimitable prairies, drifting over mile-wide rivers, climbing over mountain ranges, assaulted from without by hostile savages, and endangered, from within by dissensions and disloyalties; and we see it ultimately reaching its goal and doubling the map of the United States. And this heroic spectacle is exalting and inspiring, and makes us proud to be Americans.

The scenario of *The Covered Wagon* was adapted by Jack Cunningham from a novel by Emerson Hough; but the material might have been taken just as readily from Francis Parkman's volume, *The Oregon Trail*. It is only because Parkman happened to be an American dealing with American subject-matter that we have been a little hesitant to recognize the fact that he was one of the greatest historians who ever lived. Volume after volume of his historical writings is replete with the most thrilling and appealing type of motion picture material. Why is this material persistently neglected by our big producers, while millions of dollars are wasted every year in shoveling before the public the customary junk and balderdash? I should like to see a fine picturization of Parkman's *Montcalm and Wolfe*. Any good director could take this history as it stands and shoot it without the intervention of a continuity writer; but it is highly doubtful if the inhibitions which oppress the motion picture industry will be overcome by even so emphatic a phenomenon as the huge commercial success of *The Covered Wagon*.

The Covered Wagon is a Paramount Picture, and it is far and away the finest thing that has ever yet been launched by the Famous Players-Lasky Corporation. But the point should be emphatically noted that this picture is not a factory product, but essentially a one-man job. It was made thousands of miles away from Hollywood, under the supreme and sole direction of one person, who, luckily, was immune from conferences and independent of committees; and to the director, James Cruze, full credit must be given for an epic achievement that ranks very high in the annals of contemporary art.

Theatre, June 1923

THE THREE AGES

ROBERT E. SHERWOOD

When Buster Keaton saw D. W. Griffith's *Intolerance* seven years ago, he probably resolved that some day, somewhere, somehow he would produce a picture of that type. At the time he was still an obscure performer in a vaudeville act, so that his lofty ambitions were necessarily shelved.

Now, however, young Master Keaton has become a star, bright enough to be graduated from the two-reel class and wealthy enough to make "Independent" productions of any length that he may desire. So he has realized his boyhood dream, and the *American Magazine* can chalk up another victory for determination, gogettiveness, and clean living.

The Three Ages, in which Buster Keaton tumbles through the Cro-Magnon period, the Roman era, and the present day, is just about as incoherent as *Intolerance* and about fifty times as funny. Although one has considerable difficulty in following the weird meanderings of Buster's plot (if any), one has no trouble whatever in greeting his antics with a hearty laugh. Of the three ages, the cave-man part is easily the most comic.

Buster Keaton is one of the genuinely funny men of our time. Together with his nimble-witted director and gag-man, Eddie Cline, he has performed a service of incalculable value to mankind. He has helped to keep this much-molested human race in good humor, at a time when it has nothing but high taxes, United States Senators, coal strikes, banana shortages, wrong numbers, and Signor Mussolini to think about.

Life, October 25, 1923

A Woman of Paris is one of the two "mystery" pictures of Chaplin's career. In 1926 he produced a film called *The Sea Gull*—nothing to do with Chekhov—and engaged the young Josef von Sternberg to direct it. After one preview Chaplin decided not to release it, and the film seems to have disappeared. He did release *A Woman of Paris* three years before that, which he directed himself, but it has not been seen publicly in decades. (Contrary to the statement in the review below, he does appear in it—a small role as a station porter.) Chaplin writes: "The film was a great success with discriminating audiences. It was the first of the silent pictures to articulate irony and psychology." [23] Whether or not this is true, the quality of the reception makes it all the more puzzling that the film has been withdrawn.

The "intelligence" noted below as rare may refer to the fact that *A Woman of Paris* deals fairly realistically with sexual relations, which were treated with arbitrary neatness in American films of that day, and of many days to come.

A WOMAN OF PARIS

For many years it has been apparent in the comedies of Charlie Chaplin that Charles Spencer Chaplin takes himself seriously. Now for the first time, in a photoplay written and directed by him, but in which he does not appear, the general public has been asked to take him seriously. The result is one of the few, in the strictly artistic sense, fine motion pictures which have been produced since that potential art developed into an industry.

In *A Woman of Paris* Mr. Chaplin as a writer and director has not done anything radical or anything esoteric; he has merely used his intelligence to the highest degree, an act which has ceased to be expected of motion picture people for many years. He has written and directed a story in which all the characters act upon motives which the spectator immediately recognizes as natural and sincere, and therefore *A Woman of Paris* breathes an atmosphere of reality, and thereby holds the attention of any perceptive audience in thrall.

As a director Mr. Chaplin has attained to a great achievement, because he has succeeded in contributing his own fascinating personality and subtle intelligence to his actors in their given situation. The performance of Edna Purviance as the woman of Paris is a thing of much charm, altogether aside from her physical loveliness. The outstanding feature of the picture is the charm and natural goodness she makes convincing in spite of her relations to Pierre Revel, as played by Adolphe Menjou with great distinction. This relation of Marie and Pierre Revel is undeniably in conflict with the thesis that a union outside of marriage is invariably unhappy, is always entirely a thing of the flesh and involves indecency of mind. Marie and Pierre, while estranged in the end, are never violently sorrowful and they are certainly not excessively fleshy. Also, their feelings, if these are an indication of their state of mind, are ones of genuine affection and respect for each other. It would be wiser to say about this attachment that it is a plea for charity and understanding of such people by one who is charitable and understands them, than that it is a subtle stroke at the wholesomeness and desirability of marriage and lawful love. For the emotional disaster that overtakes Marie is due to her desire for lawful love and marriage, and in Pierre there is always an implied sympathy for the want in Marie's heart, as well as an urge to satisfy it. That this should be part of the drama of so fine a technical achievement will doubtless be regrettable to many, and a point for attack on the picture as a whole. On the other hand, there will be many who will perceive a treatment both clean and honest, a purpose both artistic and truthful. Not a spot in this polished picture is tarnished by anything cheap and vulgar, not one moment is spent in pandering to low tastes or the craving for the sensational.

A Woman of Paris has the one quality almost every other motion picture that has been made to date lacks—restraint. The acting is moving without ever being fierce; the story is simple and realistic without ever being inane; the settings are pleasing and adequate without ever being colossally stupid. The result is a picture of dignity and intelligence, and the effect is startling because it is so unusual.

The achievement of Mr. Chaplin indicates what should be obvious, that 10,000 in the cast do not necessarily make a moving drama, and directors of pictures made on that principle would do well to see this picture often and take it to heart if it is the artistic motion picture that they are striving for. The action is very simple, and to tell the story would be unprofitable, because the story is not at all unusual, which is the very thing that makes it humanly interesting. But to attain the simplicity and even flow which his picture has must have cost Mr. Chaplin much effort. He, as the director, undoubtedly deserves much of the credit for the natural relations of his characters to each other as brought out by Edna Purviance, Adolphe Menjou, and Carl Miller. It is easy to see that these actors are doing exactly what they are told, and doing it as they would in their homes, if they happened to live in such homes as Mr. Chaplin, the writer, has devised for them.

Incidentally, *A Woman of Paris* has some bits of comedy that are typical of what has made Charlie Chaplin justly famous, but the comedy is never forced in for relief but takes place as the natural thing in the situation. There is also an underlying vein of satire which is a healthy sign in any study of the interrelations of human beings in modern life.

Exceptional Photoplays, October/November 1923

Alice Duer Miller wrote light and popular novels, one of which, *Gowns by Roberta,* became the basis of the musical comedy *Roberta. Dulcy,* a comedy by George S. Kaufman and Marc Connelly, was about a woman given to platitudes.

Jackie Coogan, referred to in the last line, was the then child actor who had zoomed to popularity in Chaplin's *The Kid,* discussed on p. 115ff.

THE TEN COMMANDMENTS

ROBERT E. SHERWOOD

Emotional, intellectual or corporeal, there must be an end to all human qualities. The term "mortal," by which each dweller upon this earth is known, is in itself an admission of temporal limitations. A man may not live forever, nor may his sentiments, his point of view, or his prejudices. There is an end to the world, and to all things associated with it.

In view of which I have long realized that sooner or later I should be compelled to change my mind about those subjects upon which my opinion has been most firmly fixed: the day would come, I knew, when I should have to utter praise for a Cecil B. DeMille picture.

By an odd coincidence, this happens to be the day.

Mr. DeMille, in his time, has mutilated the works of many writers—from James Matthew Barrie to Alice Duer Miller—has sacrificed their ideas to make a Hollywood holiday. But when, in *The Ten Commandments,* he approached the words of God, he became suddenly overwhelmed with the idea that it would be better to set them forth unchanged. In this, Mr. DeMille displayed commendable originality; for no literary work has had rougher treatment from the public at large. If the mighty Cecil had seen fit to step on the Ten Commandments, he would at least have had plenty of precedent for the act.

However, there they are, all ten—count 'em—ten, presented on the screen just as they were revealed to Moses on the jagged crest of Mount Sinai. No star of the stage or the films has ever enjoyed a more spectacular entrance than that which is arranged for the Ten Commandments. Great masses of clouds form, are rent by streaks of lightning, and then are dissolved into the flaming words of God. Each of the Commandments swirls out of the heavens and hits the spectator squarely between the eyes—and each, it must be recorded, earns an equal storm of applause.

The Ten Commandments may not exercise as much influence as they should, but they are certainly good theater.

The picture itself is divided into two parts: the first, a biblical spectacle which shows, educationally, how the Commandments were made; the second, a modern story, designed to demonstrate how they are broken.

There is a vast difference, superficially and fundamentally, in the style with which these two portions have been treated. In the biblical prologue, Mr. DeMille puts on the dog heavily—reflecting the gorgeous extravagance of Pharaoh's court in pictures of incredible magnificence. Some of these are in color, and others in the usual photographic tints, an inconsistency which detracts materially from the realism of the spectacle. There are other remarkable scenes, of the Israelites wincing under Egypt's lash, of the Exodus, of the Red Sea being parted in the middle, and of the worship before the Calf of Gold.

This is all great stuff, and profoundly stirring—but it is not so very far ahead of *Intolerance,* which D. W. Griffith produced eight years ago. It is full of mechanical tricks which, while marvelous in themselves, remain just tricks: an audience invariably loses some of its illusion when it murmurs, "How did DeMille do *that?*"

In the modern story, however, Mr. DeMille displays a directorial genius which is comparable with that of Charlie Chaplin in *A Woman of Paris.* He recounts a narrative of singular absurdity, but does it so effectively that every character and every situation, however impossible, is made to seem eminently real.

The Ten Commandments, in its later stages, lacks all the bizarre ostentation which has been part and parcel of every DeMille movie since the *Don't Change Your Husband* days. He tells his story simply and with great vigor, relying on the subtle eloquence of reality rather than the megaphone blatancy of excessive splurge.

He is aided throughout the picture by the deft work of his cameramen, by the superb plot construction and subtitles of Jeanie Macpherson, and by the general excellence of the cast. Of the many stars who appear, Rod La Rocque stands out vividly. His performance of an unregenerate youth who flouts the Ten Commandments is one to be remembered as long as we old cronies sit around the fire and discuss the movies of yesteryear. Leatrice Joy is (of course) splendid, Richard Dix is seriously convincing, and Charles de Roche gives a glamorous portrait of Pharaoh the Magnificent.

From all the players, Mr. DeMille's production has derived an unusual degree of ability, sincerity, and inspiration. I'm not going to say that they "live their parts," because I don't want to steal any of *Dulcy's* stuff; but at least, they make a good bluff at it.

Here endeth to-day's lesson, and let no man say that I have never praised a DeMille production.

You may now bring forth a Jackie Coogan picture that I may pan, and my record for impartiality will be complete.

Life, January 17, 1924

This obituary is included because it is both a critique of a career and a historical marker of an attitude toward the short pictures with which the film had begun.

The *Anna Christie* mentioned here was a silent film, made in 1923, directed by John Wray, with Blanche Sweet. George F. Marion, who played Anna's father, later repeated the role in Greta Garbo's first sound film.

"PRODUCED BY THOMAS H. INCE"

With the death of Thomas H. Ince, one of the most spectacular and interesting figures passed from motion pictures. Thomas H. Ince was a personality; above all he was an institution. "Produced by Thomas H. Ince," when thrown upon the screen in connection with a motion picture, was a guarantee to millions of people that the article offered was the output of an old and tried concern. It was like saying, "Established since the beginning of motion pictures." And, indeed, in that beginning lay the past of the Ince studio.

To turn to that past for a moment from the purpose of this review, which seeks to summarize, as far as that may briefly be done, Ince's achievement in his chosen profession, one remembers "the lot" at Culver City, California, the white road winding northward along the ocean, around the bluffs, from Santa Monica; suddenly the studio buildings and the sets—French village, Chinese temple and pagodas, a House of Parliament, as the scenic needs of the pictures under production might be—appearing in a space set in the hills. One remembers the ride up the little mountain behind "the lot" in the old stagecoach driven by an "old stager" and drawn rocking along by four horses over the precipitous trail, in order to give visitors "atmosphere" and a view of the surroundings. One remembers the supers in all manner of costumes, the broncos and the cowboys; the invariable bustle; the atmosphere of making serious all the make-believe, the enthusiasm injected into the effort. In the midst of all, one remembers Tom Ince with his touch upon "the works," busy with a thousand and one things, ready at any moment's notice to dash from office to set, to pick up the megaphone where needed, to direct, expound, encourage—like a cheerleader or a coach at a football game. Beneath all this, one had the sense of an organization, a flourishing business, founded and directed so well that it would continue on a permanent basis. Time has proved that this was the true condition. Ince was a pioneer, but he ended by being also a survivor, still keeping pace with the industry and carrying to further accomplishment what he had pioneered to do. Of all the motion picture makers of that early date, only one beside himself at the time of his death remained a significant factor in pictures—D. W. Griffith. Both were part of a romance that has become a business, and both remained forces in that business. Of the two, Ince had established—perhaps not the greater name—but the greater business concern.

What, then, has Ince's contribution been to the art of making motion pictures and to the art in motion pictures? He began with two-reelers, they were good ones, he ended with *Anna Christie,* the high watermark of all his productions. The thing he could do in the beginning, he could still do, and do better, at the finish. What was this?

To go back to the first question, Ince, by organizing studio operation, by regarding motion pictures as a permanent business, and by keeping his eye out for new and better facilities, contributed largely by giving motion pictures, not the method of technique so much, but a system for putting that method to work. To the art itself, he gave faith, enthusiasm, a boundless energy, and the knowledge of a natural-born actor. One thing marked his productions from the beginning—dramatic vigor, the "punch." For this quality alone, some of those early two- and five-reelers would remain interesting today.

The Taking of Luke McVane, The Cup, and many other films characteristic of that earlier period, which if not directed by Ince were at least supervised by him, had a plot, a story, a "curtain" that sent the spectator out of the theater feeling that he had spent his money wisely, and determined to come again. In this way, Ince's business was founded through his art— for it is art to put movement on the screen that is interesting and tells a robust story. And, answering our last question, this is the thing he could put there at the end as well as in the beginning. *Anna Christie* was a witness to it, for *Anna Christie,* while Ince only supervised it and John Wray gave it able direction and subtle touches, could not have been what it was if Ince, as occasion demanded, had not thrown off his coat, seized the old megaphone, and thrown in the "pep."

Ince's early pictures were more compact and perfect than his last ones. It may be stated with some plausibility that as pictures lengthened in footage, his grasp of dramatic essentials and his directness of presenting them diminished. De Maupassant, however, was never asked to write a story as long as *Les Misérables.* Of course, he was wise enough not to try. But that may be answered by saying that Ince was in a business whose customers demanded that long and ever longer pictures be produced. Thus there crept into many Ince pictures a noticeable degree of hokum and padding. These, however, the customers also demanded, and the introduction of such things not pertaining to art therefore never hurt the commercial value of his product. When it came to *Anna Christie* he threw them away, shot for stark effects and legitimate suspense, and did as nearly as he and his studio force were capable of doing, to say Mr. O'Neill's play with pictures as Mr. O'Neill himself had said it with the spoken word. *Anna Christie* was thought to be film-food for the censors. All kinds of changes probably were planned for the screen version. Ince said no, he would make *Anna Christie.* The result—perhaps not altogether in terms of money—was something that gave Ince great prestige, that discouraged the censors, or indeed, won their commendation, because it confronted them with something that was sincere, cleanly done and convincing, and that went a great way toward reestablishing the virtue of motion pictures in the minds of intelligent and perceptive people all over the country. When Ince made *Anna Christie* he did the art of motion pictures a service and thereby the industry of motion pictures a service.

To Ince ideas probably came faster than they did to anyone else in pictures. When his enthusiasm for these ideas lasted overnight, the studio always got action. Like those of everyone else, his enthusiasm sometimes miscarried. When Ince gave way too far to a theatrical streak in him, his work became gaudy and unconvincing. Yet the strength of his pictures always hovered on the brink of theatricality. Indeed his pictures were powerful for that very reason—for his ability to come to the precipice of dramatic folly and stand there without toppling over. This was true of the psychological study, *The Coward,* of that grim presentation of war, *The Despoilers* (*War's Women*), and of a still later production, *Behind the Door.* In such productions his name was associated with actors and actresses like Frank Keenan, Charles Ray, Hobart Bosworth, Enid Markey, and Bessie Barriscale.

Ince was never the great developer of screen talent that Griffith has been; but he had the sense to choose capable actors and use them capably. At one time or another, most of the big names of the screen, and of those who went from the stage to the screen, have appeared in his productions. The biggest name he made for an actor was that of William S. Hart, in Ince's "Westerns." The finest actor, perhaps, ever to work for him was Frank Keenan. Ince and Hart, Ince and Keenan, Ince and Ray—these were combinations for the exhibitor to conjure with; and in the still earlier days, Ince and Louise Glaum—in her time, the best actress of all the screen vamps.

At the time of his death, Ince had in the making what he considered to be, and fondly hoped would prove, the monumental production over his name, *The Last Frontier*—as it was to be called. This will not have the master eye looking over its sets when the remaining scenes are taken. But in the organization he set up, and perfected, and fought for so tenaciously, must surely reside the talent and purpose which will make possible the completion of this film very nearly as Ince planned it. The thought is not to be entertained that the institution of Thomas H. Ince will pass with his passing. Tutored as they have been by his sagacity, persistence, and ability, the people he worked with, out of a sense of loyalty to Ince and loyalty to his business of which they have become a part, will surely find a way to complete not only *The Last Frontier,* but many more pictures that shall bear his studio's name. "Produced by Thomas H. Ince Studio," should be a valuable trademark on motion pictures for a long time to come.

Exceptional Photoplays, December/January 1925

GREED

ROBERT E. SHERWOOD

Ferocity, brutality, muscle, vulgarity, crudity, naked realism, and sheer genius are to be found—great hunks of them—in von Stroheim's production, *Greed.* It is a terribly powerful picture—and an important one.

When von Stroheim essayed to convert Frank Norris's *McTeague* into a movie, he assumed what is technically known as a man-sized job. There was absolutely nothing in this novel of entertainment value, heart interest, or box-office appeal—none of the qualities that are calculated to attract the shrewd eye of the movie mogul.

Nevertheless, there were the elements of fierce drama in *McTeague,* and these have been taken by von Stroheim and turned loose on the screen. He has followed copy with such extraordinary fidelity that there is no scene in the picture, hardly a detail, that is not recognizable to those who have read the book.

The acting in *Greed* is uneven: Gibson Gowland is practically perfect as McTeague, as are Zasu Pitts and Jean Hersholt as Trina and Marcus Schouler; but von Stroheim has been guilty of gross exaggeration in his treatment of the subordinate characters. They are an artificial lot, derived from the comic strips rather than from reality.

Atmospherically, *Greed* is marvelous. The costumes, the settings, and the properties are just as Norris described them. McTeague wears a plaid cap which may be rated as the most appropriate article of attire ever displayed on the screen.

There are two defects in *Greed*—one of which is almost fatal.

In the first place, von Stroheim has chosen to be symbolic at intervals, and has inserted some very bad handcoloring to emphasize the goldenness of gold. This detracts greatly from the realism of the picture.

In the second place, von Stroheim has been, as usual, so extravagant with his footage that *Greed* in its final form is merely a series of remnants. It has been cut to pieces—so that entire sequences and important characters have been left out. Thus the story has a choppy quality; many of its developments are abrupt. We see Trina in one instant the tremulous young bride, and in the next the hard, haggard, scheming shrew of several years later. The intervening stages in her spiritual decay are not shown, although von Stroheim undoubtedly included them originally.

This is von Stroheim's own fault. He must learn to acquire some regard for the limitations of space. *Greed,* I understand, was produced in forty reels, which would take eight hours to unwind; and the eight-hour day for movie fans has not yet dawned—thank God!

Von Stroheim is a genius—*Greed* establishes that beyond all doubt—but he is badly in need of a stopwatch.

Life, January 1, 1925

GREED

Greed, the much-talked-of picturization of Frank Norris's *McTeague,* is a picture of undeniable power. Erich von Stroheim has let himself go and has produced a picture which by virtue of choice of subject, treatment, and emphasis represents a logical development in the work of the creator of *Blind Husbands, The Devil's Passkey,* and *Foolish Wives.* Mr. von Stroheim is one of the great stylists of the screen whose touch is recognizable in everything he does. He has always been the realist as Rex Ingram is the romanticist and Griffith the sentimentalist of the screen, and in *Greed* he has given us an example of realism at its starkest.

Like the novel from which the plot was taken, *Greed* is a terrible and wonderful thing. *McTeague* is one of the most savage, uncompromising, ugliest novels ever written. It achieved fame and continues to be read as an example of the horrible. It must be considered in any survey of the development of the American novel.

In judging the picture which Mr. von Stroheim has made from it we must use the widest possible perspective. For motion picture art has by this time attained its majority. It is entitled to experiment in any form from the ultrasentimental to the latest fad in symbolism. The days of censorship in that sense, the feeling that motion pictures must always be pretty pictures, are over. The time has come when we can invite the spirit of Matthew Arnold to the screen to see what he saw in literature, namely a criticism of life.

Most emphatically, there is and should be a place for a picture like *Greed.* It is undoubtedly one of the most uncompromising films ever shown on the screen. There have already been many criticisms of its brutality, its stark realism, its sordidness. But the point is that it was never intended to be a pleasant picture. It is a picture that is grown up with a vengeance, a theme for just those adults who have been complaining most about the sickening sentimentality of the average film. Nobody can complain of being deceived when he goes to see it; Zola did not compete with Gautier, and Frank Norris would never have sent any story of his to *True Romance*.

Lest it be considered that so far this review has been propaganda rather than criticism, we hasten to add that *Greed* is not our idea of a perfect picture. It is sometimes easier to make a perfect picture than a real one. *Scaramouche,* which has just won the Adolph Zukor $10,000 prize, is one of those perfect pictures. It is slick and polished, deftly acted, correct in setting and costume. But it is not really very much alive. Its perfections satiate rather than stir. Von Stroheim could do that sort of thing; in fact he has done it. But it is entirely to his credit that he has preferred to do some pioneer work. His picture, it is true, has generated the heat of controversy, but the very picture people who today are saying that he has gone beyond what is permissible on the screen tomorrow will be copying him.

The picture follows the novel with considerable accuracy. It gives the essentials of *McTeague* insofar as that could be done upon the screen. Just how far von Stroheim succeeded in this respect will, however, never be known. For the original picture was made in no less than forty reels, which were first cut down to twenty-four, then to twelve or less. Inevitably much must have been sacrificed in this process of reduction, and one certainly misses some of the motivation.

But these omissions hardly impair the primitive impact of the story, and the Death Valley sequence would stand out in any picture as a sort of travelogue through Hell. Some of the details of the picture, the sheer animalism of the characters as reflected in their every manner, have been the subject of much criticism. But Stroheim set out to show that greed is an ugly cankerous thing, and in his conception everybody and everything in the picture becomes smudged with this quality. Sometimes the sense of ugliness becomes overwhelming so that it disturbs our esthetic reaction. The best form of realism in any art does not do this, and to that extent von Stroheim has failed to do what he set out to accomplish. But that is one of the penalties of experimentation and should not become an unconditional criticism of the picture.

The acting honors of this remarkable production are so evenly divided that it is hard to say whether the characterization of McTeague by Gibson Gowland or of his wife by Zasu Pitts is the more memorable. Both create the illusion that they are not acting at all. They build up the characters slowly and carefully and carry the spectator with them at every point. Jean Hersholt's impersonation of Marcus Schouler, McTeague's false friend, is hardly less skillful though it, together with the other characters, shows some of the exaggerations of low comedy into which the actors were undoubtedly pushed by von Stroheim's over-direction. There are times when von Stroheim squeezes the lemon a little too hard.

Exceptional Photoplays, December/January 1925

In the following three articles about *The Last Laugh* Sherwood mentions a number of names, some of which have faded from sight. Charles Brabin was a British-born director active in Hollywood in the twenties and thirties whose best-remembered film is probably *The Bridge of San Luis Rey.* The Rockett Brothers, Al and Ray, were producers who made *The Dramatic Life of Abraham Lincoln,* among others. George Loane Tucker was a director whose *Ladies Must Live* apparently dealt with more grimness than was the rule of the day.[24]

Blood and Sand, from Ibanez, starred Valentino. *Tess of the D'Urbervilles,* from Hardy, starred Blanche Sweet. *One Glorious Day* starred Will Rogers. *Deception* was a German film directed by Lubitsch with Emil Jannings as Henry VIII and Henny Porten as Anne Boleyn. *The Marriage Circle* was the second film Lubitsch made in Hollywood, with Adolphe Menjou.

Surely it's not irrelevant, in human terms, to note that this appreciation of German art was written by a man who, only eight years before, had been severely wounded in a war against Germany.

THE LAST LAUGH

ROBERT E. SHERWOOD

It's a good thing for the movie business that Germany wasn't entirely obliterated in 1918; for German directors, actors, and technicians have been responsible, directly or indirectly, for 80 percent of the progress that the films have made in the past five years. The ideas that have come to us in cans from Berlin have been startlingly new, definitely advanced, and, in most cases, genuinely fine. Hollywood has not always admitted openly the enormous value of these ideas, but it has shown the effects of them in countless ways.

The actual menace of German celluloid importations as competitors of the home-grown products has petered out; but we are still at liberty to live and learn—and we can learn a great deal from our late neighbors in No Man's Land. Take, for instance, *The Last Laugh*——

Here is a marvelous picture—marvelous in its simplicity, its economy of effect, its expressiveness, and its dramatic power. The men who were principally involved in its production—Carl Mayer, the author; Emil Jannings, the star; and F. W. Murnau, the director—have demonstrated that thought in Berlin is farther ahead of thought in Hollywood than the intervening seven thousand miles would indicate. These artists tell a humble story, devoid of flourishes or frills, and tell it entirely in eloquent pictures; there is not a subtitle in the entire film! Never once is the issue in doubt— never once is the motive obscure. We see what the characters are doing, and we know what they are thinking: we are permitted to fill in the whys and the wherefores from our own imaginations—a none too exacting requirement.

The Last Laugh is the story of a pompous, strutting old man who gains caste in the humble district in which he lives because he happens to be the commissionaire of the expensive Hotel Atlantic. He wears a gorgeous uniform, fit at least for an Admiral of the Grand Fleet, and as he passes through dingy streets on his way home he is awarded respectful salutes by all. He glories in his circumstance.

But the manager of the Hotel Atlantic notices that the old fellow isn't quite so spry as he once was; he falters when he lifts heavy trunks from the taxicabs, and he is easily winded. So a new commissionaire is engaged. The unhappy old man is deprived of his uniform, and, as a mark of recognition of his long and faithful service, is given a purely honorary position handing out towels downstairs in the gentlemen's lavatory!

When the full extent of this frightful fall dawns on the ex-commissionaire, and he realizes that he will be an object of derision in his own home—that there will be no more salutes—there appears in his eyes an expression that might well be stamped on every overworked ego: the fearful, bitter, shaming mark of deflated pride.

Emil Jannings plays this remarkable part with all the fine fervor that is his; but it is not to Jannings so much as to Mayer and Murnau that the real credit belongs. For they have done things with a movie camera that have never been done before. Their manipulation of photographic effects is simply astounding; they have used the lens as a great painter would use a pliant brush that produces broad strokes or fine lines, sharp angles or graceful curves. They have made a moving picture that is really worthy of the name.

After *The Last Laugh* has run its legitimate course, a fantastic happy ending is tacked on, with the implication: "For those of you who can not take their liquor raw, here is a ginger-ale chaser." This added conclusion does not affect the main picture in the least, for it is actually no part of it.

I understand that the happy ending was made in Germany solely for the benefit of possible American audiences—a gesture of contempt, and a justifiable one. When Rex Ingram produced *The Prisoner of Zenda* he ended it as Anthony Hope ended it—with a parting of the lovers. But exhibitors complained at this so vociferously that the parting was removed. The same thing happened in *Where the Pavement Ends,* another Ingram picture, in *Blood and Sand,* and in *Tess of the D'Urbervilles.*

I am not trying to argue that the happy ending is inartistic; such a contention is absurd, as various classical examples will instantly prove. But I do argue that the happy ending isn't, or shouldn't be, essential. It is forced upon all those who try to write for the screen and its influence is dangerously bad: it makes for obviousness and for that product of a rubber stamp which is known as hokum.

Evidently all movies (to be successful) must dissolve into a roseate sunset, with the pleasant announcement that all's now right with the world. But is it? I've heard different.

Life, February 19, 1925

There are conclusions to be drawn from *The Last Laugh,* which was reviewed with uncharacteristic ecstasy in these columns last week. Such conclusions, were I to pursue them as far as they might lead, would fill ten issues of *Life* from cover to cover, with no room left for the advertisements (which, obviously, would be a very foolish thing).

The fact is this: *The Last Laugh* could never have been produced in this country. Even if there were directors, actors, and camera men qualified for the heroic job (and it is my belief that there are such), there would be no producers with moral courage to back them up. What chance would Carl Mayer, the author, have in a movie studio with a story that included no love interest, no patriotism, no marital entanglements, and no particular element of hope? And yet—it seems to me that the story of *The Last Laugh* is the finest dramatic conception that has ever come to the screen.

The movie industry in this country is too heavily saturated with "Yes-Men"—time-servers—who believe, and justifiably, that the safety of their miserable jobs depends on their ability to salve the men next higher up. They must kowtow incessantly to jealous stars, pompous directors, cold-blooded distributors, and executives whose ideals are cramped by the elastic bands which surround their bank-rolls.

Occasionally some real artist tears away from the stifling influence of the great film art factories, and produces on his own account something genuinely worthwhile: Charlie Chaplin, above all others, has done this, and so have D. W. Griffith, Douglas Fairbanks, Rex Ingram, Charles Brabin, Richard Barthelmess, the Rockett Brothers, Harold Lloyd, Robert J. Flaherty, Charles Ray, George Loane Tucker, and Buster Keaton. Still more occasionally, intelligent creative effort has been turned loose within the mills themselves—by such men as James Cruze, Herbert Brenon, Frank Lloyd, King Vidor, Victor Seastrom, Erich von Stroheim, Ernst Lubitsch, and William deMille.

These are exceptions to a sorry rule. With the ubiquitous influence of the box-office and the utter ignorance of the producers (as a class), there is little chance for a good man to get going in Hollywood.

If we can't afford to originate, then the best we can do is follow in the footsteps of those pioneers who have the courage of their artistic convictions. If we are incapable of producing *The Last Laugh* in this mighty nation, we are at least privileged to profit by it.

Life, February 26, 1925

The letters are beginning to appear from those who went to see *The Last Laugh* on my earnest recommendation, and who are now hastening to hurl my glowing words back at me, with accumulated interest.

"So this is Art!" they murmur scornfully, implying that they go to the movies to be entertained and that there is enough sordidness in life without trying to reflect it on the screen.

My answer to all comers is this: I never said that *The Last Laugh* was Art, (*a*) because I don't know what Art is; (*b*) because I didn't want to damn this worthy picture with a term that is, in the public's estimation, opprobrious.

I, too, go to the movies to be entertained, and *The Last Laugh* entertained me. In view of this, what should I have said? I might have explained in my review: "I enjoyed *The Last Laugh* intensely, but I advise you not to see it because you, unlike me, are not qualified to appreciate anything that is genuinely great."

That would have been charming.

This department is not devoted to the cause of intelligent criticism; it is merely a page upon which the violent opinions of one solitary individual may find expression. I am not conducting a service for movie exhibitors— telling them what pictures will make money and what will flop—nor am I engaged in the great profitable profession of uplift.

I am here to say what I think (on a catch-as-catch-can, take-it-or-leave-it, the-Marquis-of-Queensberry-be-damned basis), and no one can tell whether

I am right or wrong—including myself; in matters of opinion, right and wrong simply don't exist.

This, of course, is the answer of all highly opinionated individuals to those who dare to disagree, and should be accepted at its face value. I don't really mean to be cross about it.

Now as to *The Last Laugh*:

It is revolutionary in technique—and by that I mean the style of its construction, direction, photography, and performance. Where our American producers must use miles of subtitles, acres of expensive sets, and mobs of extras to get over one idea, these Germans have used the simplest and most economical effects of light and shadow.

The public, of course, has been educated to accept the absurd exaggeration of Hollywood, and it can't fathom this strange simplicity. When I saw Charlie Chaplin's *A Woman of Paris,* I heard a young lady in the audience remark, "The trouble with this picture is, the characters ain't real—they don't show any emotion." She was so steeped in the movie tradition that she could think of emotion only in terms of heaving bosoms, quivering lips, and cataracts of glycerine tears.

A Woman of Paris was a financial failure; so were *Broken Blossoms, One Glorious Day, Deception, The Marriage Circle,* and *The Dramatic Life of Abraham Lincoln.* Yet these were all fine pictures—important pictures —and I don't apologize for praising them.

As I have said many times before, and will continue to say as long as I have this space to fill, the public is never friendly toward pioneers in any field of endeavor.

The public laughed at Columbus when he said the world is round, at Roger Bacon when he postulated the equality of man, at Fulton, and Langley, and John Huss, and Walt Whitman, and John the Baptist, and Socrates. The greatest tragedies in history are to be found in the lives of men who were born ahead of their time.

It is always the follow-up men who make the money. Columbus never saw any of the Inca and Aztec treasures that built the Spanish Armada; Lewis and Clark were the first to explore the Northwest, but it was James J. Hill who successfully exploited it; Lee De Forest and Atwater Kent have made more money out of the radio than Marconi ever dreamed of; and I understand that H. C. Witwer's income is larger than Ring Lardner's.

So don't crow too loudly because *The Last Laugh* is failing to earn fortunes at the box-office. Wait until we have had a chance to observe its effect on our more practical American producers—and then decide whether or not it was worth doing.

Life, May 14, 1925

Edmund Wilson, who does not need to be identified as one of the pre-eminent men of letters of his time, was an editor of *The New Republic* from 1926 to 1931.

THE GOLD RUSH

EDMUND WILSON

The most important element in American moving-picture humor is what is known technically as the "gag." A gag is a kind of comic trick, the equivalent in moving picture action of the spoken gag of the stage. When Buster Keaton on a runaway motorcycle knocks the ladder out from under a housepainter and goes off with the bucket of paint on his head or when Harold Lloyd, who has been making his escape on a clothes-line strung between two houses, the clothes-line having been cut by an enemy, swings exactly into a room on one of the lower floors in which an assemblage of spiritualists are awaiting a materialization, he is exploiting a gag; as Douglas Fairbanks is doing equally in one of his allegedly romantic pictures, such as the recent *Don Q,* in which he lassoes the spouting pipe of a fountain with the end of his whip and bends it down so that it spurts in the face of an old lady who is sitting asleep behind it. The gag is the basis of all these films; and the manufacture of gags has now become one of the most important occupations of the movies. At Hollywood, the gag-writers of the comic stars are among the most influential and most envied members of the community; for, without them, the stars would be nothing. One has seen brief flashes on the part of Buster Keaton of what seemed to be a rather high order of pantomime; but it may be said in general that the Keatons, the Fairbankses, and the Lloyds do not need to be actors any more than Baby Peggy, Rin Tin Tin, Strongheart, or Silver King. Their public do not want to see them act: they are content merely to have them astonish, as the heroes of difficult feats or the victims of unexpected tricks.

The one comedian who has succeeded in doing anything really distinguished with this comedy of gags is, of course, Charlie Chaplin. In the first place, he is, I believe, the only comic star in the movies who does not employ a gag-writer: he invents everything for himself; so that, instead of the somewhat mechanical character of the humor of even the best of his competitors, most of whose gags could be interchanged among them without anyone's knowing the difference, Chaplin's jokes have an unmistakable quality of personal fancy. Furthermore, he has made a practice of taking his gags as points of departure for genuine comic situations. Thus in his latest picture, *The Gold Rush,* he has a cabin which is blown to the edge of a cliff while the occupants are asleep. This in itself is only a gag like another: for any other comedian of the screen it would have been enough to startle the audience by showing them the shack rocking on the dangerous brink and then, by acrobatics and trick photography, following it up with other visions equally startling. But Chaplin, given his gag, which will amuse everybody in the fashion of Harold Lloyd's clothes-line, proceeds to delight, to transport his audience in a way of which Harold Lloyd would be incapable, by developing it with steady logic and vivid imagination. Charlie and his companion wake up: the panes are frosted; they do not realize what has happened; Charlie sets out to get breakfast but whenever he moves to the side of the room where his companion is—the side hanging over the abyss—the house begins to tip. He puts it down, however, to dizziness—he has been drunk the night before—and goes determinedly about his business. But when his companion—the gigantic Mack Swain— gets up, the phenomenon is aggravated: "Do you have an illusion that the floor is tipping?—Ah, you notice it, too, do you?" They jump on it to see if it is standing solid; but as Charlie jumps on the projecting side while Swain is holding it down on the other, it does not at first appear what is wrong and it is some time before the fatal combination—both men on the projecting side—almost sends them over the· cliff. They rush back to the safe half of the room and Charlie goes to the door—which is frozen shut— to see what is outside; after a struggle, it suddenly flies open and he falls out into space, only catching himself by the sill. His companion rushes down to save him but by the time he has pulled him in, their double weight has set the cabin sliding: it is anchored only by a rope which has caught to something on the ground. Charlie and his companion, abject on their bellies, try to crawl up the terrible floor, now at an angle of sixty degrees: at first, Charlie manages to remain sensible and calm, though his companion's eyes are popping: "Just go easy! A little at a time." But no matter how little they attempt, every movement makes the cabin slip. And so on, through a long and fascinating passage of pantomime.

Conversely, however, Chaplin uses gags to help him through the deliberately ironic or pathetic situations which have become more frequent in his comedies. *The Gold Rush* has some of his most ambitious—and most successful—scenes of this sort, but he seems to be afraid of losing touch with his popular audience by venturing upon these scenes without the precaution of breaking them up with gags. Thus the love story in *The Gold Rush* is on the whole treated seriously but is occasionally enlivened by such low comedy incidents as that in which Charlie accidentally saturates his bandaged foot with kerosene and then has it set on fire by one of the ladies' dropping a match. And it happens sometimes as here and in parts of his previous film, *The Pilgrim,* that the straight situations and the gags rather jar together. Chaplin has never yet dared desert his old public—the public that first saw him in Mack Sennett, the public that still go to him for the same sort of entertainment that they find in Fox and Christie comedies. But it would appear that as Chaplin has gained in reputation with the critics and the sophisticated public, he has not advanced proportionately, nor even, I believe, held his own, in the esteem of his original popular audience. The people at large do not now distinguish any difference between his rivals and imitators, on the one hand, and Chaplin, on the other. In fact, they seem to be coming to prefer the former. For Harold Lloyd and Buster Keaton have, in a sense, carried gagging far beyond Chaplin. Their films have all the modern American smartness and speed and all the modern mechanical devices. With their motorcars, their motorcycles, their motorboats, their aeroplanes, their railroad trains, their vertiginous scaling of skyscrapers, and their cataclysmic collisions, they have progressed a long way beyond Chaplin, who, though he avowedly works in the same field and appeals to the same public, has made no attempt to keep up with them, but continues with the cheap trappings and the simple tricks of the old-fashioned custard-pie comedy. But Chaplin is even older-fashioned than the old-fashioned movies; he is as old-fashioned as Karno's *Early Birds,* as the British music hall in which he first appeared and which was at least a school of actors, not of athletes. As the comedy of the movies has come more and more to depend on machinery and stunts, Charlie Chaplin has remained incorrigibly a pantomimist.

What turn his career will take in the future is, therefore, still a curious problem. He is himself, I believe, acutely conscious of the anomaly of his position. In the moving pictures, he seems hardly likely to play an important part in the artistic development of the future. His gift is primarily the actor's, not the artist's or director's. All the photographic and plastic side of the movies, which is at present making such remarkable advances, seems not to interest Chaplin. His pictures are still nearly as raw in this respect as *Tillie's Punctured Romance* or any other primitive comedy, and it is only when the subject is already a sordid one—as in *Pay Day,* with its crowded city streetcars going home after work and its grimy suffocating city flat—that the *mise en scène* has any artistic value of its own. This was particularly evident in *A Woman of Paris,* which did not have the advantage of Chaplin as the chief actor: here, for all the intelligence he brought to directing it, Chaplin was willing to allow what was intended for an attractive, for a serious picture, to go out clothed in all the hideous flat light and the putty make-up of the comic studios. On the other hand, he seems peculiarly jealous of his independence and would, I should say, be extremely unlikely to allow himself to be directed or produced by anybody else. If he is not now carrying his old public along with him, he will unquestionably in time have to give it up, but whether he will then simply retire from the screen or try something altogether different, it seems impossible to predict. In the meantime, it may be that his present series of pictures—*The Kid, The Pilgrim,* and *The Gold Rush*—with their gags and their overtones of tragedy, their adventures half absurd, half realistic, their mythical hero, now a figure of poetry, now a type out of the funny papers, represent the height of his achievement. He could scarcely do better in any field than in the best moments of these creations. The opening of *The Gold Rush* is such a moment. Charlie appears as a lone adventurer trailing belatedly after a long line of prospectors among the frozen hills: he twirls his cane a little to keep his spirits up. As he makes his way along a narrow mountain pass, a bear comes out and follows him. Any ordinary movie comedian, given the opportunity of using a bear, would, of course, have had it chasing him about the countryside for as long as he could invent gags for it. But Charlie does not know that the bear is following him: he keeps on, twirling his cane. Presently the bear withdraws into a crevice and only then does Charlie think he hears something: he turns around, but there is nothing here. And he sets off again, still innocent of fear, into the disasters that await him.

The New Republic, September 2, 1925

Joseph Wood Krutch was Brander Matthews Professor of Dramatic Literature at Columbia University from 1943 to 1952 and drama critic of *The Nation* for thirteen years. The principal "makers" of this German film were Fritz Lang, who directed, and Thea von Harbou, who wrote it. *Siegfried* was the American title of *Siegfrieds Tod,* which was Part One of the two-part film *Die Nibelungen.*

SIEGFRIED

JOSEPH WOOD KRUTCH

Siegfried, the new German movie now playing at the Century Theater, is by no means so eccentrically original in technique as either *The Cabinet of Dr. Caligari* or even *The Last Laugh.* Yet for persons interested in those much-talked-of possibilities of the movies—which, by the way, are rapidly becoming as old a story as the youth of America—it should be equally interesting. When the effects which it obtains are superior to those in the usual American film they are so because of the exercise of general artistic intelligence rather than because of ingenious technical devices, and in consequence the methods employed are applicable to the treatment of a great variety of materials instead of being suited, as was the case with the other pictures mentioned, only to stories belonging to a particular *genre*.

In the first place, the makers of *Siegfried* have striven for that unity of style in their backgrounds which is generally so completely lacking in moving pictures. Whereas the worst writer in the world is compelled, by the limitations of his own temperament, to make his descriptions represent to some slight extent one particular view of the world, the eye of the camera, unfortunately, sees everything and reproduces everything with equal clarity and equal emphasis. The actual historic spot where a thing occurred is usually the worst place on earth to act it out for the simple reason that it is generally so cluttered up with irrelevant details and irrelevant objects as to scatter the attention completely. The photograph of it represents the scene accurately but it does not, as every work of art must, represent it as seen through a temperament; for a lens has no temperament. And when, as is usually the case, this lens is turned, in the course of a single picture, now upon, let us say, the Cathedral of Notre Dame in Paris, now upon a painted studio set, and now upon a stretch of California sand which is supposed to resemble the Sahara Desert, there is added a confusion similar to that which would be produced in a novel if the descriptive passages were written alternately by Theodore Dreiser, Anatole France, and Ethel M. Dell. This fact alone would be sufficient to explain why there are very few movies which, whatever spectacular or other effect they may contain, can be said to exist at all as works of art, since there can be no art without some unity of style. Realizing this difficulty, the directors of *Siegfried* have used only carefully selected natural scenes and used those very sparingly. For the most part they have constructed what they wanted, and they have seen to it that these constructed sets, usually simple in outline and mass, represent a consistent conception of a setting for their legend. Some of the scenes are very striking, some by no means so good, but they hang together and they have a style.

In the second place, those responsible for *Siegfried* have made some advance in skill in the general conduct of a picturized narrative. Most movies, though they may have exciting scenes of combat or chase, seem to me devoid of any cumulative dramatic power. With all their quick shifting of scene, their cut-backs, and their close-ups, they do not achieve much arrangement or emphasis; when the hero opens the door of a taxicab the action seems just as significant as that when he faces the seducer of his wife. In *Siegfried* too there are passages of this meandering, pointless narrative; but there are also many scenes, like the sequence of three or four [minutes?] showing the death of the central character, which have real power.

Finally, full advantage has been taken of the unrivaled opportunity for providing an adequate musical score. The task of adapting Wagner was by no means easy, since the film, following a different version of the legend from that upon which the operas were based, has comparatively few scenes corresponding to any treated by Wagner; but Hugo Riesenfeld has done an exceedingly clever job in fitting passages from the various parts of the *Ring* as well as from *Lohengrin* to the movie, and it is, indeed, difficult to estimate just how much of the effect which the whole produces would be left if the picture were seen in perfect silence.

Four-fifths of all the moving pictures I have seen in the last ten years have bored me profoundly, and this remark applies as well to those playing regular engagements in Broadway houses as to those ordinary pictures described by their producers as no more than mere "extra super-features." *Siegfried,* music and picture, I found highly enjoyable.

The Nation, September 16, 1925

THE BIG PARADE

ROBERT E. SHERWOOD

I could not detect a single flaw in *The Big Parade,* not one error of taste or of authenticity—and it isn't as if I didn't watch for these defects, for I have seen too many movies which pictured the war in terms of Liberty Loan propaganda.

The Big Parade is eminently right. There are no heroic Red Cross nurses in No Man's Land, no scenes wherein the doughboys dash over the top carrying the American flag.

This is due primarily to the fact that Laurence Stallings wrote the story, and was allowed to select the director and the most important members of the cast. Mr. Stallings kept his story down to the simplest possible terms, avoiding anything that might remotely resemble a complication of plot, and he displayed remarkable judgment in choosing King Vidor as director, and John Gilbert and Renée Adorée as stars.

For these reasons *The Big Parade* is a marvelous picture, a picture that can be ranked among the few genuinely great achievements of the screen. The initial credit must go to Mr. Stallings, but the final honors belong to King Vidor, who thus substantially justifies all the loud salutes that, I am happy to say, have been fired in his behalf in this department. He proves here what he indicated in *Wild Oranges:* that he is a director of intelligence and imagination.

He has made war scenes that possess infinitely more than the usual spectacular thrill; he has made war scenes that actually resemble war. When he advances a raw company of infantry through a forest which is raked by machine gun fire, he makes his soldiers look scared, sick at their stomachs, with no heart for the ghastly business that is ahead. What is infinitely more important, he causes the sleek civilian in the audience to wonder, "Why, in God's name, did they have to do that?"

He has shown an American soldier, suddenly wild with the desire to kill, trying to jab his bayonet into the neck of a dying German sniper. He has shown the look on that sniper's face, and the horrible revulsion that overcomes the American boy. I doubt that there is a single irregular soldier, volunteer or conscripted, who did not experience that same awful feeling during his career in France—who did not recognize the impulse to withdraw the bayonet and offer the dying Heinie a cigarette.

Although the war scenes are naturally predominant in *The Big Parade,* the picture itself is essentially a love story—and a supremely stirring one at that. Renée Adorée, who appears for a very short time in the early part of the story, and again at the finish, manages to impress herself so vitally on the audience that her presence, in the dim background, is never for an instant forgotten. Both she and John Gilbert are brilliantly effective.

There is great work by Tom O'Brien and Karl Dane, as two rough and blasphemous but typical crusaders of the A. E. F.; indeed, the entire army that moves forward with *The Big Parade* is recognizable and real.

It is recorded that when Laurence Stallings went to Hollywood to write *The Big Parade,* he failed to endear himself to the denizens of that strange community. In fact, he intimated in print that the great majority of them were dim-wits.

This caused all the local mental giants to pray feverishly that Stallings' maiden effort as a photodramatist would prove to be a flop. It seems that these embittered yearnings are not to be gratified.

The movies need some more men who can insult them and, at the same time, produce pictures like *The Big Parade.*

Life, December 10, 1925

Ted Shane became best-known as a humorist and editor and writer on travel.

BEN HUR

TED SHANE

It would seem that, having attained his first $505,000,000, Mynheer Marcus Loew was hard put to know what to do with the odd $5,000,000. Whereupon some bright literary office boy stepped forward and proffered the suggestion that since *Ben Hur,* the mighty creation of our Gen. Lew Wallace, had not been done more than eight times during the past twenty years, and was resting peacefully and forgotten in its grave, why not do it again? Presto, chango and e voilà! Again we have *Ben Hur,* edition No. 1359m44, revived for $5,000,000 cold cash. It opened at the George M. Cohan one night last week, before a rubbernecking movie audience, which showed taste enough, at one time, to applaud the Madonna. We recommend it to you at your own risk.

To this strictly partial observer, edition No. 1359m44, represents the expenditure of $4,999,999.95 on massive effects and the remaining $.05 on drama. It resembles a tiny boy with a huge head resting on his puny shoulders. For as a hippodromic spectacle it has hardly ever been equaled, containing all the elements going to make Amazing, Gargantuan, Stupendous, and. Mighty Biblical Pageantry. Which grandeur includes: (a) a Terrifically Impressionistic Galley manned by a thousand slaves; (b) a Thundersome sea battle between the Romans and ancient pirates; (c) a horribly effective Valley of the Lepers; (d) wondrous pictorial touches taken from the life of Christ; and of course, (e) ye good old chariot race, staged in a woolworthian, mammoth stadium with every Los Angeles man, woman, and child lying about as a super. Why, in scale, the thing almost resembles Opera.

As for the $.05 worth of drama, the fault would seem to be our General Lew Wallace's. His piece of bric-à-brac romance is nothing more than a super Rover Boys story touched up with a biblical background.

Ramon Novarro plays his best as *Ben Hur* and gives the part plenty of adolescence, if nothing else. Francis X. Bushman seemed well cast as Messala, his nose at least giving him that Roman Look which a program note asserted was sought after in casting for types. Summarily, after watching this Roman Jewish Holiday, should the estimable M. Loew ever again have $5,000,000 to chuck away, why not call a conference and be a bit more careful as to just where to chuck it?

The New Yorker, January 9, 1926

BEN HUR

ROBERT E. SHERWOOD

In casting about for adjectives with which to describe the long-awaited movie version of *Ben Hur,* I find myself limited to that section of the thesaurus which offers synonyms of "big."

Colossal—tremendous—gargantuan—and just the least bit overwhelming; that is a fairly adequate summary of *Ben Hur.* Most of the time, this bigness makes for extreme impressiveness and visual thrill. At intervals it makes for confusion and fatigue.

Ben Hur, as General Lew Wallace imagined and wrote it, was a comparatively simple story of the Christ. When the novel was dramatized it became essentially a spectacle; now, on the screen, it is about one million times more of one—and the resultant orgy of huge sets, seething mobs, and camera effects contains little of the spirit of the original story.

In all other respects, however, *Ben Hur* comes up to and surpasses the prevalent expectations. Fred Niblo, it seems to me, has done a fine job with the direction. Whenever the main characters are about to be lost in the shuffle, Mr. Niblo drags them forth and returns them to the center of the screen, just to remind the audience that there *is* a plot, after all.

Mr. Niblo has not been quite so wise in his selection of players. Ramon Novarro as Ben Hur, Claire MacDowell as his mother, and Nigel de Brulier as Simonides—these three are above reproach; but the rest of the cast is insufficient, particularly Francis X. Bushman, who appears from the past to remind us that the motion picture has made great progress.

There are many beautiful and exciting scenes in *Ben Hur:* the Nativity, photographed in color, with Betty Bronson at her loveliest as the Madonna; the frightful ordeal of the galleys; a rousing naval battle with a whole fleet of triremes in action; the Sermon on the Mount.

There is also, it need hardly be added, a chariot race, which is undoubtedly the most terrific chariot race in history. Ben Hur and Messala have been arguing it out in the Circus Maximus for a matter of forty-five years now, and Messala has been beaten every time; but for all that, the old thrill is still there. When Ben Hur forces his rival to bite the dust, the cheers are frenzied.

For some strange reason, there is always the vague fear in the heart of every spectator that Messala may win. The fact that the villain's batting average, to date, is exactly .000 has no effect on his big-league standing.

Life, January 21, 1926

Richard Watts, Jr., was the film critic of the *New York Herald Tribune* from 1924 to 1936. The reason for including this particular review is in the last paragraph.

As we have seen, European films had been impressing the United States mightily through the twenties. So Hollywood went shopping for European talent, mostly German but also a few artists from Sweden, including the director Mauritz Stiller.

Stiller would not come to Hollywood without his leading lady, Greta Garbo, so, as a concession to him, she was also given a contract. Stiller's American career was not happy. He never directed a film with Garbo, although he started one; he directed three pictures with Pola Negri instead, returned to Sweden in 1927, and died soon afterward.[25] Garbo remained.

THE TORRENT

RICHARD WATTS, JR.

The "movies" continue to give away the eminent Senor Vincente Blasco Ibanez. In *Mare Nostrum* they exposed him as a Latin E. Phillips Oppenheim, and now in *The Torrent,* or as it is billed for some esoteric commercial reason *Ibanez's Torrent,* he is revealed as not above employing for his own ends the lovers separated by a stern parent and the prima donna who sings and smiles while her heart is breaking.

It should not be thought, however, that *The Torrent* is not an interesting motion picture. Pictorially it is lavish, tasteful, and always beautiful. Dramatically it is effective and succeeds in capturing to a considerable degree a half-tearful romantic spirit that is appealing. The story, it might be advisable to point out, is of a young singer whose sweetheart gives her up at the demand of his mother. Twice the lovers are about to be united, but both times the mother's influence comes between them. At the end the boy has grown into a rich, ugly, dissatisfied old man and the girl is a famous prima donna, beautiful, loved, envied, but equally unhappy.

It is an encouraging sign of the times in the cinema that an occasional ending of the type referred to as "unhappy" is beginning to creep in. *The Torrent* moves courageously enough to a close that keeps the romantic lovers separated. For this the picture, I think, deserves commendation. It is worth your while, too, for its physical beauty, its acting and its creation of an affecting sentimental mood. But it is so good that it seems all the more unfortunate that the film resolutely refuses to reach greater heights. The lovers' separations are often too patently for the purpose of carrying on the story. The subtitles are too frequently of the type of that one in which the hero asks his mother, "Is honorable love a crime?"

There is the scene of the torrent, too, which is admirably staged, but has little to do with the story. I had thought that it was the director's intent to make the torrent have some symbolic relation to his heroine, but apparently it was intended merely for spectacular effect.

In the leading role Greta Garbo, Swedish screen star, makes her American debut. She seems an excellent and attractive actress, with a surprising propensity for looking like Carol Dempster, Norma Talmadge, Zasu Pitts, and Gloria Swanson in turn. That does not mean that she lacks a manner of her own, however. Ricardo Cortez does well as the rather spineless hero.

The New York Herald Tribune, February 22, 1926

Quinn Martin wrote film criticism for *The New York World* and subsequently was a member of the Paramount editorial board.

THE BLACK PIRATE

QUINN MARTIN

While it is true that Douglas Fairbanks has ever associated himself in the cinema with story subjects and mechanical treatment designed to attract the interest of the very young as well as that of the more mature, it also is a fact that he has not neglected at any period in his career to contribute a zealous effort toward the esthetic betterment of his profession. It was, indeed, this salubriously energetic fellow who brought to the films their first compelling proof that individual movement—furious, relentless, lightning-like movement—could be photographed into the action of a pictured play and made to lend dramatic force to the whole. It was he who introduced pure fantasy to the screen, really. Until *The Thief of Bagdad* came into existence some three or four years ago, no one had ventured to project dream stuff upon the silver sheet for the entire running time of a feature-length film.

And now, in *The Black Pirate,* a cinema entirely in colors, we find the first example, so far as I know, of a so-called super-film pictured throughout in tints and hues, which is beyond question a sure, sound success.

Ranging over the last ten years there have been numerous motion pictures presented, most of the scenes of which have been either retouched with colors or so treated in the laboratories as to appear to have been painted. Not one of these, with the lone exception of a brief subject called *Marionettes,* starring Miss Hope Hampton, has seemed to me to even so much as suggest "naturalness," which, I am told, is in fact the end in view. Miss Hampton's short charmer had, no doubt, a most careful and skillful laboratory attention paid to it, and thus it surpassed its longer brothers and sisters. All these colored photoplays of which I speak were treated with vivid, brilliant, sometimes fairly blinding hues. Not only were the colors themselves far from being properly toned for naturalness; they actually could not be made to remain in their proper places. Literally, some perfectly good actor's red necktie might any moment leap downward and rest for the fraction of a minute upon the third button of his waiscoat. At times the glare and burn of the colors clashed with the eye. It simply wasn't the thing.

Mr. Fairbanks has avoided all this by first choosing a subject adaptable to his scheme, then giving orders to everyone concerned that while the entire picture was to be turned out in color, not one blazing tint was to be stamped upon it. All were to be subdued—browns, grays, unobtrusive reds. So that while the spectator fails to find any carnival hues shooting across the canvas where this cinema is shown, still the deep, rich brown of his pirate ships is there; the faded, gray and brown clothing of the players are there; the weak, green waters of the sea are there.

It is here, I think, that the star has added evidence of his own sincere regard for the development of the moving picture. It would have been a matter of no great extra expenditure of time and money for him to have plunged headlong into a picture play wrapping itself in all the vividness and variety of the rainbow's colors, depending largely upon the novelty of the object to reward him for his pains. Instead, he has taken the first step with considerable modesty. It would not be at all surprising, now that he recognizes the soundness of his theory, to see him come through with another film drama on which a wider range and a more lavish display of color is devoted.

For my own part, it is a little difficult as yet to decide as to whether the films really ought to cherish the thought of eventual colorization for all subjects. It seems to me there is room for both the black and white and the varicolored dramas. It would appear there ought really to be no greater call for universality in screen composition than in, say, canvas or drawing board composition. We admire the pen and crayon none the less for the existence of oil paint and watercolor. To be sure, there can be no question as to pictorial dimensional value as between the color and the plain cinema. In *The Black Pirate,* for example, it is found that a very definite sense of depth, rotundity, and spacing is afforded—qualities quite noticeably lacking in all but the most expertly lighted of the black and white film pictures.

I am well aware that there have been those who assert that even so delicately tinted a motion picture as is this latest one affects their eyes and positively gives them pain. For these unfortunate souls I most urgently recommend early and conscientious visits to the offices of the nearest oculists. For there can be little doubt that practically all light reflection has been reduced to a minimum. Furthermore, whatever may remain in our present-day cinema of that relic of the good old age of *The Great Train Robbery* and *Fire Engines on the Way to the Fire*—the "flicker"— has been done away with entirely by the application of the natural tints. It is going to be pretty hard for me to concede any optical hazard in the color film.

Mr. Fairbanks, seated on the back of a chair in the theater where his picture later was to be given its première, talked with me at length of his venture and his hope for the ultimate employment of natural shadings. He has no predetermined or even deep-seated theories as to what color may or may not do to (or for) the cinema. He is inclined to smile faintly over the problem. There is in his attitude an almost childlike enthusiasm in his experimentation.

His hand, brown as is his face from his almost perpetual outdoor existence beneath the warm sun of his Beverly Hills and his Hollywood, sweeps in a wide gesture toward the white sheet being set in place on the stage before us. He says, in his high-pitched, boyish voice:

"Really, I don't know what it's all about; none of us does. That's why it is all so confoundedly interesting."

But these retiring words are being spoken by a master in his own field. At the moment I can think of no one in the cinema more earnestly searching after technique and form or more honorably conducting himself for the benefit of his craft and his fellows.

The Arts, April 1926

Evelyn Gerstein was the theater and film critic of *The Boston Herald,* then the New York film correspondent of *The Boston Evening Transcript* and the film editor of the *Theatre Guild Magazine.*[26] She also contributed reviews and articles to *The Nation* and *The New Republic.*

Lothar Mendes was a German-born director who worked in

Hollywood, in Great Britain (*The Man Who Could Work Miracles*), then in Hollywood again.

VARIETY

EVELYN GERSTEIN

The first of the German invaders of the cinema was Lubitsch, then came von Stroheim; now there are Murnau, Mendes, and Dupont whose *Variety* is his first film to be shown in this country. A dark, stinging tale of life in variety, utterly devoid of the pale puerilities, the sterile conventions, that cabin and confine the cinema, it has yet captured that ephemeral thing —the favor of the populace. Dupont, like von Stroheim, is a realist, ruthless, passionate, Rabelaisian. At some time or other all of this German band have been so. Lubitsch was when he directed in Europe, in *Gypsy Blood, One Arabian Night, Passion;* there was a vitality of a different sort, a light Viennese laughter in *The Marriage Circle*. But he lost something of it between Berlin and Hollywood. And it is this earthiness, this madness that reaches to ecstasy, this foot-in-the-soil intensity that has given even the least of these German films a dynamism that the watered romances of Hollywood have never approached.

Variety is not so exquisitely chiseled or so lyrical as *The Last Laugh*. Its story is far more commonplace, a melodramatic tale of a crime of passion among vaudevillians. Drama of a different genre, sensual, voluptuous, beautiful in its nakedness as Dupont has done it; a tragedy rich with a low, lusty laughter. It moves rhythmically, relentlessly toward its end, a perfectly coördinated work of art, each detail pertinent, illuminating, carved in the round. There is no gesture that is unconsidered, no planting of the camera that is not arresting and eloquent. Almost titleless, *Variety* is pure cinema, drama wholly dependent on pantomime; on the swift ordering of moving masses, the weird, shunting play of light and shadow, all of that restless, fantastic world of mechanistic device still so little explored.

Objects tearing through space; intangible, phantom shapes; swarming, searing eyes of the audience; chattering hands; white pinpoints of light that torture "Boss" Huller as his little world collapses about him; chains and machines that leap and revolve with a terrible intensity, destroying, whipping life into a timeless muddle—all this touches on moods too fragile for words, too tenuous to imprison, distorted creations of the unconscious mind. Always, there is that endless motion, charging and rebounding, singing through space, devouring. Faces, machines, inanimate objects even, are alive, plastic, lyrical with a strange animate silence. This is Picasso technique translated to a moving screen, which as yet only Murnau and Dupont, and a few of the experimentalists (Dudley Murphy, Fernand Léger) have carried so far. *The Last Laugh* used it, too, yet that evolved into a cameo-like melody. But *Variety* is crude, barbaric, pulsing, touched with wildness, like the music of Stravinsky, at times, although it is not so self-conscious.

Unlike *The Last Laugh, Variety* was not written directly for the screen. It is an adaptation of a novel by Felix Holländer, worked into a deft, malleable continuity. The scene is Hamburg, a circus on the waterfront, a dejected caricature of a circus whose frequenters are sad creatures that once were men. Disheveled sluts, still trading their wasted bodies, angle their arms and legs while the audience applauds in beery obscenity. In command is "Boss" Huller, powerful and gentle, a sensualist, the creature of his emotions. His wife, once a trapezist, now sullen and heavy-heeled, thumps the piano. A man with restless eyes and a leery smile, just off the ship, brings a girl to Huller, Berthe-Marie, a young rounded girl who dances. The voluptuous white-armed dancer from the Barbadoes, hips bending sinuously, maddens the halfnaked men into a delirium. "Boss" can stand no more; the curtain is rung down; catcalls hurtle up from the pit; he decides to return to the trapeze with the dancer. In Berlin, "Boss," with his new partner, a petulant, untamed creature, an exquisite voluptuary, is in a circus near the Winter Garden. Then, the Winter Garden and "the three Artinellis" (Artinelli, Huller, Berthe-Marie), trapezists pursued by blinding lights and distorted perspectives high above the audience where they saw the air with their leaping bodies, unprotected even by a net below. (This is one of the most amazing stunts that trick photography has as yet manipulated.) Artinelli seduces Berthe-Marie, and "Boss," bull-necked and irresistible, knifes him in the dismal little room of the theatrical boarding house that was the setting of the seduction; then he gives himself over to the police. Then follow ten years in prison. All that has gone before is done on the screen as a flashback, as the story of Prisoner Number Twenty-eight whose face is not revealed until the end, when he is at last released at the plea of his deserted wife. Freedom, and a bent, shuffling derelict passes through the gates.

In and around this relentless tale Dupont has worked his satire, a satire candescent and pitiless, scorching audience and performers alike. Chinese jugglers, trundling grimacing clowns, a serpentine dancer, a nude girl reflected on a dozen opera glass lenses, fat-chinned women, beery men with protuberant bellies, sycophants, fatuous fools . . . louts . . . the camera shrieks it . . . have been limned with the power and ferocity of a Daumier. And with what rich blacks Freund, cameraman also of *The Last Laugh,* has lighted it, blacks that even Renoir would have envied.

In "Boss" Huller, another emotional instrument of fate, Emil Jannings, for the first time acting without make up, has once again created a man. There is more drama, more tragic force, more joyous abandon in his broad, powerful back than in the faces of most actors. An actor with an imagination and restraint that transmutes each thing that he touches into something alive and rounded; a man with an unerring dramatic instinct, a leaping sense of humor, he is without an equal, whether it is in the playing of a decadent Louis, an old doorman with querulous eyes, or the passion-ridden bouncer of a circus. Without him it is difficult to imagine *Variety*. Miss Lya de Putti, by now well intrenched in the American movie colony, is an interesting and exotic beauty who ranges inordinately from the luxuriantly oriental, a woman out of Conrad, even to a plain-faced and callous, but always animated, screen actress. She plays with a temper and abandon that none but a European actress ever has, an emotional intensity that seems always destined to be lost with importation to our shores. Warwick Ward, the hollow-cheeked villain of the piece, will doubtless be made still another of the Byronic permanents of Hollywood as soon as the deliberating movie makers can arrange it.

Here, in *Variety,* the cinema has at last depicted sex without self-consciousness and adolescent pruderies. It is the motif of the piece, riddling, overpowering, the basic theme of this tragedy of the backwashes of show business; a tragedy that but for the grace of God and Herr Dupont might have passed into another shoddy anecdote of the sort that delights the readers of the journals for "people who think." But through the sardonic and unflinching lens of Dupont and Freund it has been charged with something of genius, warmed with a tormented, vital beauty having nothing at all to do with the feeble, chastened myths that make the "movies."

It is said that when *Variety* descends upon the dark corners of this country, especially the free and censored states of Massachusetts, Ohio, and Pennsylvania, the entire Hamburg episode will be dropped. The piece will open with Berlin and the circus where "Boss" Huller and Berthe-Marie, discreetly married, are paired performers. But no one expects intelligence or the toleration of art in dark places. It would be incongruous to countenance *Variety* in hamlets where babies are admitted as naturals only for week-day showings, and even travelogues are stripped of their bathing sequences on Sunday. The great Berlin-to-Hollywood emigration grows more staggering day by day. But, in the face of it, it is wiser to forget what happens to directors in that fleshly paradise by the western sea where studio politics is the only intellectual diversion, and the director is merely an unhappy soul lost among the magnates in a Minotaur's cave.

The New Republic, July 28, 1926

Polikushka was directed by Alexander Sanin. *Taras Bulba* is presumably the film known in the USSR as *Taras Shevchenko,* directed by Pyotr Chardynin. The last line of the review is from Nietzsche's *Thus Spake Zarathustra.*

POTEMKIN

EVELYN GERSTEIN

Even in its disordered decade or two the cinema has known its cycles. Each country, in turn, has left an impression upon it, although not always in full tone. And now, even as the Germans are reaching their apogee in camera virtuosity and whimsical machine age fantasias, the Russians have given birth to *Potemkin*—a film which, because of the magnificent ugliness of some of its realism, as well as the blatancy of its Soviet trademark, has been in grave danger of coming permanently under the censor's ban, as far as America is concerned.

Potemkin has already been shipped away from the shores of England and the borders of Germany. Even their shameless dictators of sorts have shivered at the fearless tread of this intoxicated witch child of the Soviet. In its galumphing Tartar rhythm they saw nothing but the seeds of revolt. For *Potemkin* has been limned with vitriol. It has no story; it is simply the pictured narrative of the mutiny on the cruiser *Potemkin* during the last days of the Russo-Japanese war, drawn from the official log and the impressions of eye-witnesses. But it is revolution! Not the anæmic and picaresque dumb show patented in Hollywood, but a black, cosmic flurry.

There are no stars, no actors, even; only the crew, the ship, and the sea, the lonely harbor of Odessa with its restless, charged multitudes pouring over the breakwater at the first whispers of revolt. It seems impossible that this is the creation of a director, cameramen, and extras. There is something too tenuous and elemental to have been manufactured. It is like some grotesque record of a gargantuan news photographer with a genius for timing and composition. The Russians have always had this penchant for realism, especially in their drama. It illumined even those early dark and naïve little "movies" that the Muscovites produced a few years ago, *Polikushka, Taras Bulba,* and the rest. But *Potemkin* has something that they barely gave promise of. There is the same instinctive feeling for drama, but it has ripened. Here is a cinema masterpiece, architectonic, self-conscious, as all art must be. It has movement, tempo, rhythm, compositional beauty. Technically superb, it has no hollow virtuosity. *Potemkin* and its young director, Eisenstein, are cinema wise.

Potemkin, outside of Russia, would be only a vodka dream. Even in that proud and often nebulous Berlin from which all good Ufa films come, there is no such directorial freedom. The Germans are more sophisticated in their use of the camera, in the management of lights, and in sheer mechanistic device. *Potemkin* is often badly lighted; this may be due to the state of the present print, however. But Eisenstein has a musician's feeling for tempo; his rhythms throughout are amazing, flexible, trenchant, cumulative. It is impossible to imagine the terrific power there is in the slow, steady rise of the guns, or the crazy speeding of the baby carriage down those hundreds of steps, into infinity.

The *Potemkin* is at sea. There is mutiny in the air; sullen, emaciated faces. An officer insults a young sailor. Foul meat is thrown to the men. The air grows choking. A weasel of a man, bearded, monocled, the ship's doctor, is told to examine the meat the men refuse. Through his glass he sees worms. He denies them. Men begin to gather on a lower deck. They slip away as an officer approaches. Everything as usual, engines pounding evenly, as usual. But there is mutiny in the air. Everyone on deck. Inspection, drill. Those who refuse to eat the meat are lined up. The Admiral, stout, peremptory, with flowing whiskers, measures his men. He commands them to throw a sailcloth over the mutinying group. They bind them to the rail. "Shoot!"

The mutiny is under way. No one shoots. Then all is confusion, scrambling through the hatches, the crew against the officers, man against man. From every angle the camera glances down at them, recording revolt. Man, mere man, starved, brutal, frightened, clamorous, triumphant, whipped to madness—man fighting for his life. The sailcloth, like a live thing, curls against the rail. The doctor is tossed into the sea; only his glass, caught in the ropes, remains swinging. Then the crew's leader, their first, is killed. The ship is theirs, but their spokesman is gone. They place him in a barge which moves silently, guarded by its rows of uncovered men, into the harbor of Odessa. It is like the funeral of an ancient king of the sea, a legendary ruler borne out on his pyre.

They come down from the city, slowly at first. The dead sailor is laid out under a canopy at the end of the breakwater. An old woman shriveled, weeping, lights the candles on each side of him. The whisper of their first casualty. Young students, blazing-eyed, parliamentary, a woman with a child, women with parasols, women bareheaded in shawls, a few scoffers who are beaten into respect; from all corners of the city, over the bridge, under the bridge, storming the long breakwater, they come. It is like some prehistoric snake, this winding stream of human beings, as impossible to check as the rivers that rush to the sea. The city is in revolt. Food for the crew. . . .

Hundreds of little boats rush out of the harbor, gallantly, as closely pressed as the wild ducks edging south in the fall. Crates of live chickens; a pig gently carried by a woman; food, food, food! And then as those on shore wave their support, there is a change. A cripple moves suddenly. The armed guard press slowly, pitilessly, down the broad stone steps, abreast. Only terror now. A woman rushes down the steps with her child. She misses him. He has been shot down. She runs with the boy in her arms, chattering, pleading, into the fire of the guard. A beautiful young mother in a mantilla, wheeling a baby carriage, falls on the stones. Down, down, gathering speed in its flight, whistles the carriage.

The ship again. The officers have reached the rest of the fleet to warn them of the mutiny. The fleet is bearing down on the *Potemkin*. "All against one. One against all." Everything asleep on the *Potemkin*. Suddenly the news reaches them. Engines pounding, the ship moves forward at full speed. The others come nearer, nearer. The camera slips from one ship to the other, from the startled furrows made by their prows to the thumping of the *Potemkin*'s engines, the furious energy on board as everyone rouses for the fight. Slowly, with a diabolic slowness, the big guns are lifted, higher, higher, till they meet the firing range. "Shall it be a broadside or . . .?" The others flanked by smoke screens bear down on the *Potemkin*. . . .Everything is ready, guns lifted, lambent. . . . And then the men on the other ships wave their sympathy. The revolt has spread. The *Potemkin* is saved.

It is only at this point that the film denies history and suggests propaganda. The revolt was in fact a temporarily successful one, but the mutineers were not joined by their fellows. Instead, the *Potemkin* escaped through the bombarding lines and was interned.

Now that the Russians have captured the cinema there is no end to what they may do. *Potemkin,* evolved under economic duress, probably with wretched studio facilities, still towers above all other "movies." Its purpose and method are so utterly different from those of the Germans that comparison is futile. It stands alone, a solitary cinema masterpiece. It makes no compromises; it is rid of childish romancing. One must be of a stout heart to survive it. These Russians will go far in the films. They have no censorship; a country that is still semibarbaric, untouched by the decadence that has swept over western Europe, its strength untried, an artistic conscience. A film such as this could never have come from a country that is in its last stages of sophistication. "One must have chaos in one to give birth to a dancing star."

The New Republic, October 20, 1926

Ernestine Evans had been a critic and a reporter and a correspondent in Russia, at the time of the revolution, for *The New York Herald Tribune* and *The Nation.* At the time of this writing she was on the staff of the *Christian Science Monitor.*

The forthcoming Eisenstein film mentioned below was *The General Line.* The offer from United Artists never materialized, and Eisenstein did not reach the United States until four years later.

Will Hays was the first president of the Motion Picture Producers and Distributors Association.

POTEMKIN

ERNESTINE EVANS

The Film Arts Guild and the Russian organization, Sovkino, have given a private showing of the Russian film, *Armored Cruiser, Prince Potemkin,* to three hundred invited guests. The picture is for sale in America. Max Reinhardt and Douglas Fairbanks unite in saying that it is great art, the best motion picture either has ever seen. Already it has had, as well, a tremendous commercial success in Germany despite defeats in certain German cities by political censorship. Will Hays, who seems never to forget that the average mental age of the American public is fourteen years, and is so very careful lest the movies help mature us, was not present on Tuesday. There is no final word therefore as to whether the picture is to become a legend among the cognoscenti, or be the sensation of the movies this year.

In making the picture Director Eisenstein used members of the Moscow Art Theater and hundreds of nonprofessional actors from the Proletcult (Organization for Proletarian Culture). The story, based on the official report in the Admiralty files of the Czar, and on the recollections of eyewitnesses and participants, describes the revolt of the sailors of the armored cruiser *Potemkin* of the Black Sea fleet outside the harbor of Odessa during the 1905 Revolution, the demonstrations of the common people at the tent-bier of the sailor who led it, the attack on the mourners and revolutionists by the Cossacks, and finally the escape of the cruiser *Potemkin* with the connivance of comrades on the other cruisers of the fleet to the Rumanian port of Constanza. Here is epic material, full of pity, terror, and truth.

Someone muttered in the audience, "This is only newsreel." There could be no higher praise for the reality conveyed. So it was, indicating at last in which direction the art of the movies is to lie, if the screen is to be something more than a vehicle for exploiting the personalities of stars and a distractor of the public gaze from public and private conflicts. There was no star in the picture, unless perhaps the cruiser itself, or the sailors, or the masses of Odessa. Certainly not the sailor who rose to give command and who died in the fighting. The eyes of the audience beheld, sensed, understood all that happened on those significant three days. Captions were few and simple, muted down, whispered directions to those who have forgotten history. The continuity halts nowhere for explanations. The eye but followed as the ear might hearken to a tune. The sailors, at work, asleep in hammocks in sultry and cramped quarters, waking, going to their decks and engines, to roll call, grumbling about the rotted meat. The doctor, looking at the meat through his glasses. Nests of wriggling maggots. The doctor says the meat is good, to wash it off in salted water. The sailors know that in the prison camps of Japan their comrades are better fed. The commander of the cruiser will have none of grumbling. It smacks of mutiny. He commands the firing squad. . . . Sailcloth is thrown over the malcontents. "Fire!" "Fire!!" . . . Fire!!!" . . . But comrade will not fire upon comrade, and the revolt has come. Words convey but feebly the tremendous impression of being everywhere at once which the all-seeing camera was able to give.

This was more than newsreel. The camera, like some holy invisible, watched and recorded. Of all this population that Director Eisenstein commanded, not one lingered before the camera. Life was the thing—masses of men, sweating at the furnaces, at mess, fighting; faces, arms, legs, engines, thermometers, the big guns with nostrils scenting danger, the restless flow of the common people of Odessa across the narrow file of the breakwater to where the dead sailor lay in common state; the faces of the mourners, the student and revolutionist exhorters; the crowd in panic— things like these have never been seen so well in life or theater before. Nor has machinery, monster and servant in the modern world, been so emotionally comprehended, or the relations between those who physically manipulate it and those who own it been so dramatized.

The audience was divided between those who were nervous and puzzled by the social conflict which was the theme of the film, and those who were deeply moved not only by the revolutionary theme but by the revolution in movie technique bringing in its wake a vision of the new developments in the one art the machine age can call its own. Whether the public sees this picture or not, it will before long experience the influence of the new technique, the use of masses, the feeling for motion and machinery, a new swiftness and naturalness. Director Eisenstein, when he has finished the picture he is now making in Moscow, a film concerned with cattle-breeding and cream separators, I am told, will spend six months in Hollywood. He has been granted leave of absence by the Soviet Government to direct one picture for United Artists.

The Nation, September 15, 1926

Even Keaton's admirers could falter; Sherwood was not alone in the views expressed below. In an international poll of critics in 1972, *The General* was voted one of the ten best films of all time. *Hands Up* is deservedly forgotten.

THE GENERAL

ROBERT E. SHERWOOD

Buster Keaton shows signs of vaulting ambition in *The General;* he appears to be attempting to enter the "epic" class. That he fails to get across is due to the scantiness of his material as compared with the length of his films; he has also displayed woefully bad judgment in deciding just where and when to stop.

In the latter connection, some one should have told Buster that it is difficult to derive laughter from the sight of men being killed in battle. Many of his gags at the end of the picture are in such gruesomely bad taste that the sympathetic spectator is inclined to look the other way.

The General has some grand scenes. Two aged locomotives chase each other through the heart of the Civil War zone, and the ingenuity displayed by Buster Keaton in keeping these possibly tedious chases alive is little short of incredible.

In spite of its pretentious proportions, *The General* is not nearly so good as Raymond Griffith's Civil War comedy, *Hands Up.*

Life, February 24, 1927

Besides extensive work as theater and film critic on New York newspapers, Frank Vreeland wrote and directed film documentaries, novelized many film scripts, was a member of the Paramount editors board for six years, and wrote *Foremost Films of 1938.*

METROPOLIS

FRANK VREELAND

On Saturday night, after the first view of *Metropolis,* I picked myself up out of my seat at the Rialto feeling like a limp rag, or a withered flower or a wilted critic. I had the persuasion that, emotionally, I had been hung up by the thumbs through this stupendous German picture. Likewise, I had the sensation that this sardonic Ufa dissection of our mechanical age, while monumentally sign-posting the perilous way that material civilization is going, had also poured most of the gigantic machinery which it holds right into my lap. So towering and overwhelming and unique is this imported Wellsian picture, with which Famous Players–Lasky expect to stop New York in its tracks for an indefinite space at the Rialto. It's an eye crasher.

Most of all did I have the impression that here at last the movies had truly and immemorially justified themselves, with a smashing, reverberant idea that might have swept, all glowing and palpitating, out of the boldest pages of H. G. Wells. Spacious and searching, with its often blazing revelation of the blight of efficiency without a soul, it is an idea that crunches upon the consciousness, in spite of having been spouted before by college debaters and others.

At length the screen, through the directorial genius of Fritz Lang, has pulled itself by its bootstraps out of the present morass of sexy stupidities, out of its ceaseless hackneyed groveling before the inanities of Mme. Elinor Glyn's *It.* Here in *Metropolis* is an imaginative but belated recognition that life can sometimes contain more than necking parties de luxe.

With splendid photography, with majestic, invincible spectacles, with trenchant acting by Brigitte Helm, Alfred Abel, and Gustav Froelich, Lang proclaims thunderously that the silver sheet can be the magnificent parade ground for living ideas far more than the constricted speaking theater. It can unfold in *Metropolis* a vivid panorama interpreting the world today that makes the frantic efforts of the modern expressionistic school of playwrights seem like mildewed feeble drivel.

This bizarre film may bewilder some at first, because it is frankly a story of the future, without any modern trick framework to make the usual puerile connection with the average subway straphanger. Its main drift is that the standardizing efficiency of our age, stressing material advancement rather than spiritual progress, carries the seeds of its own destruction in its metallic bosom. To impress this graphically *Metropolis* visions a mammoth city of a later century, teeming with mechanical marvels and owned by one callous, superefficient master—who bears in the person of his German impersonator a haunting suggestion of Henry Ford.

Bloodless pinnacle of a soulless age, he has reduced life to a deadly uniformity for his myriads of grubbing workers, who exist like moles underground while on the upper crust the few elect persons feast at the flesh pots rabidly. Masterman's one soft spot is his affection for his son, who falls in love with a spiritual girl of the working classes, beloved by the sweating, dreary laborers as she tries to put a god into their machine. Because she inspires the awakened son to espouse the common cause and turn hired hand, and because the underdogs are muttering, ominously, Masterman has her hidden away, while her image is reproduced by an inventor in a mischievous, heartless mechanical girl, responsive to Masterman's bidding and cowing the throngs who worship her.

But this Frankenstein monster is true to her breed and works evil for her creators. Under her baneful exhortation rebellion flames up and the workmen nearly smash Metropolis. The picture, however, is not revolutionary at bottom, for it winds up with Capital and Labor shaking hands. Also, it has a happy ending for the two lovers, though a tragic one was quite in order. But the box office is one of the symbols of modern efficiency which even this picture can't ignore.

Those who recall Wells's early novel, *When the Sleeper Wakes,* and are conversant with his "Story of the Days to Come" in the volume called *Tales of Space and Time,* will find them here translated into marvelous photography in a world of beings living in a state of suspended animation. The overalled, numbed workers, the swart underground habitations—all are from Wells. Wellsian books have always been popular in Germany, and there can be no doubt that they spurred Lang to dream this powerful picture into existence. Possibly also, he was influenced by a now forgotten romance of Atlantis, *The Scarlet Empire,* written twenty years ago by Richard Parry and flooding the lost continent to its destruction, just as the maddened workmen here flood their own subterranean city, forgetting their deserted children and leaving them to be heroically and damply rescued by Masterman's son.

The very scenes are like Wells illustrations, dazzling and far-flung and a little sinister, with soaring pyramids of skyscrapers to make the most advanced architect a little dizzy. In refulgent cliffs, they hang above breathless canyons wherein meander hordes of weird motors, aerial interlacing runways, and flying bridges, where express trains streak, while through them busy airplanes loop and dart like dragonflies. Below these vibrate colossal machines, so Brobdignagian that the screen is all too small and seems to bulge with them. One has the feeling that these devouring industrial dinosaurs, wreathed in cruel gusts of steam like Moloch, grind out collarbuttons or something equally puny.

All these scenes are studio sets, sometimes in miniature, and yet one never tires of them, so marvelous and massive and meaty are they. Camera angles assert themselves, yet here they are, oddly enough, justifiable. For they assist the drama, especially in those vistas where the son, Eric Masterman, tears about like a tiny atom adrift in a chaotic world to save his sweetheart from the Lon Chaney inventor.

The New York Telegram, March 7, 1927

Channing Pollock, who wrote the *Metropolis* subtitles, was a prolific playwright in the first third of the century, author of *The Fool, Mr. Moneypenny,* and *Many Mansions.*

R. U. R., a Czech play by Karel Capek, was produced in New York in 1923. The initials stand for Rossum's Universal Robots; the play is the source of the word "robot."

METROPOLIS

EVELYN GERSTEIN

Hollywood lives for money and sex. It borrows or buys its art. It is the Germans who are the perpetual adventurers in the cinema. They gave the camera its stripling mobility, its restless imagination. They played with lights in the studio and achieved innumerable subtleties in the use of black and white as a medium. Even in their scientific miniatures they have worked with a virtuoso camera. And it was the Germans who injected fantasy into the cinema.

Metropolis, for all its thesis and its subtitular dialectic compounded for American comprehension by the enlightened Channing Pollock, is much more akin to the romantic vagaries of *Siegfried* than to the realities of *The Last Laugh.* For Fritz Lang, who directed both *Siegfried* and *Metropolis,* is not a cinema radical. Like Murnau in *Faust* he thinks in terms of sheer visual beauty, composition, and group rhythms rather than of dynamics. He is still of the theater of Reinhardt in the fluency of his groups and the rhythmic progression of his pageant. Although Karl Freund, the cameraman for *The Last Laugh* and *Variety,* has worked here in the same capacity, *Metropolis* lacks cinematic subtlety. It is only in the shots of machinery in motion and in the surge of the revolutionists that it is dynamic. The camera is too often immobile, the technique that of the stylized theater.

Yet here for the first time the chill mechanized world of the future, which only barely revealed itself in *R. U. R.,* has been given reality. Here is the city, that tormented circus of buildings which touch the sky, of tunnels that disrupt the places under the earth. Through the air man has hurled his obstructions, his bridges and traffic ways. Yet only the machines seem real; gigantic purring gods grinding down life. Machines, machines, machines, sliding through the earth, challenging the cosmos, pounding out human resistance as they set the awful tempo of life.

There is no loveliness here, except in the garden of the rich, high above the levels of the city, where space and light are not mortified for efficiency. Below the surface of the earth the workers and their children crawl through a timed eternity, strapped to the dynamos like so many numbered robots. There is no rest, no beauty, no life below the gardens of the higher levels. Man is inanimate. Life is metronomic. It is only the machines that are alive. The machines and the careless children of "Brains."

As Lang has directed it, *Metropolis* is more stylized fantasy than realism. Even in the torrentous revolt of the workers as they pour through the machine-rooms, alive, demoniacal, there is an air of unreality. This is not revolution as the Russians stage it. It has neither taste nor smell. Yet it is magnificent. Even the most careless groupings are beautifully composed. Lang is too much the artist to deny the imagination.

R. U. R. was a satire, but *Metropolis* is utterly devoid of humor. Thea von Harbou, its author, wrote it originally as a novel and then adapted it to the screen. Only her concept of Metropolis itself is intellectual. The rest is sentimental symbolism. There is no individualization within the type. Her persons are puppets. There is the Capitalist, his Son, Mary the spiritual leader of the workers, et al. The Son is the eternal mediator who, with the help of the woman Mary, although only after a revolution intervenes, brings "brains" and "brawn" together for the final fade-out.

Perhaps it is because of its original form that *Metropolis* lacks concision. One of the most interesting episodes of the entire film is that in which the inventor transmits the shape and likeness of Mary to the woman of his creation by encircling bands of electricity, yet it is only partially developed. The robotess, or creature of human invention, breeds revolution and is stoned by the mob, but the formula which gave her life is never mentioned again. The inventor is himself hurled from the cathedral roof by the blond and shining John, the hero; but what of the formula?

It is Metropolis itself, the city of domed basements and curving machine-rooms, of massed buildings that conceal the sky, of aeroplanes that ply their corner-to-corner traffic, of trains that seem to shoot into unmeasured and untracked space, that makes Fritz Lang's film so significant.

The Nation, March 23, 1927

Welford Beaton founded the *Film Spectator* in Hollywood in March 1926. He felt that criticism was too concentrated in the East and that the film capital should have a critical journal of its own. His goals, he said, were "basely commercial," to help the industry make more money.[27] But his criticism and that of other contributors was reminiscent of the trade journals of twenty years before, in the *New York Dramatic Mirror* and *The Moving Picture World,* where American film criticism had begun: that is, there was a great consciousness that the trade critic's best way to help the industry was to write the most rigorous, informed criticism that he could, emphasizing expertness about films and studios and picture people, without slavishness to business criteria.

As for Beaton's last comment: Erich Pommer spent two periods working in Hollywood, in the twenties and after the Second War, but produced nothing there comparable to *Metropolis.* Josef von Sternberg wrote of Pommer that he was as knowledgeable a producer "as any I had ever known in the sense that he not only knew how to bring together cinematic values but recognized that his function at best was to aid the director, not to dominate him . . ."[28]

METROPOLIS

WELFORD BEATON

Only those who view with pessimism the fate of the human race can derive satisfaction from *Metropolis* as a piece of fiction, but those who are pessimistic regarding the development of the screen must become optimists when they view it. It is an extraordinary motion picture, in some ways the most extraordinary ever made. One must admire the minds that conceived it and brought it into being. Erich Pommer, the supervisor, and Fritz Lang, the director, are raised to a new dignity in screen art by this production, the former for the magnitude of his conception, the latter for the greatness of his screen interpretation of the conception. It was a brave thing to undertake for it was an adventure into a realm of fiction that it is hazardous to exploit. I have my own ideas regarding the trend of civilization and the state it will have reached when our great-great-grandchildren are adults. You also have your opinion. No doubt it differs from mine.

Erich Pommer has his, and it may differ from both yours and mine. He puts his in a picture and asks you and me to accept it. I, for one, will do no such thing. I refuse to believe that a century hence workingmen will be slaves who live underground. If Pommer wished to produce a story laid in a mythical country, and showed me bullfrogs driving rabbits tandem, I would not quarrel with him, for it is his own mythical country and I must accept all that his brain peoples it with; but when he says, "This is what your descendants will be doing one or two hundred years hence," I refuse to follow him, for definite knowledge on the matter being unobtainable, I do not see why I should dismiss my own opinion and accept his. The whole trend of civilization is in a direction opposite to that which *Metropolis* takes, which makes the picture nonetheless entertaining, for at least it stimulates discussion. I do not believe that we ever will advance to a time when capital concerns itself with laborers as individuals whose bodily comforts and domestic welfare are of major importance to it from a sociological standpoint; but I do not believe for a moment that it will forget that it can realize upon its investment in labor only in the degree that the laborer is efficient. In *Metropolis* we have laborers reduced to their lowest point of efficiency. The improvement in transportation makes reasonable the prediction that in another century or so men can live hundreds of miles from the scenes of their daily occupations. This will tend to spread the population over great areas and give each man his quota of sunshine and garden. *Metropolis* assumes that civilization will burrow below the surface of the earth and that men will become clammy things with colorless skins and white eyes. It assumes also that men will work long hours, in spite of the fact that the tendency toward shorter hours is marked. None of the things that *Metropolis* says time will do to society seem reasonable to me. Capital never will make slaves of workingmen because it is not good business to do so. For all these reasons I could derive no satisfaction from following the story of the picture. But as a picture I found it fascinating. Let us consider it purely as a picture and not as a piece of literature.

Metropolis was made to be released in twelve reels. Such was the footage in which the whole story was told. All the intimate phases of the story, the development of the love of the boy for the girl, the views of the home life, and the social existence of the characters were sacrified to production when five reels were eliminated from the original film to bring it down to the standard seven-reel feature length. I believe that the American version would have been a much better picture if the human element had not been reduced so greatly. When Channing Pollock revised the film to make it fit our conditions— a job that brought him twenty thousand dollars and his name in gigantic letters on the screen—no doubt he was persuaded by

Paramount's salesmen that production value was what the public craved, consequently he eliminated everything that would have given the story any plausibility. Lang's direction reveals more aptitude for movement than for acting. All his mass shots and those in which the machinery was featured were handled in a manner that shows that Lang is a master in the treatment of such subjects, but when he directed his actors he was not so much at home. The father gives a convincing performance, in a quiet, repressed way that makes the portrayal a powerful one. The son overacts all the way through, and gives a performance that entirely lacks conviction. Apparently the director allowed his actors to give their individual conceptions of the characters, without regard for their relation to one another. *Metropolis* is rather an argument for dual direction. If Lang's efforts with the material aspects of the production had been supplemented with a Lubitsch's skill at making the characters human we would have had a better picture, although the story militates against it being a perfect one. When Ufa made *Metropolis* it did not arbitrarily place its time one thousand years hence. As I understand it, Erich Pommer's idea was to depict life one or two centuries hence. Paramount's press agents, with their usual flair for exaggeration, made it ten centuries, thereby preparing the public for something more weird than it received. Technically the picture is a revelation of what can be done with models and a camera. The scenes of city life, airplanes passing among buildings, taxicabs dashing along elevated streets, pedestrians moving along sidewalks, were done so realistically that they must astonish anyone who is not familiar with the manner in which such things are done. It will interest Hollywood to know that these scenes were shot as we shoot our cartoon comedies; cardboard cut-outs being advanced after each shot. It cost less to shoot the scenes by this method than it would have to have used moving models, even though it took no less than nine months to complete them. The most striking shots in the picture were those showing the illuminated rings passing up and down around the dummy to which the face and form of the girl were being transferred. I have no idea how it was done. Another effective shot was that showing several columns of people converging on the tower of Babel. It gives the impression that many thousands of people were used. If you looked closely, however, you could detect evidences of it being a divided shot, or whatever it is called—the same bunch of people being shot half a dozen times. No matter what degree of entertainment you derive from *Metropolis* you must give it credit for being a great intellectual feat as well as an example of the extraordinary possibilities of the screen. It is to be hoped that some day Erich Pommer will find himself so situated in Hollywood that he can attempt something else equally daring and ambitious.

The Film Spectator, September 3, 1927

Harry Alan Potamkin introduces a new note in film criticism, a tone of nativity, possibly because he was one of the first serious critics born in the twentieth century after the motion picture had become an inseparable part of the environment. It seems appropriate that his first appearance here is a discussion of another film critic, with comment on others, thus testifying to the growth of a language of film discourse. Potamkin was twenty-seven when he wrote this and had six more years to live.

Exceptional Photoplays had become the *National Board of Review Magazine* in 1926. Examples of Bakshy's work appear in later pages.

ALEXANDER BAKSHY

HARRY ALAN POTAMKIN

No American has captured in the written word the qualities of cinema so well as has Alexander Bakshy, a Russian-English critic. Mr. Bakshy's brief essay, "The Kinematograph as Art"—written in 1913, published in *The Drama* (Chicago) in 1916 and in his volume *The Path of the Russian Stage* in 1918—is an amazing statement of the cinema and an anticipation of its present and imminent problems. Bakshy almost fifteen years ago recognized the movie as an art medium, but did not speak vaguely or too broadly. Bakshy more than a decade ago indicated the folly of the literary intrusion. He was not carried away by *Cabiria* as was Lindsay. Not even d'Annunzio belongs to cinema. Yet Mr. Bakshy kept his poise when he touched upon the intrusions. Unlike numerous other commentators, he was not shunted into an abuse of the inherent movie. He recognized that the usual attack is not the movie's peculiar concern, that it is really an attack upon evils not peculiarly the movie's. He understood that there is no quarrel between the mechanical and the nonmechanical, but between the artistic and the nonartistic. He remarks upon the necessity for independent film artists. The problem of commercial concentration was present ten years ago.

But the importance of Bakshy's contribution does not rest in these pointers to the negative aspects of cinema procedure. It consists of an immediate recognition of the character of cinema pantomime that is almost prophetic. Cinema pantomime, he said more than a decade ago, "is the most abstract form of pantomime," and should be left "to the dancers, clowns and acrobats who do know something about the laws of movement." This is a recognition manifested in the success of the greatest of the movie pantomimists, the low comics. Bakshy saw in the ballet the rudiments of cinema rhythm. Quite a few years later the Léger Murphy *Ballet Mecanique* appeared.

Bakshy resolved the optical problems of the film into simple terms of camera—a decade ago an amazing apprehension. What director today knows that the camera and not the picture is the medium? Bakshy anticipated by more than ten years the silhouette film; France produced a multiple reel movie of silhouette cutouts in 1926. He anticipated also a problem soon to threaten us, the natural vision film. Since its origins the movie has been abused by inventors and investors. The talking picture, the colored picture, the stereoscopic picture. Bakshy met the problem of the natural depth, three-dimensional film, not by opposing it, but by separating the cinema into two kinds of pictures: the one plane, flat film—which should be our present one—and the stereoscopic, depth film. A moving picture and a moving sculpture. This moving sculpture is quite different from Lindsay's sculpture-in-motion. Lindsay's is based on an analogy with sculpture; it is, in fact, only that sculpture in motion. Bakshy's conception is of three dimensions interrelated by motion, interrelated so as to create a rhythm, preconceived by the regisseur and sustained and exploited by the camera. The art training of a Lindsay is not such as would be very helpful to cinema, even were cinema only an extension of the graphic. And it is certainly evident that his understanding of art does not include a familiarity with its divisions and their circumscriptions and particular concerns. Bakshy is intimately cognizant of what belongs to each of the different plastics. He sees the confusion of plastics in futurism, which wanted to give kinematographic value to sculpture and painting. Time has been included as an element in painting by every important painter. But futurism wanted to *realize* time, not *visualize* it. To the movie the realization of time pictorially belongs—in other words, actual rhythmic motion. In his recognition of categories, Bakshy emphasized the fact that the movie is a medium, not of colors, but of tones or color-values. The French critics understand this, although French movies are full of color impurities. American journalistic critics, however, are unable to make the distinction. Mr. Quinn Martin waxes eloquent upon the adventurousness of Douglas Fairbanks in furthering technicolor.

The work of Mr. Bakshy indicates what movie critics should be doing. Nor has Mr. Bakshy withdrawn. He has extended his consideration of the cinema. Last year he advocated the exploitation of the screen as the receptive medium. An elementary use of this in the enlarged film was made in *Chang* and *Old Ironsides*. But Mr. Bakshy advocated a multiple screen for purposes of rhythm, relationship of minor to major actions, and climax. The unit could be separated into its elements and fused. Undoubtedly, someone will make use of this idea. And that is the point of Mr. Bakshy's importance. He is not a weathercock but a prophet. Criticism is altogether too redundant now. No one thinks it important to do anything else but repeat what has been said many times before. Criticism must save its wind. It must also have something to do with the generating of the wind. Its prophecy, however, must not be concerned with presentiments so as to appear miraculous, but subject itself to the discipline of its category. It must be a criticism in terms of the inherent qualities of the thing criticized. In this instance, the movie. From a scrutiny of the movie and what criticism of pertinence it has called forth, certain tenets can be drawn. These tenets must be qualified, extended, and applied, both by the practician in the cinema and the critic. In fact, the critic must be a practician as well. That is, his criticism must be such as to be immediately convertible into practice. Mr. Bakshy's criticism is of that kind.

National Board of Review Magazine, September 1927

German directors were principal objects of the Hollywood shopping tours referred to on p. 171. German film had become a standard and German origin a talisman. Will Rogers said of one of his pictures in 1922, "If you think this picture's no good, I'll put on a beard and say it was made in Germany, and then you'll call it art." [29] No German director brought to the United States was more talented than F. W. Murnau.

The distinguished poet and literary critic, Louise Bogan, was moved by Murnau to one of her infrequent essays in film criticism.

SUNRISE

LOUISE BOGAN

Mr. Murnau's talent as it appears in his direction of *Sunrise* is a talent that takes the camera on neglected rather than new terms, making it primarily an eye for motion-beside-within-motion, a retina reflecting an intricately flowing world. The camera moves as the eye, and the eye, with the camera, makes journeys, steering gently along the path of the subject it follows, is caught into long perspectives that plunge into the screen, swerves around corners, becomes involved in elaborate fleeing lights and shadows, all the exciting mixture and quarrel of vision. Here is camera technique pushed to its limits, freed from pantomime and parade against a world as motionless as a backdrop. In the same way that a man walking becomes a more complicated and dramatic mechanism when seen from a moving train than from an open window, so the people in this adapted Sudermann story are heightened and realized in their joy and despair by having their action set against action.

Not since the earliest, simplest moving pictures, when locomotives, fire engines, and crowds in streets were transposed to the screen artlessly and endearingly, when the entranced eye was rushed through tunnels and over precipices on runaway trains, has there been such joy in motion as under Murnau's direction. He slaps down the cramping cubes of sets and makes, whenever possible, walls of glass and steel that imprison in their clear geometry the intersection of long smooth lines of traffic, people walking, trains gathering speed. When the rare shot shows human gesture against a static background, the stillness is an accent, after the rush of a full moving screen. He knows every complication and subtlety of his method—his people walk over uneven rather than level ground, along paths slightly devious. The earth has mist over it, and breath comes visibly from nostrils. Distortion he uses but rarely, and then only as the object naturally might be distorted against the eye.

The story of the young peasant who is seduced into the thought of murdering his wife by the woman from the city is given in unbroken sequences, a continuity of the eye, throughout half its length. The husband and the city woman embracing in the dark fields, the wife in her clumsy dress seated in the boat with rocking water behind her, the blind face of the husband as he rows back to land after his murderous resolution breaks, and, above all, the two agonized young creatures huddled on the platform of the trolley car with the landscape pouring by them through the car windows—all these scenes have a plasticity, a beauty not easily named or described. They have economy as well as reckless daring in presentation, and are, at the same time, completely true to their medium.

The last half of the picture moves more heavily. It has less freshness and more obvious invention. The episodes of the photographer's studio and the barber's shop are ordinary in conception and detail. Fortunately, however, here the emphasis is laid upon the young peasant couple, and the energy and youth of George O'Brien and Janet Gaynor make even the duller moments come alive. Murnau's imagination is whetted by speed and confusion; his camera should always be taxed to its capacity. His real power again comes through when, at the end of their day, the young pair are set against every conceivable effect of light on darkness. Rockets

leap upward; bonfires burn on the water's edge; there is monstrous lightning; and, at the last, a crowd of lanterns is held up over still black water.
Night and storm revolve behind the frightened man and woman, and the
picture springs back to an intensity hardly to be believed.

Sunrise is not fortunate in its art director. It has had contrived for it a
village evidently molded from marzipan, artificial trees—one remembers
the real tree blowing beyond the prison window in *Variety*—and a claptrap moon. Mr. Murnau does not need this "art" super-imposed upon his
reality.

The New Republic, October 26, 1927

SUNRISE

Mr. F. W. Murnau's first American picture is in many ways a fascinating
achievement. It bears the impress of an artist of rare sensibility. If there
still remained any need of pointing out that the director is the most important factor in creating a picture this would be a convincing illustration.
Any picture which is worth discussing at all always bears the unmistakable
imprint of its director.

Murnau has already shown us his hand. In *The Last Laugh* he created
a character portrait which has remained unique on the screen. It was a
deliberate, loving study with a slow development in which the physical as
well as the psychological background counted largely in the happy result.
In his memorable *Faust* the pictorial element and the reproduction of a
certain medieval atmosphere presided over by the spirit of Albrecht Dürer
to a considerable extent outweighed the character development though
this was, of course, no great departure from the Goethe original in which
types rather than individuals are dominant. Neither *The Last Laugh* nor
Faust were notable for plot action or for the typical swift movement of
the movie.

Now in *Sunrise* we are again confronted with the unmistakable Murnau
mood. In treatment and atmosphere it recalls the purely American *White
Gold* in which the direction of William K. Howard reached such a sudden height. The analogy between *Sunrise* and Dreiser's novel, though it
has been very generally pointed out, is not very vital. The hero-villain of
An American Tragedy wished to get rid of the woman because he feared
the consequences of his relationship with her on purely selfish grounds in
relation to his future career, whereas the husband in *Sunrise* is acting under the spell of a siren whose will has almost obliterated his own.

The comparison with *White Gold* is much more pertinent. There we
had a largely actionless story in which everything is subordinated to the
creation of a mood and a quality of slow and brooding suspense which

directors, usually whipped on by their production supervisors to make sure of their lunch, rarely attempt to achieve. *Sunrise* has a good deal of this quality. Much has been made of Murnau's complete freedom in making this picture. We may assume therefore that he chose his own story. American scenario editors would not be very likely to go to the bat for Hermann Sudermann's *A Trip to Tilsit* with its rather foreign psychology, its morbidity, and its unhappy ending. But it is directly in the Murnau tradition. It deals with types rather than with characters and depends upon the creation of a certain scene, upon camera painting, if we may use that as an equivalent for word painting, a not too fortunate phrase of the literary critics.

As in his *Faust,* Murnau in *Sunrise* let himself go for the first reels in a pure ecstasy of mood. He shows us the home of his peasant hero, the fickle face of the lake which can change from idyllic tranquillity to sudden storms, the loving but passive wife, and the sharp passionate edges of the woman from the city whose desire has somehow been perversely stirred by this loutish lover. For a long time nothing happens, things are merely seen and felt with the dominant note lying entirely in the man's indecision as the siren slowly works upon him to drown his wife as if by accident and to flee with her to the city on the proceeds of the sale of his farm.

Then the action starts, still slow and fumbling, as the man makes his bungling preparations to drown his wife while taking her across the lake for a trip of pretended reconciliation. The dramatic action is still negative as the husband, facing his wife's confident smile of love which gradually changes to an expression of terror as she dimly senses his murderous impulse, finds that he cannot go through with it.

At this point the pace of the picture changes entirely. The wife, in her mad rush to escape from her husband, boards a passing trolley car. He manages to catch up with her. She is still in a panic at his strange behavior and repulses his conciliatory advances. He continues his pursuit through the station and the traffic jam of the metropolis. He seeks to recapture a lost love while she is intent to avoid a love which apparently has turned into murderous hate. The movement of the picture is now correctly conditioned by the psychological reactions of the characters.

The husband succeeds in recapturing the confidence of his wife. She no longer fears him. They abandon themselves to the raptures of a second honeymoon and revel in the childish amusements of a sort of glorified Coney Island. Again the movement of the picture is adjusted to the mood of the characters.

There is something very touching about the way these two troubled souls find each other again in these garish surroundings. They are out to have a good time, somewhat deliriously perhaps, and make a point of sampling every variety of amusement that the place offers. One of the best bits of comedy comes when a trained pig from a sideshow gets loose. Now pigs is one of the subjects that the man knows all about, and in a long and hilarious chase sequence the scampering animal is triumphantly recaptured. Here is legitimate comic relief adroitly introduced.

From this mood of laughing hearts and renewed conjugal felicity there is a swift transition with tragic implications. As the happy couple recross the lake at night a sudden storm engulfs them. The husband drags himself up on the shore with his wife apparently lost. The lady from the city who had spurred him on to contemplate the murder goes to meet him thinking that he has made clever use of the storm to hide his crime.

Right here Mr. Murnau puts on the brakes. As the husband is about to choke the lady to death news comes of his wife's rescue. A certain letdown in the tension is undeniable. Yet much happier endings have left us infinitely sadder. For the psychological situation of the grief-maddened husband killing his temptress had been clearly indicated. There was no compelling need of following Sudermann's piece of sensationalism through to the bitter end. *A Trip to Tilsit* is hardly a tragic masterpiece. It was not a case of making Hamlet kiss his uncle. And as it stands *Sunrise* remains a fine and sensitive picture often delicately wrought and pictorially beautiful.

National Board of Review Magazine, October 1927

THE JAZZ SINGER

WELFORD BEATON

The Jazz Singer definitely establishes the fact that talking pictures are imminent. Everyone in Hollywood can rise up and declare that they are not, and it will not alter the fact. If I were an actor with a squeaky voice I would worry. There is one scene in *The Jazz Singer* that conclusively sounds the knell of the silent picture: that showing Jolson at the piano, playing idly and talking to his mother. It is one of the most beautiful scenes I ever have seen on a screen. How anyone can view it without seeing the end of our present noiseless screen entertainment is something that I can not understand. What immediately succeeds it is so flat by comparison that it becomes ridiculous, and you can not point to any art that has clung to anything ridiculous. The whole program that we saw at the Criterion makes silent pictures out of date. The curtain-raiser, a short reel in which the story is told entirely by voices, shows what can be done; and to argue that the public will be satisfied with motion only after it has been shown that voices can be added is to argue that the mind of the public has become stagnant. I am in a combative mood about speaking pictures because I just have left the office of a producer who proved conclusively that such screen entertainment never would be popular, and who urged me not to advance a contrary view, because it would give my readers the idea that I am an impractical dreamer. The silly ass! I suppose that if he had been toddling about when Bell invented the telephone, he would have produced proof that the public never would accept it. It is possible to tell stories on the screen better with voices than without them, and to declare that the public never will demand the best is to combat all the history of human achievement. If I were a producer I would give sound devices my major attention and I would develop artists who can talk and directors who know color, for if there be anything certain about the future of pictures it is that in two years or less we will be making talking pictures in color and that no others will be shown in the big houses. *The Jazz Singer* demonstrates how sound devices will change motion picture technique. They will allow simultaneous action. A scene shows a Jewish congregation singing, and we hear the singing. We see a cut to another scene while we still hear the voices, registering that the service continues in progress while the boy visits his home; then we come back to the congregation and end the sequence when the singing ceases. Off-stage sounds will be reproduced without cuts to show their origin, which will simplify shooting. When we have a scene showing people standing in a window looking down on a band which is marching on the street below, there will be no need for a cut to the band, as we can hear it and do not need to see it. No sound device that I yet have heard is perfect, but all of them are good enough even in their present state of development to be used generally. As speaking pictures become better known the public will demand them, and producers who do not keep up with a public demand will be forced out of business by those who do. It is the same way with color. It will take only a few all-color features to make the public clamor for more of them, and the way to make most money is to give the public what it clamors for. It will be only a short step then to a demand for action, sound, and color in the same picture.

Usual motion picture standards cannot be applied to a criticism of *The Jazz Singer*. What it lacks in story interest is compensated for by the fact that it is a pioneer in a new screen adventure, and every reel of it is interesting on that account. We have lots of pictures showing people singing songs, but this is the first time we have heard some of the songs. In silent pictures the singing is indicated by cuts to the singer, while in *The Jazz Singer* the camera is held on the singer until the song is completed, the most obvious variation in screen technique, for which the general use of sound devices will be responsible. I noticed that apparently no effort was made in the long shots to synchronize the lip movement of the singers with the words they recorded, a defect that was minimized by quick cutting. And it was the only defect I noticed in the Vitaphone. The reproduced musical accompaniment was a notable feature of the evening's entertainment. An attachment that will bring symphony orchestras into moving picture houses will make the program more attractive. I would like to see the Vitaphone applied to a story with more universal appeal than *The Jazz Singer* possesses. It is too Jewish, a fault that I would find in it if there were too much Catholic, Mason, or anything else. Al Cohn made a worthy adaptation of the story and Alan Crosland directed it well, although he gives us many more close-ups than were warranted. Most of them mean nothing. There is one that emphasizes the fact that no intelligence is exercised in their use, and that those who cut them into pictures do not know what they are for. Jolson returns to the home he left when a boy. In the early sequences the home is planted and the boy's place in it shown. When Jolson returns he embraces his mother, and the embrace is shown in a large close-up which effectually blots out the home and gives us only the two heads. Such treatment destroys the spirit of the scene, as so many close-ups do. The scene should have been presented in a medium shot which preserved as much of the home as its frame would have permitted. Jolson did not return only to his mother; he returned to his home as well as to her, and the spirit of the scene demanded that a portion of the home in which we had seen him as a boy should have been part of the picture of the reunion. The facial expressions of the mother and son were matters of no value to the scene, for we could imagine what they were. The only value of the scene was the presence of the two once more in the home in which we had been accustomed to seeing them, and the close-up robbed it of that value. I was not impressed particularly with Jolson as a screen actor. He is too jerky, and is entirely devoid of repression. I like his voice when he does not stress the sobbing quality. May McAvoy is the girl and is as delightful as she always is. Long before I started the *Spectator* May became one of my screen favorites, and her every appearance strengthens my liking for her. The love element in *The Jazz Singer* is handled admirably. Warner Oland gives a feeling and convincing performance as Jolson's father. Despite the handicap of a comprehensive beard, he gives a telling impression of the proud old Jew, his eyes being used effectively to register his emotions. Eugenie Besserer makes an impressive and sympathetic mother, and Otto Lederer contributes another strong characterization. *The Jazz Singer* will have a definite place in screen history, and Warner Brothers are to be congratulated upon blazing a trail along which all other producers soon will be traveling.

The Film Spectator, February 4, 1928

Bakshy is introduced by Potamkin on p. 191.

THE CIRCUS

ALEXANDER BAKSHY

Looking at our great and incomparable Charlie Chaplin I feel like patting myself on the back. Did I not argue as long as fifteen years ago that the ordinary "legitimate" actors should be barred from the motion picture? It was of these actors that I said in 1913: "Are they aware that the cinematograph play is the most abstract form of the pantomime? Do they realize that if there is any stage on which the laws of movement should reign supreme, it is the cinematograph stage? If they did they would not have monopolized the cinematograph play, but would have left it to the dancers, clowns, and acrobats who do know something about the laws of movement." A few years later came Charlie, the perfect clown and acrobat, and by way of confirming my dictum at once leapt to such heights of artistic distinction that ever since there have been only two kinds of motion picture actors: Charlie Chaplin and the rest. The classification is based not only on the singularity of Chaplin's genius, but equally so on the singularity of his methods as an actor. This fact, however, is often ignored. Chaplin's mannerisms, the peculiar traits of the screen character he has created, have been imitated and plagiarized times without number. On the other hand, his consistent pantomime acting (I cannot recall a single picture in which Chaplin moves his lips as if actually speaking), his emphasis on expressive movement (his gait, for instance), and his puppetlike, essentially nonrealistic treatment of his role—these are the characteristics of Chaplin's acting which have found but few imitators, and certainly none to show anything like Chaplin's appreciation of their meaning and importance.

In *The Circus,* his latest picture, Chaplin is again at his very best. His inexhaustible comic imagination has provided the picture with a more than ample supply of side-splitting "stunts" of characteristic Chaplinesque quality, the most striking of these being the scenes at Noah's Ark and the lion's cage. The "big scene" of the picture, in which Charlie performs some amazing feats in tightrope walking (with the help of an attached wire), is funny too, but suffers somewhat from the attempt to join the wistful buffoonery of Charlie's little trick to the cruder and different fun of his helplessness in disengaging himself from the attacking monkeys. And through all these mirth-provoking scenes there flits the unforgettable image which has so endeared itself to the world—the image of a childishly simple and quixotically noble Pierrot who occasionally borrows the impishness of Harlequin.

In *The Circus* Chaplin's is a solo performance. The rest of the actors are not more than competent, and the direction of the picture as a whole lacks distinction. This last feature is disappointing. Chaplin showed his mettle as director in *A Woman of Paris,* and though there is no place for realism of this kind in his own grotesqueries, there is place in them for something which he is pre-eminently fitted to accomplish. His style of acting and all his dramatic upbringing proclaim Chaplin for what he actually is: a superb vaudeville comedian. We have motion pictures that are equivalent to comedy and drama. But we still have no motion picture vaudeville, i.e., entertainment shunning illusionist effects and making its appeal direct to the audience simply and solely as entertainment. I cannot help hoping that perhaps one day Chaplin will turn his mind to this richly promising field of experimental effort. There is waiting for him a full-size job worthy of his genius.

The Nation, February 29, 1928

Stark Young was the drama critic of *The New Republic* from 1921 to 1947, except for one season, 1924-25, when he was the drama critic of *The New York Times.* He wrote occasional film criticism.

THE CIRCUS

STARK YOUNG

One of his friends said that a good part of the fascination that Byron exerted on so many people who came in contact with him arose from the power he had of a certain dangerous intimacy.

I have often thought of that observation with regard to Charlie Chaplin. When you talk with him you sense at the very start an impulse to make the connection between the two of you direct and alive, a hunger that the moment should be pure and glowing, and the exchange between you and him open like a passage in art.

As we talk, I always have a sense that there is much that is not coming into what is said, facts, if you like, that are overcrowded, and facts that are so stressed and illuminated as to become different from what they might be for anyone else who knows them. But I never think of this as false, or that the truth is being distorted. I am convinced that it is a high and passionate sincerity that fills this conversation of Charlie Chaplin's, sincerity such as only an imagination like his could come at. I mean that, where exchange and *rapport* between two people, even those who trust each other, is often halting and half-divined, however true it intends to be, this moment between Charlie Chaplin and me, so evolved from his imagination and so driven with the necessity to express himself, has in it a great completeness and absorption; the thing between the two people involved is alive for both, and therefore full of its own truth. He will speak of his personal affairs, of events and of persons that delight, embitter, or destroy him, with a warmth, sting, despondency, exact poetry, or gay wit that is meant to make me see them in the liveliest degree possible, and that, therefore, seeks to engage me through the regions where my response would be most likely and natural. He does not take his color from me, but from my color he takes what he needs to express himself to me. He says what he wants me to believe of what he is telling me and, at the same time, I can see that it is what he himself wants to believe of it through me.

To that talk he gives himself with a fluency and precision and rich-mindedness that must be rarely equaled. The soul of it is shy, but the blood excited; the points are quick and telling; the word sense is remarkable; the variety ranges from a beautiful, warm elevation and eager enthusiasm to the devil's own Rabelaisian articulation; and one of its secrets is that it cannot do without you.

This complete and shining persuasion and perfect conviction of sympathy and contact could not happen without a sharp air of frankness, of saying anything called for. It needs the sense of a sort of universal lyric candor by which whatever is said seems to be free of the speaker, no longer personal, as moving and alive to the one who hears as to the one who speaks. In Byron this dangerous frankness came from pride, passion, and a vehement sense of his inability to present to the world a just picture of himself, to do "himself justice," as Lady Blessington said. In Charlie Chaplin, shot about by a restless, intense, and fertile mentality, quivering, sensitive, hurt in his early years, proud, egotistical, loving what is gentle, warm, and laureate in life, imprisoned in a mask, this power of frank intimacy was made possible only by an immense success in the world, as life itself was made possible to him by success.

I remember four years ago one afternoon we were talking about this picture of *The Circus* that has now arrived at a public showing. I had spoken of the end of *The Pilgrim,* that place where, after the kind official had got him to the Mexican border and he could run for his life and so keep out of jail, Charlie must stop to pick a flower and turn back to present it before he sets out down the road to the vague freedom ahead of him. It was one of the best motivations in modern drama, I said. "Well, you see, he just wanted to give, he felt at the moment that he must give," Charlie Chaplin said. One of the most tragic and touching and wittiest, I said. He remembered tears had come in his eyes when he had thought of it, he said. Then he began to speak of *The Circus,* the clown idea, the comic images of action that should express what he wanted to express. Incident after incident, motive after motive were working out in his head, and everything was seen, at that stage, not as some action or gag, but as ideas, pictures, states of feeling, ironic poetry, poignant finalities; and about them Charlie Chaplin, tracking out his conception of the play, lighting his way from point to point in the design of it, was clear and shrewd like a fine artist, never soft, but bitter and deep like a poet. The only thing extraneous to the dramatic idea was the necessity he felt for engaging me in it for the moment, and this in a way was part of the idea after all, or was so, at least, for so long as he was talking to me of it.

I mention this conversation about *The Circus* because it may serve to dispose of such people as like to flout what they call Charlie Chaplin's esthete critics, and because of those who try to deride all attempts to assert profound meanings for these Chaplin films, and all attempts to turn their details into significant symbolism—which last I, for one, should never do; they are too perfect images, too aptly expressive and too final to be mere symbols. By a perfect image I mean a motive, an action, a personage or event that parallels a thing in nature, a hill, a tree, the wind blowing; it can be taken simply in itself, it carries for the simplest person, and carries with it its elemental idea, which it is inseparable from. But at the same time it is capable of the whole idea; it can exist with or without amplification or comment; it can hold as much meaning as you put into it.

The Circus, as we see it at the Strand, is, for the most part, purer in the old-style Chaplin than *The Kid* was or *The Gold Rush.* The acrobatic ability is the same as always, the flitting unreality of the figure and the elusive music of the movement, the poignant, shy motivation, the way of mocking life and breaking its heart, the astonishing effect of brevity and completeness in single incidents, the uncanny accuracy of effect where exactness is wanted, as, for example, where in front of the sideshow the supposed dummy figure fools the officer and knocks the man on the head at regular intervals till he falls over. The affair with the conjurer's table, where Charlie stumbles on to the forbidden button and lets loose the birds, rabbits, pigs, geese, balloons and so on, and in dismay tries to put them back while they fill the world around him—as we, all our lives, are loosing wings and absurdities and small bestialities that surprise and dismay us, flying about our heads and wriggling under our fingers—this motive is the most boldly imagined that I remember in any Chaplin film.

There are two things that, though easily understood, perhaps, as privately compensatory and as easily condoned, are regrettable, and need either to go farther and be more complete in their own kind or to come out of the next Chaplin venture. One is the less abstract general make-up, the entire mask of the face and figure, including the movement and pantomime now and then. The other is the conscious and elaborate pathos that appears two or three times, most of all in the scene near the very end, where the circus wagons have all passed, taking along with them the beloved girl, who has been given to the other man by Charlie, and we see him sitting alone, the paper torn from one of the clown properties, with the sole star on it, on the ground at his feet. Such effects as this will carry Charlie Chaplin's pathos to a wider public, no doubt, and so may serve to add to him a slightly different sort of popularity. But the whole world, often unconsciously perhaps, has already felt his pathos in its truest kind, and the scene mars what has just gone before in *The Circus*: he has no need of that sort of fact.

Meanwhile remain the directness and finality of those conceptions and those images that express them—the figure with the pile of plates running from the mule that is also so interested and hostile; the ghastly tightrope walking with the monkeys climbing up over him, stripping off his elegance and crazy exaltation; the turns in the mirror maze; the flights with the trapeze belt; and that constant tipping of his hat, at an insult, an order, an audience's applause, a race with the thief, as if always there must be that little leaping up to happiness and what is sweet in life, always the rebuff, always that foolish leaping up again.

Seeing *The Circus* more than once, and thinking on this art of Charlie Chaplin's that I see in it and of him also, I think of how much went to the creation of a single movement, a single perfect invention or motive or image, even a pause; exactly as so many centuries went to the development of an organ like the eye, or as so many forces, seasons, wind, rain, and so much of the chemistry of dust, went to the half-lights in the depths of a flower. I wonder if art is always like this, if it is something out of the memory, a voice of something past, the immortal come to us out of death; I wonder if art is like the return of a soul to its old life, of a ghost to its memory.

The New Republic, February 8, 1928

William Edward Hickman was a California murderer.

THE CROWD

WELFORD BEATON

Even if *The Crowd* were not as good as it is, Metro would deserve a lot of credit for having made it. It is a peculiar organization. In rapid succession it turns out pictures that give little evidence of the expenditure of any thought on them, and then it comes along with something like *The Crowd* that is so full of thought that it will not be a box office success, in spite of the fact that it is one of the finest and most worthy motion pictures ever made. King Vidor's conception was an extraordinary one and he has put it on paper with a degree of faithfulness and conviction that could be attained only by a master craftsman. When he reached into the crowd his hand fell on the shoulder of one of its standard parts, and out of that part he made a motion picture. His hero is one of the men upon whom nature relies to keep intact the integrity of its crowds, a man without either virtue or vices, and lacking the mental equipment to lift himself by his thoughts above the level of the others whose elbows always were touching his. With this thought, and with his average man, Vidor proceeds to write an essay and spread it on the screen. In so doing he presents us with two performances of extraordinary merit, those of Eleanor Boardman and James Murray. The acting of these two young people is enough in itself to make a picture notable purely as a picture, but a dozen such performances in such a picture could not make it notable as screen entertainment. It has the fundamental weakness of attempting to interest us in something inherently uninteresting. We are not interested in average things, whether animate or inanimate. We are interested in anything in the degree that is above or below the average. We are interested in Lindbergh because he is a fine, brave boy who soars above the average; we are interested in Hickman because he is a beast so far below the average that he attracts our attention. We are not interested in young Johnny Sims, one of several hundred clerks in an insurance company's office. He is one of hundreds in the same office and of untold millions throughout the world, and there is nothing about him to attract our attention. Vidor presumed that we would become interested in Johnny when he was pointed out to us, but pointing at him does not make him more interesting. I am aware that great plays and great books have been written about average people, but in them the average people did things or thought thoughts that we would not expect from average people, proving, after all, that they were not true to the average. *The Crowd* gets all its merit from the fact that it deals with people who do not rise above or fall below the mean average. In short, it tries to interest us in the most uninteresting thing on earth: an average product. The most successful picture always will be the one which deals with the most interesting subject in the most interesting way. It cannot be a picture that possesses only one of these superlatives. There are some things so uninteresting that they cannot be made interesting by any kind of treatment. The average man is one of them.

But *The Crowd* was a fine thing for Metro to do. I am afraid, however, that the poor box office record that it is going to make will have a blighting effect on the organization's output. In the future when a director wishes to get Mayer's permission to make a picture with a thought in it, *The Crowd* will be trotted out as proof that the public does not wish to think. The Vidor picture would not have been made if the Metro executives understood the business they are in. If they knew anything about screen fundamentals they would have seen that the picture could not be successful. While we go to the film houses mainly for entertainment, we go to them also for inspiration. The reason the public enjoys a picture whose logical ending is happy, more than it does one which, to be logical, must have an unhappy ending, is the inspiration it derives from the former. Johnny Sims and his friends are paying over 90 percent of what the world pays to see motion pictures. The screen has become practically their only source of inspiration. The discouraged stenographer is inspired by the fact that the stenographer in the picture marries the boss, and the traveling salesman is given fresh hope when he sees Dick Dix or Bill Haines, playing a salesman, cop the millionaire's daughter in the final reel. Johnny Sims sees that there is a future for him when the picture shows the clerk becoming vice-president and marrying the president's daughter. But what does anyone get from *The Crowd*? The comfortable citizen who drove to the theater in a car of his own and who can sleep at night without worrying about the grocery bill sees paraded before him on the screen every heartache he and his wife endured during the years of their upward struggle. Out of locked closets come specters of the past that the screen breathes life into and makes real again. And what do the friends of Johnny Sims get out of it—the young people who constitute the crowd? The only thing that keeps their heads up and eyes front is the thought that some day they will rise above the multitude, as the heroes in motion pictures always do. But this picture has no such inspiration. With extraordinary vigor and conviction it plants the utter futility of endeavoring to battle one's way to success. It shows that the crowd is too powerful to be combated, and it breathes hopelessness and despair. All these drawbacks are accentuated by the excellence of the production from a motion picture angle. I do not think a finer example of intelligent direction ever reached the screen. As an example of cinematic art *The Crowd* is a success, but as a medium of screen entertainment it will be a failure. It is too depressing and carries realism just a little further than the public will prove willing to follow. But it should not discourage further adventures into realism, which should be applied to themes that strike a more optimistic note. Metro is to be commended for discarding the superlatively happy ending that was tacked on to *The Crowd* at one stage of its evolution. It ends now just as it should.

At the time of one of its previews *The Crowd* had a wildly ridiculous ending tacked on to it, as I pointed out at the time. I suppose it cost some thousands of dollars to shoot. It destroyed in half a reel what King Vidor so powerfully built up in seven. The impossibility of it was so obvious that finally even the Metro executives saw it. They recalled the prints that had gone out, and replaced them with the version that was shown in Los Angeles. It is not an unusual thing for a studio to make two or more endings of a picture, and to give each one a chance to make good at a preview. It is a sensible practice that should be adopted by other arts. Take architecture. At present, when an architect is planning a twelve-story building he builds from the basement up, and designs a roof that is in keeping with the rest of the structure. That is, he thinks it will look well. Anyway, the contractors go ahead and finish off the building with the roof that the architect deemed the most logical for it. Picture people would have used more intelligence in finishing the building. How could the architect know that Iowa tourists would like the roof he designed? Logical? My dear boy, you and I know that the architect has the right idea, the artistic idea, but we are not erecting buildings for you and me. We must think of our public, dear fellow. And to please the public several roofs would be built, one after the other, and each given a turn on the top of the building until the final choice was made. My illustration is not an extravagant one. Despite the fact that alternative endings have been shot for some of our best pictures, I maintain that such a practice is an artistic idiocy and an economic folly. There is but one ending that any story can have: that dictated by logic. There may be discussion during the story-building stages of what ending logic would dictate. Opinions would differ, but before shooting begins such differences should be composed and the picture given the ending that the majority mind decided was the logical one. To shoot two or more endings is a childish practice, a sad confession by the production staff that it does not understand the story it is putting on the screen.

The practice is an offshoot of executive indifference to waste. Dollars are the cheapest things to be found on any of the big lots. On the payrolls are men who could recognize the proper ending for a given story, but in the executive offices are men who are afraid of themselves and who squander scores of thousands of dollars each year while trying to make up their minds, with which they are furnished quite scantily. When exhibitors fail to be impressed by the cost of a picture, a move may be made to reduce the cost. Metro will sell *The Crowd* to exhibitors on the strength of the large sum it took to make it, which puts a premium on extravagance. Exhibitors reason that if it took that much money it must be good, and buy it on that theory. They should remember that the cost figure presented to them by the salesman consists of three parts: the amount that what reaches the screen really cost; the amount wasted; and the amount that the liar who sells the picture throws in for good measure.

The Film Spectator, April 14, 1928

Part Three

SOUND

The *Scientific American* for May 20, 1893 carried an article that began:

At the regular monthly meeting of the Departments of Physics of the Brooklyn Institute, May 9, the members were enabled, through the courtesy of Mr. Edison, to examine the new instrument known as the kinetograph. The instrument in its complete form consists of an optical lantern, a mechanical device by which a moving image is projected on the screen simultaneously with the production by a phonograph of the words or song which accompany the movements pictured. For example, the photograph of a prima donna would be shown on the screen, with the changes of facial expression, while the phonograph would produce the song; but to arrange this apparatus for exhibition for a single evening was impracticable. Therefore, a small instrument designed for individual observation, and which simply shows the movements without the accompanying words, was shown to the members and their friends who were present.

The "complete form" of the instrument remained "impracticable" for almost thirty-five years, although experiments in sound film were constant. In fact, Harry Warner, one of the Warner Brothers, the firm that made the theatrical breakthrough with sound, was so weary of experiment that when his brother Sam told him about Vitaphone he was skeptical. "I had heard and seen talking pictures so much that I would not have walked across the street to look at one," he said of himself in 1926.[1] But Vitaphone changed his mind, and after some trials, his studio made *The Jazz Singer* (p. 197). The Vitaphone process used synchronized phonograph records. It was soon replaced by Movietone, the first process to use a soundtrack placed directly on the film.

The sound revolution entailed huge new investments by manufacturers and exhibitors, career reversals and accelerations, esthetic revision, and immense discussion. Here is one comment.

THE "TALKIES"

ALEXANDER BAKSHY

It is a sad reflection on the limitation of intellectuals and artists all over the world to see history repeat itself in the contemptuous resentment with which they are greeting the arrival of the talking picture. Just as twenty years ago when the silent movies began to stir the world, so today the patrons of art and the theater refuse to see in the talking picture anything but another vulgar product of our machine civilization. But so, too, does history repeat itself in the eagerness of the commercially minded not to miss their share in the windfall of the talking picture, however little they may understand the problems which arise from the use of the new medium, or be able to see where to look for their solution. Thus between the incompetence of the commercial entertainer and the superior self-righteousness of the intellectual, the talking picture is apparently doomed to grope blindly for several years before it reaches anything that may be properly described as an original form of drama. That it will reach this goal eventually does not seem to me in the least doubtful.

In the meantime let us consider the prospects of the talking picture. So far its greatest successes have been scored in a field which does not quite come under the definition of "talking." Pictures like *The Singing Fool* or *My Man* are really "song pictures." The fact, however, that they succeed in conveying their appeal to the audience is vastly significant. Lacking as they are in color and depth, they still capture something of the personality of the artist. No doubt Al Jolson and Fannie Brice are more intimately felt and radiate more genuine warmth when one sees them on the stage. At the same time even on the screen they are unmistakably their peculiar and likable selves. The loudspeaker, though still very imperfect, serves them much more loyally than it does the "talking" actors, since singing reproduces better than speech.

With the inevitable technical improvement in the production of human voice and in the effects of color and stereoscopic depth, the song picture of today will naturally expand into a full-blown musical comedy. So long as this *genre* of entertainment rests its appeal on the singing of popular stars and the gyrations of pretty chorus girls, the screen musical comedy will be able to depart little from the orthodox methods of the stage. In this respect it is in the same boat as the screen drama which would also take the stage for its model. For it has been laid down by our estheticians that in copying the stage the talking picture would lose all claim to be regarded as a medium of art. Though why should it? A perfect copy is obviously as good as the original, and it is absurd to claim that no reproduction can be perfect. Besides, in the case of the talking picture one does not so much copy an original stage production as imitate the stage form—which, if a sin, is certainly not a cardinal one.

At present the trouble with the talking picture is to be found less in its attempts to imitate the stage than in its numerous technical imperfections. It is safe to predict that within the next ten years these will be removed. And it is only then that the real esthetic problem of the talking picture will become apparent. The ability to give a perfect imitation of the stage or to create a new and completely original dramatic form means nothing unless it is inspired by the genuine spirit of art. It is here that one becomes seriously alarmed. In the coming fight between Hollywood and Broadway it is ten to one that the former will be victorious. But if the defeat of the Broadway journeymen can hardly be regarded as a great loss to art, the victory of the Hollywood robots will undoubtedly endanger the future of drama on the stage as well as on the screen. The talking picture is merely a mechanized tool; but the Hollywood manufacturers of films represent mechanized brains, and what this means to art we have already learned from the experience of the silent movies.

In this rather dismal picture of the future there are two important factors which have yet to be taken account of, and which are likely to counteract if not completely overcome the influence of Hollywood. The first of these is the remarkable growth in volume and quality of amateur production together with the rapid spread of little cinema houses. Before many years are past these developments will seize the artistic leadership in the movies and will force Hollywood to accept their superior standards. The second factor is the inevitable evolution of the talking picture in accordance with the laws of its own nature. This undoubtedly will exercise a far-reaching influence on Hollywood methods. When the talking picture mechanism is made perfect, the really important development will be along lines which are already beginning to reveal themselves and which will definitely direct the talking picture away from the stage and toward a new, authentic motion picture drama.

This evolution is inevitable. It is dictated by the inner logic of the medium. Analogies between the stage and the screen assume that they deal with the same material. But they don't. The material of the screen is not actual objects but images fixed on the film. And the very fact that they have their being on the film endows these images with properties which are never found in actual objects. For instance, on the stage the actor moves in real space and time. He cannot even cross the room without performing a definite number of movements. On the screen an action may be shown only in its terminal points with all its intervening moments left out.

Similarly, in watching a performance on the stage the spectator is governed by the actual conditions of space and time. Not so in the case of the movie spectator. Thanks to the moving camera he is able to view the scene from all kinds of angles, leaping from a long-distance view to a close-range inspection of every detail. It is obvious that with this extraordinary power of handling space and time—by elimination and emphasis, according to its dramatic needs—the motion picture can never be content with modeling itself after the stage. The fact that it has now acquired the power of speech will certainly not make it any more willing to sacrifice its freedom and individuality. Nor is there any need for such a sacrifice. Dialogue can be concentrated—reduced to a number of essential statements—as effectively as action, just as it is done now in the dialogue titles of silent pictures. Then, the talking picture will also develop the specifically cinematic method of "close up." It will be able to focus an individual utterance, and at the same time put out of focus all the other voices—a procedure unquestionably in advance of the method of the "realistic" stage which, in order that certain characters may be heard, enforces a most unrealistic silence among all the other characters. And such being its technique, the spoken drama of the screen will obviously and inevitably develop into something original and non-stagy—something that will be instinct with the dynamic spirit of the movies.

The Nation, February 20, 1929

History, never shy of paradoxes, supplied a neat one just after the sound revolution: one of the best of silent films arrived from abroad.

THE PASSION OF JOAN OF ARC

EVELYN GERSTEIN

There is now being shown in New York a remarkable French film, *The Passion of Joan of Arc.* It was directed by Carl Dreyer, and is the same film which was banned by the censors in England, apparently on "patriotic" grounds because it shows the English soldiers in a none-too-pleasant light. Dreyer's is still another version of the Joan legend, or rather an original point of attack, for he has built his entire drama about the last six hours of her life, the inquisition, and the trial, the burning at the stake —the passion.

This is a cinema masterpiece of its sort—one has come to use the word sparingly these days—but a masterpiece that will probably be without issue. For the very technique that has made it so impelling and ruthless, a technique that Dreyer has evolved with diabolic skill, could not survive in different hands, and with a theme less dignified and moving. Fundamentally, the film is uncinematic, done in a succession of amazing close-ups (Joan herself is only shown three times in full length); a succession of beautiful images, filmed against a white backdrop without benefit of make-up, and animated only through the mobility of the faces, and the fluency of M. Maté's camera.

It is an abstract film, depite the fact that the drama is both actual and subjective. Dreyer has conceived it entirely from Joan's point of view, both physically and emotionally. She is always photographed as if looking up, and we are always below the judges, looking up at them, so that they appear to us in the same relation that they do to Joan. It is a Joan already crushed before the film even commences, tortured, eternally supplicating. As the granitic faces of her accusers, like sculptures in motion, close in on her with a swift relentlessness, they crush us as they do her. As they emerge from the void, each in turn to confront Joan's consciousness, they take on the resistless quality of bronze and stone.

Dreyer, guiding his camera by the intensity of the drama, sweeps from mouth to mouth, lighting on a significant detail, a fraction of a face that he throws across the screen on the diagonal, as Joan would have seen it. His is a visual continuity, rather than an actual one. Gigantic, grotesque, the judges swoop across the screen with a thrust that has its own dynamic quality.

The film, as a whole, and each particular grouping, has the luminous clarity of Flemish painting—Dreyer himself is Danish—a mannered realism that is quite uncompromising in its insistence on physical detail. The actors who try to entertain the crowds before the burning have the picaresqueness of Jerome Bosch. *The Passion* is a triumph of the particular over the general. Image succeeds image according to the dictates of a highly sophisticated, self-conscious art sense. Like Flemish painting, it never gives one the feeling of spontaneity or fluid mass that Eisenstein and the Russians do. It is not reality as the Russians see it. Dreyer's mobs are always composed of individuals. But, like Eisenstein, he has a superb sense of casting to type. Each picture is a portrait, and the film is composed of them; still portraits, made dynamic through Dreyer's amazing cutting and camerawork.

The acting is quite without flaw. Mlle. Falconetti, as Joan, with her marvelously mobile face and the heavy, muscled hands of the peasant, is always the Italian *Mater dolorosa*. M. Sylvain's Bishop Cauchon is very subtly done. But *The Passion* is pre-eminently a photographer's achievement, and Dreyer, with his own technique, has for once given the cinema a three-dimensional film that needs neither color nor sound to augment its catharsis.

The New Republic, April 10, 1929

H. D. (Hilda Doolittle), one of the leading Imagist poets, was American-born and lived in Europe. She wrote the following for *Close Up,* an English-language film journal published in Switzerland. She saw Dreyer's film—under another title—before it reached America, which explains the date of her article as against the previous one.

THE PASSION OF JOAN OF ARC

H. D.

The Passion and Death of a Saint is a film that has caused me more unrest, more spiritual forebodings, more intellectual rackings, more emotional torment than any I have yet seen. We are presented with Jeanne d'Arc in a series of pictures, portraits burnt on copper, bronze if you will, anyhow obviously no aura of quattrocento gold and gold dust and fleurs-de-lys in straight hieratic pattern, none of your fresco that makes the cell of Savonarola make the legend of Savonarola bearable even to this day. Jeanne d'Arc is done in hard clear line, remorseless, poignant, bronze stations of the cross, carved upon medieval cathedral doors, bronze of that particular sort of medieval fanaticism that says no and again no to any such weakening incense as Fra Angelico gold and lilies of heavenly comfort. Why did and why didn't this particular Jeanne d'Arc so touch us? Jeanne d'Arc takes us so incredibly far that having taken us so far, we are left wondering why didn't this exquisite and superb piece of screen dramatization take us further? Carl Dreyer, a Dane, one of the most superb of the magnificently growing list of directors, is responsible for this odd two-edged sort of feeling. His film, for that, is unique in the annals of film art. The passion of the Jeanne is superbly, almost mediumistically portrayed by Mlle. Falconetti. Heart and head are given over to inevitable surrender. Heart broke, head bowed. But another set of curious nerve-reactions were brought into play here. Why is it that my hands inevitably clench at the memory of those pictures, at the casual poster that I pass daily in this lakeside small town? Is it necessary to be put on guard? *Must* I be made to feel on the defense this way and why? Also why must my very hands feel that they are numb and raw and bleeding, clenched fists tightened, bleeding as if beating at those very impregnable medieval church doors?

For being let into the very heart, the very secret of the matter, we are left out of . . . something. I am shown Jeanne, she is indeed before me, the country child, the great lout of a hulking boy or girl, blubbering actually, great tears coursing down round sun-hardened, wind-hardened, oak-tree hardened face outline and outline of cheek hollow and the indomitable small chin. Jeanne is first represented to us, small as seen from above, the merest flash of sturdy boy figure, walking with chained ankles toward judges (too many) seated in slices above on ecclesiastical benches. Jeanne is seen as small, as intolerably sturdy and intolerably broken, the sort of inhuman showing up of Jeanne that from the first strikes some note of defiance in us. Now why should we be defiant? I think it is that we all have our Jeanne, each one of us in the secret great cavernous interior of the cathedral (if I may be fantastic) of the subconscious. Now another Jeanne strides in, an incomparable Jeanne, indubitably a more Jeanne-ish Jeanne than our Jeanne but it just isn't our Jeanne. Worse than that it is a better Jeanne, a much, much better, more authentic Jeanne than our Jeanne; scathing realism has gone one better than mere imaginative idealism. We know we are outwitted. This is a real, real, Jeanne (poor Jeanne), little mountain Newfoundland puppy, some staunch and true and incomparably loyal creature, something so much more wonderful than any greyhound outline or sleek wolf-hound is presented us, the very incarnation of loyalty and integrity . . . dwarfed, below us, as if about to be tramped or kicked into a corner by giant soldier iron-heeled great boots. Marching boots, marching boots, the heavy hulk of leather and thonglike fastenings and cruel nails . . . no hint of the wings on the heels of the legions that followed the lily-banner; the cry that sang toward Orleans is in no way ever so remotely indicated. We are allowed no comfort of mere beatific lilies, no hint of the memory of lover-comrade men's voices, the comrades that Jeanne must have loved loyally, the perfect staunch child friend, the hero, the small Spartan, the very Telisila upon the walls of that Argos, that is just it. This is *no* Telisila upon the walls of Argos, no Athene who for the moment has laid aside her helmet for other lesser matters than that of mere courage and fidelity. This is an Athene stripped of intellect, a Telisila robbed of poetry, it is a Jeanne d'Arc that not only pretends to be real, but that is real, a Jeanne that is going to rob us of our own Jeanne.

Is that the secret of this clenching of fists, this sort of spiritual antagonism I have to the shaved head, the stares, defiant bronze-statue, from the poster that I pass on my way to market? Is it another Jeanne in me (in each of us) that starts warily at the picture, the actual *portrait* of the medieval girl warrior? The Jeanne d'Arc of Carl Dreyer is so perfect that we feel somehow cheated. This must be right. This must be right . . . therefore by some odd equivocal twist of subconscious logic, *I* must be wrong. I am put in the wrong, therefore I clench my fists. Heaven is within you . . . therefore I stand staring guiltily at bronze figures cut upon a church door, at friezes upon the under-gables of a cathedral that I must stare up at, see in slices as that incomparable Danish artist made me see Jeanne in his perhaps overdone series of odd sliced portraits (making particularly striking his studies of the judges and the accusers of Jeanne, as if seen by Jeanne herself from below) overwhelming bulk of ecclesiastical political accusation. I know in my mind that this is a great tour de force, perhaps one of the greatest. But I am left wary, a little defiant. Again why and why and why and just, just why? Why am I defiant before one of the most exquisite and consistent works of screen art and perfected craft that it has been our immeasurable privilege to witness?

One, I am defiant for this reason (and I have worked it out carefully and with agony) I and you and the baker's boy beside me and Mrs. Captain Jones-Smith's second maid and our own old Nanna and somebody else's gardener and the honeymoon boy and girl and the old sporting colonel and the tennis teacher and the crocodile of young ladies from the second pension to the left as you turn to the right by the market road that branches off before the stall where the old lady sells gentians and single pinks and Alpenrosen each in their season (just now it is somewhat greenish valley-lilies) are in no need of such brutality. No one of us, not one of us is in need of this stressing and stressing, this poignant draining of hearts, this clarion call to pity. A sort of bugle note rises and with it our own defiance. I am asked to join an army of incorruptibles to which long and long since I and the baker's boy and the tennis champion in the striped red sash have given our allegiance. This great Dane Carl Dreyer takes too damn much for granted. Do I *have* to be cut into slices by this inevitable pan-movement of the camera, these suave lines to left, up, to the right, back, all rhythmical with the remorseless rhythm of a scimitar? Isn't this incomparable Dane Dreyer a very bluebeard, a Turk of an ogre for remorseless cruelty? Do we have to have the last twenty four hours' agony of Jeanne stressed and stressed and stressed, in just this way, not only by the camera but by every conceivable method of dramatic and scenic technique? Bare walls, the four scenes of the trial, the torture room, the cell and the outdoors about the pyre, are all calculated to drive in the pitiable truth like the very nails on the spread hands of the Christ. Do we need the Christ-nails driven in and pulled out and driven in and drawn out, while Jeanne already numb and dead, gazes dead and numb at accuser and fumbles in her dazed hypnotized manner toward some solution of her claustrophobia? I am shut in here, I want to get out. I want to get out. And instead of seeing in our minds the very ambrosial fields toward which that stricken soul is treading, foot by foot like the very agony toward skull-hill, we are left pinned like some senseless animal, impaled as she is impaled by agony. This is not *not* good enough. There is some slur on the whole of human consciousness, it is necessary to stress and stress and stress the brute side of mystic agony this way. Somehow, something is wrong here. An incomparable art, an incomparable artist, an actress for whom any but praise were blasphemy . . . and what happens?

I do not mind crying (though I do mind crying) when I see a puppy kicked into a corner but I do mind standing aside and watching and watch-ing *and* watching and being able to do nothing. That is something of the antagonism I think that crept in, that is something of the something that made me feel I ought to go again, to be fair, to be *sure* what it was that upset me, perhaps cowardice on my own part, some deep subconscious strata or layer of phobia that I myself, so un-Jeanne-like, was unwilling to face openly. I said to myself next morning I will get this right, I am numb and raw, I myself watched Jeanne d'Arc being burnt alive at Rouen last night . . . and I myself must go again . . . ah, that is just it. We do not go and see a thing that is real, that is real beyond realism, AGAIN. I said I will go again but I did not go again. I did not and I don't think I failed any inner "light," any focus of consciousness in so ceding to my own new lapse. I can NOT watch this thing impartially, and it is the first film of the many that I have consistently followed that I have drawn away from. This is perhaps the last and greatest tribute to the sheer artistry and the devilish cunning of the method and the technique of Carl Dreyer. I pay him my greatest compliment. His is one film among all films, to be judged differently, to be approached differently, to be viewed as a master-piece, one of the absolute masterpieces of screen craft. Technically, artisti-cally, dramatically, this is a masterpiece. But, but, but, but, but . . . there is a Jeanne sobbing before us, there is a small Jeanne about to be kicked by huge hob-nailed boots, there is a Jeanne whose sturdy child-wrist is being twisted by an ogre's paw because forsooth she wears a bit of old hard hammered unwieldy bulk of gold upon one finger, there is a numb hypnotized creature who stares with doglike fidelity toward the sly sophist who directs her by half-smile, by half-nod, by imperceptible lift of half an eyebrow toward her defaming answers, there is a Jeanne or a Joan whose wide great grey eyes fill with round tears at the mention of her mother ("say your pater noster, you don't know your pater noster? you do? well who taught it to you?") there is Jeanne or Joan or Johanna or Juana upon Jeanne or Joan or Johanna or Juana. They follow one another with precision, with click, with *monotony*. Isn't that a little just it? There is another side to all this, there is another series of valuations that cannot perhaps be hinted at consistently in this particular presentation of this one kicked little puppy of a Jeanne or a Joan or a Johanna. Isn't it just that? Isn't the brute side of the flawless type, the Jeanne d'Arc of all peoples, of all nations, the world's Jeanne d'Arc (as the world's Christ) a little too defiantly stressed, a little too acutely projected? I know after the first half of the second reel all that. I know all, all that. Just that round child face lifted "who taught you your pater noster?" gives me all, all that. I do not mean to say that there could have been any outside sort of beatific screen craft of heavenly vision. I don't mean that. But Jeanne kicked almost, so to speak, to death, still had her indomitable vision. I mean Jeanne d'Arc talked openly with angels, and in this square on square of Danish protestant interior, this trial room, this torture room, this cell, there was no hint of angels. The angels were there all the time and if Jeanne had reached the spiritual development that we must believe this chosen comrade of the warrior Michael must have reached, the half-hypnotized numb dreary physical state she was in would have its inevitable psychic recompense. The Jeanne d'Arc of the incomparable Dreyer, it seems to me, was kicked toward the angels. There were not there, nor anywhere, hint of the angelic wing tip, of the winged sandals and the two-edged sword of Michael or of the distillation of maternal pity of her "familiar" Margaret. Father, mother, the "be thou perfect" perfected in Jeanne d'Arc as in the boy of Nazareth were in no way psychically manifest. Such psychic manifestation, I need hardly say, need be in no way indicated by any outside innovation of cross lights or of superimposed shadows. It is something in something, something behind something. It is something one feels, that you feel, that the baker's boy, that the tennis champion, that the army colonel, that the crocodile of English and Dutch and mixed German-Swiss (come here to learn French) feel. We are numb and beaten. We won't go a second time. The voice behind me that says wistfully, taken unawares, "I wish it was one of those good American light things" even has its place in critical consciousness. For all our preparation, we are unprepared. This Jeanne d'Arc is sprung on us and why should it be? There is a reason for most things. I think the reason is that it doesn't link up straight with human consciousness. There is a gap somewhere. We criticize many films, sometimes for crudity, sometimes for sheer vicious playing up to man's most febrile sentiment, sometimes for cruelty or insincerity. We criticize Jeanne d'Arc for none of these things.

The Jeanne d'Arc of the incomparable artist Carl Dreyer is in a class by itself. And that is the trouble with it. It shouldn't be.

Close Up, July 1928

The Marx Brothers could no more have been silent-film comedians than Fred Astaire a silent-film dancer. They arrived with sound, with large theater reputations, and with the intense interest of a sophisticated group of critics.

Among them was Gilbert Seldes. During a long and varied career, Seldes was an editor, a novelist, a playwright, and a critic of several arts. He is especially noted for his early advocacy of a serious view of the popular arts. Among his many books are *The Seven Lively Arts, The Movies Come from America, The Great Audience,* and *The Public Arts.*

THE COCOANUTS

GILBERT SELDES

The best way to clear one's mind of the concept of the talkies as spoiled movies is to see some which are developed stage-presentations, dramatic or musical. After six months of watching on the silent screen the everyday offerings which small communities can afford, I find myself interested in the talkies and much less offended by the talkie-stage-movie. I have still to discover a full-length talkie which has any virtue of its own.

Of the musicals, I chose *The Cocoanuts,* because I wanted to see the Marx Brothers again and because Robert Florey, who made *The Death of a Hollywood Extra* for some ninety dollars and threatened the complacency of the movie magnates, was associated with the making of the talking version. If I had not also seen Paul Fejos's *Broadway,* I should have believed that the talkies were really the death of the film, because Mr. Florey's work is almost invisible. There is one shot of a lot of chorus girls photographed from above; as they emerge from a cluster, their arms make an interesting design for fifteen seconds; the rest is the most ordinary kind of old-fashioned moving picture technique.

The Marxes came off handsomely; Groucho's is the first voice I have heard from the screen in swift chatter—not as swift, not as crisp as his wisecracking on the stage, but better in these respects than all the other deliveries I have encountered; Chico, who seemed to me to take a giant stride last year, keeps up the pace in this picture; and Harpo is extraordinarily funny and endearing, but the semiclose-ups take away some of the mystery of his expression. He was badly served because the director chose to play one of his famous scenes so that it remained invisible to the audience. I mean the one he imported from vaudeville where he stands with bland innocence written all over his face and cascades of cutlery, watches, jewelry, and other valuables pour from his clothes. With Harpo's back turned, the scene on the screen looked as if someone else were throwing knives.

Apart from that, it should be noted that the director never made up his mind whether he was making a movie or photographing a musical show; for the most part the production might as well have been a moving picture of what took place on the stage. The movie added nothing; the talking was exactly what it had been. All the virtues of the offering are due to G. S. Kaufman, Irving Berlin, the Marxes, and the other collaborators in the original stage show.

The New Republic, June 12, 1929

The lesser-known or unidentified persons below include: Charles S. Gilpin, the first performer of O'Neill's *Emperor Jones;* Jean Toomer, the author of a notable novel called *Cane;* Eastman Johnson, a nineteenth-century painter of black subjects; Octavus Roy Cohen and Hugh Wiley, who wrote purportedly humorous stories about blacks for *The Saturday Evening Post;* Léon Poirier, who made many documentary films, among them *La Croisière noire;* A. E. Gonzales, who wrote and edited books about Gullah blacks; Reed Smith, who edited South Carolina ballads; Ben Burbridge, who produced a film called *Gorilla Hunt;* Sir Alan Cobham, who made a film called *With Cobham to the Cape;* and Josephine Baker, a black American cabaret singer who had a dazzling career in Paris.

The Emperor Jones was filmed in 1933 with Paul Robeson, directed by Dudley Murphy.

THE AFRAMERICAN CINEMA

HARRY ALAN POTAMKIN

The Negro is not new to the American film. The late Bert Williams appeared in a film before the war. But this did not get very considerable circulation due to southern antagonism. It was the first of the Johnson-Jeffries fight that thrust the Negro out of films and created the interstate commerce edict against fight films. Sigmund Lubin produced all-Negro comedies in Philadelphia before the war. The Negroes themselves have been producing pictures on the New Jersey lots, deserted by the white firms that migrated to California. These companies have starred actors like Paul Robeson and Charles Gilpin in white melodramas like *Ten Nights in a Barroom*. White impersonations of Negroes have been frequent, either in farces or in the perennial *Uncle Tom's Cabin*. Negro children have in the last years been appearing in such slapstick films as Hal Roach perpetrates with his tedious and unconvincing Gang. The treatment of Farina is typical of the theatrical (variety and film) acceptation of the Negro as clown, clodhopper, or scarecrow, an acceptation which is also social. No objections have been raised by the solid South to Farina's mistreatment by the white children (to me a constantly offensive falsehood and unpardonable treachery of the director) nor to Tom Wilson's nigger-clowning.

The present vogue for Negro films was inevitable. The film trails behind literature and stage for subject matter. There has been a Negro vogue since the spirituals were given their just place in popular attention. Many Negro mediocrities have ridden to glory on this fad. Many white dabblers have attained fame by its exploitation. The new Negro was suddenly born with it. Cullen and Hughes were crowned poets, but Jean Toomer, a great artist among the Negroes, has not yet been publicly acclaimed. He first appeared before the hullabaloo was begun. The theater took the Negro up. First Gilpin, and eventually came *Porgy*. Now the film. Sound has made the Negro the "big thing" of the film-moment.

Of course, the first Negro film in the revival had to be *Uncle Tom's Cabin*. I praise in it the gaiety of the first part and the friendly, unsupercilious treatment of the Negro and the general goodwill of the actors. I condemn in it the perpetuation of the claptrap sentimentality. This is not the day to take Harriet Beecher Stowe too seriously. *Uncle Tom's Cabin* should have been produced as folk composition, or better not at all. It is not important as matter or film. Sound is bringing the Negro in with a sort of Eastman Johnson–Stephen Foster–Kentucky Jubilee genre, or with the Octavus Roy Cohen–Hugh Wiley crowd satisfiers, where the Negro is still the nigger-clown, shrew sometimes and butt always. And Vidor's *Hallelujah* with a good-looking yaller girl. As for me, I shall be assured of the white man's sincerity when he gives me a blue nigger. I want one as rich as the Negroes in Poirier's documents of Africa. I am not interested primarily in verbal humor, in clowning or in sociology. I want cinema, and I want cinema at its source. To be at its source, cinema must get at the source of its content. The Negro is plastically interesting when he is most negroid. In the films he will be plastically interesting only when the makers of the films know thoroughly the treatment of the Negro structure in the

African plastic, when they know of the treatment of his movements in the ritual dances, like the dance of the circumcision, the Ganza. In Ingram's *The Garden of Allah* the only good movement was the facial dance of the Negro performer.

The cinema, through its workers, has been content to remain ignorant. It might have saved itself a great deal of trouble and many failures and much time had [they] studied the experience of the other arts. Well, what can the Negro cinema learn from the White Man's Negro and the Black Man's Negro in art, in literature, in theater?

Graphic art: The Greek and Roman sculptors of black boys were defeated because they did not study the structure of the faces. In modern art, there is Georg Kolbe's fine *Kneeling Negro*. There are Annette Rosenshine's heads of Robeson and Florence Mills—elastic, lusty miniatures. And there is the vapid, external, gilded Negro by Jesper in the Musée du Congo, Tervueren, Belgium. Compare. If you want to see how a principle can be transferred and reconverted, see what the late Raymond Duchamp-Villon learned from African sculpture. Relaxation among angles. Study Modigliani for transference to another medium. In painting examine Jules Pascin's painting of a mulatto girl and Pierre Bonnard's more stolid Negro. But always the source: the sculpture of the Congo, the Ivory Coast, the Gold Coast, the bronzes of Benin, the friezes of Dahomey. Observe their relation to the actual African body, coiffure, etc., to the dance. What do you deduce?

Literature: In America I know of but one white man's novel that has recognized the Negro as a human-esthetic problem—which he must be to the artist—and not either a bald bit of sociology or something to display. I refer to Waldo Frank's *Holiday*. This eloquent though monotoned book is not a bare or ornamental statement of the interrace. Its concern is not with the culmination of the tragedy in the lynching, but with the relationships involved. The horror and the sacrifice of the lynching are certainly unavoidable, but greater and above these are the relationships, and the denial of the beauty of these relationships by the final mob act. This is the one book I know of that has recognized the entirety as ultimately human relationship, which determines the esthetic unity. There is not in this book the ethnographical-archeological-sociological preoccupation that obscures the major motif in the other books. This is a novel, it is art, it is distillation, condensation, purity. Shands, Stribling, Peterkin, Van Vechten all strive to reveal their intimacy with the details of life and vocabulary of the strange folk they present. Shand's *Black and White* and Stribling's *Birthright* do free the central motif from a number of these interferences, leaving a clearer path to the culmination. But the motif should determine the book, which it does not in either case. Peterkin wishes to be genuine (but to be genuine is not to be unselective) and sympathetic and impartial. This makes her work a less questionable enterprise than Van Vechten's *Nigger Heaven,* the conscience of which must be severely doubted. *Black April* is better than *Green Thursday.* The former obscures the relevant data with data on folk idiosyncracies. It is the artist's business to evaluate the relevant data that he may be better able to know its potentialities, and not to record every detail contributing to the formation of that material. *Green Thursday* indicated no sense of the potential materials, their convertibility and relevant form. They were dark waters poured into Hamlin Garland jugs or Mary Wilkins-Freeman ewers, taking the form and conveyance of the receptacles.

Theater: The film may find instructive analogies and sources in three plays: *Earth* by Em Jo Basshe, *Porgy* by the Heywards, and *The Emperor Jones* by Eugene O'Neill. *Earth* is an instance of a play with a concept in its theme, but no recognition of that concept perceptible in the language or human-arrangement of the play. The theme was meant to articulate the struggle with the Negro between paganism and Christianity. Instead it is a struggle of personalities we witness. The theme indicates what the Negro film promises in the way of experience, when the philosophic cinematist will be present. *Porgy* is more immediate indication. It lacks all concept. It lacks significant intention. It lacks a valuable narrative. Its tale is that of Culbertson's *Goat Alley* and the old white melodrama—the wicked man, the lured girl, happy dust, the cripple, sacrifice, vengeance. But its virtue is folk, always a good source. It has caught the folk in its rhythm, and whatever idea the play possesses is in its rhythm. This "rhythm as idea" makes of it a better play than Torrence's *Granny Maumee,* in spite of the latter's effort to convince us of folk authenticity. The tragedy of *Porgy* is no more important than the tragedy of *Goat Alley.* It is rendered more poignant simply because it has taken place in a folk structure to whose rhythm the individual participants contribute. That is why the character of the crab-vendor, suggested by one of the actors and inserted into the completed play, does not obtrude. It is of the total folk structure and easily finds its place in it. In the Theatre Guild production the play failed as a rhythmic unit, leaving us to enjoy, not the entity, but the details. This may be due somewhat to breaks in the authors' construction. The authors and the director failed to sustain the rhythmic counterplay between Crown's sacrilege and the Negroes' religion in the hurricane scene. This was a play meant to be produced not mimetically but choreographically, and moreover—as folk—to be stylized. It laid too much stress on a bad story, the songs were not intervalled with precision, and—most serious of faults—the diction was stereotype. This last, of course, has nothing to do with the production, it is the authors' weakness. The authors confess they did not take advantage of the original Gullah dialect because it would be incomprehensible to an audience not familiar with it. Should Synge have avoided the Gaelic on the same score? Synge exploited, and converted the difficult speech, suiting it to the language of his audience, which was his language medium, and attained thereby a tremendous eloquence. Any author, intuitively gifted and philologically and rhythmically aware, could go to the documents and records of a Gonzales, a Bennett, or a Reed Smith and recreate a diction at once original, relevant, convincing—and comprehensible. Yet Peterkin and the Heywards, operating in the very environment of the dialect, could do nothing with it but run away from it. These immediately foregoing words are full of meaning to the Negro film with speech.

Coming to the Negro talkie, we can find no more complete entrance than by way of *The Emperor Jones*. In itself *The Emperor Jones* is not particularly Negro. One may question the thesis of atavism which runs through it, as one may easily deny the too patent psychology. But it is excellent theater, a theater of concurrent and joining devices. It is, in fact, better cinema than theater, for its movement is uninterrupted. The uninterrupted movement can be borne only by the film and screen, for the necessity of changing sets obliges an interruption in the theater. There is a central motive of the escaping Jones. The theater has not the capabilities to reveal the textural effects necessary to the drama, such as the increasing sheen of sweat on the bare body. Here is your "photogenic" opportunity! The theater can never equal the cinema in the effect of the gradual oncoming dark, also a dramatic progression in the play. The ominous and frightful shadows, the specters of the boy shot at craps, the phantom gallery—the cinema has long been well-prepared for these. And now the sounds. The play is dependant on the concurrences and reinforcements of sounds. The sounds are part of the drama. The drumbeats, the bulletshots, the clatter of the dice, the moan of the slaves, and the recurring voice of Jones, his prayer—what a composition these offer for a sound-sight-speech film! This is the ideal scenario for the film of sound and speech. Here silence enters as a part of the speech-sound pattern, and becomes more important than it ever was in the silent film! Here one can construct counterpoint and coincidence, for there is here paralleling of sound and sight and their alternation. There is intervalling, a most important detail in the synchronized structure. But all this does not end *The Emperor Jones*. It must be Negro! How? We can switch back to my earlier words: "The Negro is plastically interesting when he is most negroid. . . ." The Negroes must be selected for their plastic, negroid structures. Jones should not be mulatto or Napoleonic, however psychologic requirements demand it. He should be black so that the sweat may glisten the more and the skin be apprehended more keenly. He should be woolly, tall, broad-nosed, and deep-voiced. The moaning should be drawn from a source in the vocal experience of the Negro, the medicine doctor's dance from a source in choreographic experience. But beware! We do not want ethnography, this is no document. I am not asking for the insertions of *Storm over Asia:* I am asking for a tightly interwoven pattern. The sources are only sources. Folk, race are not complete in themselves. Dialect is not an esthetic end. I am not asking for the duplications such as Langston Hughes writes. We shall have enough of these, and they will be nothing but records, and records lacking even intelligent selection and commentary. What I have said in my remarks upon the Negro in art and literature will indicate what the ideal Negro film must not be and must be. The documentary film is ethnographic. The documentary film is a source, but even in a document one cannot place everything and there must be concessions to the form. In the constructed film of the Negro, the art film let us say, the problem will always be, not the Negro in society, but the Negro in the film. The problem will not be that of Edward Sheldon's *The Nigger,* filmed years ago with William Farnum (Fox Film, *The Governor*). That sort of play in reality omits the Negro, just as *A Doll's House* actually gave us no woman but a thesis. We are, I hope, far away now from films about "the black peril"—although *The Birth of a Nation* is still with us and "the yellow peril" is a constant offering. The problem of intermarriage and interrace is not likely to be honestly dealt with on the American screen for a long time, but I do not complain of that—the problem play has generally been dull drama, it would be even duller cinema. When the cinematists have shown that they have intelligently examined the Negro as subject matter, that they know a great deal about him and his experiences, then the problem film of the Negro can be attempted, for the problem will be comprised then, and only then, in a complete experience of a people. It is indeed reassuring that literature in dealing with the Negro has become more sympathetic. The sympathy, however, has not extended as yet to the formal material, the convertible raw stuff—it is humanitarian, and that is good. But in the humanitarian sentiment one still detects considerable patronage, indulgence, condescension, and an attitude hardly judicious, that of the examiner of an oddity. In the documentary films of Burbridge and the Cobham journey, the captions are frequently supercilious, and in a document of a polar trip, a bit of nondocumentation is perpetrated for humor: a Negro hand runs off scared upon seeing a polar bear, safely bound, hauled upon the deck. These Caucasian evidences will persist a long time, and wherever they will persist there will be no proper attitude toward the Negro as subject matter.

Then is the hope in Negro films turned by Negroes? That would be a hope, if the American Negro had given evidence of caring for and understanding his own experience sufficiently to create works of art in the other mediums. But the American Negro as graphic artist has shown very little awareness of this experience; as writer he is imitative, respectable, blunt, ulterior, and when he pretends to follow Negro materials, he does little more than duplicate them. Of course there are exceptions. The exceptions, I believe, will eventually create the rule. But that rule will be created only by artists who are strong enough to resist the vogue which would inflate them. We are now entering into a vogue of the Negro film. Perhaps when that is over, the true, profound, realized Negro film will be produced, and perhaps Negroes will produce them.

It will have been observed that my preoccupation has been constantly with relationships. I have been preoccupied with relationships only because they are constantly present. The relationship between the African dances and the sophisticated Charleston and the Black Bottom is unavoidable, the relationship between native Negro song and jazz is evident. We are always what we were: that is perhaps a platitude, but it is also an important truth for the Negro film. It suggests a synthetic film, a composite film, in which the audience's experience of a girl by Tanganyika becomes the audience's experience of an idolized Josephine Baker. Folk, race dominates the world. There is a theme. And the movie with its devices for simultaneous and composite filming offers the opportunity. Someone might similarly make an incisive film deriving the hooded Ku Klux Klan from the leopard-skin-hooded vendetta of the black Aniotas of Africa. In that way lies penitence for *The Clansman* which became *The Birth of a Nation.*

Close Up, August 1929

HALLELUJAH

WELFORD BEATON

Hallelujah is a magnificent motion picture, a magnificent tribute to the genius of King Vidor, and a magnificent achievement that reflects the greatest credit on Metro-Goldwyn-Mayer as a producing organization that is striving for the best there is in screen art. Not even superlatives can do it credit. It is a gorgeous poem of the South, both dramatically and pictorially. Its all-Negro cast gives us some superb performances, and Gordon Avil with his camera gives us a succession of views of surpassing beauty. The story is a gripping one, emotional, dramatic and human, and even though the production is strong in atmosphere and many of the scenes are notable for their composition, lighting, and photography, Vidor tells the story briskly and without circumlocution. Eastern writers who have seen the picture disagree about the faithfulness with which Vidor has caught the spirit of the Negro and presented it on the screen. Not being qualified as an authority on the subject, I cannot take sides in the controversy, but I am content with what he gives us. If he has caught the spirit accurately he is to be congratulated upon the efficiency with which he screened it; and if he failed to catch it accurately, he is to be congratulated even more upon the extraordinary attractiveness with which he gives us his conception of the South. There is no doubt about the honesty of the camera, which caught scenes that make the picture an entrancing journey through an idealized South. In addition to dealing with the joys and sorrows of the colored people the production follows the progress of cotton from the field to the factory, to that extent giving the film an educational value. As is the case with most of the productions that have come to us from the cradle of the sound device, this one in places is more noisy than it need be, and the sharp cutting that apparently was necessary to bring the picture down to length causes too many abrupt terminations to entertaining musical numbers. At first I thought a weakness of the story would be its difficulty in enlisting our sympathies for characters who have no personal appeal to us, but soon I found myself being swept along with the current of the story, and admiring greatly the superb performances of Daniel L. Haynes and Nina Mae McKinney, who have the leading parts. I even went so far as to sympathize with the villain, William Fountaine, and I loved the dear old mammy of the picture, Fannie Belle DeKnight. Harry Gray, Everett McGarrity, and Victoria Spivey also are to be credited with splendid performances. But Vidor is the man to whom the major praise must be given. As a creation it is entirely his, as he wrote as well as directed the story. He has a place of his own among American directors. He is as fearless as are those foreign directors who give us beautiful works of screen art that enrich the screen even if they do not enrich their producers. I can not imagine that *Hallelujah* will fail to earn a large profit, but even if it should fail to do so, it is of tremendous value as a contribution to the art of the screen. There is one sequence in it which I think is the finest thing ever done by an American director. Toward the end of the picture the villain lures the girl away, and the hero, after the girl dies, goes out in pursuit of the man who wrecked his home. The villain flees in terror through a swamp that Avil has photographed with extraordinary effect. Behind him comes the relentless pursuer. The villain runs, stumbles, and sometimes falls, but the pace of the hero always is the same, a deliberate, deadly, menacing advance straight toward his quarry. The sequence is directed and cut in a manner that makes it an outstanding example of the steady building of dramatic intensity. Directed less skillfully and acted with less understanding, it would not justify the footage devoted to it, but as handled by Vidor, Haynes, and Fountaine, it is extraordinarily effective. In sharp contrast to this sequence is the note struck in the one which follows it, and with which the picture ends. The homecoming of Haynes, after serving a term in prison for the murder of Fountaine, is another fine bit of intelligent and human direction. It gives us again a shot which we saw earlier in the picture, a camera etching of superlative beauty in which Avil seems to have caught the whole spirit of the picture. *Hallelujah* should go into every motion picture theater in the world.

The Film Spectator, November 2, 1929

ARSENAL

ALEXANDER BAKSHY

They are still coming from Russia, those breathtaking revelations of genius that make cinematic history. You may doubt this statement if you see *Arsenal* only once. I was doubtful myself when I saw it for the first time. But I have no doubts now after my second visit to the theater. *Arsenal* is one of the most beautiful pictures that have ever been shown. In Russia today they judge works of art by their social significance; the artist, like any craftsman, must execute a "social order." Dovzhenko, the director of *Arsenal,* has fulfilled this requirement, I understand, to the complete satisfaction of his customer. But he has done more. He has produced a piece of palpitating reality that transcends its immediate political message and reaches into the ideal realm where rights are rights and wrongs are wrongs simply because the artist willed them to be so.

I am not sure, for instance, that communism as a religious cult is any less grotesque and funny than is the cult of nationalism. What does it matter? When I see *Arsenal,* communism is right with me and nationalism all wrong, and I laugh at the Ukranian patriots glorying in their embroidered shirts and cascades of patriotic oratory, or hate their cool executioners who shoot Bolsheviks like rats, while my heart goes out to the poor dying soldier who in his deathbed letter to his parents inquires if he may kill officers and bourgeois if he meets them in the street. There it is. The artist has made you accept his characters in the light in which he wants them to be seen, and you surrender yourself to the spell of his art because he has succeeded in creating an independent ideal world, entirely self-sustained and coherently compact, which has its own life and its own emotional logic.

It is strange that one should be so conscious of this inner unity, seeing that the first impression one gets from *Arsenal* is that of utter incoherence.

There is hardly any story in the picture. Groups of soldiers fight other groups of soldiers, incidental characters spring up from nowhere and disappear into nowhere, and you hardly know who is who or what it is all about. But once you have become familiar with the faces and grasped the general line of action, every character and every scene falls into its proper place as part of an emotional pattern. It is the great achievement of Dovzhenko that he has built this pattern and bound his picture together by means of a purely cinematic treatment of rhythm. Nothing so rich in contrasts, so subtle in nuances, has yet been done on the screen. The fury of the revolutionary struggle, its tragedies and humors, are all brought out by variations of rhythm that range from complete stillness with characters posing like statues, to breathless speed carrying all before it like so much litter in a gale. The episode of a runaway train, outwardly unconnected with the story, acquires symbolical significance as a rhythmic accent in a symphony of struggle that is the real story of *Arsenal.* There are two or three scenes in which symbolism appears to be somewhat forced, the characters, standing still in unnatural positions, doing symbolical duty in a picture of life that is essentially realistic; but if this is a blemish it is a minor one. The picture as a whole is an amazing performance, no less rich in its technical resourcefulness than in its dramatic sense of human character; and it is splendidly acted.

The Nation, November 27, 1929

MGM, Garbo's employers, were apprehensive about her accent and delayed her first sound picture. As late as 1929 she made her last silent film, *The Kiss,* which was also the last silent film for MGM.[2] Her next film was *Anna Christie.*

The following review celebrates what was in fact only one-third of Garbo's vocal debut. She also made German and Swedish versions of *Anna Christie.*[3] The German version, which opened in New York on January 5, 1931, was directed by the Frenchman, Jacques Feyder, and had an entirely different suporting cast. The Marie Dressler role was played by Salka Viertel, who later was coauthor of five screenplays for Garbo, *Queen Christina, The Painted Veil, Anna Karenina, Conquest,* and *Two-faced Woman.*

Katharine Cornell was a theatrical star for three decades, beginning in the 1920s.

ANNA CHRISTIE

RICHARD WATTS, JR.

The most eagerly and fearfully awaited cinema event since the talking pictures got into their stride took place yesterday, when the voice of that fascinating, inscrutable, almost legendary personage, Miss Greta Garbo, was heard upon the screen for the first time. It is pleasant to report that, in a day when so many tragic blows are being delivered at the prestige of some of the most appealing of film stars, Miss Garbo proves entirely triumphant in her defiance of the microphone. Her voice is revealed as a deep, husky, throaty contralto that possesses every bit of that fabulous, poetic glamor that has made this distant Swedish lady the outstanding performer of the motion picture. There is the vague, intangible, mythical, poetic quality in her tones that only the incomparable Miss Cornell offers upon the stage, and there is combined with it the same strange, paradoxical mood of realism that her stage parallel offers. It is impossible to believe that any Garbo addict will be made unhappy by hearing his heroine speak.

As for her acting, which it is so difficult to separate from her utterly distinctive personality, it can be accurately said that it is excellent. There is a moment or two when she seems less than expert, and there are times when you suspect that she is too poetic a creature for the grim, sordid role she is playing. At almost every turn you will guess that her next screen appearance in the sentimental drama *Romance* will be considerably more striking. Yet there is never an instant in *Anna Christie* when you doubt that Greta Garbo is the outstanding actress of the motion picture world.

As the screen transcript of an important play, *Anna Christie* is entirely successful, for the film version is accurate, handsomely produced, well acted, and faithfully managed. The only trouble is that you are bound to suspect that the O'Neill drama is not quite the masterpiece you had once imagined. The superiority of its first act over the remaining section is more obvious than ever; something of the original bite is gone, and there are times when its dramatic methods seem as archaic as those of Pinero. Nevertheless, it remains an earnest, sensitive, and effective drama that is one of the landmarks in the American theater. Whatever you may say against it, there is never anything commonplace about *Anna Christie*.

Nevertheless, it is as a Garbo vehicle, rather than as a production or a story, that *Anna Christie* is important. It might, therefore, be easy to overlook the excellence of such unsung citizens as the members of the supporting cast. Permit me, then, to remind you that George Marion, as the heroine's father, is as fine and moving as he was in the original version; that Charles Bickford is a perfect Matt Burke; and that Marie Dressler is admirable as the ancient harlot of the narrative. The important thing about *Anna Christie,* though, is that the scene where Miss Garbo makes her first appearance and walks about the screen for almost a minute before beginning her first speech contains more suspense than you can find in any talking motion picture yet made.

The New York Herald Tribune, March 15, 1930

Of all the major comics up to this time, Laurel and Hardy got the least serious criticism, probably because they were the last of their peers to make feature-length films. In 1931 they made their first feature, out of economic pressure, not out of impulse. Years later, Laurel said: "We should have stayed in the short-film category. There's just so much we can do along a certain line and then it gets to be unfunny. . . . We didn't want to go into feature-films in the first place, and even though I've got some favorites among them, I'm sorry we ever did go beyond the two- and three-reelers." [4]

One critic who paid attention to their short films, at least briefly, was Pare Lorentz, who later became a documentary filmmaker. His work includes *The Plow that Broke the Plains* and *The River.*

Amos and Andy were blackface radio stars, immensely popular in a daily serial. Moran and Mack were blackface vaudeville stars. James Parrott was the brother of the silent-film comic star, Charlie Chase, whose real name was Charles Parrott.

BLOTTO

PARE LORENTZ

I am late getting around to Laurel and Hardy. I always suspect all clichés. I have never joined the Amos-'n'-Andy school, and I did not belong to the now deceased Moran-and-Mack League. However, without a doubt, the two-reel comedies of Laurel and Hardy are the funniest and the best-directed short movies being made today. The director, James Parrott, has developed a peculiar methodical, simple routine for his comedy team. The last one I saw, *Blotto,* had very few gags and not much of a story. But the gags were pulled so deliberately and with such finesse, I wonder that Mr. Parrott does not establish a new school of movie direction.

Judge, May 10, 1930

FREE AND EASY

PARE LORENTZ

If one is to judge by the insulting letters that have littered the office these past weeks, the women of the nation were more excited by the sound apparatus of Miss Garbo than they would be by the deportation of Rudy Vallée (which, I am sorry to say, does not seem to be an imminent event). I am not going on about the Garbo situation, but if the letters continue to come in I am going to turn them over to Doctor Jung and his associates. I'll stand just so much abuse. As a matter of fact, I would not have given the coming of the Garbo voice a second thought had it not been for the fact that her owners also saw fit to record the vocal efforts of Buster Keaton, an event that should have been heralded with pall-bearers and wreaths. I have always enjoyed the antics of the frozen-faced comedian and consider his major epics of several years ago among the best movies ever produced in this country. Yet the Gold Coast boys are so fascinated with their electrical toys, it seems to make no difference to them what an actor has done—if he can't dance and sing a theme song he just isn't worth his salt.

Keaton's new movie is called *Free and Easy.* As far as I could see, the movie was presented merely as an excuse to advertise the theme song which, by a strange coincidence, is called "Free and Easy." In the so-called experimental days of the talkies the theme song was more of a trick than an asset, but by the golden alchemy so common to the movies it has been discovered that theme songs, properly plugged, are worth millions of dollars, so that from the time you pass through the lobby of a cathedral of the motion picture until you stagger away from the organ concert each week you are forced to hear a dozen versions of a new, tiny song.

Keaton not only talks; he sings and dances. He does them all well, but he emerges in this new state as just a fair hoofer with a bass voice (and we can at least be thankful it's bass). He is no longer the enigmatic personality, the persevering, misunderstood stranger with a knack for falling on his ear. He is a hoofer, and there are thousands who can do his tricks just as well. It might interest his employers to know that there is a comedian of the stage called Harpo Marx who has been successful for years yet has never been forced to speak or do a tap dance. It seems to me Keaton would have been worth twice as much as a comedian if, in a day of talking pictures, he had remained silent, but I suppose it is too much to ask of the boys to expect them not to use their toys while they have them.

Free and Easy has some wretched dancing, a long and tiresome story about a Kansas girl who tries to break into the movies, and a plot that borrows most of its effects from *Merton of the Movies.* Keaton is funny at times, but his most valuable asset—pantomime—is gone. I still think his one-man baseball game in the Yankee Stadium, a scene in his silent *Cameraman,* was one of the funniest bits ever done in a movie. Such things do not belong to the dancing and grumbling era of the films.

Judge, May 17, 1930

Bakshy's reference point below, *Journey's End,* was a film based on a highly successful play about British soldiers in World War I by R. C. Sherriff.

ALL QUIET ON THE WESTERN FRONT

ALEXANDER BAKSHY

According to one of Bernard Shaw's pet theories, the stage in the matter of ideas is usually ten years behind literature. It would be difficult to say how far behind the movies are, for as a rule they care precious little about ideas. But there is one exception. Let the idea attract public interest, let the book in which it has found expression be a best seller, and no expense will keep the film companies from producing the book as a movie as quickly as they can get the rights. During the past year the Great War was the most popular subject in literature, and for once, to refute Bernard Shaw, also on the stage; and so *All Quiet on the Western Front,* as well as *Journey's End,* has already found its way to the screen. Need it be added that both cost tremendous sums to produce (it is said, two millions in the case of *All Quiet*), and that both have been unprecedented box office successes?

There can be little doubt that Remarque's *All Quiet* is not a great literary masterpiece. At least this was the conclusion that I arrived at after I had found that nearly every page of the book required a special focusing of imagination in order to bring out in clear relief the episodes and facts that stud the author's guileless and inarticulate prose. Nevertheless, there is no denying the interest and importance of the story as a human document. No book had spoken so courageously and, granting the necessary effort of mental readjustment, so vividly of the sheer horror of war—of man's relapse into bestiality with its frenzy of fear and rage, of his physical suffering and moral prostration. It is just as such a document that *All Quiet* emerges in a film of the same name—a terrifying document that reveals the carnage of war with staggering force. Battle scenes have been represented in many a picture, but *All Quiet* surpasses them all in the stark horror and madness of the business of fighting. Although the picture is not devoid of gentler moods, and is sprinkled generously with captivating humor, the predominant impression is that of life in the raw, of existence stripped of all adornments and bared to the bone. For this reason the total effect produced is not so much the tragedy of war as its callous bestiality. One is staggered, and shaken, and almost ready to sob, but one is not really thrilled. It is probably because of the elemental quality of its material that *All Quiet* is not so good a drama as *Journey's End;* but its appeal is more immediate, and technically it is a superior piece of cinematic craftsmanship, for which achievement Mr. Milestone, who directed the picture, deserves unstinted praise.

The Nation, June 11, 1930

Ernst Lubitsch, who had been a Reinhardt actor in the theater and a screen comic before he began directing films in his native Germany, was one of the talents brought to Hollywood by the American shopping tours of Europe in the twenties.

The Dance of Life, directed by John Cromwell, was a musical based on the Broadway hit, *Burlesque.*

MONTE CARLO | *ANIMAL CRACKERS*

ALEXANDER BAKSHY

Musical comedy is not a subject to be approached lightly by a critic. He may be excused writing about it in the facetious tone characteristic of the genre itself, but may he be serious about it? At the risk of appearing a low-brow to some and a bore to others, I propose to be nothing but serious in discussing *Monte Carlo* and *Animal Crackers.* After all, entertaining as these two pictures are, the question why they are not more entertaining does not seem to be particularly funny, except for the comedy, of course, that belongs by the very nature of things to all doings of Hollywood.

Strictly speaking, the problem is not the same in both pictures. *Animal Crackers* is essentially a farce in which a quartet of delightful loonies is let loose regardless of consequences. The loonies being those excellent entertainers, the Marx Brothers, the only quarrel I can pick with the picture is the tameness of its direction outside of its dialogue and gags. A little detail, the painted mustache of Groucho's make-up, may serve to illustrate this point. That a character supposed to be merely a freak should be stamped as a stage comedian is an incongruity to be explained only by the inability of the actors and director to shake off their memories of the stage.

Incidental in *Animal Crackers,* this problem of the stage and its conventions becomes the dominant factor in *Monte Carlo.* Here we are presented with the deft and at times very witty efforts of that grand master of Hollywood, Mr. Ernst Lubitsch, to acclimatize the familiar musical comedy to the screen. Be it remembered, the musical comedy in question is not that of *The Jazz Singer* or *The Dance of Life,* where singing and dancing flowed naturally from the fact that the characters were singers and dancers. No, in *Monte Carlo* as in his earlier *Love Parade,* Mr. Lubitsch is out to capture the very spirit of the artificial, conventional musical comedy, with its music and dancing as means of dramatic expression independent of the realistic requirements of the plot. It must be admitted that these realistic requirements have balked Mr. Lubitsch, as they have balked others. In fact, every time he introduces singing (in solos, duets, and even choruses) he feels obliged to disguise the procedures by some device, at which he is often extremely ingenious. It must be even regretfully stated that most of Mr. Lubitsch's ingenuity in *Monte Carlo* is directed at disguising the staginess of the musical comedy convention, whereas in *The Love Parade* he allowed himself a few brilliantly successful flings at something more creative and original; viz., at combining independent sounds and images by the process of cutting. Seeing that the final solution of the problem of musical acting on the screen can be found only in the direction of such assembling of sounds and images, I am baffled by the shortsightedness of the Hollywood producers who have not set a single director to explore to the full this tremendous field of cinematic possibilities.

The artistic justification of musical comedy on the theater stage lies in its frank emphasis of its staginess. But no actor on the screen can make the audience accept him as an actor. He is and will always remain a character. On the screen the power of direct contact with the audience can be wielded only by one person, the man who pulls the strings behind the scenes, the director. For this, however, he must stress the arrangement, the graphic pattern of his images on the screen in their relation with sounds. There is much more to be done in this direction than merely to diversify visual images that are strung together by a continuous dialogue, song, or orchestral accompaniment, as in most of *Monte Carlo,* or to combine independent characteristic sounds into a dramatic unison, whether simultaneous as in the train scenes in *Monte Carlo* or consecutive as in the barking dogs and other episodes in *The Love Parade.* Particularly do I look forward to the technique of the "split screen," which more than any other method promises to develop a purely cinematic convention of musical comedy and drama.

The Nation, October 1, 1930

Earlier this year, in *Pagany,* Spring 1930, Potamkin had called D. W. Griffith "the first great composer (not artist) of films," a concept pertinent to the following review.

The New Masses was a Communist magazine whose high points of circulation and influence were in the Depression years. Stephen Vincent Benét, author of stories and poems, had written *John Brown's Body,* a novel-length epic poem that was a rousing best seller. *China Express* was a melodrama directed by Ilya Trauberg, an Eisenstein disciple.[5]

STORM OVER ASIA | ABRAHAM LINCOLN

HARRY ALAN POTAMKIN

In the first chapter of the history of the art of the motion picture, the name of David Wark Griffith will be important. He was the first to suspect the scope of the new medium, and, although the new devices he introduced were conceived by him solely as expedience, they have been utilized by other succeeding directors as experiences. These directors are mainly the Soviet artists. The American movie has not extended in the least the work of Griffith and his early contemporaries. Pudovkin, among the Soviet directors, has developed the early American film to its ultimate. *Storm over Asia* is the culmination of the romantic technique of the Griffith-Western period. As a culmination or perfection of the primitive film it is a reflection upon the inertia of the American movie. As a perfection of the film of muscular impact, it is still unsuited in method to the profound material of the Soviet kino.

I first saw *Storm over Asia,* intact, in Amsterdam. I have seen it three times since. My reaction has been always the same. An exciting film, which beats any American audience-film. It makes the boasted dramatic technique of America appear a schoolboy's exercise. Griffith's *Lincoln,* in comparison with it, is a mooning idyll. Yet both Pudovkin and Griffith suffer commonly from a sentimentalism which expresses itself in bad "figures of speech" and oversimplification. The theme in Pudovkin's film is tremendous: imperialism. In Griffith's film it is trivial: the Lincoln of the least of the epigrams—a Lincoln that any child beyond the fifth grade in school would disown. Pudovkin, like every Soviet director, had a social theme to convert into a dramatic instance. Griffith had a sentimental figure out of a fairy tale. In the particularization of the theme, the film itself, Pudovkin selected frequent symbols below the level of the theme, and stressed too ardently the personalities and their narrative, so that very often the theme —the implication of the narrative—is not perceivable in the occurrences. That is one reason the film, while possessing strength, physical strength, lacks poignancy, penetration. *China Express,* in contrast, while not grand, remains a more poignant, permanently appealing, film upon imperialism.

In Griffith we see what Pudovkin might have been in America 1910-30. In Pudovkin we see what Griffith might have been in the U.S.S.R. Griffith, possessing social sympathies, expressed these in platitudes on "tolerance" and "free speech," and read his American history in the terms of *The Clansman* (the Ku Klux Klan and the Confederacy, in whose army his father was a General), and in the terms of the crudest Lincoln myths. His films in the past have been innocuous idylls and grandiose panorama, allowing him distinction for his instincts of composition. *Lincoln* has everything of the sentimentally idyllic, and nothing of the grandiose. It is an unintelligent Drinkwater chronicle-play on the screen, despite Stephen Vincent Benét's hand in the scenario (why "despite?"). The fact that it draws tears is rather against it than for it. The pathos of a tremendous social occurrence should not be refined or lachrymose, but revealing. The social occurrence seldom gets a chance here. Slogans of spurious manufacture explain the motivations of the Civil War.

The legend of a people may offer as much substance for revelation as the actual unmythical source. But such revelation demands a critical understanding which alone assures a surpassing of the elementary myth. Griffith possesses no critical penetration. The nostalgia of a dessicate aristocracy seeps through the film: in the silly pretense with music to toleration of the black (what an hypocrisy after *The Birth of A Nation*); in the tiresome reiteration of the virtues of the protagonists—Lee especially, etc. Griffith, still bound to the conceptions of refinement and good taste (a tradition set by him by now noxious in the American movie), thwarted a player of more eloquent talents, Walter Huston. And the innovator of the silent film contributes nothing to the improvement of the garrulous. The simple-minded spectator will carry away with him an amiable sentiment toward North and South, emancipation and slavery, and the Union forever! The close, with Lincoln's monument, is a palpable bid for patriotism. Who says the American movie is against propaganda?

A last tribute: to Soviet photography in *Storm over Asia,* as against the sickening "artisticalness" of the Menzies-Struss collaboration in *Lincoln.* To the authentic types (they become prototypes) in *Storm over Asia* as against the dubious histrions of *Lincoln* (notice Abe Lincoln's lip-rouge). The selection of types among nonprofessionals has taught the Soviet director to select the authentic even among professionals.

These two films call forth speculations upon the nature of propaganda, which concides with the nature of art. *Storm over Asia* asks: "How much immediate impact, how much aftereffect? Cannot what drives in too forcefully, just as easily drive out? Is not propaganda the accumulation of what is implied?" *Lincoln* says: "The less critical the propaganda, the less valid art it demands."

The New Masses, October 1930

Morocco marked the American debut of Marlene Dietrich. The German film that had brought her to Hollywood, *The Blue Angel,* was not released in the United States until a month later.[6]

MOROCCO

WILTON A. BARRETT [7]

Many discerning commentators have felt, some even from the time of the early *Salvation Hunters,* that in Josef von Sternberg our screen had found its most interesting exponent—an experimentalist whose work would sooner or later parallel in its creative aspect the work of artists in other fields and mediums of expression. *Underworld* went far to substantiate this feeling. It had form, dramatic meaning, esthetic purpose. It recognized the box office, but it did not truckle to it. It was a silent film. Then came sound and dialogue. In its effort to reproduce the stage, the cinematic pattern of the motion picture, painfully developed through a span of thirty and more years, slipped back overnight to the verge of its crude beginning. What would Mr. von Sternberg do with the destroying devils of the mike, the disk, and the sound track?

Mr. von Sternberg, it would seem, set out to find a proper use for them with a keen determination to preserve the cinematic pattern. He saw dialogue and sound as adjuncts and not as principles of fundamental change. After a period of testing in which he produced several worthy sound films, he now comes before his public with *Morocco*.

It is our purpose only to hint at its plot material and the interest and authenticity of his characters. Neither, striking as they undoubtedly are, by themselves make it the outstanding film that is a definite step forward in the art of motion pictures, one of the most noteworthy films, many will think when they have studied it, that the sound screen has yet produced. However, some outline must be undertaken in order to give the tonal background to a sketch of the technical perfections of the production.

To the hot Algerian locale, then, comes a strange, exotic person, a young actress of the trooper's stage, adventuring, her antecedents never more than obliquely indicated. Once installed as a singer in the local cabaret, she comes by a great passion for a common soldier of the Foreign Legion, a company of which happens to be quartered in the town. A wealthy artist now falls in love with her, offers to marry her. The soldier having failed in his promise to desert and take her back to Europe, she consents to this marriage. But she ends up by following the Legionnaire into the desert, when he marches away the second time with his company, tramping after him with the native women, the camp followers, who cannot give their men up.

Thus, like all motion pictures of the front rank, the material is that of the screen alone, the narrative thread an exceedingly simple one. It amounts to the way it is embroidered. And here the result is that cinematic pattern we have mentioned, brilliant, profuse, subtle, and at almost every turn inventive.

Morocco sets its sound in the background. Its speech is purely that of pictures, except where the pictures can be told more effectively by sound. For example: the Legionnaire is sent forward to capture a machine gun nest. You hear the put-put-put of the gun, at first in the distance, then nearer, nearer, as the soldier, whom you always see, creeps closer to it. The effect is wonderfully heightened, partakes of reality itself, gives the immediacy of self-experience. The capture of the gun is left in the air with a fading screen, and the suspense is kept like a bridge over to the following sequence of events. This sort of thing is unfailingly terse, cinematically economic, a cunning grasp of the power of suggestion as made possible by the image in motion and the sound that in the context of that image, and in association with it, can make another image of its own. It is the sort of thing that points the way to the method of the motion picture of tomorrow, and makes of *Morocco* a stimulating forerunner.

And again with the use of dialogue in this film: when a character speaks it is merely in substantiation of the thing the action has made you see and know. The artist gives his engagement supper to his friends. All is sumptuous, splendid, covered with light, gaiety, and tender feeling. The tragic past of his fiancée is gone. Then the drums of the returning Legionnaires are faintly heard. You get the sensation of the stirring city in the warm night outside. And Jolly must tear herself away, must go to find her lover. There is no word spoken. Eloquently the silent screen speaks to us as of old. And when she is gone, you get the shot of the long, richly laden table with its startled, embarrassed guests, and its host at the head, left to his contemplation of the situation. He rises, for he must follow Jolly, just as she must follow the soldier, Tom Brown. Then Menjou, who plays the artist lover, says, and from the screen emanates not a mechanical voice out of the flat middle of a shadow, but living words from the human lips, quiet, moving, and immensely real: "You see—I love her." How terse and how explanatory—yet it is the picture, the cinema, the parade of images, convoluting yet always leading to that moment, and not the sound device, that makes the simple utterance so effective. One could go on finding in this film a textbook and finding in the firm and sinewy grasp of its director the resolve to bring the motion picture, with the new powers that science has given it, back to its own.

And because the readers of this review will possibly wish to know a few more things about *Morocco* other than these notes regarding its technology, it should be said that the photographic quality is frequently of the best (another point of return to the highest traditions of the screen before the advent of sound made cameramen careless and slovenly); that its atmosphere is not manufactured out of heated hokum, but arises from what seems, no matter how strange, to be real and in its place; and the acting of the cast—well, go see the picture when you have the chance, for under the handling of Mr. von Sternberg, Menjou is at his level best in a role that could easily have become maudlin if not unbelievable, and Gary Cooper achieves a rough naturalness that gives one understanding and holds one's interest; but Marlene Dietrich, the newly risen star, shines forth, a personage indeed, something different on the screen, an actress to wit, a symbol of glamor, like whom there is but one other in motion pictures—and when you see *Morocco,* you will be reminded who that is.

One word more. As a study of the attraction that a man and woman of a certain type may have for one another—that can tear a woman from whatever of safety and pleasure her existence holds—*Morocco* is not unsubtle in its psychological reading. And this it is, perhaps, that leaves us feeling that we have seen something true if strange.

National Board of Review Magazine, November 1930

Richard Dana Skinner, one of the founders of *The Commonweal* and its drama critic from 1924 to 1934, sometimes wrote on film.

The version of *The Blue Angel* reviewed here, with much of the dialogue in English and some in German, is no longer shown.

Josef von Sternberg, not an idolator of actors, said of Emil Jannings that he "had every right to the universal praise that was his for many years, and his position in the history of the motion picture is secure, not only as a superlative performer but also as a source of inspiration for the writers and directors of his time." [8]

THE BLUE ANGEL

RICHARD DANA SKINNER

Like the first talkie of Greta Garbo, the first sound film of Emil Jannings is a notable event. In the present instance, the vehicle for the occasion is a maudlin and humorless affair, produced under Ufa auspices, in which, after the Berlin fashion, sensual details are freely played up for their own sake and with a disagreeably leering quality. But that fact does not lessen by one iota the actual worth of Janning's own performance, nor the significance of the fact that plays can be written in which, by clever arrangement, the apparent barriers of language can be surmounted successfully and plausibly.

The story, which is the rather trite one of an old man making a tragic fool of himself over a cabaret singer, is placed in Germany. The old professor (Jannings) is a teacher of English literature, who insists that all the boys in his class talk English. The cabaret singer (Marlene Dietrich) is supposed to be an American. This combination of circumstances gives a reasonable excuse for English being spoken in every scene that counts. The few passages in German are so easily understood by the pantomime that the entire effect is authentic and unforced. Exceptionally fine photography, swift and intelligent sequences, and a minimum of dialogue all contribute to make the picture an excellent and hopeful product from the purely technical aspect.

But since technical excellence is marred so frequently by the detailed material, it is only the work of Jannings that deserves comment for its own sake. Speech helps, if anything, his mastery of screen technique. He is an artist of detail down to the least motion of his hands. When, for comedy, he repeats a certain scene, such as the morning opening of his classes, he is careful to give just the right bit of variety and change. He fully conveys the man of routine habits, without the absurdity of identical actions. In the tragedy which follows his marriage to the cabaret singer, in his slow decline to a low comedy actor, and in his final madness and death, he reaches rare heights of tragedy. It is good to know that he can now be numbered among the few great artists of the talking screen.

The Commonweal, December 31, 1930

THE BLUE ANGEL

A picture which features the welcome return of Emil Jannings to the screen in a talking part and which at the same time shows us another step in Marlene Dietrich's meteoric ascent to stardom presumes that we are witnessing an event of importance.

That presumption is entirely correct. *The Blue Angel* is surely one of the outstanding pictures of this season's screen offerings. Strictly speaking this is a foreign picture. For it was made in Berlin. But it is a foreign picture with English speech, occasional German interpolations being used for the sake of atmosphere and realism.

Certainly it is astonishingly well suited both to the capacities and the limitations of Emil Jannings. For here again we have a story of the disintegration of a fine character to the point of complete degradation with a tragic flash of his former self at the end which heightens the dramatic contrast. And again the emphasis is upon character delineation rather than upon action, so that the star's slow, deliberate method and his gift for portraiture are given full opportunity to score.

In the matter of the dialogue and the talking sequences it is even more subtly adapted to the requirements of Mr. Jannings. He plays the part of a professor of English in a German high school. That rather familiar type in the German school system is likely to be correct but halting in his English, to be far from idiomatic, and to be all the more sure that he is right because he knows his Shakespeare better than you do. Though slightly comic it is an ideal part for a man like Jannings who was always diffident about his English in real life and who for that reason passed from the American screen with the advent of talking pictures.

Jannings proceeds to give us the schoolmaster par excellence. He is pedantic, brusque, with a certain ludicrous dignity, and he is cordially hated by his pupils. He is greatly perturbed to find them circulating a post-card of an alluring cabaret performer in "The Blue Angel," a dive in an unsavory part of town. Rather inquisitorially investigating their evening activities, he meets the temptress and is promptly ruined by a combination of his own suddenly awakened sensual weakness and the code of respectability to which his superiors adhere. With a few changes of locale and character one can, of course, make comparisons with Jannings' previous picture, *The Way of All Flesh*. These comparisons, however, need not be invidious, and the contrasting element of dialogue provides a sufficient difference to make this latest picture refreshing.

The Blue Angel is notable from the directing angle on account of von Sternberg's clever combination of talking and silent film technique. He uses dialogue sparingly and climatically and employs long sequences of purely cinematic storytelling. In other words, he allows the camera to tell the story whenever possible rather than letting the actor tell it vocally. That, in a nutshell, is the goal of good talking pictures today, now that the ghost of the all-talking picture has been laid.

Certain talking sequences, or sometimes merely single phrases, are in German. This in no way detracts from our understanding of the action. For they are used purely for atmosphere, at times when the action fully conveys the meaning. Thus, for instance, the Professor's housekeeper addresses him in German through the door of his bedroom. But her manner and the breakfast tray in her hands plainly shows that she is telling him that it is time for him to get up and have his breakfast. A policeman in the cabaret who is being berated by one of the performers tells her, in German, to keep her mouth shut. It is perfectly obvious to any English-speaking audience that that must be exactly what he is telling her. Intrinsically these German sequences have the same effect which silent sequences would have. It is unnecessary to make them vocal except for atmospheric effect. But the atmospheric excuse is sufficient, for though the hero is a professor of English, teaching English to his pupils and succumbing to an English traveling cabaret entertainer, he moves in an environment of German speech. As long as pictures have become lingual there is no reason why they should not also become polylingual when the story logically calls for it.

Occasionally Mr. von Sternberg's directorial style leads him into slow tempo as if building up for a dramatic suspense which never quite comes off. This is all the more noticeable in a picture which has a minimum of action and a surplusage of characterization and atmosphere. These defects were perhaps abetted by Jannings. One sometimes wonders whether Jannings, especially since he became an undisputed star, has not always set the tempo of his pictures, however his director might cry for speed. His slow, deliberate method of acting and gesticulating at times anticipated the talking picture while he was still acting on the silent screen.

Marlene Dietrich, whose performance in this picture ranks her very close to the star, gives an excellent account of herself. Her rendition of the part is both trivial and tragic. She is the accidental cause of the Professor's downfall, and he is merely an incident in her career of seduction, but at the same time her manner suggests that she is an instrument of destruction inevitably making for evil whether she wants to or not.

Her work as we have now seen it in both *The Blue Angel* and in *Morocco* certainly stamps her as an actress of unusual merit. But it is hoped that the powers that be will not force her to repeat the same type of part in her future pictures or label her as a second so-and-so. Her talents are sufficient to allow her to stand on her own merits.

National Board of Review Magazine, January 1931

SOUS LES TOITS DE PARIS

ALEXANDER BAKSHY

René Clair, the author and director of *Sous les Toits de Paris,* enjoys the combined benefits of talent and good fortune. He has produced a picture that in many ways is a little masterpiece, and he has been lucky enough to be the first artist in a field that has been dominated by Hollywood robots. Indeed, so great is one's relief and delight at seeing a fresh mind, unencumbered with hollow conventions and equipped with taste, subtle wit, and imaginative insight, apply itself to fashioning a work of art that the shortcomings of the picture inevitably recede into the background. There I shall leave them for the moment, to stress the more important fact—the fascination and charm of René Clair's offspring.

The quality of the picture is revealed almost from its opening scenes. The characters have hardly been introduced when the story halts on a scene in which a group of Parisian tenement dwellers, led by a young peddler of songs, engage in solemn singing in the fashion of the Salvation Army. The length of the song, the dulness of the music, and the solemnity of the singing would have been enough to condemn this scene for any Hollywood talkie. But here comes the miracle of art. By introducing a slight action, so slight that it is almost entirely confined to an exchange of glances between the peddler and a prowling pickpocket, the artist sets off the vital force. Instantly the characters become intensely alive, the singing acquires the quality of suspense, and the whole scene begins to sparkle with humor and to throb with the pulse of human life. By vivifying touches such as this, one scene after another is transformed into a palpitating reality. We observe their effect in the episode of the two friends interrupting their altercation to turn on the fashionably dressed passers-by who stop to gaze at them; in the scene of another fight where a gramophone keeps wailing after the tune has played itself out, and where the face of a silent café habitué plays a gamut of expressions that follows the action with a tale of its own; and in several other episodes throughout the picture, too numerous to be listed here. All this testifies to the freshness of approach and the sense of vital and significant detail with which René Clair treats the material of human life. His imaginative vision of this life is the source of the authentic Parisian atmosphere that distinguishes his picture, that makes it so stimulating in its sober earnestness.

But greatly as I admire this creative interpretation of the material of life and the flawless acting in which it is embodied I am not prepared to regard *Sous les Toits de Paris* as an important advance in the solution of the problem of cinematic form in the talkies. René Clair undoubtedly achieves a fair measure of success in blending scenes with dialogue with scenes without dialogue. He succeeds, however, only by the extensive use of music, of which, as it happens, he has an abundant supply in his story and setting. But even he is occasionally obliged to resort to music as mere accompaniment, as in the old silent pictures; and this method, if applied to less musical stories, would be dodging the issue of cinematic dialogue.

The Nation, January 7, 1931

The gangster film was not an invention of the thirties—there had been dozens of them during the twenties—but two factors seemed to fertilize it especially now. The addition of sound had given it new life; the machine gun could now be heard. And the Depression seemed to inflame a civic frustration in the public that found a special satisfaction in vicarious civic violence.

LITTLE CAESAR

RICHARD WATTS, JR.

From *Little Caesar,* W. R. Burnett's much-admired novel about the rise and fall of a homicidal gang chieftain, comes the truest, most ambitious and most distinguished of all that endless series of gangster photoplays which have been inundating us in recent years. So many pictures celebrating the adventures of America's most picturesque banditti have been manufactured and their formula has become so stale that it is difficult to believe that a fresh and distinctive work on the subject is currently possible. But *Little Caesar,* by pushing into the background the usual romantic conventions of the theme and concentrating on characterization rather than on plot, emerges not only as an effective and rather chilling melodrama, but also as what is sometimes described as a Document. Chiefly, though, it is made important by the genuinely brilliant performance that Edward G. Robinson contributes to the title role.

Ever since Mr. Robinson created the part of the sinister Nick Scarsi in that memorable stage melodrama, *The Racket,* he has seemed doomed to play evil gang leaders. He has played them in dozens of films, shrewdly and competently, but he has done the same role so frequently that it appeared not unlikely that he, too, was beginning to run to formula in the part; that, having acted the same character over and over again, there was the danger that it would become a routine. In *Little Caesar,* he dissipates any such suspicion. Not even in *The Racket* was he more effective. Taking one of the most familiar roles in the universe, he makes it seem fresh and real. By a hundred details of characterization, he transforms a stock figure into a human being. And, heaven knows, he doesn't make Little Caesar human by suggesting any softness in him. Never does he cease being a savage and terrifying killer, a man who is all the more sinister because of his reality.

If you happen to be interested in my idea of good acting, let me recommend to you the scene in which Little Caesar, broken and beaten, lies on the dirty bed of a flop house and overhears the reading of a newspaper story in which Police Sergeant Flaherty accuses him of cowardice. When you watch him writhing there in impotent rage over the insult and uttering grotesque animal outcries of pain and indignation, you are seeing a scene which almost any actor would ruin, but which Mr. Robinson makes the most effective current moment in the cinema.

Little Caesar is the first of the gangster pictures to capture any of that realistic sense and that menacing, rather shocking credibility that Edward Dean Sullivan gets into his books about Chicago crime. The viewpoint of the photoplay is strikingly effective. As closely as the censors will permit, it adopts something of the manner of Fielding's *Jonathan Wild* and permits us to see how its hero-villain sees his career as a triumph of integrity, character, and good old ambition, as proof that hard work, earnestness of purpose, and an avoidance of bad habits will carry the worthwhile fellow to the top. It has irony and grim humor and a real sense of excitement, and its significance does not get in the way of the melodrama.

Hollywood, it seems, can always cast a racketeer picture realistically and in *Little Caesar* the types are admirably chosen. It is, of course, Mr. Robinson's film, but the lesser roles are capably handled. That increasingly competent actor, the younger Douglas Fairbanks, is particularly good, and so are Stanley Fields and George Stone. Thomas Jackson again plays a soft-voiced detective perfectly.

The New York Herald Tribune, January 10, 1931

John Mosher, author of a collection of sketches called *Celibate at Twilight,* was the film critic of *The New Yorker* from 1928 until his death in 1942.

LITTLE CAESAR

JOHN MOSHER

In *Little Caesar,* the new picture at the Strand, you may find some insight into the criminal mind which will be useful in your dealings and contacts with this social system of ours. Since his appearance on the stage in *The Racket,* Edward G. Robinson has grown to be the leading authority on the behavior and mannerisms of those gunmen and gangsters whose doings often occupy the attention of the press. Evidently all his experience and research work in such a field are now employed in the study of Rico Bandello, the central figure of this movie.

Little Caesar (from W. R. Burnett's chronicle) is the story of the Chicago career of an enterprising young man from a small town who climbs high, step by step, in the world of gangsters until he steps just a bit too far when he shoots the Crime Commissioner. The picture does not indorse his activities, and he dies at last miserably in a vacant lot under the machine-gun fire of the police. Aside from the most unobstrusive sub-plot involving Little Caesar's comrade, admirably played by Douglas Fairbanks, Jr., and a nightclub dancer, the movie is almost a case-history, a straight document of the gunman's life. It is not as a glamorous affair nor as a story of adventure that this picture is interesting.

The piece is not so intensively or thoroughly worked out, I feel, as to be the final word on this absorbing topic, yet Mr. Robinson's diagnosis of our Little Augies and perennial Gyp the Bloods is so simplified and so articulate as to be the outstanding characterization of the kind at the moment. You will gather from his portrayal that these sinister persons have the most curious, childlike qualities. The most naïve vanity seems to be the moving spirit of his Little Caesar. His eyes glitter at the sight of a scarfpin in the tie of his superior, and nothing will stop him until he has then disposed of that gentleman and assumed his leadership and his jewels. When he reaches high pinnacles where he must don a dinner coat, with spats, he is fearful that he looks a fool yet is fascinated by the elegance of his own appearance. Mr. Robinson makes this more sensitive side of his character amusing, yet hardly poignant. He is doubtless correct in the suggestion of a stupidity behind this slick and adroit gunplay which is this Caesar's solution of all problems. What he does is to make the gunman certainly no hero in a world of appealing glamor, and very probably his analysis is accurate.

The New Yorker, January 17, 1931

THE PUBLIC ENEMY

RICHARD WATTS, JR.

There is, about *The Public Enemy,* a quality of grim directness, Zolaesque power, and chilling credibility which makes it far more real and infinitely more impressive than the run of gangster films. It is the inevitable conclusion of pictures dealing with this highly colored phase of contemporary Americana that there is something just the least bit romantic about the annals of the gunmen, strive as the producers may to add to their work the correct moral that crime doesn't pay. Even *Little Caesar,* the best of these photoplays and the first one to attempt an honest, ironic dissection of the gangster mind, could not, despite its efforts, quite keep from its malignant little murderer a touch of Napoleonic romance. *The Public Enemy* is not as strikingly dramatic a motion picture as *Little Caesar,* but certainly it is the most ruthless, unsentimental appraisal of the meanness of a petty killer that the cinema has yet devised.

Its central character is a homicidal little rat, and there never is any effort to show him as anything else. *The Public Enemy* is merely his biography. You see him first as the tough boy of the neighborhood, a petty thief operating in the department stores of his vicinity. You watch him graduating into the bigger business of robbing a storage loft, follow him through his subsequent career as rumrunner and killer, and in the end see his bullet-riddled body dumped down, rather melodramatically, in front of his mother's door by a rival mob.

All of his story is presented simply, directly, and more in the manner of sociological document than of a picturesque and exciting melodrama. No doubt the most impressive thing about the picture is that complete refusal to sentimentalize its central figure. Even *Little Caesar* showed its hero in the moment when he was too romantic to shoot down the friend who had deserted, and granted him a touch of tragic grandeur in that incredulous dying speech of his: "Mother of Mercy, can this be the end of Little Caesar?" In the new picture there are no such extenuating episodes. Its title character does attempt to be reasonably decent to his mother, but that represents the only effort made to show him as even comparatively human. From the time that you see him engaged in his first robbery to the moment when he walks out on the girl he is about to win in order to shoot down the horse that had thrown the head of his gang, he is utterly merciless, utterly homicidal, and utterly real.

In the all-important title role, James Cagney, a splendid actor who hitherto never has been properly appreciated by the producers, plays with a simple, relentless honesty that should immediately place him among the personages of the screen. Certainly only Edward G. Robinson has played one of these modern urban assassins with a similar power and veracity. There is another superior performance by Edward Woods as the slightly more human companion of the boy torpedo, and most of the other members of the cast likewise are excellent. It seems to me, however, that Miss Jean Harlow completely ruins the scene in which an attempt is made to show the comparative values of shooting and loving in the animal mind of our amiable hero.

William Wellman, whose direction has not always been applauded in these columns, has handled the picture admirably, bringing out all its qualities of grimness and ferocity. *The Public Enemy* doesn't always succeed in being what is known as a good show, and it might well have been cut down a bit, but it is powerful and impressive—well, not entertainment, but at least drama.

The New York Herald Tribune, April 24, 1931

James Shelley Hamilton had succeeded Alfred Kuttner as head of the committee in the Exceptional Photoplays Department of the *National Board of Review Magazine.*

THE PUBLIC ENEMY

JAMES SHELLEY HAMILTON

The Public Enemy tries to give the impression of being something of a sociological document, presenting—editorially—its story and characters as a problem which the country must, *must,* MUST solve. This emphasis, contained in a foreword and an afterword, is all very well, but the picture does very little to solve it. It differs from most of the other pictures in showing its gangsters from boyhood, when the first seeds of evil were planted, and how associations and opportunity nourished those seeds into first-class specimens of modern crime. This attempt to uncover first causes is pretty superficial and unconvincing: Tom Powers seems to have been a bad lot from the beginning, cruel, and a bully, with a natural instinct for taking what he wanted without any qualms about how he did it, or about other people's rights. His home life was certainly not a nursery of crime, for his brother, with no other advantages but what his own special interests and ambitions created for himself, turned out to be as upright a young man as ever graced the screen. The moral may be that boys should not be allowed on the streets—in this case it is not a moral with a very sharp point, for no active boy could be blamed for staying away as much as possible from a home so saturated with the kind of monotonous cloying sweetness that Beryl Mercer always exudes when she is given a mother part to play. The truly logical inference from the picture is that criminals are born, not made, which is no striking help toward the solution of the gangster problem.

The real power of *The Public Enemy*—and it has a certain power, of the hit-you-between-the-eyes kind—lies in its vigorous and brutal assault upon the nerves, and in the stunning—stunning in its literal sense—acting of James Cagney. Incidents culled from the actual records of gangsterdom, which no writer would hope to make credible if he merely imagined them, are put on the screen with astonishing effect, and the position of women in the gangster's life is exhibited from an angle that the motion picture has hardly ventured to approach before. No girl, no matter how waywardly romantic, is likely to get any illusions about the thrill of being a gangster's moll from seeing how the ladies fare in this film. Women, on the whole, will probably find the picture an exceedingly unpleasant thing to look at.

The central figure is acted by James Cagney, who did more than anyone else to make *The Doorway to Hell* an interesting picture. Here he is a fairly thorough little rat, hard-boiled, vicious, cruel. As a piece of acting it is remarkable in its vividness and consistency. As a character its effect is rather mixed—somehow it manages to create a kind of sympathy, not through understanding of the circumstances that are implied to have created such a man but by the subtle appeal that loyalty to friends and to a code always makes. The strongest impression is not that a gangster inevitably gets bumped off, but that there was something likable and courageous about the little rat after all.

In direction the picture is competent but not remarkable. It permits some rather painful doings on the part of Beryl Mercer and Jean Harlow, but it handles the men very effectively. And it keeps pretty closely to motion picture technique, telling its story with the camera without leaning too much on stage devices of dialogue.

The National Board of Review Magazine, May 1931

Francis Fergusson, one of the very best American drama critics, wrote a monthly column of theater reviews for a time in the 1930s, from which the following is excerpted.

CITY LIGHTS

FRANCIS FERGUSSON

If any excuse is needed for discussing [Charlie Chaplin's] latest film in notes supposedly devoted to the stage, it is that his method provides a model many stage artists would do well to study. It is lucky for us all that he developed as a speechless clown, and that he was wise enough not to make his new film "talkie." He never tells us about anything, he shows us something, and we laugh or cry. Words are hard even for a poet to bring to life, and a writer of dialogue can hardly hope to attain anything like the immediacy of a good image, much less of an authentic moment of acting. All he can hope to do, scratching his head in his large Hollywood suite, is figure out how to make the story clear, and Chaplin, the pantomimist, needs no help with that.

He took into his own hands both the directing and scenario-writing and made one of the better Charlie Chaplin legends. His girl, a blind flower-seller, loves him as long as she can't see him. His rich friend embraces him when drunk and kicks him downstairs when sober. In the midst of one of his few beatific moments, while he contemplates his lady love, a cat in an upper window knocks down a flower-pot that cracks him rudely on the head. This gives him a chance to make the best of things until the last close-up of Charlie watching the girl (whose sight is restored) realize what a hobo she has loved. Then he shows us an ironic gleam in the eye, like Chaplin stepping from behind the tramp make-up and confessing that he knew from the first what a sinister business life was. Notice—for I suppose that by the time this is published everyone will have seen *City Lights* —notice how well he understands how often to repeat his absurd misfortunes. Twice, while he is trying to rescue his drunken friend, they both fall into the harbor. When he is contemplating a picture in a store window, and stepping back, like a connoisseur, to get the proper light, a trap door opens behind him. He plays with this for a long time—sometimes the trap closes in time to receive him; sometimes he stops right on the brink. At last he falls in. The dénouement is as clear and well developed as the end of a theorem of geometry; but the repetitions serve not only for clarity, but to emphasize that cruel, laughable absurdity which is integral with the story and the character.

Of course, Chaplin uses some of the dead trappings of the movies—he has not completely vitalized his medium. His music, though extraordinarily well related to the changing moods and rhythms of the pantomime, is trite movie music; his blind girl, though very good of her kind, is a film ingénue; and his interiors are overstuffed screen luxury or papier-mâché screen picturesqueness. And then, Chaplin's poetry is confined to the character of Charlie Chaplin the hobo and his adventures. This figure moves, like Don Quixote in Kansas City, against an accurately photographed background of prize-fighters, rich men, and snappy street crowds such as we see daily. Mr. Chaplin does not depend, like Miss Cornell, on the moribund drawing-room tradition with its old-fashioned *décor*. He is not a star with a perfunctory vehicle, but he is an artist who has managed to set a comic legend in streets and among characters that we all know.

The Bookman, April 1931

LE MILLION

ALEXANDER BAKSHY

René Clair's *Le Million,* like his earlier *Sous les Toits de Paris,* is one of those rare pictures that make you their willing captive immersed in their mood and letting yourself be carried away on the wings of their fancy. In *Le Million* the fancy is much more exuberant than it was in the other picture, but it enforces submission upon you just as effectively, so that like everybody else around you, you inevitably exclaim: "What charm! What invention! What fun!" This spontaneous reaction, confirmed by the laudations you hear on all sides, is sufficient proof of the unique qualities of the film. It is the work of an artist who sees beyond the obvious and who can view the comedy of life with a good-natured cynicism that proclaims its authentic "sophistication." From under this gentle leg-pulling there gradually emerges a fantastic world inhabited by not quite normal human beings who now and again burst into dancing and singing that reveals their hidden kinship with puppets. It is René Clair's great achievement as an artist that, though his characters' behavior is at times so grotesquely fantastic, it never appears incongruous with their surroundings or inconsistent with their more normal actions. But the achievement is a tour de force that only disguises its fundamental weakness.

The problem that René Clair sets himself to solve in *Le Million* is the old one of screen musical comedy. It has repeatedly been proved that the forms of singing and dancing seen in stage musical comedy are intolerably false and incongruous when transferred to the screen. The only successful treatment so far devised by Hollywood has been the use of plots in which singing and dancing are a natural part of the action. Stories of backstage life have been particularly in vogue in this connection. The field, however, is a small one, and it has been explored so thoroughly that with the public grown indifferent to such stories Hollywood has practically stopped making musical pictures. Now René Clair attempts to justify musical comedy by means that are directly opposite to those of Hollywood. Instead of making singing and dancing more natural, more in accord with the daily life of his characters, he makes the daily life of his characters more unnatural, more in accord with stage singing and dancing. Thus the story of a lost lottery ticket becomes a series of madcap adventures in which the normal is hardly distinguishable from the eccentric. Clair's success in this daring experiment reveals the measure of his talent as an entirely convincing and vastly entertaining interpreter of human foibles. But his fantastic treatment is even more restricted in its application than the naturalistic one of Hollywood. Moreover, his approach to the problem of musical comedy is confined to the choice of subject, whereas the only way to solve the problem is to discover a cinematic form that would make dancing and singing spring as freely from the nature of the screen entertainment as they spring from the nature of the stage performance.

The Nation, June 10, 1931

LE MILLION

FRANCIS FERGUSSON

If René Clair's new show, *Le Million,* is better than most Hollywood comedies, it is because he is still supported by the Molière formula, which is far better theater than our own funny-paper slapsticks. *Le Million* is the story of a young man who wins a lottery, and loses his winning ticket, which everyone in Paris then tries to steal. By chopping this film into a series of neatly built scenes; but putting it all in a snappy rhythm, like a quick march, and setting part of it to music; and by using his setting like the traditional French stage with three doors, out of which angry people are always popping, René Clair shows that he is simply transferring the old comedy to the screen. In this he is successful within the limitations of his scenario. It is a relief to meet unsentimental juveniles, treated as part of the whole satire. Our Hollywood film makers never manage to make their young things as human as this, perhaps because they are farther geographically and culturally from the source of classical comedy.

The Bookman, August 1931

MONKEY BUSINESS

JOHN MOSHER

Somehow the movies have managed to pull themselves together and produce a bit of entertainment for us. The particular prize of the week is the Marx Brothers' picture *Monkey Business,* which I think is the best this family has given us. Not that their own contributions here differ essentially from what they have done before. Groucho is still bland and garrulous, and Harpo silent—with his perennial moment at the harp, pursuing his ladies, like the gentleman in the ode, never triumphant though winning near his goal. The only novelty might seem to be the privilege allowed the generally somewhat slighted Zeppo—as a favor, perhaps, for having been good and quiet for so long—of a good beating in the grand finale. The advantage of this picture does not lie so much in any superior novelties on the part of the Messrs. Marx as in the fact that this is a movie contrived directly for the screen and not a rehash of a libretto. Formerly, when the Marxes were on the screen the picture was hilarious, but immediately after their departure it would slump, until their return, in a morass of musical-comedy plot.

Beginning aboard a steamer, where the four worthies are stowaways ("The stowaways of today were the stockholders of yesterday," remarks Groucho), including a scene with the passport officials which may well express the suppressed frenzy of every traveler, going on to a racketeers' ball, ending somehow in a barn, the story manages to keep the pace of fast burlesque. Considering that the fugitive Harpo is always silent, the whole picture is practically a monologue by Groucho. He talks, talks, talks. "Can I buy back my introduction to you?" he inquires. "Married in rompers? Pretty country!" he exclaims. It is crazy nonsense put over without a halt. Only in the matter of the photography, of the camerawork itself, does the picture fall below standard. I suppose a glamorous landscape would be hardly the proper setting for the Marxes, but a certain finish might have been given to the film, I think. There is something a bit shoddy and casual about the sets, for instance; something perfunctory, which is regrettable.

The New Yorker, October 17, 1931

Kenneth White, who taught philosophy at Harvard University for three years, was a playwright and the author of two volumes of poetry, *October Vigil* and *An Array for One.*

ANIMATED CARTOONS

KENNETH WHITE

The spontaneous manner in which Krazy Kat once crossed a chasm by catching hold of a question mark visible in midair before his eyes marks as distinct a movie manner as the earlier Mack Sennett comedies or the antics of the Keystone Kops. The ridiculousness of animals suggesting the conduct of humans was, long before the movies, an obvious means of getting laughter, pointing a moral, or telling a story; but the animated cartoon introduced a new element into the old method. By the addition of movement and the multiplication of scenes, the possibilities for comic fantasy were enormously increased. Then, with the introduction of sound and music to accompany and point up the movement of the characters in a scene, the rhythm of the fantasy could be stabilized and emphasized; even stylized to the point where Madame Lopokova's recent back-handed compliment to the American dance, in which she pronounced Mickey Mouse "America's greatest dancer," has considerable meaning.

The antics of Mickey Mouse very definitely resemble the movements of a ballet dancer: each movement is calculated, each movement has a definite point and each movement is rhythmical and positive. This, at least, is the resultant economy seen in a cartoon. The reason for the economy derives from a method far removed from that of the ballet, in a medium essentially static, in contrast to the movement of the ballet. The method by which every cartoon is constructed sufficiently indicates the medium. A brief Mickey Mouse film is made up of a series of drawings and tracings, of "cells," and each cell contains a variation, sometimes only a minute variation, on the preceding drawing or cell. These cells, without the transforming agency of the camera, would be nothing in the world but a lengthy comic strip with all the transitional movements depicted. It is directly from the comic strip that the animated cartoon derives its economy, as well as its slapstick and even some of its peculiar fantasy. The fundamental likeness between a comic strip and animated cartoons would be apparent if, for example, Rube Goldberg's "Inventions" were filmed as cartoons. And certainly such a series, for a few times anyway, ought to be highly amusing. What the animated cartoon has that the comic strip of Goldberg and Herriman has not, is variety, movement, rhythm, and completeness.

The rich humor that Mickey Mouse and his confrères, Bimbo, Krazy Kat, and the others indulge in has the same source as the comic strip's, in a logical ridiculousness; but the distinct humor of the animated cartoon can be presented only by the movies. For its effectiveness, motion and change are necessary, even occasional exact repetition that only the camera can perform. Certain kinds of American humor, like that of Donald Ogden Stewart, correspond, in general method, to the humor of the cartoon. Stewart and other writers like him develop a humorous point not by the addition of other humorous ideas but by expanding and distorting the humorous point to its farthest logical absurdity. But no one can elongate a dachshund in prose, or tickle a fireman with flames. No comic strip artist can startle a tree into scared life by a thunderstorm. Only the camera can enrich and amplify a fantastic idea until all the possible humor is exhausted from it.

There is a further enrichment in the animated cartoons that seems not to be found in any other place: their humor tends to the frankly bawdy. Not so long ago the coy rhythms of Carolyn Cow troubled the censors. Still, in spite of the censors, the umbilical emphasis in the clogging that so perpetually occurs in the cartoons continues, and villainous animals' pants, in full view of the public, are taken down and the exposed area spanked by an angry populace of flames. It is, undoubtedly, these irate flames, and startled trees, heart-broken hydrants, dancing piano stools, helpful pianos and all their perversities, reluctances, and contributions that make the cartoons the hilarious fantasies they are.

It seems a shame, then, that all the cartoons are becoming alike, that the variation among the different series is so slight. In a way, it was bound to happen; the immediate possibilities of sound and music were so quickly explored, once they were added to the cartoons (and resulted in two fine Silly Symphonies, *Spring* and *The Skeleton Dance*) that further experiment and manipulation seem unnecessary. The very stylization, perhaps the almost faultless rhythm, that gave the cartoons their character was certain to give rise to a formula which afforded easy repetition for mass production. It is even possible that visualized fantasy has such definite limitations that once a formula which gives the occasional illusion of variety has been arrived at, there is no more to be done. No one of the elements that go to make up the cartoon—sounds, music, characters, gestures, gags—can be altered separately without altering the whole thing. And the range of sounds in a cartoon is probably limited to the tinkling of bells, the clatter of bones, the screams of a whistle, etc. True, combinations of images and sounds might be worked out in a manner which hasn't been tried before; but here too the range will be fairly quickly exhausted. The main use of music appears to be to accompany singing and dancing and to maintain or emphasize the rhythm of the piece. The gags, of course, depend upon the ingenuity of the makers. Men like Goldberg and Small (who draws Salesman Sam) would undoubtedly have something to contribute. There is one possibility which Disney and the other artists have not made all they could out of. The inanimate objects which now play a subordinate role in the cartoons could be elevated to stellar parts. The abduction of a steam engine by a water tank, or the adventures of a no-account ash-can might make an amusing series of cartoons, provided their makers did not commit the error of giving the characters voices and lines to speak. If the characters in animated cartoons must speak, the sexless tones of Mickey and Minnie Mouse appear to be about the best solution.

Whatever does happen to the cartoons will have to happen within them. There is no outside help at all to be had, unless from some of the better comic strip artists. The cartoons are a tight, difficult medium; nothing quite like them exists even in the movies. If they were like any other single medium, certain influences would be sure to have an effect upon them. The problems of variety and development that they present, however, are the result of synthesis and combination, and they must be solved as if they were the result of a unique medium.

It seems unlikely, too, that the cartoons can contribute directly to the method of ordinary motion pictures. The whole comic strip method, which is, of course, at the basis of the animated cartoon, is foreign to that of movie making. The economy of means which good movies display is utterly different from the economy of the cartoons. The kind of visualization a director is said to need is quite different from the visualization a comic strip artist needs, even when the comic strip artist is drawing scenes to be photographed for an animated cartoon; the whole process of composition, and later, of editing, is of a totally unlike sort. The very precise, pert relation that must obtain between sound and images in the animated cartoon so that they click together like the point of a good joke and the immediate laughter can have little use in the movies proper, unless the movies are to copy directly the methods of the cartoon. When, in an ordinary movie, sound is intelligently used it increases the dimensions of the image; in a cartoon, the dimensions remain the same. Even the fantasy of the movies must be constructed on a different plane; not, of course, in the heavy-handed manner of the long-gone *Thief of Bagdad,* but more properly of Lubitsch's comedies. It isn't possible to reduce the problems of one medium to the problems of another and hope thereby to solve them. Certain hilarious scenes in René Clair's recent *Le Million* might suggest a likeness of spontaneous horseplay to the doings-about in a Mickey Mouse cartoon. But a resemblance could be traced equally well between the French picture and some of Mack Sennett's comedies. The likeness lies not at all in the method but in the swiftness and complex change of movement; in other words, the likeness lies in common farcical principles from which the animated cartoon, as well as the comedies, draws for its effectiveness.

The effectiveness of the animated cartoon cannot, for all the banality it now exhibits, be denied. It is a distinct addition to the movies, and the skill and ingenuity of its creators—the cartoon was distinguished even before the advent of sound—cannot be overestimated. What remains to be seen is what will be done with a medium in which the technical method has been so aptly and slickly worked out.

The Hound & Horn, October/December 1931

SCARFACE

JAMES SHELLEY HAMILTON [9]

Scarface has had a troubled prerelease career—rumors have emerged of cuts and retakes to make it publicly acceptable. What the censors and soft-pedalers have done to it is only a matter of conjecture: from the internal evidence of the picture itself it seems likely that only incidents too hectic and too unpleasant have been removed. There is no perceptible sign that anything has been done to avoid offending those mysterious powers by which gangdom is permitted to flourish—those powers are left as mysterious as ever. Perhaps a different ending than was originally made has been given to it—the conventional sop that the wicked must inevitably perish. It may easily occur to the suspicious on seeing the conviction and hanging without any glimpse of the face of Tony, the central figure in those scenes, that the scenes were made as an afterthought when the face of the actor who played Tony was no longer available. Did the picture intend to show what so often happens in life, the criminal triumphant over law to the very end?

Whatever the difference between what it is and what it started out to be, as a film it is as good as any gangster film that has been made. It is more brutal, more cruel, more wholesale than any of its predecessors and, by that much, nearer to the truth. It is built with more solid craftsmanship, it is better directed and better acted. Such characters as Tony and his sister and the chief, Lovo, and his girl, were created with an understanding of what human beings really are, and they are splendidly acted by Paul Muni, Ann Dvorak, Osgood Perkins, and Karen Morley. The incidents through which the story unfolds are dependable enough—most of them came recognizably from events known to all newspapermen. The more important thing is that they hang together with the coherence of actual life. The only really troublesome weaknesses in the story are in the extraneous moralizing speeches, unexceptionable in their morals but quite out of place in the drama, indubitably thrown in for whatever they might be worth as a "lesson." The lesson of such films is never taught by incidental sermons but by the life that we see being lived.

National Board of Review Magazine, March 1932

SCARFACE

JOHN MOSHER

Of *Scarface* there has already been so much said, so much heard about the objections of censors, and so many sensational rumors about its production—such as that the corpse flung from a taxi in one scene is no dummy but a remnant actually procured from some convenient morgue—that the poor film itself had hardly a chance of real success. It seems to me, however, that it has weathered all this unfortunate advance hullabaloo very satisfactorily. It arrives on the scene too late, of course, for its own good. It has obviously been shaved and trimmed a bit here and there, which you notice at times uncomfortably; although it is unusually long and has so many killings, as it is, you wonder what violence on earth could have been omitted. In general, too, I should say that it lacks the brilliance of acting and detail that *The Public Enemy* and *Little Caesar* both had, and that it now seems a sort of résumé of all the gunmen pictures we have seen, surpassing the average film of this sort only in the matter of length and in the quantity of gore. Pineapples have been flung around as freely as custard pies were twenty years ago, and we have become inured to the machine guns and silk shirts of gangsters, and in them intrinsically there is no longer novelty, or even any great concern. That the picture is topical, perhaps—there are items from the news such as the famous Saint Valentine's Day slaughter in the Chicago garage and the death of O'Banion among his roses—adds but a mild spur to your interest.

Paul Muni plays the Tony Camonte, a scar on cheek, with talent, especially in the earlier sequences; later, his juvenile appearance as leader of all the gangs is a little against him, as I am under the impression that such officials are generally middle-aged persons inclined to the paunch. This is a little captious however, I suppose, but on the other hand I was unduly amused by the little "secretary" who would shoot the telephone when the connection exasperated him. It seemed an idea. As a palliative for all the shootings and rumpus, there are now and again thrown on the screen somewhat formal and discreet reminders of the "callous indifference of the government" to the behavior of these hoodlums. The censors, I should think, might have judged that this picture so completely exhausted the field of activity it presented as to prepare the way for those perfumed and gentle idylls of innocent romance they appear to desire.

The New Yorker, May 28, 1932

Lincoln Kirstein is world renowned as a ballet impresario, probably the most distinguished since Diaghilev. He has also had a considerable career as poet and editor and critic. He was one of the founders of *The Hound & Horn,* a quarterly published from 1927 to 1938, and subsequently one of the editors of the quarterly *Films.*

JAMES CAGNEY AND THE AMERICAN HERO

LINCOLN KIRSTEIN

The art of dramatic expression may be conceded as international property. The tradition of the drama from the classical unities and the five-act Elizabethan tragedy to the three-act English comedy of social problems and manners is, in the West, surely a continental heritage. There's hardly a single American play that can stand against the second best of Europe. America, however, has developed the movies, and is developing the talkies. The Germans, the Russians, occasionally the French, can take our Hollywood-forged instrument and make a finer thing with it than we have so far dared, but in spite of that, the industry is our creation, and its worldwide expansion is due to our ingenuity. America as yet has hardly produced a picture that generations could watch with pleasure. Hollywood has, in short, given us no *Hamlet,* no *Cherry Orchard,* nor anything nearly so well organized, but it has contributed sharp American types that we can recognize with intense pleasure.

Each movie type has several faces. There is a hero who has been a nice-looking juvenile from Wallace Reid to Douglas Fairbanks, Jr.; he has two or three dialects of action from fresh, rough-and-ready to wistful and sappy. He has had his attendant heroines from the Gish girls to Janet Gaynor. Then there are the type villainesses, or heavies, from the vamp who was Theda Bara to the anomalous villainess-heroine type of Greta-Dietrich. And they have had their corresponding villains. There are a few other masks—the comedians, for example, each with a little more solid differentiation due to a technical development.

Every so often in this carefully bred descent of types there is a line of sports, of powerful exceptions. For example, figures arise, not with "sex-*appeal*" as Gilbert Seldes pointed out, but with "sex-*menace*"—which is something else again. Rudolph Valentino had sex menace; so has Clark Gable. It is silent, imperious, will not be denied. Valentino was exotic, foreign, scarcely American. Gable is hardly exotic; he is as American as Eugene O'Neill. He is a strong silent man, or he is the 1931-32, maybe -33 model of a strong silent man.

The strong silent man is the heir of the American pioneer, the brother of Daniel Boone whom James Fenimore Cooper immortalized as the American type for Europe. The strong silent man has been a trapper, a cowboy, a miner, a railroad man, a soldier, a sailor, a U. S. Marine. He has become, now, a surgeon, an architect—even a movie director. The strong silent man means America just as a hunting squire means England, a man in a silk hat and waxed moustache means France, and a bullfighter Spain. He is more American than Uncle Sam, and now he's a gangster—or was. The public is supposed to be fed up with gangster films, so he talks tough-guy and is a taxi driver or an automobile racer. The origin of the lean, shrewd, lantern-jawed, slow-voiced, rangy, blond American pioneer was in the New England adventurer in the West. The type has become a short, red-headed Irishman, quick to wrath, humorous, articulate in anger, representing not a minority in action, but the action of the American majority—the semiliterate lower middle-class.

James Cagney, while he is neither typically strong or silent, does excellently as the latest titleholder of a movie-type which either has become or is derived from a national type. Cagney, in a way, creates his own type. After the creation we can put it in its proper niche in the Hall of Fame of our folk legends. Cagney is mick-Irish. He was trained as a tap dancer. He has had a small experience as a "legitimate" actor. He is the first definitely metropolitan figure to become national, as opposed to the suburban national figure of a few years ago, or of the farmer before that. He is, or has been, quick shooting, while old Bill Hart was straight shooting. He snarls, "If I taut yuh meant dat why I'd . . ." instead of "When you say that, Pardner, smile." He twists a grapefruit in his lady's face, which is the reverse and equivalent courtesy of the older "ladies first" school of etiquette. It delights and shocks us because it is based on the reverse of chivalry. Cagney may be a dirty little low-life rat, a hoodlum, a small-time racketeer, but when his riddled body is propped up against his mother's door, mummied in bandages and flecked with blood, we catch our throats and realize that this is a hero's death.

Cagney, in spite of the coincidence of his character with the American tough guy, whether it's a racketeer or taxi driver, is an independent actor in his own right and as finished and flexible an artist as there is in the talkies today. He has resisted every attempt to have himself exhausted by being made to act the same character in every play. Few new actors ever can survive the prestige of their first success. Cagney has an inspired sense of timing, an arrogant style, a pride in the control of his body, and a conviction and lack of self-consciousness that are unique in the deserts of the American screen. We may think of the stock gestures of an Elizabethan bravo, slapping the rapier into scabbard, cocking his hat, or leaping to his horse, as typical active Elizabethan. In America there are men and boys lounging in front of drugstores, easing down off trucks, lifting up the hoods of their engines, sighting for a cue on a billiard table, tossing down their little pony of raw whiskey, or even shooting through the pocket of their double-breasted Tuxedos. When Cagney gets down off a truck, or deals a hand at cards, or curses, or slaps his girl, or even when he affords himself and her the mockery of sweetness, he is, for the time being, the American hero, whom ordinary men and boys recognize as themselves and women consider "cute." It is impossible to tell at once whether his handshake is cordial or threatening. He is "cute"—the way Abraham Lincoln said a certain trapper was "cute," that is quick, candid, and ambiguous. Cagney is not a man yet, but neither is he a juvenile. He has not allowed himself to rely too much on the good stories and brilliant dialogue that he has been given. In his next picture we will see him as an automobile racer; after that as a prizefighter. No one expresses more clearly in terms of pictorial action the delights of violence, the overtones of a semiconscious sadism, the tendency toward destruction, toward anarchy which is the basis of American sex appeal.

The Hound & Horn, April/June 1932

Margaret Marshall was the associate editor of *The Nation,* then its literary editor, from 1938 to 1953.

A NOUS LA LIBERTE

MARGARET MARSHALL

With his third film, *A Nous la Liberté,* René Clair establishes himself as the most accomplished and intelligent exponent of the art of the cinema. This is not to say that he is unsurpassed in all aspects of filmmaking. The Russians provide richer photography; the Lubitsch "touch" has a human warmth that Clair lacks—and probably scorns. The interesting fact about M. Clair is that he has mastered his technique as a whole so thoroughly that he is now able to employ it freely in creating a style of his own. In his hands the film, about which so little in the way of definition or scope has been understood, much less formulated, emerges almost for the first time as a separate and fully developed form of artistic expression.

M. Clair made it clear in his first picture, *Sous les Toits de Paris,* that the film as a form of art must not be confused with the necessarily static stage play. Motion, both obvious and subtle, is the distinctive element of the camera as a medium, and it is in terms of motion that M. Clair has worked out his motion picture technique. *In Sous les Toits* he achieved a stylized realism to which photography is intrinsically adaptable; and he achieved it not through any resort to stylized settings or bizarre photography such as were employed, for example, in *Dr. Caligari,* but through constant variation of perspective, composition, and light. Also, he made use of motion itself, particularly of the motions of the body and of facial expression, which can be exploited fully only by the moving camera and which for the illumination of character are the most effective and economical medium. The plot was simple and fast and ended in irony. He used dialogue sparingly; his use of music was conventional and direct, consisting of a "theme song" and occasional rhythmic accompaniment to action in the tradition of musical comedy.

Le Million was another experiment, this time in fantasy. Again, the effect of fantasy was achieved not through any trick of setting or photography but by the mobile use of the camera before referred to. The chase, which is equally suited to the mood of fantasy and the technique of the moving camera, played a large part in *Le Million.* Music, in the second picture, if my memory is right, was used incidentally and for broadly humorous purposes. The plot was ingenious, fast, and again ended in irony. *Le Million,* though it seemed slighter, was a more finished production more surely handled than *Sous les Toits;* it was a second important experiment in M. Clair's developing technique.

A Nous la Liberté combines the stylized realism of *Sous les Toits* and the fantasy of *Le Million*. Implications as well as events are allowed to assume dramatic and convincing shape. From a realistic scene the spectator is led quite imperceptibly into the fantasy of implication until the two are inextricably fused. For instance, the scene in which blackmailers threaten the wealthy factory-owner is presented realistically. But, later, the chase in which the gangsters pursue their victim through the halls of his factory becomes pure fantasy as M. Clair multiplies into abstraction the blank walls and staircases which are real enough to begin with, and extends the chase to fantastic limits of time and space. Finally, in the scene in which the blackmailers, after the pursuit, find themselves locked in the great vault which is filled with money they are powerless to take away, realism and fantasy, event and implication merge. The same technique is employed in the sequence which leads to the film's climax. In an extremely realistic and highly amusing scene the owner of the factory is shown announcing to his full-dressed directors and leading citizens his invention by which phonographs can be made without human labor. As he speaks, a wind rises. It blows open a case of mille-franc notes which during his pursuit by the blackmailers he has managed to hide on a roof in preparation for his escape. The notes, one by one, are blown past the noses of the distinguished guests. Here fantasy begins, and the sequence ends in a wild chase in which banknotes are pursued by respectable gentlemen while the wind blows harder and harder and dignity becomes a silk hat rolling in the dust, a swallowtail flapping in the breeze. The result, obviously, of Mr. Clair's combination of realism and fantasy is satire of a high order.

The story of *A Nous la Liberté* is simple, written by Clair himself directly for the screen. Two friends in prison plan to escape. One gets out, the other is caught. Through a series of accidents the first becomes owner of a phonograph factory so large in scale that its employees, like its machines, are automatons. It is here that the two friends meet, when the second one, having been released from prison, is picked up as a vagrant in a field adjoining the factory and hustled into a job. The adventures of the two until the day when the factory-owner, who is about to be arrested as an ex-convict, gives his plant to the workers and escapes from his factory prison with his dreamy companion, who has failed in love, are as hilarious as they are ironic. For despite the intellectual cast of the film, its characters are flesh and blood; its action is as fast and as funny, even aside from its implications, as Chaplin at his best. More deftly than ever M. Clair has created a film in terms of motion in which the expression of the eyes and the movements of the body play a great part. The music which was a song in *Sous les Toits* becomes in the third picture an extremely clever ironic musical accompaniment written by no less a composer than Georges Auric —which like the dialogue never obtrudes upon but heightens the excitement or humor or suspense of a given scene.

The technique of René Clair as displayed in *A Nous la Liberté* is much closer to the technique of music than of any other art. The picture has a theme, the theme of prison, which is first stated simply and then repeated throughout the picture with variations of rhythm and elaboration, rising to a climax in the scene before described in which mille-franc notes, silk hats, and respectable gentlemen whirl within the prisonlike walls of a great modern factory dedicated to mass production and profit. Throughout, also, there is a constant contrapuntal interplay of regimentation and human fallibility, efficiency and impulse. The winking of an eye, a fluttering handkerchief, a flower; any one of these can—and does in M. Clair's gay world—set a whole system at naught.

But just as surely and just as gaily the system sets at naught all human values. For M. Clair's irony is complete and impartial. The flowers and birds with which he elicits human longing are invariably paper flowers and music-box birds. Without a word he implies that the workers who own the factory which turns out phonographs and profits endlessly without their help may find dancing and fishing a little tiresome. Finally, at the end, he catches the former factory-owner, who is "free" once more to roam with his friend, looking wistfully after a passing limousine. Yet M. Clair is no cynic. Cynicism, like pessimism, presupposes the possibility of perfection. Because M. Clair entertains no such possibility, except in the field of art, his gaiety is pure, entirely devoid either of morals or malice.

The Nation, June 8, 1932

HORSE FEATHERS | AMERICAN MADNESS

ALEXANDER BAKSHY

When the Marx Brothers are in a picture, the picture is all in the Marx Brothers. This means more than their own prominence. They could not, of course, be in a picture without making themselves its heart and soul, its center of interest. But it means that the other people with whom they surround themselves, though in the picture, are not of it. This is a pity. It makes the peculiar brand of lunacy which these gifted actors have made their own lose some of its point. It makes it appear as the mere antics of funny men, as pure clowning, where it could have been something far more interesting, a lunacy run riot and setting its entire little world on its head.

There is a suggestion of such lunacy in the opening scene of *Horse Feathers.* Groucho as the newly installed president of a college, after addressing the students on the benefits of education in his inimitable vein, breaks into a dance, and the entire faculty of solemn and bewhiskered professors follows suit in the mock style of a finale of a musical comedy.

But the situation is not followed up. The students remain mere spectators in a show, and the professors are never given another chance to indulge in a few jolly capers of their own. Imagination staggers at the thought of what the campus life would have been like had Groucho conducted a course on love with the expert assistance of the college widow who figures in the story, creating perhaps a few more widows from among the professors' wives; had Harpo been appointed to the combined professorship of dog-catching and harp-playing; and had Chico been made the head of the college speakeasy and a professor of bootlegging. But the Marx family makes no attempt to put college education on a sound basis. Instead it engages in a series of escapades which, mad and highly amusing as they are, do not amount to much more than just delightful fooling. Harpo's gags come off perhaps best of all. His method of catching dogs with the help of a butterfly net and a variety of portable lampposts to suit dogs of different sizes, and his drive around the football field in a garbage-man's cart looking for all the world like a chariot driver of ancient Rome, are two of his happiest conceits. But I wish for once he had left out his solo number on the harp. It may be fine music, and it may be perfectly in its place in a vaudeville act, but it does not belong in a picture like *Horse Feathers*. In fact, the main flaw in all Marx Brothers pictures, if one can be so ungrateful as to pursue this subject, is the inability of these unique comedians to think of the film as being essentially different from the vaudeville stage.

American Madness also deals with madness, but of a different kind. The film relates the story of a bank conducted by an extremely able, honest, and likable president, but brought to the very brink of ruin when exaggerated reports of its losses cause the panic-stricken public to make a run on its funds. The story is sheer propaganda for the banks, and in some of its episodes falls short of the plausible, but it is skillfully told, capably acted, particularly by Walter Huston as the president, and directed with real distinction by Frank Capra. The scene of the run on the bank is film art at its best.

The Nation, August 31, 1932

GRETA GARBO

STARK YOUNG

Since Miss Greta Garbo came to America some years ago, her fame has grown and grown. In her last picture, a Hollywood and rather nursery version of Pirandello's *As You Desire Me,* she has come to the end of her contract and to her highest success; the piece has passed from one end of the country to the other in triumph, and Miss Garbo has gone back to Sweden, to return or not to return as the case may be. During all this time her position has steadily advanced. As to her drawing capacity I know very little, these are delicate and falsified matters on the whole, and what drawing power means, crowded box offices, I am still uncertain. I remember once, coming back from Italy, half an hour after Gibraltar, and just as we were passing the coast of Spain, with a vista magnificent and everchanging, how most of the passenger list had hastened below decks to see Jackie Coogan. There is no proverb about the ears and eyes of people being the ears and eyes of God. Miss Garbo's box office realities, nevertheless, are very great and, I feel sure, have steadily increased, or there would not be so many pictures of her promulgated or efforts at spreading news, such news, that is, as can be snappily concocted, about her, all of which costs the producers money.

Certainly it can be said that Miss Garbo is unique among Hollywood ladies and curiously untouched by its vulgar silliness of report and its obvious and intimate Kodak and journalism. Meantime she supplies an odd comment on our public, with regard to its popular philosophy, its esthetic theory, and its soul. Both satire and poetry and common dream are involved.

By Miss Garbo's being a comment on the popular philosophy of a great people and a great democratic legend I mean two things. The first is in a lighter vein. The managerial publicity for Miss Garbo, based soundly enough on facts, has created unceasingly the theme of her solitude. She does not make a part of crowds; she has moments when she likes to be alone; she flees publicity; she likes to live privately. In general this is a thought that almost strangles our average citizen. What, not go to a committee, not ride forth, not take a part in the community; if you can sing, not do it on the radio; if you are blessed with a motor, not speed somewhere; if you have a house, not create a swarming for it; if you have emotions, not carry them and tell! At any rate, conceive of someone who stays in when he could go out, who could see people but thinks it a kind of communion, peace, rest, or right to be alone sometimes! This has made Miss Garbo almost a national puzzle. It could have been explained away by making her a freak or a high-hat. But she is neither. She is not even sick; Swedish people are athletic. We must swallow it, then, as a cosmic mystery, this successful star really likes at times to be alone.

In the course of democratic thought another point, much more serious, has arisen. What are artists? Are they any different from anybody else? To this challenge many of our artists of the theater have arisen. They are as everyday as everybody. I was told in Grand Rapids once of a singer from the Metropolitan who, at a Rotarian dinner in his honor, told the diners that he was just like the rest of them, no different, singing was his business just as bonding, banking, running a laundry, was theirs. This was no doubt true, but it does not affect the question. One of the things to ponder in the theater now, in the opera especially, is the vast melee of fallen stars. They are not fallen from fiscal stardom, they are fallen from glamor. As stars they are known for their hits, their successes, their salaries and contracts, sometimes for their personalities, real or created by their agents and managers; they remain just folks like the rest of us. That is the great balm. But they are not the glamor and wonder of the heart, not any longer. As the dramatist tells us in *The Swan,* royalty, like swans, should stay well away from the bank; seen close at hand they are apt to be at best but waddling animals. So it is in the theater ultimately, but not in democratic theory.

The sarcasm of all this is that Miss Garbo contradicts the whole business. We know very little of her, not really. Visitors to Hollywood do not see her. Junior League conventions, given a dinner by the producers, with all the screen stars lined up as *hors d'oeuvres* and flashlights as souvenirs, miss this one relish in the lot; they see everybody but Greta Garbo, and though they like the haircut of some great artist, they depart with a certain awe about this refusing Swedish player. A little actress, renting Miss Garbo's house, may get a picture published of Garbo's bed, renting publicity. Nor do we see photographs of Greta Garbo meeting someone at the train or drinking Swedish punch with a millionaire, or buried in the midst of a pile of books (wooden movie properties), or any other blessed fiddledeedee for the popular heart. There were tricks in plenty among the old stars. Patti was not without her special coaches and her parrots and imperial gems, nor did the Barnum method leave untouched the great figure of Bernhardt, who carried in her his soul's epic.But when all was said and done, their splendor and ability shone at the proper shining time. These ancient tricks are tired now, overworked, and most stars are starry in long-runs, incomes, romances, and scandals. It can be said that to Miss Garbo some of the glamor, old-style, baffling, full of dreams, imaginings, and wonder, has returned. If nothing else, in many instances, she is a blessed rebuff to the back-slapping and personal-friend-of-mine citizens that appropriate the artists of the theater, who in their turn are too scared of their positions, too greedy, or too mediocre themselves to do anything different. It would be a sad day in our midst if our great ticket-buying public should learn one chief and simple fact about art, which is that a great artist is like everybody else but is not like anybody else. Alas, equality and the folks!

Esthetically, the case of Miss Greta Garbo is a kind of joke on the whole theater public. The realism-democracy theory that the great public holds concerning the theater tells us that acting is just being natural, being the character, things as they are, none of the spouting and artificiality of the old fellows. Down deep, this prose-nature business is the last thing wanted; most people, however flat, want art to be art, without offending them by being anything different from anything else. The lurking dream is there, nevertheless, the desire for creation anew, the fresh world of fiction, flux, or ideality. What they think they want would be best found in the zoo, since nothing so acts like an elephant as an elephant. What they really want is the difference between the moon in the sky and the moon in the water; they want a new birth with a nameless difference; they want resemblance with escape. What they declare and actually seek is what they won't like when they get it. The public arrives by things outside of its declarations, and obeys constantly forces it could never understand. In whatever style, what people want in acting is acting. Miss Garbo solves this problem without seeming to, and, for that matter, even when she is not acting at all. At the very start her foreign accent gives her a certain removal. It is not necessarily a style, a treatment, a definite elevation, or distillation; it is primarily a physical fact that removes her from the ordinary and makes possible the illumination, unreality, and remoteness that we thirst after. That remote entity of her spirit, a certain noble poignancy in her presence, a certain solitary fairness, a sense of mood that is giving and resisting at the same time: these defeat and break down the poor little common theory of naturalness and prose method. This player is not hoity-toity or highbrow or any of that, the public feels; she is not unnatural; she is like somebody, they don't know just who, but still——. Her mere physical factual distance from the audience parallels the distance that style in art assures and that instinct expects, so that what they would deny in theory they now run after in fact.

This is leaving out of account the side of the public's relation to Miss Garbo that is so much to its credit. People's souls sense in her some concentration of magnetism that they value. There is a muteness, inaccessibility, and beauty that attracts both men and women. She presents an instance of the natural and right progress of the poetic: from the concrete toward ideality. There is in her work no cheapness of attack, it is clear that her services could not be obtained for such effects. Her mind is not patently technical, her spirit not easily flexible, so that it is mainly a larger something that comes off to the audience, and in the future there will be a fuller development and radiance of her natural resources according to her own study, training, and the influences to which she is subjected.

As to Miss Garbo's performances, her creations of the roles assigned her, they have been variable. Such a role as Mata Hari, in a silly play, with a cast made up largely of lollipops and a brindling, venal atmosphere of Hollywood danger and war, was not for her, though the piece could have been written for her particular qualities. *Romance* was a cruel venture to subject her to, not because she could not have played some Nordic artist, beautiful, absorbed, passionate, and changing, but because she was burdened with creating a child of the sun, rich, impish, swanlike, and typical, cosmic as legend, and this had no relation either to her realm of feeling and beauty or her external technique. In Pirandello's *As You Desire Me,* Miss Garbo for the first time came, in my opinion, into her own, so far forward indeed that this discussion of her must remain inadequate. For the first time she seemed to me to show in her playing an inner delight and happy dedication to the love and joy of it. Her stage movement has grown lighter and more varied; the line of her hands has taken on a new and vivid life; and the diversity in technical attack and in the player's vitality seemed to me much greater. The secret luminous center of such playing cannot be conveyed, of course, any more than its shining fluency can be forgotten. Something is given in this playing of Miss Garbo's that I have not seen given before, and from the moments of her playing it seemed to me something radiant returned to her; she seemed to me not another person but a new artist in her art.

The New Republic, September 28, 1932

TROUBLE IN PARADISE

RICHARD WATTS, JR.

The Lubitsch magic is again in evidence in the new picture at the Rivoli Theater and thereupon *Trouble in Paradise* becomes a thoroughgoing delight. In fact, it must even be described by that cryptic and slightly embarrassing word "civilized"—meaning, of course, that it is one of those deft, silken, and debonaire comedies which delight the reviewers, make money in New York, and dwindle helplessly in the countryside. In his slyest and most knowing manner, Lubitsch—who is, taking one thing with another, the master of them all—lights upon a slender and less than novel tale of a gentleman bandit and his beautiful prey and, by his great gift for the subtly amusing treatment of sex problems, transforms it into a brillant excursion into cinema light comedy.

In the new film you will find that charming English actor, Herbert Marshall, as a dashing and polished international thief whose picturesque exploits are the talk of the underworld in Venice, Paris, Geneva, and Constantinople. Assisting him as partner and sweetheart is the blonde Miss Miriam Hopkins, who picks pockets and rifles safes while talking of her intimate acquaintance with the minor nobility. A happy and successful pair, their Eden is turned into rather a purgatory of doubt and difficulty when Mr. Marshall, bent on robbing the handsome Miss Kay Francis of a slice of her fortune, has the misfortune to grow slightly sentimental about the lady.

Such a story is, of course, entirely familiar in the cinema, but in Lubitsch's hands it takes on curious qualities of freshness. In the first place, he refuses, even in the more amorous moments, to sentimentalize the romantic episode. Then, too, his sly, impish touch, which lights upon a thousand facets of incidental wit, has a way of changing even the most routine incidents into marvels of dashing good humor. There have, with the passing of years, been innumerable imitations of the Lubitsch manner and what we inevitably refer to [as] the Lubitsch touch, but the German still remains the unapproachable master of the frivolous spirit in the cinema.

The photoplay is, among other things, a triumph for Mr. Marshall, who plays the central role of the fable with all of that dashing likableness and easygoing expertness which have made him so welcome a stage visitor. Miss Francis is excellent as the potential victim of the brigand, and Miss Hopkins plays the role of the sly accomplice with effective humor. Minor roles are well played by Charles Ruggles, C. Aubrey Smith, Robert Greig, and, much to my surprise, Edward Everett Horton. As you may have gathered, I liked *Trouble in Paradise.*

The New York Herald Tribune, November 9, 1932

TROUBLE IN PARADISE

ALEXANDER BAKSHY

One may wish there were more sting, more sarcasm, in Ernst Lubitsch's polished wit, but we must take the man as he is, and with all his limitations Lubitsch seems to be the only director in Hollywood who talks the language of adult people and whose suave and subtle humor betrays a keen if cynical mind. His cynicism has earned him the title of the acknowledged master of "sophisticated" comedy. Yet in the last analysis it is probably the least important element in his make-up as an artist. It shines only by contrast with the primitive earnestness of Main Street. Regarded by itself it suggests no more than the attitude of a good-natured gourmet who enjoys the oddities of the human scene. I have no quarrel with Lubitsch on this score. His intellectual mood has at least the grace of a certain refinement. I am more thrilled, however (if the word "thrilled" can be applied to the titillating sensation produced by his work), by the masterly skill with which he tells his afterdinner stories, the skill of a raconteur who makes his points without raising his voice.

Trouble in Paradise is one of the gossamer creations of Lubitsch's narrative art. The story, it goes without saying, is a trivial anecdote which deals with some adventures of two society crooks. It is unnecessary to relate it in detail, and it would be impossible in this brief notice to describe the innumerable touches of wit and of narrative skill with which it is unfolded. The opening scene gives the key to the treatment of the story. It shows us a man collecting garbage whom we presently discover to be a Venetian garbage man carrying away his spoils in a gondola to the accompaniment of a raucous song. And so, throughout the picture, we see the adroit and impish Lubitsch turn his slightly crooked mirror now to one episode, now to another. It is all thoroughly delightful.

The Nation, December 7, 1932

I AM A FUGITIVE FROM A CHAIN GANG

WILTON A. BARRETT [10]

In this visual recounting of the case history of a boy—a boy returned from the war, feeling himself changed and out of key in a world changed too, leaving home, going on his own to struggle and fit himself to the new scheme of things, finding work scarce, traveling here and there to get a job, going broke and, innocently getting caught in a lunch-wagon hold-up, arrested, sentenced, and sent to serve ten years in a chain gang, escaping, changing his name, and in another state, through his innate honesty and ability, winning a place of trust and respect in the community, then, through the cupidity and vengefulness of his wanton wife, discovered and re-arrested, surrendering himself to the state in which he was convicted, on the promise that he will be pardoned after serving ninety days, finding himself condemned to the chain gang again, the prison keepers revenging themselves upon him because he had given the newspapers the story of chain gang conditions, denied his pardon by the authorities, and, with the ghastly and hopeless knowledge that he is doomed to serve out his time, desperately making his escape again, and, broken with terror and despair, becoming a haunted fugitive from justice, skulking day and night, lost to his friends, the girl who loves him, and to society—in this film of social injustice, iniquity, and the grinding down of an unfortunate individual, a film so sincere, real, inevitable, compassionate, restrained, and moving, the American motion picture comes into its estate as a medium for expressing the forces of social behavior and corrective social thought, of performing the function which intelligent people have been saying it must perform if the screen is to realize its place as a serious art that uses the

dramatic materials of our national life and institutions, methods and problems, not thereby to surrender one tithe of its status as a great entertainment but in order to heighten that status by giving its art a social and more
human meaning. Surely such people and those in the ranks of picture
patrons as well will perceive in this picture a conscience that calls for
respect and a verity that lifts it to a high level of dramatic entertainment.

We have heard—and this department in certain cases has agreed—that
the Russian cinema has marked highwater in the creative achievement of
motion pictures. If it has done this, it is because—granted that a properly
conceived technique has fashioned it for extraordinary dynamic thrust and
therefore effective compact—it has dealt intensely, imaginatively, and
provocatively with the material of human beings in relation to the social
organism, with what happens to the souls of people, with what destroys or
enlivens souls, with what society can do to souls through blindness or
stupidity or selfishness or malice and sheer rage; it is because the Russian
cinema, even when adulating and centering on a special cause, idea, or
social scheme about which there is justifiable disagreement, has spurned
the putty and paint, the prettiness and pretentiousness, preferred to follow
uncompromisingly the bitter grain of life, and so remained authentic in
theme and passionate in utterance. But with this film of bitter life before
us, made in America, in Hollywood, praise be, there can be no hesitancy
in saying that our picture producers, when they get the slant, the courage,
and the will, can turn out just as important films as can anyone, anywhere,
in the world (as indeed—but often with too little proof—our producers
have been contending all along). *I Am a Fugitive from a Chain Gang*
proves the contention amply and is to be enthusiastically commended for
its courage, artistic sincerity, dramatic vigor, high entertainment concept,
and social message—the last a word we don't like, but have in all conscience to use.

And yet why not? It would be denying the full flavor of this powerful film
to deny its earnestness and propaganda value. But what does that mean?
—or does it mean that Hauptmann's *The Weavers,* Ibsen's *Ghosts,* Gals-
worthy's *Justice* are not excellent plays and superlative entertainment
because they happen to deal with certain evils of society and do so convincingly and intentionally? Does it detract from a film, then, when it says
something? *I Am a Fugitive from a Chain Gang* says something—something about a human being foiled in finding his own expression, trying to
go straight when fell circumstance says, "You have gone wrong," trying
to remain human in a world that has turned inhuman, and in the end being
overcome, as human beings are, by a nemesis—which in this case is only
another name for man's ignorance, trickery, and failure to save members of
his own tribe from distress when he finds himself organized into a society

whose tragedy it still is not to be able, while seeking the path to righteousness and justice, to pull up its roots from the swamp of man's old primitive intolerances and brutalities. The tragedy of a scrubwoman can be as great as the tragedy of Lady Macbeth, as Hauptmann, we believe, has said, and a man caught in a prison, trying to escape from it and failing to do so, can be as awakening to our sense of the unfortunate, terrorful, pitiful, and therefore cleansing, as King Oedipus trying to escape the Furies. When a motion picture can make us feel and recognize this, it has not only said something, it is something.

In writing of such a film—with its links of strong, cinematically wrought episodes building to the chain that finally fastens James Allen to his fate forever, with its sparse and telling use of sound and dialogue which slowly gathers to a monotone like the silence of ended life, with its swift and eloquent photography, and the splendid, sincere acting that marks its players throughout—it goes without saying that its director, Mervyn LeRoy, its scenarists, Sheridan Gibney and Brown Holmes, the photographer, Sol Polito, the star, Paul Muni (a moving performance his, indeed), and the entire supporting cast, have royally contributed to the dignity and tragic beauty of the work as a whole. And then—the producing company is to be congratulated and applauded, for in deciding to make, and in making, I Am a Fugitive from a Chain Gang, it has performed a service in behalf of the dignity and meaning of the art of the American film.

National Board of Review Magazine, November 1932

I AM A FUGITIVE FROM A CHAIN GANG

PARE LORENTZ

There were two ways in which director LeRoy could have made this picture. He could have ripped the high lights from the startling novel of the same name written by a convict escaped from the chain gang and told in brief episodes the story of this man's life. As the story is a horrible one, he could have used the man as an instrument against his background and, like the Germans and Russians at their best, manipulated people as group actors, making the prison, and not the actors, the object of the film.

But unfortunately he had to expect a profit from his labor and try at once to tell a dramatic story and still to dramatize his prison. He managed to dramatize his hero, and he certainly did not soften the background, but in doing this he failed to characterize the brutal guards, the horrible complacency of state officials, their utter detachment from society.

I don't hold with the radical school of critics that indignation *per se* is art. However, I don't join hands with the arty boys, either, who maintain that all indignation is cheap, inartistic simply because it attempts to grind an ax. Actually *I Am a Fugitive* is not a moralizing treatise. But you can't see it without feeling that it is a savage document against existing penal systems, nor can you ignore daily evidence that such systems are operating in our great commonwealths every day in the week.

I quarrel with the production not because it is savage and horrible, but because each step in an inevitable tragedy is taken clumsily, and because each character responsible for the hero's doom is shown more as a caricature than as a person. The men do not seem real. The chain gang certainly does. You may very well say you want to go to the theater to forget trouble. But *I Am a Fugitive* has no moral treatise. Personally I think you'll find it more dramatic than, say, a current play dealing with Chinese peasants, or Irish drunkards, or French maids, or middle-class neurotics.

Vanity Fair, December 1932

Victor Fleming's *The Wet Parade,* cited below, was made from a novel by Upton Sinclair and starred Walter Huston.

CAVALCADE

PARE LORENTZ

There are two, possibly three, reasons why every newspaper reviewer in the Eastern U. S. went wild with enthusiasm over the motion picture *Cavalcade,* and called it everything from the finest picture ever made in the English language! (*sic*) to a dramatic masterpiece matched in cosmic importance only by Shakespeare's best works.

One reason for this unanimous accolade is that *Cavalcade* is a "good" movie. The other, and most obvious reason, is that Noel Coward, a very shrewd man, wrote a shrewd patriotic spectacle, and if there is anything that moves the ordinary American to uncontrollable tears, it is the plight —the constant plight—of dear old England.

In picture form, *Cavalcade* is a superlative newsreel, forcibly strengthened by factual scenes, good music, and wonderful photography. It is marred by pat and obvious dramatic climaxes, and by a conclusion which is anticlimactical and meaningless. And when one forgets the pace, the flow, and the really dignified and lovely quality of the picture—which is easier said than done—one can hear some very cheap theatrical observations from that choleric old empire-builder, Mr. Coward.

There was many a sob in the audience during the charming scene which dramatized the funeral of the great Queen, Victoria. But why? The scene itself reached no dramatic ceiling. And it was not a tragic death. I do not want indirectly to deprecate a fine production with a speech (which I am ready to deliver at the drop of a hat) on the silly deference most of our writing boys show visiting Englishmen, and I mention the sobs attending this one scene in the movie as an indication of the fact that, while the audience was moved, Hollywood, and the cast and crew hired out there, deserved no little credit for it.

The music, and the extraordinary pictorial dignity, made death itself dramatic: the scene gave one a melancholy, impressionistic feeling of the passing of all things. And this same fine work on the part of director Frank Lloyd and his assistant, William Cameron Menzies, made the war scenes equally as impressive, even though one could not help but remember that the brave laddies who relieved Mafeking were engaging in one of the most ignominious wars England ever staged.

As far as the subject matter was concerned, I personally enjoyed the scene in *The Wet Parade* of a Tammany celebration in 1912 more than any of the chapters of English history dramatized in Mr. Coward's spectacle. Yet seldom has a movie company released a finer technical production than *Cavalcade,* and Mr. Lloyd, who once did a charming and unusual and really legitimate movie called *Young Nowheres;* and Mr. Menzies, who, since the beginning of Hollywood, has been the one man in the business who has brought imagination, skill, and a sense of beauty to the most neglected department in the industry—scenic-designing—deserve the highest praise for their work.

Mr. Lloyd might have spared us the brokenhearted mother waving her little flag Armistice night, and he might have aided Mr. Coward if he had put the tinkly song, *Twentieth Century Blues,* in an earlier section of the picture. Furthermore, he might have greatly aided Mr. Coward if he had cut a shoddy bit of theatrical nobility and denied us the sophomoric toast, given in conclusion by the old father and mother, in which they hope "grace and dignity and peace" may be restored to old England. I can repeat, but not print, what the shade of Ben Jonson and his boys must have said to that.

As for Mr. Menzies, I don't think his work could have been improved upon. If you remember *The Thief of Baghdad, Robin Hood,* and *Bulldog Drummond,* you may recall that the sets were half the shows. Mr. Menzies made them, and I hope he makes many more.

I have one more complaint to register and then you can go and cry your eyes out at the sight of "the march of time measured by a human heart—a mother's heart." (Advt.) Ursula Jeans, especially imported from London for *Cavalcade,* was cold and unattractive. With the aid of a good hairdresser, a modiste, and a George Kaufman to direct her, she might be able to compete with any one of forty young actresses already sold down the river to Hollywood.

Vanity Fair, March 1933

SHE DONE HIM WRONG

PARE LORENTZ

Sex has not entirely disappeared from the screen, but like the horse in transportation it is a minor necessity in the movie industry these days. An old-fashioned reactionary myself, I must say that I find the new fashion in picture plots a mixed blessing, and it was a pleasant surprise to discover Mae West, swan bed and all, in a movie version of her great play, *Diamond Lil.*

With less care, the whole production might have become one of those "For Men Only" jobs, or worse yet, it might have been one of those self-conscious satires on the Gay Nineties: one of those dull plays in which even the extras think themselves too, too funny in make-up, and consequently go about giggling with uncontrollable laughter at the whole thing.

She Done Him Wrong is played straight, and to the hilt, and as a result it is good fun. Miss West sings "Easy Rider," "I Like a Slow Man," and "Frankie and Johnny" as though Stanford White and Harry K. Thaw really were sitting in the front row. John Bright kept a good melodramatic pace in the manuscript. The production itself is surprisingly good: the sets and lighting, and the general direction, handled by Lowell Sherman, are way above par.

What most producers will fail to understand is that this picture is not just smutty, and that, although definitely a burlesque show, it has a certain beery poignancy and, above all, a gusto about it which makes it a good show.

Vanity Fair, March 1933

KING KONG

RICHARD WATTS, JR.

It seems that King Kong was a prehistoric ape fifty feet tall and that he had the misfortune to fall in love with Miss Fay Wray. For the 70,000 centuries or so of his existence before meeting Miss Wray his life had been a comparatively placid one, enlivened by occasional brawls with brontosauri, tyrannosauri, and other of the amiable fellow inhabitants of his lost island. His simple needs in the way of feminine companionship were supplied by the savage natives of the place, who offered an occasional woman of their tribe to him as a sacrificial offering, and his pride was sufficiently ministered to by the awe with which the islanders regarded him. Then he had one look at the ingenue blondness of Miss Wray and became so enraptured that the first thing he knew he had been captured, taken off to New York as a circus exhibition, and was battling for his life against a fleet of airplanes while clinging desperately to the top of the Empire State Building.

There is something about Miss Wray that appeals to "movie" monsters. It was not more than a few weeks ago that she was being pursued by Lionel Atwill as a mad waxworks proprietor with a detachable face, and not long before that an insane scientist was planning to drain her blood for one of his experiments. Never, though, has this fatal lure of hers led into such predicaments as she faces in *King Kong*.

She is comparatively happy, starving in the streets of New York, when a screen director hires her to appear in one of his travel films and from then on life becomes a series of screen nightmares. She is captured by savage natives, is trussed up and tossed as a sacrifice to the fifty-foot ape, is carried off in Kong's hand as he wanders about the forest primeval, and has to watch her captor as he battles his fellow monsters in a series of bouts that should delight the artistic soul of Mr. Curley, the wrestling promoter. Then as a climax to her pleasant adventures she is carried by Kong up the side of the Empire State Building when he visits that impressive structure as one of the few guests not greeted by ex-Governor Smith, and must cower beside the mooring mast as a fleet of airplanes opens fire on Kong with machine guns.

In the end, of course, she is rescued and married off to Mr. Bruce Cabot, the juvenile, but I should like to know more about what sort of wives women who have been scared by giant apes make. Fortunately Miss Wray is of the placid type, so that her adventures apparently disturbed her only momentarily, but somehow I would imagine that they might have some sort of deleterious effect on her nervous system. It seemed to me that Mr. Cabot and Mr. Robert Armstrong as the screen director who captures Kong were rather handsomely casual about their exploits too.

As you can see, *King Kong* is pretty much in the tradition of Conan Doyle's *The Lost World,* as done in the silent films seven or eight years ago. There has, however, been nothing like it since, and with the cinema going in for parlor realism these days, the picture emerges as an interesting and effective stunt, produced with considerable imagination. It strikes me, though, that Radio City where it is being shown, is a trifle ungrateful to the elevated lines after they went to the trouble of painting all their structures around Rockefeller Center. For one of the scenes shows Kong wrecking an elevated train in a manner that may make the more sensitive passengers who happen to see *King Kong* rather nervous in the future.

The New York Herald Tribune, March 3, 1933

William Troy is best remembered as a literary critic; his posthumous *Selected Essays* won a National Book Award in 1968. From 1933 to 1935 he was film critic of *The Nation*.

KING KONG

WILLIAM TROY

At least one of our national characteristics is illustrated in the RKO-Radio production of *King Kong* which loomed over the audiences of both Radio City movie-houses last week. It is a characteristic hard to define except that it is related to that sometimes childish, sometimes magnificent passion for scale that foreigners have remarked in our building of hundred-story skyscrapers, our fondness for hyperbole in myth and popular speech, and our habit of applying superlatives to all our accomplishments. Efforts to explain it have not been very satisfactory; the result is usually a contradiction in which we are represented as a race that is at once too civilized and not civilized enough. If Herr Spengler interprets the extreme gigantism of the American mind and imagination as the sign of an inflated decadence resembling that of Alexandria and the later Roman Empire, others discover in it the simpler expression of a race still unawakened from childhood. At Radio City last week one was able to see the contradiction pretty dramatically borne out; an audience enjoying all the sensations of primitive terror and fascination within the scientifically air-cooled temple of baroque modernism that is Mr. Rockefeller's contribution to contemporary culture.

What is to be seen at work in *King Kong* is the American imagination faithfully adhering to its characteristic process of multiplication. We have had plays and pictures about monsters before, but never one in which the desired effect depended so completely on the increased dimensions of the monster. Kong is a veritable skyscraper among the apes. In his own jungle haunts he rules like a king over the rest of the animal world; and when he is taken to New York to be exhibited before a light-minded human audience he breaks through his chromium-steel handcuffs, hurls down two or three elevated trains that get in his way, and scales the topmost heights of the Empire State Building with the fragile Miss Fay Wray squirming in his hairy paw. The photographic ingenuity that was necessary to make all this seem plausible was considerable, and in places so remarkable as to advance the possibility of a filming of certain other stories depending largely on effects of scale—*Gulliver's Travels,* for example, and possibly even the *Odyssey.* But unfortunately, it was thought necessary to mitigate some of the predominant horror by introducing a human, all-too-human theme. "It was not the guns that got him," says one of the characters at the end, after Kong has been brought to ground by a whole squadron of battle planes. "It was Beauty killed the Beast." By having Beauty, in the person of Miss Wray lure the great monster to his destruction, the scenario writers sought to unite two rather widely separated traditions of the popular cinema—that of the "thriller" and that of the sentimental romance. The only difficulty was that they failed to realize that such a union was possible only by straining our powers of credulity and perhaps also one or two fundamental laws of nature. For if the love that Kong felt for the heroine was sacred, it suggests a weakness that hardly fits in with his other actions; and if it was, after all, merely profane, it proposes problems to the imagination that are not the less real for being crude.

The Nation, March 22, 1933

M

RICHARD WATTS, JR.

The German picture enigmatically called *M* is not only an overwhelming horror tale, but it is one of the most poignantly pathetic documents of humanity ever filmed. A story of a lustful, hideous, inhuman murder, it manages to be at the same time so sympathetic and understanding a study of a savage, pathological killer that it becomes a genuine tragedy as well as an essay in savagery. It strikes terror into the heart of the beholder and still succeeds in extending the borderline of human sympathy almost beyond the breaking point. It contains pity and horror and grim irony, and all of these difficult, tortured qualities are combined into a great whole by the brilliant direction of Fritz Lang and the superb acting of Peter Lorre. *M* is one of the great motion pictures, a Teutonic film to stand beside *Maedchen in Uniform* in its quality, if not in substance and manner, and perhaps to cause one amazement that it should, with all its knowing compassion, come from a land of hatred and bitterness.

M is the story of the child murderer of Düsseldorf. It was not so many years ago that the newspapers were filled with stories of the savage killings of small girls and of the desperate and unavailing efforts of the police to find the maniacal assassin. Without showing you one of the slayings, without anything of the explicit horror of the American films of the terror school, this film manages to create at the outset the hideous suspense and the utter monstrosity of the murders. A child's toy balloon floating off into the air, a child's rubber ball rolling down a hillside, the sound of the murderer's hysterical whistle—by these quiet bits of suggestion, not by any display of detailed frightfulness, the whole mood and the spirit of the Düsseldorf murders are created and maintained.

After the film has presented the mood of the murders it goes on to present their immediate implications—the terror of the populace, the suspicion and the mass hysteria that result from the savage reign of assassination. Then comes vengeance. The criminals of the town have come under suspicion and they resent the fact that such things should place a curb upon their activities. Thereupon they organize, and the associated beggars place a cordon around Düsseldorf and set out to track down the killer. Finally they locate him and drag him off, screaming, not to the police, but to a "kangaroo court," where they are to try him for his crimes.

There is something overwhelmingly terrible and sinister about the tracking down of the mad killer by organized crime, and Fritz Lang, the director, has captured all the dramatic qualities of such a situation. Then there is the trial, where the doomed murderer pleads for his life, telling the criminals in his piteous outcry that, while they commit crimes because they want to, he is guilty because he is driven to it.

It is here that the amazing sense of pity in the film is revealed. For this hideous murderer, this merciless slaughterer of the young, who whistles snatches from *Peer Gynt* at his work, somehow becomes a pathetic, understandable, tragically human figure. You see the pathological helplessness of the man and the poor, distorted, crippled qualities of mind and soul that have driven him to the murders, and, while you never lose your sense of horror about the man and his deeds, you do begin to find a strange, grudging compassion for him.

The man is played with almost incredible insight and understanding by Peter Lorre, who gives what must certainly be the most terrifying performance in screen history—terrifying not because of what he does so much as because he shows you how pathetically human such a beast can be. It is a most chastening experience for any of us. . . . Incidentally, the English titles by Wolfe Kaufman are sharp and incisive, but I wish there had been more of them.

The New York Herald Tribune, April 3, 1933

M

WILLIAM TROY

M, the German-language film, is based on the crimes and the final apprehension by the police of the famous child murderer of Düsseldorf. Certainly no subject could be more inherently horrible, more dangerously open to a facile sensationalism of treatment. Yet such are the tact and the genius with which Fritz Lang has handled it that the result is something at once more significant than either the horror story, pure and simple, represented by *Caligari* and the *Rue Morgue,* or the so-called psychological "document" of the type which Germany has sent us so often in the past. The result is, in fact, a film which answers to most of the demands of classical tragedy. In the first place Lang has concentrated his interest not on the circumstances but on the social and human consequences of the crimes. We are shown a whole city thrown into panic by what is for every class the least pardonable of all acts of violence. The police have failed in their efforts to find the criminal; the underworld of crooks, thieves, and beggars, in order to guarantee their own security, organize themselves in a man hunt. At the end it is the latter and not the police who ferret out the guilty one in the dark recesses of a factory storeroom. All this, of course, provides a formal suspense more sustained than would any playing on the usual modes of physical horror. It also provides a certain nervous relief. The horror, as is proper and necessary in the films, is conveyed by implication rather than representation. It is implied through a very few miraculously appropriate symbols—a child's toy balloon caught in a telegraph wire, a child's ball rolling to a stop from the scene of the crime. Bloodlust is identified with the strain of Grieg which the criminal whistles whenever the passion is upon him. The whole pattern—lust, the victim, and the circumstances—is symbolized in the frame of glittering knives in which the criminal, staring in a shop window, sees the image of his latest victim reflected. Because these symbols are one and all visual or aural, peculiar to the talking screen, they serve to make *M* of the very highest technical interest. But they are not enough to explain why it may also be considered a great tragedy. For the crystallization of these symbols in an emotion absolutely realized in the spectator and effecting in him a genuine Aristotelian catharsis, the flawless acting of Peter Lorre is perhaps finally responsible. In his rendering of the paralysis of frustrated lust in the scene on the café terrace, for example, he gives us an intuition of the conflict of will and desire such as we are accustomed to only in the great classic dramas when they are played by great tragic actors. And in the last scene, when he stands at bay before the assembled underworld seated in judgment, his wide-eyed, inarticulate defense is made the equivalent of those long passages of rhetoric at the close of Greek or Elizabethan plays in which the hero himself is forced to admit his helplessness before the forces which have undone him. The modern psychopath, through Peter Lorre's acting, attains to the dignity of the tragic hero. It does not matter that the forces are no longer on the outside. They are perhaps the more ruthless for being inside him. The *moirae* may be given different names by the doctors, the judges, and the audience, but they have lost none of their ancient inevitability.

The last thing that may be said about *M,* therefore, is that it confirms our belief in the continued vitality of the tragic emotion. Few other attempts to substitute for the old gods, fates, or destiny a modern fatalism of psychological mechanisms have been so successful. The difficulty has seemed at times (as in O'Neill's *Electra*) that the latter are too subjective ever to take the place of the former. But it may only have been some failure or insufficiency of the artistic process at work. It may be that Fritz Lang and Peter Lorre are better artists in their fields than most of those who have sought to revive tragedy in our time. Or it may be—and *M* gives strength to the supposition—that the cinema is able to supply a language for modern tragic experience that is at once fresher, more various, and more poetic than the flat statement of naturalistic drama. Our speech, we are often enough told, has suffered in the marketplace. Our language symbols are abraded and our rhythms dissolved. But through the distinct symbols and closer pantomimic acting possible on the screen the whole world of tragic reality may once again be reopened to us.

The Nation, April 19, 1933

Comradeship (Kameradschaft), cited below, was a German film directed by G. W. Pabst.

M

PARE LORENTZ

Ordinarily, I do not like to waste space writing about the significance of foreign pictures. During the year we get no more interesting pictures from Europe than we do from Hollywood; along with them we get as much horrible junk as was ever turned out by any local company. It has become a cliché on the part of a great many profound commentators to use the phrase, "the Germans and the Russians," as an all-inclusive recommendation; and, as few people ever see foreign pictures, most moviegoers probably have the notion that, somehow or other, those fellows certainly can put it all over us when it comes to making pictures, but they'd better stay where they came from.

Actually, there isn't any *group* distinguishable as "the Germans and the Russians." You can look at a hundred German pictures, and you'll find that a majority of the directors are patently imitating Hollywood. And while the Russians have had a world at the service of their cameras, the sum total of their good productions can be added on one hand.

There are two or three men in Russia, one in France, one in England, a half dozen in Germany, and about four in Hollywood who have conceived and executed some originality in motion pictures, but even that originality has been more literary than technical: that is, where Pudovkin, or Murnau, or Chaplin may have designed a camera trick or a cutting trick any good director immediately could seize upon, it is only when an educated man uses such skill to turn a personal, literary idea into a movie that we have that rare thing, a fine movie. Thus, it is not so much technical originality, but René Clair, that made *A Nous, la Liberté* good; Murnau, and not Flaherty's photography, that made *Tabu* a lovely thing; and it is Fritz Lang, and not "the Germans," who is responsible for a picture, long famous in Europe and Hollywood, called *M*—a movie which already has greatly influenced good directors, and which, along with its esoteric technical innovations, also is a beautifully balanced melodrama, well worth space in any language.

M is a dramatization of a sex murderer (apprehended some years ago) known as the Düsseldorf murderer.

Lang immediately has a cultural advantage over local contemporaries, both in his understanding of the character and in his audiences. Known to them only as a "fiend slayer," few local audiences will find anything in this murderer that will agree with their impressions of how a fiend slayer feels, or how he acts. I imagine that's why the censors let it through; looking for bloody gangster monkeyshines, they found only a pudgy, pop-eyed, simple-faced young German with a puzzling predilection for little girls. With the exception of one scene in which he displays a spring knife, there is no obvious indication of crime or sex in the picture. There is one scene in which he is frustrated, and collapses in a café—and another in which he confesses and reenacts his crimes—that is tragically real, and, to a civilized person, about as horrible as anything you ever want to see.

The photography is straightforward and austere. There is no acting in the picture. Every character, from the murderer to the most insignificant extra, is beaten into subordination. You feel as though you were watching a newsreel. Never for an instant do you say—ah, what an actor! There are no camera angles, no whirling cogs, no Coney Island tricks with faces thrown out of focus.

This newsreel quality of *M* does force an admission that some Germans and Russians are able to get an unusual quality into even mediocre pictures, such as *Comradeship.* That quality is subordination. A German director, now in Hollywood, was talking last winter about the amazing use of dialogue in *M,* and how Lang puts the audience right into his scenes by never showing the speaker—or, by thrusting his camera into a group of people, and making them so absolutely natural that the audience feels that it, too, is actually seeing and hearing with the cast.

We agreed that you could not make such a picture in Hollywood, even if the producers kept their hands off the production, simply because in all America you could hardly collect a hundred actors and put them in a picture and keep them from acting. In a job such as *I Am a Fugitive* every man and woman within a hundred yards of camera range is acting his head off, figuring that he is a Clark Gable, or a Garbo, as the case may be, who needs only to project himself strongly enough to have the director send posthaste for him to sign that big contract.

This is not just a Hollywood characteristic (although it is the main reason why Clair and Lang and Pabst can make pictures which ring absolutely true, and which are so convincing one forgets one is seeing a dramatic production, while our best productions are obvious and theatrical). As my friend pointed out, it is true of most American art. He directed a successful show some years ago, and spoke about his troubles with the cast. "They have no humility." A crackpot theatrical producer, given a fragile little comedy, rehearses his cast with all the temperament and unreasonable tyranny of a Stanislavski producing *The Seagull.* The author of a successful puzzle book overnight assumes alcoholic temperament that would shame a Hearn or an Oscar Wilde. The play, the job, itself, is never the thing.

It is this humility on the part of Europeans that causes the local boys to scratch their heads and sagely explain everything by saying "the Russians and the Germans." Even when Hollywood does go, we won't be able to make an *M,* unless independent companies allow their directors to do away entirely with actors, and (which is the only sensible way to manufacture movies at all) pick types and faces off the streets.

Meanwhile, until the millennium, Hollywood's poverty has been a minor blessing. Starved for pictures, theater owners will show anything, and we can expect to see the best things the Russians, the Chinese, the Irish, and the Zulu Islanders have to show us; a condition impossible in the good old blackjack corporation days.

Vanity Fair, May 1933

One of the authors of *Kuhle Wampe* was Bertolt Brecht.

L'AGE D'OR | *KUHLE WAMPE*

WILLIAM TROY

The purpose behind the two private film societies founded this season was admirably illustrated and realized in their last programs, both of which happened to be shown on the same Sunday. Neither *Kuhle Wampe* nor *L'Age d'Or* was the sort of picture to be seen at any of the commercial houses; the unrelenting honesty of the first, the intense eclecticism of the second, would have proposed too many difficulties. Yet both represent certain interests and tendencies in the current European cinema which it is important for us to recognize if only, as in the case of the second film, that we may avoid them. In their choice of offerings the Film Forum and the Film Society also confirmed the suspicion hinted at in this column that they are to be sharply distinguished in the nature of the attack they are making on commercial film standards in this country. The difference in their directions, it may be said, reflects what is undoubtedly the dilemma of the noncommercial or "artistic" film all over the world at present. *Kuhle Wampe* and *L'Age d'Or,* seen on the same day, leave one with the impression that the cinema is at the crossroads.

The general parallel for such films as *L'Age d'Or* and the recent *L'Affaire est dans le sac* is to be found in most of the aristocratic art and literature of our time. Like the music of Stravinsky, the painting of Picasso, the writing of Joyce and Eliot, these pictures derive their theme and technique from the disintegrated consciousness of the modern world. More particularly, however, they may be related to that explosive, ill-mannered, and entirely superficial movement in postwar French letters known as *surréalisme*. As a literary movement, of course, *surréalisme* endured no longer than it deserved. It had amounted to nothing more than a belated exploitation of the humorous possibilities inherent in the dissolved syntax and violently juxtaposed imagery that had been introduced into French style a half-century before in the apocalyptic recordings of Rimbaud and the Comte de Lautréamont. Although these stylistic peculiarities had originated as the expression of the tortured sensibilities of really serious artists, they degenerated in the work of Tzara, Breton, and others of the *surréaliste* group into something that can only be called humor, a particularly brutal and ghastly brand of humor.

The first thing that must be said about *L'Age d'Or,* then, is that it is a distinctly "literary" film. It is not so much an attempt at a cinematic translation of the *surréaliste* vision as a literal dramatization of a typical "narrative" of the school. It is, of course, impossible to offer a synopsis of the scenario prepared by Messrs. Buñuel and Dali. Let it be enough to say that in between a prologue and an epilogue which bear no logical relation to the main story, is to be seen a phantasmagoria of violence, lust, blasphemy, luxury, and unmotivated crime such as has never before been projected on the screen. Whatever interest all this may have resides in the subject matter, or the particular disarrangement of it, rather then in any special effects of camera style or technique. Except for occasional shots—a man lying face downward on the ceiling of a room, blood gushing from a man's face in the middle of a love scene—and the irrelevant accompaniment of the *paso-doble* at the end, there is little dependence on strictly visual or aural methods of communication. There is mention in the program notes of Buñuel's remarkable use of screen metaphor. Presumably the objects thrown out of the window by the protagonist were intended to be metaphorical symbols of some kind—the Christmas tree phallic, the effigy of the archbishop religious, and so on. But these symbols pictorially realized are actually no more effective than the words for them on the printed page. No added value is given to them by the photographic process either separately or in relation to the whole. Yet in these symbols, if anywhere, we are to look for some continuity of meaning. If we take the archbishops, the Christ-like figure at the end, and the cross as symbols of an inverted religious mania, the picture becomes no more than a pathological document—Black Mass, *rive droite,* 1928. If we take them, on the other hand, as constituting a viciously satirical anticlericalism, the picture is open to the charge of propagandism. No matter how we interpret them they fail to take on a significance which gives either unity or meaning to the picture as a whole. The complete absence of any value or values to which they may be related results in a dissolution of form which makes any kind of unified response impossible.

The recognition of the importance and necessity of just such values in the subject is responsible for the very real effectiveness of Dudow's *Kuhle Wampe.* Indeed, its theme is precisely the realization by a group of young people in Germany that their survival depends on their ability to work out some elementary values of living for themselves in the midst of a senile, decaying world. Although the picture is in an unfinished state, there is enough adherence to the theme throughout to give it a substantial unity. In fact, it is sustained adequately in the single character of Anni, as beautifully rendered by Hertha Wiele, in her efforts to retrieve her demoralized family by moving them to the unemployed colony outside of Berlin, her uncomplaining acceptance of her personal problems, her relations with the jobless mechanic to whom she is married. Here the meaning is brought out pictorially through the richly detailed but highly selected documentation of the surfaces of life as it is lived by this submerged section of lower-class German society. The social criticism, if one must find it, is implicit in the representation. It rises out of the materials; it is not imposed on them as in so many Russian films. And this is true despite the long discussion of world affairs in the subway train at the end; for even here, where the social implications of the picture seem most conscious, the ideas expressed are subordinated to the characterization of the speakers. Everything is kept in a proper relation to the young couple's desperate search for a value— a search which gradually acquires the force of one itself, which is, indeed, a value in itself.

The choice before the more serious cinema at the moment is pretty well illustrated by these two pictures. Either it must go in for whatever elements of humor, fantasy, and sophisticated cleverness may still be extracted from the representation of modern chaos; or it must go in for an ever deeper and more honest exploration of particular terrains of contemporary experience. Certainly such a picture as *Kuhle Wampe* shows us the great opportunity the films have to make us *realize,* in the strictest sense, the exact substance of that experience, to render it with such fidelity that we may possibly be able to see new values in the actual process of shaping and asserting themselves. And by this, of course, is meant something quite different from the superimposition of any particular set of intellectual ideas—like Marxism, for example. The Russians have shown us often enough how disastrous this can be to the development of the cinema as a truly creative art. For some time to come, perhaps, the film, like all other branches of art in our time, will have to remain skeptical of the various systems of dogma available, to keep very close to the reality in order that whatever values it may finally give rise to will be the surer and more acceptable.

The Nation, April 5, 1933

THE PRIVATE LIFE OF HENRY VIII

RICHARD WATTS, JR.

Mr. [Charles] Laughton, who apparently was born for the express purpose of playing Henry VIII, seems to have stepped right out of the Holbein portrait of the connubial Tudor for his performance in this finest of English motion pictures, and immediately there is every reason for bringing up all the critical superlatives about acting. The photoplay is a handsome, striking, and richly atmospheric chronicle of its times, which deserves every credit as a distinguished example of the cinema's ability to recreate an epoch. Its sixteenth-century England, with its color, its cruelty, and its gross heartiness, is quite brilliantly depicted, and the story of the monarch's domestic life, from the execution of poor Anne Boleyn to his last henpecked days with domestic Catherine Parr, is admirably told. But, with all of the film's other virtues, it is Mr. Laughton's really magnificent performance which makes *The Private Life of Henry VIII* so distinguished a drama. Here is acting in its richest and grandest manner.

If there is any fault to be found with Mr. Laughton's portrayal by the most captious critics it is that he makes the monstrous monarch too likable a figure to check with the facts of history. With that possibly partisan exception, there can be nothing but the most ecstatic praise for a characterization which suceeds in being at the same time real and vivid and humorous and understanding and enormously human. Mr. Laughton's Henry is a lecherous scoundrel, selfish, unfeeling, and gross, but there is about him the petulant air of a spoiled child which makes amazingly for compassion. The manner, also, in which Henry is shown as an amorous old fool, completely at the mercy of the most obvious feminine trickery, tends to make him, if far from an heroic, then at least a slyly likable character. Then, too, the characterization succeeds in combining the best phases of stage and screen acting, so that the performance should appeal with equal sucess to playgoers and to those few stalwart worshippers of the oldtime screen who feel that acting should be effective in its pantomime as well as in its handling of speech.

As in all chronicle dramas, the narrative of the new film is episodic and without climax. You see Henry on the eve of the execution of Anne Boleyn, waiting for the fall of the headsman's ax so that he can marry the pretty, heedless Jane Seymour and then follow his domestic life—which, thanks to the number of attendants pursuing him about, could be called "private" only in irony—when, after the death of Jane in childbirth, he marries and divorces Anne of Cleves, marries and executes Catherine Howard, and marries and is bossed by Catherine Parr. His various marital adventures become almost individual one-act plays, held together by the presence of their hero-villain. The best of the episodes is the one in which the plain German girl, Anne of Cleves, who wanted to go away with the man she really loved, plays cards with Henry on their marriage night and wins her freedom from him. Here is as brilliant a high comedy incident as Lubitsch ever achieved in the days of his great silent comedies. The next most popular incident is certain to be the one in which the Tudor dines sumptuously and rowdily, tearing apart his meat with beautifully savage gusto.

The dialogue of the film is excellent, keeping a fine balance between the two possible dangers of making the speech either too archaic or too studiously modern for comfort. As I have probably hinted, the picture is completely Mr. Laughton's, but the other roles are ably handled in every case. It is worth noting, incidentally, unless the work is deceiving us, the court of Henry VIII was simply overrun with good-looking women, and that at least three of the queens were exceptionally beautiful. The best feminine role, that of the sly Anne, is delightfully played by Miss Elsa Lanchester, who is also Mrs. Laughton. Miss Merle Oberon is a lovely and pathetic Anne Boleyn; Miss Wendy Barrie, whose name I don't believe, is pretty and straightforward as Jane Seymour, and Miss Binnie Barnes is a handsome and striking Catherine Howard. Don't you believe that the English can't make motion pictures.

The New York Herald Tribune, October 13, 1933

Meyer Levin's career includes work as reporter, actor, documentary filmmaker, and novelist. Prominent among his novels are *The Old Bunch* and *Compulsion.* Through much of the 1930s he was the film critic of *Esquire.*

Zeppo is not in the mirror scene. It is between Groucho and Harpo, joined eventually by Chico.

DUCK SOUP

MEYER LEVIN

. . . The musical field needs to lie fallow. The last flowers were sort of pale-like. Take, for instance, the latest offering of the Four Marx Brothers: a blurp called *Duck Soup,* and their worst concoction. The story is a feeble effort at satirizing dictators: Groucho, ruling over one of those mythical musical-comedy kingdoms, has adventures with a rich widow and a foreign ambassador.

The Marx Brothers ought to get wise to the fact that Harpo, and not Groucho, is the genius in the family. Groucho's gags grow staler, and his puns flatter, in every picture. Yet he has more to do in each new opus; his jabber disastrously slows the pace. Harpo's appeal is directly to our instincts. He does everything we are inhibited from doing. If he sniffs a pretty female, he makes a beeline for her, eyes ablaze, arms open. He takes a fiendish delight in destroying things; his pockets are full of outlandish contraptions, idiotic inventions. He is, in short, the boy in man, for once allowed exuberant life. At times Harpo impresses one as having a gift comparable to that of Chaplin. But where Chaplin's humor is sad-eyed, based on negation, Harpo's humor is positive, ablaze with his frenetic appetite for life; he isolates the sheerly idiotic joy of life. The brothers ought to try building one picture around Harpo.

Duck Soup contains a really hilarious scene. Zeppo and Harpo, both disguised as Groucho, confront each other as in a mirror. They go through a convulsive series of facial contortions, nose-thumbings, twirls, hops, leaps, crawls, in perfect parallel, trying to catch each other out.

Esquire, February 1934

The Invisible Man has a distinction in addition to those mentioned below: It is the only film in which an actor made his screen debut in a leading role without being seen, until the very end.

THE INVISIBLE MAN

WILLIAM TROY

There are two very good reasons why the version of H. G. Wells's *The Invisible Man* is so much better than this sort of thing usually turns out to be on the screen. The first is that James Whale, who is responsible for the direction, has taken a great deal of pains with something that is usually either reduced to a minimum or altogether ignored in these attempts to dramatize the more far-fetched hypotheses of science—namely, setting. Ordinarily we are precipitated abruptly and without warning into the strange and violent world of the scientific romancer's imagination. We are given no time to make our adjustment to the magic of this new world which is so different from the world to which we are accustomed. The result is, of course, that we never truly believe in this new world: it is too abstract, too intellectually conceived, to take us in very sucessfully through our feelings. For this reason one is always tempted to lay down as a first principle for writers and directors dealing with the extraordinary, the principle that to respond to the unusual we must first be reminded of the commonplace. And James Whale's success in observing the principle makes one more convinced than ever that it should be regarded as a general one. He begins with a carefully documented picture of a small country inn in England: the people, the furnishings, the whole atmosphere are not only instantly recognizable but also so particularized as to have an interest in and for themselves. The background is solidly blocked in so that we have no uncertainly as to the reality of the people and the places with whom we have to deal. Everything is made ready for the invisible man to step in and perform his marvels.

Now the only problem for the director was to make the best possible use of his idea—an idea which happens to be ideally suited to the talking screen insofar as it is impossible to imagine it being equally well treated in any other medium. For the wretched scientist who had made himself invisible still has a voice. A body without a voice we have had on the silent screen, but not until this picture have we had a voice without a body. And in Wells's novel the sight of the printed words on the page cannot be so disturbingly eerie as the actual sound of Claude Rains's voice issuing from empty chairs and unoccupied rooms. The problem for Mr. Whale, then, was to miss none of the opportunities for humor, pathos, and metaphysical horror which this rare notion opened up to the sound camera. How admirably he has succeeded it is impossible to indicate without reference to the numerous instances in which his ingenuity surprises our habitual sense patterns. It will be enough to mention the books hurled through space by an invisible hand, the cigarette smoked by invisible lips, the indentation in the snow of the shattered but still invisible body. Also one must point to the effectiveness of not showing the visible features of the scientist until, in the last few feet of the film, death restores them to him. Of Claude Rains's richly suggestive voice it is not too much to say that it is hardly less responsible than the direction for the peculiar quality of the picture as a whole. The preternatural compound of Olympian merriment and human desolation which are its overtones lends a seriousness that would otherwise be lacking. But taken either as a technical exercise or as a sometimes profoundly moving retelling of the Frankenstein fable, *The Invisible Man* is one of the most rewarding of the recent films.

The Nation, December 13, 1933

George Jean Nathan, the drama critic referred to below, was celebrated for cosmopolitan taste and urbane wit.

SUGAR AND SPICE AND NOT SO NICE

GILBERT SELDES

It is surprising that no one has yet pointed out the simple and astounding reason for the success of Mae West in the movies. In the thousands of columns written about her two things have been said again and again:

that she is voluptuous and that she is vulgar, one of which is hardly true, the other hardly important. She has been treated as the 1934 harder, more sophisticated version of the old movie vamp, as if she weren't exactly at the opposite pole, in technique and intent, from the whole Theda Bara school; and the revolution she may cause in the movies' morals and appeal has not yet been suspected, least of all in Hollywood. Miss West constitutes, in my opinion, a threat to the Hepburns, the Crawfords, the Garbos, the Shearers (lumping in these plurals themselves and those who aspire to be like them) and, in fact, to every woman player except Marie Dressler and that superb, almost anonymous Negro whose great mahogany shining face and divine smile are among the major pleasures of dozens of films through which she passes. Indirectly—and this comes under the head of good news—she may undermine the crooners and the pretty boys who play male leads, although the name seems a technical error.

Before proceeding to the heart of the Westian mystery, it is worth while looking for a moment at her predecessors in popular favor. The vamp, first type, is irrevocably linked to Kipling's poem and Theda Bara's sinuous graces; the second development, little noted at the time, came with Lubitsch's *early* pictures, starring the dark and, in those pictures, truly voluptuous Pola Negri; the third began the downfall, since the concentration was on the movies' discovery of It, associated, of all things, with a hoydenish little girl, suggesting that the entire male population of the United States was likely to fall in love with an immature and brash little morsel obviously incapable of the arts of seduction and endowed with a merry twinkle which instantly negatived all the laboriously learned tricks supposed to represent an abundant sexuality; the fourth stage came with the talkies when Lubitsch moved from historical romances of great mistresses to polite sophisticated comedies (note a specific loss of sex interest as the interest in comedy grows, the two being mutually hostile), and the pictures as a whole were happy to reproduce on the screen the hits of the Theatre Guild (the two are again mutually hostile). Linking the movies and the talkies is the profound influence of the magnificent and magnificently beautiful Garbo who has always acted as if the human species, male and female, gave her great pain, out of which she has managed to make herself the nearest thing to a tragic actress on the screen, and following her, the impishly seductive Marlene Dietrich who began as the ideal mistress, lustrous, silky, handsome as hell, and friendly; and who has managed, in her version of *The Song of Songs,* a hotly sexual story, to suggest that the chief interest of the men in the picture was in the tilt of her head.

In this last phase the moral interest in sex has not been underplayed. The eminent elder who announced, on one occasion, that the theme of *Lysistrata* made it forever unavailable for the movies, has not been able to keep from the screen a vast number of pictures in which it is suggested that men and women have a physical appetite, one for the other, and that, for the satisfaction of this appetite they steal, betray, and murder to attain their ends, and, having attained them, are often a little less than constant. There has been sex which began in the pictures as a SIN—a theory out of which a great many people derive pleasure, a perfectly workable theory which the movies had to drop only because some fifty million of its spectators seemed to have dropped it on their way to make the world safe for democracy. Having lost that solid principle, the movies were incapable of proceeding to the next step—the step Miss West has taken for them, which I will soon define. They stopped halfway with the implication that sex is a pastime and a swell thing to talk about. At that halfway spot, almost all the women in the movies went completely upstage, giving the spectator to understand that they were too witty, too highbred (or should it be high-toned?), too intellectual, too dainty, too delicate, too something, whatever it was, to waste themselves on the likes of the men offered for their entertainment. The notorious incapacity of movie actresses to convey any real emotion is partially responsible for this impression, but not entirely. Let the reader recall the films he has seen in the past five years and try to remember a scene (something seen, not heard) in which a movie actress actually gave the impression that the character she was playing really was in love with a man, really desired him in the common way of human desire. Love, said the correct Dr. Johnson in his dictionary, is the passion between the sexes. How many times have you recognized that passion on the screen?

I do not mean to suggest that all the actresses and all their directors suddenly decided that it is polite to be perverse and that an interest in the opposite sex is frightfully bourgeois and old-fashioned. Some of this there was, as there was on the stage, and George Jean Nathan has properly protested that the average audience is not for long going to be taken in by love scenes played between epicenes to each of whom the sight and sex of the other is an affront. Girls obviously most at home in a riding habit or a gent's dinner jacket have appeared in silks, furs, and chiffons, and been ridiculous, but a good actress can, at a pinch, simulate an emotion and transfer it; the trouble on the Hollywood screen is that no one believed in the reality of the emotion.

Enter Miss West. Miss West had made whatever reputation she had by a vigorous, downright, honest exploititaion of the commodity which, in her splendid simplicity, she had made her own, even using it for the name of one of her plays: *Sex*. At the time Miss West was being harried and chivvied about by the Law, it occurred to me that mere dirt could not account for her magic spell and I timidly printed the suggestion that she was a superb actress who, if she had come from France, would have been all-hailed for her consummate art and her divine vulgarity. (I was probably wrong about her vulgarity—she has a commonness and a coarseness of fiber which are not vulgar; but I was right about her talents, and if the producers of movies had read *The New Republic* eight years ago, instead of fan magazines, they might have picked her up then on my tip.) I was not, however, as penetrating then as I now can be: the core escaped me. Today it is all daylight.

Among Miss West's other plays was one which never was permitted to come to Broadway: it was called *The Drag,* and it treated (contemptuously) the race of fairies. Miss West, an astute manipulator of the public's sensations, was not above using the contemporary interest in pansies for her own purposes, but she indicated a stern moral disapproval of any departure from the most ordinary of sexual interest. To her mind, sex was a great power, delivering men into the hands of women who——

Who gave them joy! That is the astonishing, the unheard-of, the still incredible suggestion Mae West makes every time she appears on the stage or screen. Indifferent to the sinfulness, if there is any, of sex, she proclaims by every look, smile, wink, by every change of gait or twist of the hand, by every wriggle of the cooch dancer transferred to Park Avenue penthouse, that sex is a pleasure. This wholly revolutionary discovery is, so far, hers alone, although Clara Bow, the It girl of a decade ago, is doing a half-portion imitation already, an imitation of the means without the meaning. "Come up and see me some time" gurgles the voice of Mae West, suggesting for the first time on any screen that mutual sexual satisfaction will result from the encounter. There are other suggestions in the invitations of the Westian screen character: men are delivered into the hands of women so that women may serve them, protect them against their enemies, take their crimes upon their own shoulders—whatever Miss West's melodramatic imagination may bring forth. But the essential thing remains the promise: if you will sleep with me, we will both enjoy it. Miss West breaks down the Law, not inscribed in the Constitution, but more potent than any statute, that women must take no pleasure in sex and must only with reluctance and distaste gratify the rude desires of men.

You see at once that this smashes the whole movie technique of seductiveness based on the principle that women care nothing for sex and therefore run away from men and have to be cajoled, tricked, and seduced. Miss West gives that show away entirely. Ninety-nine of a hundred movies with a love interest (or, more briefly, ninety-nine of a hundred movies) arrive at a triumphant conclusion when the lovers embrace after hesitations, refusals, and certain artificial barriers have been removed (the war, the Depression, the collision of the sun and the planets all figure in the movies only as barriers to true love which does not, however, indicate anything more that the willingness of a young woman to be alone, in an hotel lobby or a motor car, but never a bed, with a young man). By exposing the awful secret that women may desire men as much, or nearly as much, as men desire women, Miss West makes hash of all these pictures. Her pictures begin with Lady Lou or whoever it is as the mistress of a man who rejoices in her and whom she either will or will not throw over in her laudable impulse to give joy to as many of this sad world's men as possible. She makes the advances more directly than any character of Bernard Shaw's; she pursues, and when she runs up against the timid type engendered by years of going to see sexless plays and pictures, she "learns them" how good and pleasing sex can be.

What are the movies going to do about it? With their usual lack of intelligence they will probably hunt for large women with amiable breasts, good hips, and a beckoning look. They will persist in thinking that Mae West is voluptuous and imagine that if they bring on the screen another woman in her physical proportions, they will repeat her effects. It will be a pleasure to miss some of their flat and icy beauties, wandering through emotions in which they do not believe, with their noses in the air, as if the thought of going to bed with anyone were an impropriety; but the satisfaction which men have found in Miss West's pictures will not be duplicated unless the same simple attitude of mind will also be duplicated. I mentioned some months ago the pleasure men found in Cagney, an assertion of the male's dislike for the tampering female. The parallel pleasure in Miss West rises from the feeling that no man would need to slap her down.

In Miss West (and Miss Dressler) the movies also return nearer to the heart of the average woman. This is important because women go to the pictures more often than men, and producers have worried whether the Mae West type wouldn't offend women or would lack the glamor of the more familiar stars. Well, the movies have glamored themselves completely out of the range of the washerwoman's or the housewife's imagination; only a stenographer can still hope to attain the exquisite heights of the Shearers and the Crawfords. It is a relief to women to see a woman, rather like themselves, get a hundred men with a look of the eye and an easily imitated wiggle of the backside. This is humanity, this is realism, this is the truth—for them. There is no glamor in it, perhaps, but there is the possibility of going and doing likewise. So the women like Mae West, hailing her as one of themselves who made good. Miss West may have accomplished a revolution in American manners (nocturnal) no less than in American movies.

Esquire, March 1934

Otis Ferguson was the film critic of *The New Republic* from early 1934 through 1941, when he enlisted in the Merchant Marine. He was killed in 1943. In addition to his film reviews, Ferguson also wrote highly regarded criticism of books and the theater and jazz.

IT HAPPENED ONE NIGHT

OTIS FERGUSON

It is a little late in the day for mention of *It Happened One Night,* but since the picture is still floating around the little houses and since it would be a pity to miss it, I should like to plump for it here, and strongly. Considering its subject, it is better than it has any right to be—better acted, better directed, better written. The plot has to do with a girl who escapes the rigors of life on her father's yacht and takes a long-distance bus for New York, where she proposes to join a villain she has just married. She runs into a fired newspaperman who at first is rather hard on her but soon turns out to be a very number-one sort of chap indeed, and everything runs along nicely until the two have surmounted about everything and are nearly home. But then, everybody being in love with everybody else in pleasantly conclusive fashion, there enters more confusion as to who loves whom and why than might be expected of a Molière comedy. Barring the incidents of the bus ride, the outlines of the story have a deadly enough familiarity all through anyway. What the picture as a whole shows is that by changing such types as the usual pooh-bah father and city editor into people with some wit and feeling, by consistently preferring the light touch to the heavy, and by casting actors who are thoroughly up to the work of acting, you can make some rather comely and greenish grasses grow where there was only alkali dust before. The cast was particularly sound from top to bottom. Claudette Colbert sensed what was required of her, and did it very well, though I do not care for her much as a person—not as much in fact as for Walter Connolly, who was delightful. Clark Gable was the outstanding feature, managing to be a rowdy and a perfect gentleman and a newspaperman and a young lover, all in the same breath and the most breezy and convincing manner imaginable. And now having adjudicated and discriminated and in a word defined the picture with proper regard for this and that, I am reminded that such a picture cannot be defined at all until we find a way of describing whatever it is that makes first-rate entertainment what it is.

The New Republic, May 9, 1934

IT HAPPENED ONE NIGHT

WILLIAM TROY

Among the more gratifying phenomena of the current season has been the growing recognition of *It Happened One Night,* the Frank Capra production of last year, as one of the few potential classics of the recent cinema. Having been selected as the best American picture of the year by the National Board of Review and other organizations, and having earned for its director and players a handsome collection of gold medals, it is at the moment in its third week of revival at a New York playhouse—a tribute usually reserved for certain films of Chaplin and certain cartoons by Walt Disney. What is perhaps most gratifying about all this is that it has come about without any of the usual ventilation of superlatives which attends the birth of a masterpiece in the American screen world. Nothing in the subject, the personnel, the surrounding circumstances of this particular film offered the least pretext for the beating of the big drum. There had been a whole succession of pictures based on the picaresque aspects of the cross-country bus; neither Claudette Colbert nor Clark Gable was a reigning favorite with the great popular public; and Frank Capra was merely one of several better than average Hollywood directors. In brief, the wholly spontaneous response with which the picture was received could be traced to no novelty or originality in its component elements. A second viewing of it confirms this truth at the same time that it enforces the realization of how difficult it is, at the present stage of motion picture production and appreciation, to determine what it is precisely which makes a good photoplay. It is true that the story, which is a mixture of both farcical and realistic situations, is exceptionally well put together from almost every point of view. It is developed with the galloping pace that good farce requires, and the timing of individual scenes is invariably well managed. But it is hard to distinguish between the work of the scriptwriters and the work of the director, who is perhaps even more responsible for maintaining an unerring accuracy of tempo throughout. And is it quite fair to ignore what the players may be contributing to the same effect? Although neither Miss Colbert nor Mr. Gable had demonstrated any particular comic talent before this picture, their playing here is at every step exactly in tune with the mood of the occasion. As for the content of the film, which may possibly be distinguished from the treatment, one can remark only that it is authentically indigenous without being in any way novel or striking. An honest documentation of familiar American actualities becomes, in a Hollywood film, more absorbing than intrigue in Monte Carlo or pig-sticking in Bengal. Also one might point out that the manner in which this material is utilized for comic purposes strikes a nice balance between pure farce and serious social satire. The result of the balance is something less tiresome than the first, and less precarious to the comic intention than the second. But the effort to fix and label the particular quality which separates this film from the dozen or more substantially like it in recent years is bound to end only in an admission of critical humiliation. A good photoplay, like a good book or a good piece of music, remains always something of a miracle—in the least sentimental sense of that word. Beyond a certain point the mind is forced to bow down before its own inability to unravel and put together again all the parts of the shining and imponderable whole with which it is dealing.

The Nation, April 10, 1935

Howard Barnes joined *The New York Herald Tribune* in 1929, succeeded Richard Watts, Jr., as film critic in 1936, and from 1948 to 1951 was both film and drama critic.

Contrary to the statement below, *Mother* was made as a silent picture. Sound effects and a running commentary were added for the delayed American premiere, which took place after the advent of talking pictures.

The New Babylon was directed by Grigori Kozintsev and Leonid Trauberg, *The Road to Life* by Nikolai Ekk, and *Marionettes* by Yakov Protazanov.

MOTHER

HOWARD BARNES

The belated exhibition of Pudovkin's *Mother* in this city not only distinguishes the season with a great screen work but serves to define clearly the magnificent cycle of motion pictures produced under Soviet auspices. This gripping film realization of Maxim Gorky's novel possibly ranks lower than *Potemkin* or *The End of St. Petersburg,* but from an esthetic standpoint it is in every way their equal. It typifies all that the Russians succeeded in creating out of the cinematic medium and at the same time places a rather definite period to a particular era in motion picture development.

For *Mother* under the conditions of its present showing, is almost a posthumous chapter in one of the great flowering periods of the cinema. It was singularly appropriate that the Russians chose the motion picture to make an artistic record of their revolution. A highly mechanical form, requiring a large collective effort, and a new, exciting, dramatic medium, it proved remarkably pliable in the hands of people to whom the changes in social and economic structure in which they were participating were an obsession, even a religion. The result was a splendid development of technique that captured revolution in more or less enduring terms as it had never been recorded before.

It was obvious that the Russians should turn to the hour of their triumph for the first of their film works, and understandable that these should prove the greatest of their contributions to the screen. Eisenstein in *Potemkin* and Pudovkin in *The End of St. Petersburg* fashioned masterpieces of the cinema that rank with the greatest works ever produced by the films. A passionate concentration on their material, coupled with brilliant imagination and artistic integrity went into their efforts. Lesser sagas of the revoluton were produced, some of them excellent and few of them bad, and then came such variations of the theme as *The New Babylon,* a bitter commentary on the Paris commune of 1871, Pudovkin's *Storm Over Asia,* and *The Road to Life*

Of late, however, the Soviet studios have given hints that the cycle of revolutionary film dramas is ended. Not only have the epochal events of 1917 been exhaustively recorded, but the U.S.S.R. has settled down into a more or less ordered existence under Stalin's guidance, and people are searching for other motivations in living than class struggle and the triumph of the proletariat. The most recent importation from the Soviet studios, a satirical musical comedy, *Marionettes,* is an index to the new point of view of the Russian movie makers.

Mother, however, belongs definitely in the era of great revolutionary screen dramas. Dealing with the smoldering turbulence of 1905 and 1906 in Russia that served as training ground for the sucessful 1917 revolution, it tells simply and compellingly of an unsuccessful workers' uprising. Through the large pattern of mass oppression and violence, Pudovkin has woven in sharp outline an individual tragedy that reflects and heightens the effectiveness of the farmer. Those students of the cataclysmic changes that shook Russia in 1917 who have discovered most of the seeds for them in the earlier revolt will find them briliantly illustrated in *Mother.*

Its removal from the present or recent past has given the work a splendid objective quality. Although its climax is tragic, the motion picture as a whole has a conclusive unity which was lacking in many of the Russian revolutionary films. There is no tampering here with the essential historical facts such as occurred in Eisenstein's *Ten Days That Shook the World,* from which Trotsky was elided for the sake of internal propaganda. At the same time there is no overwhelming bias to give the material an air of grotesque caricature. The random trailers of Soviet achievements that the Acme [Theater] has appended to the drama to stir its audiences are ridiculously out of place.

Whatever value *Mother* may have as a stirring document of oppression and revolt, it is equally significant as an assured work of art. Although the Russian dialogue has been prohibited in its current showing, it belongs distinctly to the era of talking motion pictures. Curiously enough, the accident that finds the film inaudible here serves to emphasize the extraordinary genius of the great Russian directors in making the difficult transition from the silent film technique to the muddied period of the articulate cinema.

There has been no question to Pudovkin that the phonographic recording of sound was little more than a substitute for the printed titles of the pre-talking picture days. With no excessive use of pantomime, he has managed to create an arresting pattern of visual images that move to their own climax in dramatic action without an imperative need of audibly recorded explanations. Unable to believe that the esthetic of the silent cinema was not the chief consideration in the creation of motion pictures, he has fashioned a model of the talking motion picture that should prove enormously valuable to cinema studios in all parts of the world.

In *Mother* the arrangement of the action has not only the cumulative crescendo that is known in high-brow circles as "montage," but it has an unerring composition that only the most talented of directors have been able to capture on the screen. The angle from which Pudovkin has shot his characters in each scene, the painstaking care with which he has arranged each background, the breathtaking beauty of his cinematic interludes manage to create not only mood and dramatic motivation, but a continuous line of pictorial splendor that is in itself almost sufficient for a spectator.

The acting in the production is all that one might have expected from witnessing the zealous fervor that animated the participants in earlier Russian motion pictures. Particularly striking is the performance of Nicolai Batalov, the collective manager in *The Road to Life,* who creates a poignant and unforgettable portrait of the young strike leader, shot down just as he escapes from prison. Vera Baranovskaya, as the mother who betrays her son unwittingly and makes heroic amends for her mistake, is magnificent, and A. Tchistiakov does a splendid job as the sullen and beaten father who is bought as a strike-breaker for a glass of vodka.

It is the perfect fusing of acting, photography, direction, and narrative that succeeds in making *Mother* a definite masterpiece of the screen. Not only does it have the passionate sincerity that marked the preceding Russian tracts on revolution, but it demonstrates the unerring skill of the Soviet directors in handling the medium of the cinema. It is scarcely conceivable that the brilliant technique they have developed will not make enduring marks on more mundane material than the epochal events that intrigued their interest during the heyday of Russian film.

The New York Herald Tribune, June 3, 1934

Little Man, What Now? and No Greater Glory, both directed by Frank Borzage, were made from novels by Hans Fallada and Ferenc Molnár. The pre-Eisenstein *Ivan* mentioned here was directed by Yurii Tarich.

MOTHER

WILLIAM TROY

By far the most important event to be reported this week is the final release in this country of V. I. Pudovkin's greatest picture, *Mother,* based on Maxim Gorki's novel of the 1905 revolution in Russia. A second view of this film at the Acme—it was shown before a private audience at the Film Forum a few seasons ago—leaves no doubt as to why it was suppressed for so long a time. Here is a film in which the distinction between propaganda and art seems to break down, in which the propaganda *emerges* inevitably out of the experience that is represented. Instead of being merely elocutionary, like so many recent Russian films, it is eloquent—in the best sense of expressing its meaning through such a complete realization of its materials that no statement is necessary. It persuades rather than convinces, which is equivalent to saying that it arouses and directs certain fundamental feelings in such a way that the mind of the spectator is carried along, like the river in the picture, to the intended conclusion. Its meaning cannot be separated or even distinguished from the fabric of the experience. It is implicit in the ramshackle backgrounds, in the expressions on the faces of the bosses and the workers, in the most casual gesture of the old mother, who innocently betrays her son to the police. In a word, it is communicated on the unconscious rather than on the conscious plane of the spectator's response, and for this reason alone the picture falls more clearly within the domain of art than that of propaganda. And since art is infinitely more subversive than the most devastatingly logical propaganda, the authorities were quite right in considering it more dangerous than any other sent over by the Soviet Republic. If it could by any chance be seen by as many people as will see *Little Man, What Now?* and *No Greater Glory,* it would undoubtedly prove by its effects on the American consciousness its distinct superiority both as art and as propaganda.

None of the recent products of the Soviet studios has presented anything like the same possibilities of danger, and one need not look very far for the reason. The difference between Pudovkin's early masterpiece and such films as *Ivan* and *Arsenal* is that while the former deals with events already completed in the past, corroborated, so to speak, by their historical actuality, the latter deal with events whose real termination lies in the future. In *Mother* Pudovkin's imagination was turned backward to an already realized past; in his soundfilms it is turned toward the future—that future which tends always to become an abstraction no matter how many factories and power dams one builds for one's particular Utopia. Memory is still the mother of the muses, in the cinema as in other forms, and the artist is likely to produce better results when his orientation is backward to the real past than when it is forward to an ideal future.

Moreover, by his success in this early film Pudovkin himself contradicts his theory that the screen should endeavor to "depersonalize" its actors in order to make them more representative of the masses and mass movements. Theoretically, the objection is once again that we are moving from the concrete to the abstract, from that to which we can respond with our whole being to that to which we can respond only with our minds. But Pudovkin actually illustrates in the effectiveness of this film the superiority of the older method of bringing out the general theme in terms of the individual and the personal drama. Both Baranovskaya as the mother and Batalov as the son are too good actors not to contribute something of their own to the whole. This is not to detract in the least from the genius of the director: the acting in *Mother,* like everything else, is a completely integrated element. Particularly admirable in this respect is the pictorial symbolism—that most tempting of pitfalls to the ambitious director. Here the symbol is never static, applied, something outside the movement and structure of the whole. The river is, of course, a symbol—a progressive symbol of stagnation, disintegration, and release—but it is also causally related to the action of the story. To mention any single element in this film, therefore, is to be forced to discuss it as a whole. One covers everything perhaps by saying that it remains one of the half-dozen greatest claims to being considered seriously as an art that the screen has so far established.

The Nation, June 20, 1934

Novelist, poet, playwright, psychologist, educational philosopher, linguistics scholar—to all these accomplishments of Paul Goodman's, and others not named, must be added film critic. This essay dates from early in his career.
Le Sang d'un Poète is by Jean Cocteau.

FAULTY CINEMATICS IN HOLLYWOOD

PAUL GOODMAN

1. The major causes for the corruption of the cinema at the present time leap to the eye and need not be described. On the one hand, the commercialism of Hollywood, "quickie" production and mass-distribution; on the other, the depravity of the public taste—each of these aggravating the other and driving it from bad to worse. Again, there is the primitive, unschooled state of the art itself, and at the same time the complexity of the technique—these also interacting to produce monsters, most often lame and timid, sometimes extravagant, never just. But now I should like to consider briefly still another form of corruption, interesting as a violation of an esthetic rule, and it is this: The movies at present more and more desert proper cinematic matter and treatment, and lean more and more heavily on the novel, the stage, or even abstract ideas. The directors are not creators of cinema at all, but mere translators into images whose function is to remind us of what has been created in some other medium. Whether they lack confidence in cinema itself, or hope to capitalize on what is well-known and established, they tend to use film in a wholly mediate way. What sin of esthetics is committed here? Is it not increasing the separation (perhaps always necessary to some degree) between the matter and the form?—so that the screen becomes uninteresting in itself and is always looked at for the sake of something else.

2. In the beginning of their career, following, we might say, "the generous instincts of youth," * the movies speedily hit on several techniques

---

* That is, at the start, to win any attention the movies had to offer something new, peculiar to themselves. Later, being accidentally able to undersell the stage, they began to drive the theater out of business and sell that product in a debased form.

and kinds of subject-matter that were like nothing that existed before. For example: the sweeping panoramas of the Wild West thrillers and the riding lickety-split behind Harry Carey or William S. Hart; or, again, the panoramic military-scenes of *The Birth of a Nation,* the easy execution on the screen of what poor Meissonnier tried all his life to do on canvas. Another cinematic invention was subtle and elaborate pantomime, the play of face and hands, made possible by close-ups and other filmic means of drawing attention to one part of the body. Such incidents—among a thousand—as Chaplin's dissection of the clock in *The Pawn Shop,* or the dance of the dinner-rolls in *The Gold Rush,* probably were not to be seen before. Still a third great invention was the Chase—the great artistic motif really perfectible only in music or the cinema—brought to such a technical height by the redoubtable Harold Lloyd and made a fine art in René Clair's *Le Million* or *Le Chapeau de Paille d'Italie.* Even the so-called star-system, with its rather frank exhibition of male and female seductiveness, from Theda Bara on, did not fail to exploit the camera. (All these examples, it is clear, might be deduced from one cinematic property: the mobility of the camera-eye; it can come close, draw far off, see at an angle, or race along.)

3. More sophisticated discoveries concerned not, as here, the objects of the camera-eye, but the properties of film itself. (Note the remarkable fact that we learn about the instrument only after using it.) An obvious example was slow motion and accelerated motion, reverse motion, and even the dead stop. Another example—I need hardly point out of what far-reaching importance—was the discovery of the possibility of constructive-editing, montage, laying all the emphasis on cutting, juxtaposition, pace, build-up. And this exploitation of mere film, as film all depended on the simple truth, brought out by the experiments of Kuleshov and others, that to the spectator it makes no difference what originally went into the camera, but only what eventually appears on the screen.

4. But not to multiply instances, I think it is clear what general sort of thing is denoted by the words cinema, cinematic (a proper definition, of course, would come only after arduous investigation); and it is equally clear wherein Hollywood is sinning at the present time. The pace and rhythm of most recent films comes hardly at all from the movement of the objects and almost never from the technique itself, but mainly from the story, the dialogue, the character-development, or in propagandist films, the moral—a movement not seen on the screen, but "suggested" by the screen. Panorama also has gone overboard, while montage and so forth belong to a system of ideas quite foreign to our directorial minds. Now it is commonly held that it was the advent of talking-pictures that marked the beginning of the retrogression in cinematics; but I believe that

the disease antedated the talkies. It was present in the old tendency to "adapt" the novel. Dialogue administered the coup-de-grace by offering the possibility of filming stage plays. Today these two art forms divide the field: those portions of a film which are not stage-dialogue are photographed novels or "epics," as they are called. (Need one point out, all question of cinematics aside, that this mixture of the concentrated drama and the diffuse and complex novel works to the disadvantage of both?)

5. Now what I don't meant to say is this, that it is illegitimate to use film (or any other medium) in a mediate way, concentrating the attention not on the medium but on the presentation. On the contrary, the great principle of evaluation is the result, and where a great esthetic effect has been achieved, it is not always useful (though always good) to point out that the means may have been indirect. But in the present case, considering the current output of Hollywood—it is not pointless to indicate that an obvious esthetic canon is being disregarded, namely: that it is dangerous to separate the end of an art too far from the means—particularly when, as in the case of the cinema, the technical means are so complex . . . Again, it is rarely self-evident what subjects and techniques are cinematic and which are not. (Who, for instance, would have foreseen the effectiveness of a dead stop, until it appeared in the last episode of *Le Sang d'un Poète?*) Indeed, it is precisely the work of a director to discover the cinema where you would not expect it; this is what the creation consists in. To lay down the law in fact rather than in principle stifles the artist. But here again, applying the argument to Hollywood, there seems only too little danger.

Trend, May/June 1934

Andre Sennwald, who had been a reporter on *The New York Times* since 1930, became the film critic in October 1934. In January 1936 he died of gas poisoning in his apartment, aged twenty-eight.

THE GAY DIVORCEE

ANDRE SENNWALD

Last season it was the "Carioca" which persuaded the foolhardy to bash their heads together. Now the athletic RKO-Radio strategists have created the "Continental," an equally strenuous routine in which you confide your secret dreams to your partner under the protective camouflage of the music. For expert instruction consult the agile team of Fred Astaire and Ginger Rogers in *The Gay Divorcee,* which put everybody in a bright humor at the Radio City Music Hall yesterday. According to the song writers: "It has a passion, the Continental, an invitation to moonlight and romance; it's quite the fashion, the Continental, because you tell of your love while you dance." Anyhow, it provides Mr. Astaire with a musical theme to match his nimble feet, although, when executed domestically, it probably will lack something of his polish.

With the addition of the final "e," this is a liberal screen version of the intimate musical comedy in which the same Mr. Astaire appeared several seasons ago. With a commendable sense of dramatic criticism, the cinema workers have set out to improve on the original by the comprehensive addition of scintillant dance numbers and fresh tunes. From *The Gay Divorce* only one song remains, Cole Porter's "Night and Day." The studio balladists contribute several excellent chansons, including "Needle in a Haystack" and "Don't Let It Bother You." The cinema brewmeisters hurl them into the composition of an entirely agreeable photoplay which sings, dances, and quips with agility and skill. Both as a romantic comedian and as a lyric dancer, Mr. Astaire is an urbane delight, and Miss Rogers keeps pace with him even in his rhythmic flights over the furniture. The audience meets Mr. Astaire and *The Gay Divorcee* at their best when he is adjusting his cravat to an elaborate dance routine or saying the delicious things with his flashing feet that a librettist would have difficulty putting into words.

Underneath the glimmering surface this is still the thinnish tale of bedroom confusions in an English seaside resort. Guy Holden, the American dancer, is pursuing the usual young woman with the usual lack of success. When she turns up at the hotel for the purpose of inventing the technical grounds for a divorce from her geologist husband, Mr. Holden is just a toe and a heel behind her. Consequently, when he turns up in her room at midnight, she mistakes him for the hired corespondent. Like the gentlemen who put the story together, you can imagine the sort of comic misunderstanding this sort of thing can lead to. But, like the carefree team of Rogers and Astaire, *The Gay Divorcee* is gay in its mood and smart in its approach.

For subsidiary humor, there are Alice Brady as the talkative aunt; Edward Everett Horton as the confused lawyer with his first case; and Erik Rhodes (from the stage show) as the excitable corespondent, who takes the correct pride in his craftsmanship and objects to outside interference. All of them, plus the "Continental," help to make the new Music Hall show the source of a good deal of innocent merriment.

The New York Times, November 16, 1934

IT'S A GIFT

ANDRE SENNWALD

Perhaps if the W. C. Fields idolaters continue their campaign on his behalf over a sufficient period of years his employers may finally invest him with a production befitting his dignity as a great artist. In the meantime such comparatively journeyman pieces as *It's a Gift* will serve very adequately to keep his public satisfied. Although the new Fields picture is seldom equal in comic invention to the master's possibilities, it does keep him on the screen almost continuously, and it permits him to illuminate the third-rate vaudeville katzenjammer of the work with his own quite irresistible style of humor. To the student of comedy who is able to tell a great funnyman from a merely good one that is a way of saying that *It's a Gift* is the first "must" assignment of the new year.

You ought to be informed that the slightly phoney name of Charles Bogle, which appears among the credits as the author of the story, is really Mr. Fields himself, lurking modestly in the corridors of Paramount's Writers' Row. This time he is the vague and fumbling Mr. Bissonette, who is the proprietor of a small-town general store, as well as the helpless victim of a shrewish wife. *It's a Gift* tells how Mr. Bissonette, after being badgered and hounded beyond his generous powers of endurance, finally boards a rattletrap flivver with his family and sets off across the country to a California orange plantation which he has purchased with the proceeds of his late uncle's will.

That is approximately a skeleton of the narrative, and as usual it is singularly useless as a guide to Mr. Fields's behavior. *It's a Gift* immerses the beery, adenoidal, and bulbous-nosed star in a variety of situations which he promptly embroiders into priceless and classic comic episodes. You find him torturing the laws of logic and gravitation in his efforts to shave himself while being annoyed by his young daughter. There is the extended account of his futile struggles to catch some sleep on the porch after he has been driven from his bedroom by Mrs. Bissonette's constant nagging. With the one exception of Charlie Chaplin, there is nobody but Mr. Fields who could manage the episode with the blind and deaf man in the store so as to make it seem genuinely and inescapably funny instead of just a trifle revolting. Then, with Baby LeRoy for his straight man, he goes quite mad during the infant's extensive operations in the store, finally closing up shop in despair and leaving behind him a sign explaining that the store is closed on account of molasses.

The great man's assistants in the new comedy provide him with excellent foils. As the nagging wife Kathleen Howard is so authentic as to make Mr. Fields's sufferings seem cosmic and a little sad despite their basic humor. As the thickwitted grocery clerk, Tammany Young is an effective lunkhead, and Charles Sellon, as the blind man, is quite as irresistible as he was last month as the wheel-chair invalid in *Bright Eyes.* The fact is that Mr. Fields has come back to us again and *It's a Gift* automatically becomes the best screen comedy on Broadway.

The New York Times, January 5, 1935

THE PROUSTIAN CAMERA EYE

PAUL GOODMAN

1. When any particular story is suggested for a moving picture, it is for reasons more or less relevant to the properties of cinema itself. The filming of the Landing of the Pilgrims (as in the series *The Making of America*) or of other such educational short subjects, is obviously on the principle that we learn better by images than by sentences and "one picture is worth a thousand words." Or again, when for financial or moral reasons, certain subjects are eagerly exhibited, and rigorously censored, it is because the screen, by its peculiar ability to excite the senses and rouse the emotions without in the least tiring the active imagination or the intellect, has become the most popular entertainment of our time. In the case of a few subjects, however, such as the great novel of Proust or T. S. Eliot's poem *The Waste Land,* it would seem that the repeated remark, "This would make a good picture!" is more immediately relevant; here, the works themselves seem cinematic.

Now already here, let me say parenthetically, we are taking for granted a very moot point, namely: whether cinema ought properly to borrow from books at all, any more than it should borrow from the theater (which it almost certainly should not). But since I do not want to discuss this at present, but some other time, let us assume the following truism: that any book is susceptible of filming to the degree that its own technique is cinematic, and some books are more so than others.

2. One of the properties of cinema that is considered peculiarly Proustian is its flow. The fluidity of shadows on a screen is, to some people, a perfect model of how we think; and this flowing association of ideas has only one dimension, Duration. Slow motion, accelerated motion, at the crisis perhaps a momentary dead-stop: all these are at the same time good cinema and the being of thought. Add the other devices that make the screen so fluid, the fade-out, the mix, the super-position; everything appearing and dissolving, with occasionally a sharp cut to another scene,

"just like thought." So the Proust novel itself has been compared to a kaleidoscope. And lastly, in this remarkable theory of thought, the screen can be hazy (sentimental or otherwise bewildered) or definite and sharply focused, and this is of course the difference between a "confused" and a "clear and distinct" idea!

Music too, however, could be said to represent thought, and so, in general, any medium that is both fluid and contrapuntal. But the flow of music is usually supposed to imitate "feeling," while the flow of images is supposed to be "thought." This is on the principle that people "feel" by a series of rhythmic motor sensations, whereas they "think" in terms of an association of pictures. (The error throughout is that sensation or passive imagination is mistaken for thought).

3. Now a second property of cinema that could be called Proustian (or vice versa, a trick of Proust's that is cinematic), is quite the opposite of the previous one: it is the *idée fixe*. Here, no matter what the point of departure, the mind is continually brought back to one dominating motive, a ruling passion or an overpowering experience, that colors everything else. These dominating ideas give body, and a cumulative effect, to the thought that seemed all flowing and transient. A device employed to this end by Proust is the "petite phrase" of Vinteuil, recurring again and again. But it is in cinema especially that the attention can be focused on one motif amid the most heterogeneous action. The technical devices used are the close-up, the quick flashback continually repeated, the training of the camera-eye on one significant feature (say, a worker's clenched fist) while the voices of the dialogue roam from one thing to another. Eisenstein is at the present time the great master of this technique—which like everything else, however, he often spoils by bad taste.

By means of this perfect expression of the *idée fixe,* the cinema is curiously adapted to the presentation of hysterical compulsive actions, lapses of memory, neurotic tics of every kind. The sidelong glance of the Baron when first seen by Marcel, this alone betraying his hidden mania (*A l'Ombre des Jeunes Filles,* vol. 2), would probably be better shown on the screen than in prose.

4. Another quality of Proust that is also a property of cinema is surprise, the unexpected revelation of traits of character or of relations between things, a revelation subtly prepared for, but breath-taking when it comes. Such an episode, for instance, as when Marcel, in the last volume, finds himself at a masque-ball where all the dancers have powdered their hair and made up their faces; and then suddenly he sees that it is not a masquerade at all, but all his friends grown old in a flash. Merely for mechanical reasons, this scene could not possibly be presented on the stage, but on the screen it is a simple quick-dissolve. For in cinema it is not

what actually stood before the camera, but what comes out of the cutting-laboratory that finally appears; the most startling juxtaposition and double-exposures are feasible, so that mechanical difficulties practically disappear. Another aspect of the same quality of surprise, easily translated into cinema, is wit, which is juxtaposition that is unexpected but appropriate. (Cf. the stunning moment in Cocteau's film, *Le Sang d'un Poète,* where the dreamer, who has just shot himself, unexpectedly removed the blood from his brow, showing it to be a paper wreath). This is the respect in which *The Waste Land* would be good cinema. Another side of the same thing is striking metaphor, e.g., the stone lion that suddenly roars like a cannon in *Potemkin* . . . But this property of cinema is extremely relevant to the filming of Proust, for from one point of view, such surprises, reversal of all prior judgments, and sudden enlightening of what was previously obscure, are precisely what "the Proustian monadology" consists in.

5. The last Proustian property of cinema that I want to mention is that the camera eye is a spectator, almost a spy. This is the newsreel quality of cinema; it faithfully copies off the events taking place before it, without distortion or bias of its own. In most other arts and in most writers, we are given an interpretation of the object; we see it through the active inter-vention of the artist—the brushstrokes of the painter or the purpose of the writer, to tell an entertaining story, for instance; but in Proust, and in photography, the effect depends on the sentiment that this is experience itself, the object as it swam into the field of vision—but not looked at square, of course, for then it promptly hides and you see nothing of it, but spied on; out the corner of one's eye, just as Marcel spied through the window at the loves of Vinteuil's daughter. When, in *Sodome et Gomorrhe,* Marcel spies on Jupien and the Baron, it is as if the camera-eye were in the alleyway, a passive plate of impressions . . . Not, on the other hand, that Proust is "photographic," as we speak of realism as photographic. (Nor, for that matter, can a good newsreel be made by just turning a camera, without choosing the angle and editing the film). On the contrary, it has just been maintained that it is the "surprises," the unexpected and enlightening juxtapositions, that are the Proustian quality of Proust (and the cinematic quality of a newsreel). But the paradox is, that these very surprises and juxtapositions, so unnaturalistic, would fail to be effective unless we knew they were photographic. In most writers, the virtue of wit is to be constructive, to present a witty object to somebody else's mind; in Proust, the Narrator is perfectly passive, but to his continual surprise his passive mind itself turns out to be witty . . . I am afraid that this is rather less than clear; but the only point relevant to this discussion is this: that a certain "passivity of the camera eye" is characteristic of Proust.

6. These four comparisons—the Proustian free-association with the

dissolving flow of cinema, the Proustian *idée fixe* with the focusing of the camera, the Proustian revelation with the unexpected juxtapositions of the cutting-room, and the passivity of the Proustian narrator with the "photographic" quality of the newsreel—these four, although not exhaustive, suffice to show in principle what is meant when it is said that *A la Recherche du temps perdu,* or any other novel, is cinematic in technique, or "would make a good movie."

Trend, January/February 1935

THE INFORMER

WILLIAM TROY

At last this season is privileged to view a Hollywood production which for sustained brilliance of technical accomplishment can bear comparison with the best recent importations from other lands. The picture is the work of John Ford, a director who has done distinguished work before, its story is based on one of the better novels of that sometimes powerful, sometimes incorrigibly meretricious Irish realist Liam O'Flaherty. *The Informer* in Dudley Nichols' excellent version, gives a more dramatic, a more richly documented, and an even more terrifying impression of the Black and Tan troubles in Ireland in 1922 than one received from Mr. O'Flaherty's novel. This is the result partly of the greater objectivity imposed by the screen medium, partly of Mr. Ford's superior detachment toward his materials. Gypo Nolan, the underworld drifter who sells his comrade for twenty British pounds, gains in reality through being presented in terms of direct action rather than in the often diffuse interior monologues of Mr. O'Flaherty's more Dostoevskian manner. Victor McLaglen, under the superb direction, contributes to this impression of a greater solidity and roundness by giving one of the most memorable screen portrayals of the year. It matters little that the megalomania with which he endows the twisted little introvert of Mr. O'Flaherty's conception gives to the character a somewhat more heroic quality than is appropriate. The modifications of the original are all in the direction of a better realization of the character and theme in strictly cinematic terms. At the same time Mr. Ford has not ignored the drama played out in Gypo's consciousness before, during, and after the betrayal. In fact, the greatest importance of the film consists in its experimentation with the means of rendering subjective moods and states of mind on the screen. What may be called the total mood, the emotional ambience surrounding the theme and the subject, is created and sustained by the lighting—a uniform semidarkness splotched here and there with the sinister glow of street lamps. Not only does the dimness through which people and objects are glimpsed intensify the atmosphere of hushed terror of Dublin under the Black and Tans, but it also serves to reflect the miasmic confusion of Gypo's guilt-laden consciousness. By this means outer and inner world are interfused; rarely has an American picture achieved such a consistent unity of emotional tone. It is reinforced rather than broken when doors thrust open in the fog reveal by contrast the lighted interiors of police stations, restaurants, and bawdy houses. (The scene in the middle-class lupanar is one of the most unforgettable, as it is certainly the most astonishing, in the recent American cinema.) But it is not by lighting alone that Mr. Ford has built up the unity of effect which makes this film so remarkable. Using musical accompaniment in the way that it was most effectively used in the silent film, recording Gypo's "second voice" or voice of conscience, and trailing both music and voices on the soundtrack as a dissolve device, Mr. Ford has striven to integrate all the newer resources of the medium and restore to it that identity which it has tended to lose since the introduction of sound. What is most significant of all perhaps is Mr. Ford's rediscovery of the uses of silence. Not only is the dialogue reduced to a minimum, but it is sometimes blocked out entirely for the sake of pantomime and other effects reminiscent of the silent film. At times this leads to results which may be considered artificial and unnatural, which can be defended only as a type of stylization. When Gypo comes to the revolutionary headquarters to be examined, he and the others are forced to stand silently for several moments while a picture of his betrayed comrade burns in the fireplace. But the intention behind the effort is one of the things which make this film the best that has come out of Hollywood in a very long time.

The Nation, May 22, 1935

THE INFORMER

OTIS FERGUSON

The picture that John Ford has made out of Liam O'Flaherty's *The Informer* opens a lot of new possibilities for Hollywood, tackles something that is really fine, and manages several memorable scenes. But because it deals with the sort of thing that must be handled adequately if it is to go over, its persistent inadequacies make it more disappointing than many pictures with less to recommend them.

The story gets off to a beautiful start, riding along on the unfamiliar color and excitement of the period when the Terror was in Ireland, tightening on the country and walking through its streets in armed squads. And it carries well through the early part of that evening when Frankie Mc-Phillip (Wallace Ford is excellent in this part) came in from the hills, to slip home in the fog and be sold to his death, with the Tans piling out of their lorries to surround the house, and Gypo Nolan, the betrayer, watching the clock at headquarters in a cold sweat. For dramatic vigor and beauty of composition there have been few sequences to compare with the one that ends with the camera looking from behind Frankie down into the court where the Tans look up with their machine gun.

So far, the atmosphere and the scene of a tragic character have been well built. But shortly after Gypo has stumbled out with his blood money, there begins a train of happenings many of which hang fire altogether—the result partly of faulty casting, partly of bad plot treatment. Margot Grahame has a weak part as Gypo's girl, and fits it; Heather Angel is a personal nonentity; the rebel leader (Preston Foster) is hollow, and his chief aide spoils a fine likely face by pantomiming with it, while Una O'Connor as the mother is a constant irritation. These people all play inevitably into the story, and are abetted by the director, who must needs drive every nail down three inches below the surface; hence whole organic stretches are made flabby or (as is the case with the last episode in church, the intercession of Katy) actually distressing. What is more, there is constant reliance on symbolic fade-ins and ghostly voices, on an elaborately cued and infirm musical score, and on the device of squeezing the last drop of meaning or sentiment out of a ten-minute sequence by hanging onto it for a quarter of an hour. It hardly seems that the man responsible for these cheap shifts could be the one who schemed the earlier episodes, the extended revelry of the middle parts, and the final trial scene.

But any one of the ham touches would be negligible—all of them taken together might even be discounted—if the central part had been sure of conception and if McLaglen had been all the way up to it. I kept feeling that he lacked the final subtlety requisite to making the crude lines of this character wholly true. In attitudes he is at times superb, but he simply does not carry the thing along. Partly because of this, partly because of the direction, the doom Gypo Nolan is preparing for himself does not seem inevitable, and one gets the feeling of impatience that always comes when what should be a natural downfall seems to be turning into a dramatic pushover.

Hollywood deserves a lot of credit for tackling such a job, and thereby opening a new field for pictures; but I do not feel that the film itself does right by a story so powerful and moving as that of a man who was driven by hunger and suspicion into the tragic foolishness of turning informer in the Irish Terror.

The New Republic, May 29, 1935

THE MAN ON THE FLYING TRAPEZE

ANDRE SENNWALD

It is possible that the final bibliography of Mr. [W. C.] Fields's work will list his new picture as one of his most important screen triumphs. For years the great comedian has been building his humorous effects out of futility, frustration, and abject despair. In *The Man on the Flying Trapeze* —which has almost as little connection with the film's theme as *Dante's Inferno* had with the works of the late Alighieri—he finally asserts his battered ego in one of the most satisfying scenes in recent motion picture history. After suffering numerous indignities at the hands of his spiteful in-laws, he runs amuck for a few magnificent seconds, slugging his brother-in-law into insensibility, and aiming a brillantly erratic haymaker at his terrified mother-in-law. Not since Mr. Fields punctured Uriah Heep in *David Copperfield* has the screen presented a denouement of such curiously poignant rightness.

The Man on the Flying Trapeze, although it is marred by that cheapness of manufacture which we have come to expect in Mr. Fields's pictures, provides some of the richest humor that has reached the screen in months. If you are properly versed in the W. C. Fields tradition, you will know at once that the Charles Bogle who is credited with coauthorship of the story is really the modest star himself. The photoplay is less a connected narrative than a string of episodes describing a typical day in the life of Mr. Ambrose Wolfinger, a browbeaten husband and minor office-worker. It is one of the faults of the film that some of the situations are dragged past the saturation point, and there is a distinctly inappropriate scene in which Mr. Fields goes in slapstick pursuit of an automobile tire. But the comedy is frequently hilarious, and it always possesses those over-tones of pathos and futility which we Fields idolaters recognize as his cynical comment on the world around him.

The episode in which Mr. Wolfinger goes berserk is, of course, the high-point of the photoplay. For sustained humor, though, the enterprise is at its best in the opening sequence. It seems that two sentimental thieves have invaded Mr. Wolfinger's cellar and, having plundered his applejack, are engaged in a nostalgic rendition of "On the Banks of the Wabash." The subsequent events in which Mr. Wolfinger joins the marauders, is bludgeoned into appearing against them in court, and is finally jailed for manufacturing applejack without a permit, make for delightfully madcap comedy. Then there are the woeful developments in the life of Mr. Wolfinger after he begs the afternoon off from work in order to attend a wrestling match, his excuse being that he must bury his mother-in-law. You will understand his dilemma when you learn that the family is deluged with floral wreaths and that his abstemious mother-in-law reads in her own obituary that she has died the victim of poisoned liquor.

It is characteristic of Mr. Fields's humor that its roots are deeply imbedded in the common experience of us all. His difficulties with the traffic policeman become a biting comment on the arrogance of that race of supermen. The scenes at the wrestling match capture the lunatic flavor of the sport, even to the unintelligible blur of the announcer when he introduces the contestants. And, finally, his brutal treatment at the hands of his nagging wife, his scornful and domineering in-laws, and his dictatorial boss contain the kind of burlesque which comes dangerously close to realism. There is a helpful group of supporting players in the new film. Whatever its faults, *The Man on the Flying Trapeze* is easily the best of the summer comedies.

The New York Times, August 3, 1935

THE THIRTY-NINE STEPS

ANDRE SENNWALD

Alfred Hitchcock, the gifted English screen director, has made one of the fascinating pictures of the year in *The Thirty-nine Steps.* If the work has any single rival as the most original, literate, and entertaining melodrama of 1935, then it must be *The Man Who Knew Too Much,* which is also out of Mr. Hitchcock's workshop. A master of shock and suspense, of cold horror and slyly incongruous wit, he uses his camera the way a painter uses his brush, stylizing his story and giving it values which the scenarists could hardly have suspected. By comparison with the sinister delicacy and urbane understatement of *The Thirty-nine Steps,* the best of our melodramas seem crude and brawling.

If you can imagine Anatole France writing a detective story, you will have some notion of the artistry that Mr. Hitchcock brings to this screen version of John Buchan's novel. Like *The Man Who Knew Too Much,* the photoplay immerses a quite normal human being in an incredible dilemma where his life is suddenly at stake and his enemies are mysterious, cruel, and desperate. Richard Hannay, a young Canadian, is sitting in a London music hall when a man is killed, whereupon a young woman confesses the murder to him and begs him for sanctuary. In his rooms she explains that she is playing a lone game of counter-espionage against foreign spies who have stolen a valuable military secret and are preparing to take it out of the country. Then the enigmatic lady is herself murdered, leaving Hannay with the meager information that his own life is now in danger, that he will learn the secret of the Thirty-nine Steps in a certain Scottish hamlet, and that he must beware of a man whose little finger is amputated at the first joint.

That is the situation, and for the next four days Hannay finds himself in the most fantastic predicament of his life. The police are hunting him for the murder of the young woman, and the spies are hunting him because he knows too much. His career is a murderous nightmare of chase and pursuit, in which he continually escapes by inches from the hangman's noose and the assassin's bullet. Mr. Hitchcock describes the remarkable chain of events in Hannay's flight across England and Scotland with a blend of unexpected comedy and breathless terror that is strikingly effective.

Perhaps the identifying hallmark of his method is its apparent absence of accent in the climaxes, which are upon the spectator like a slap in the face before he has set himself for the blow. In such episodes as the murder of the woman in Hannay's apartment, the icy ferocity of the man with the missing finger when he casually shoots Hannay, or the brilliantly managed sequences on the train, the action progresses through seeming indifference to whip-like revelations. There is a subtle feeling of menace on the screen all the time in Mr. Hitchcock's low-slung, angled use of the camera. But the participants, both Hannay and his pursuers, move with a repressed excitement that adds significance to every detail of their behavior.

Robert Donat as the suavely desperate hero of the adventure is excellent both in the comic and the tragic phases of his plight. The lovely Madeleine Carroll, who begins by betraying him and believes his story when it is almost too late, is charming and skillful. All the players preserve that sureness of mood and that understanding of the director's intention which distinguished *The Man Who Knew Too Much*. There are especially fine performances by John Laurie as the treacherous Scot who harbors the fugitive, Peggy Ashcroft as his sympathetic wife, Godfrey Tearle as the man with the missing finger, and Wylie Watson as the memory expert of the music halls, who proves to be the hub of the mystery.

The New York Times, September 14, 1935

WORDS AND MUSIC

OTIS FERGUSON

In pictures, it would be natural to expect that the best thing this country could turn out would be the musicals. We have a first-class body of popular-song writers, the best jazz bands (marvelous enough in themselves), literally millions to squander on choruses, singers, hoofers, and people like Busby Berkeley and Hermes Pan, who live apparently for nothing else but to turn these things into production numbers. And in Hollywood we have a tradition of flash comedy that isn't to be equaled.

But what comes of all this? Something like *Roberta* or *Flying Down to Rio;* something that is colorful or vibrant in this or that part, but as a whole pretty vacuous and dull. So that when a picture like *Broadway Melody of 1936* happens along, with a consistent brightness about it, the show is so much more than was expected as to seem enough. And when there is a picture that is splendid with the presence of Mr. Fred Astaire, people will get violent and say to stop grousing—what do you expect from a musical anyway?

And that is the main trouble: you can't expect anything. A musical rarely attempts to be more than a ragbag of various show tricks; and even when it does, there is no relation between its comedy, which is mostly wisecracks, and its songs, which are mostly sugar. As for possible plots, there are two in use: the Hymie-the-Hoofer type, where the boy makes the grade with his act; the My-Gal-Daisy-She-Durrives-Me-Crazy type, where the boy makes the girl. These are naturally followed with no conviction, the chief problem in any given picture being how to bring in the first number. Somehow, before the film has gone many feet, somebody has got to take off from perfectly normal conversation into full voice, something about he won't take the train he'll walk in the rain (there is suddenly a twenty-piece band in the room), leaving everybody else in the piece to look attentive and as though they like it, and as though such a business were the most normal of procedures.

From this first number it is customary to push on to the second. The boy, for instance, refuses to meet the girl, who refuses to meet him. So they fall in love. Singing together in close harmony for the first time, without knowing it, they sing:

> How sweet to meet
> My pet unmet
> I kiss your feet
> Madame.

And the band has got five more pieces, including marimba and steel guitar, and a chorus of forty voices resolves one of the spare seventh chords downward, *piano, pianissimo:*

> We kiss your feet'n fite'n fotum. We
> kiss. We-e-e kissyourfeetmadame—

and the line spills out into formations that would cover a four-acre lot.

In short, the second number. Having reached this point, anybody can ad-lib the rest, there being nothing to do now but keep the girl from falling into the boy's lap, by many ingenious devices—such, for example, as having him misremember where he put it. If the picture is R.K.O., the chances are the lap will have been mislaid in the butler's pantry, which is the cue for some good and funny business with Eric Blore; and just as you go out of the room, there is E. E. Horton, a nervous wreck; and there can possibly be another touch of comedy before the girl slaps his face and takes off for Lucerne, thus introducing the lonesome, or I-Yearn-for-Lucerne, number.

This business of the comedy element in musical comedy, incidentally, is a ticklish business, because often there seems to be none. *The Gay Divorcee* was a musical built and directed primarily as comedy. *Top Hat,* an attempt to repeat on it, throws in practically the same stock company (Horton, Blore, Erik Rhodes, etc.); but it goes back to the old hit-or-miss method of letting the cast get as many laughs as it can and throwing in a two-line gag whenever anybody thinks about it. *Broadway Melody of 1936* is more in the tradition of the stage revue, and by far the funniest show around. It has, for example, made a place for such charming and individual drollery as that of Robert Wildhack, professor of soft-palate calisthenics, or the snore—austerely scientific in procedure and powers of research, rich with illustration, *e.g.,* the varieties of the labial, or ah-pooh, type, the thin or blonde snore, and the various expirational classes: the whistle, the wow, the straight plop, etc. This is an absolutely star performance and worth the price of the show by itself, although the story derives a lot of meaning from the parts of Jack Benny and Sid Silvers, and some brightness from the tap dancing of Buddy Ebsen and Eleanor Powell. As music, its numbers are flat and stereotyped, lacking even the tailored verve of the several pieces Mr. Berlin wrote for *Top Hat.*

But when we come to the subject of music in the musicals, we come to the first consistent expression of popular songs and rhythms that this medium has seen, namely Fred Astaire. From the crowds he draws, I should say that Astaire must mean many things to many people—as, for example, glamor to married ladies in for the day from Mamaroneck, real elegance to telephone girls whose boys suck their teeth and wear pinstripe suits, etc. But one thing he manages above all others, and that is the best visual expression that has been generally seen in this country, of what is called the jazz. As an actor he is too much of a dancer, tending toward pantomime; and as a dancer he is occasionally too ball-roomy. But as a man who can create figures, intricate, unpredictable, constantly varied and yet simple, seemingly effortless, on such occasions as those when the band gathers together its brasses and rhythm section and begins to beat it out

—in this capacity he is not to be equaled anywhere: he brings the strange high quality of genius to one of the baser and more common arts. Some of the aspects of jazz—its husky sadness, its occasional brawling strength —do not appear in Astaire; but its best points are sharp in such of his steps as those of the softshoe sandman number and in the number where the lights go down, just before the line of men, with top hats and sticks, swings up the steps, over the rim of the stage. Fred Astaire, whatever he may do in whatever picture he is in, has the beat, the swing, the debonair and damn-your-eyes violence of rhythm, all the gay contradiction and irresponsibility, of the best thing this country can contribute to musical history, which is the best American jazz.

The New Republic, October 2, 1935

Clifton Fadiman has been a book publisher, book editor of *The New Yorker,* a radio quiz host, and a judge for a book club. He has also been a prolific critic and journalist.

The songwriters referred to are Johnny Green, Bert Kalmar, and Harry Ruby. Kalmar and Ruby wrote songs for four Marx Brothers films, *Animal Crackers, Horse Feathers, Duck Soup,* and *A Night in Casablanca.* As for the last paragraph, the Marxes subsequently made pictures on two of the three subjects mentioned, *At the Circus* and *The Big Store.*

A New High in Low Comedy
(A NIGHT AT THE OPERA)

CLIFTON FADIMAN

Just to remove that frightened, I-think-I-hear-Gilbert-Seldes look from your face, allow me to issue at once these flat statements:

1. No attempt is herein made to trace the origin of the Marx Brothers' humor to the *commedia dell'arte* of the sixteenth century.

2. Their impertinent treatment of the social proprieties is not construed either as a revolt against the constrictions of American life, or as proletarian propaganda.

3. Groucho's intransigent attitude toward his lady stooge, and Harpo's conception of a woman as merely something up which to clamber, are not explained as symbols of frustrated American manhood crying out against female domination.

4. There will be no witty references to Marxists.

Nevertheless, the thesis of these comments is that the Marxes are now quite funny enough to be taken seriously. Suppose they were called Fratellini or Grock or any other name that did not exude a ready-to-wear atmosphere. And suppose these arrived here from Paris, all a-bulge with profound statements out of Bergson concerning the inner nature of comedy. Would there not be considerable genius-hailing and reverential analyses in alert periodicals (such as *Stage*) and comparisons with Mr. Chaplin, etcetera? But the poor Marx boys have for over a decade been a native institution and, as with most native institutions, we may have grown a little too used to them. If so, *A Night at the Opera* ought to shock us into new awareness, for not only is it the funniest and most technically finished picture they have ever made, but to my mind it marks a distinct step forward in American film comedy. It should be clear that, aided by the convulsive gags of Mr. Kaufman and Mr. Ryskind and the sleek direction of Sam Wood, they have now established themselves as just about the finest low-comedy and middle-comedy artists in the world, with the returns from Lapland still not in.

For a time Mr. Fields seemed to be offering serious comic rivalry. But since it was decided for him in *The Man on the Flying Trapeze* that he should tug at our heartstrings, do everything slowly four times, and be a large-as-life "significant" actor, much of his appeal has withered. The fact remains that he is not yet ready to do a Chaplin. Now that he has wandered into these remarks, it is worth pointing out how neatly opposed is his humor to that of our heroes. His is the comedy of careful understatement; that of the Marxes, of prodigal overstatement. His face habitually reveals an expression of quiet resignation; that of Groucho is nothing but an exaggeration, whereas Harpo's cannot be exaggerated, being a kind of *ne plus ultra* in faces. Even in his juggling act Mr. Fields seems to move slowly; the Marx gestures are rapid, explosive, extravagantly unnecessary. There is something eminently *reasonable* about Mr. Fields; it is the rest of the world that is unreasonable. But the Marxes are so defiantly unreasonable that the reasonableness of all things non-Marx suddenly becomes flat, stale, unprofitable—and ridiculous. (The ethical effect of any Marx picture on the spectator is to awaken in him bitter doubts as to whether it is worthwhile not to be a fool.) As philosophers, Mr. Fields would be a Stoic, the Marxes Anarchists. (This sentence may be pasted in your hat and the hat thrown away.)

The basis of their comedy of overstatement is not hard to see. Groucho is funny because, among other reasons, he cannot stop talking; Harpo because he cannot talk at all. One overstates garrulity, the other, reticence. (Chico, a great comic *per se,* acts also as an essential bridge between the two, his comparative sanity setting in bolder relief the pantalunacy of Harpo and Groucho.) But Harpo as overstater is positive as well as negative. He overstates with props. He enlarges things till the proportions are grotesque. It is a nice question as to which is funnier: Groucho in the new picture regretting that he has not longer arms to use in trying to read a contract, and turning around to ask whether anyone has a baboon in his pocket; or Harpo, in *Duck Soup,* courteously pulling out a blazing acetylene torch to help someone to light a cigarette. It's the same joke, of course.

Every Marx situation has its element of exaggeration, but I do not think the *frères* have ever been provided with more fantastic enlargements of experience to play against than in *A Night at the Opera.* Perhaps the high point of their career is the stateroom scene, which will chortle down the corridors of time. In this scene the three brothers, the juvenile lead (who sings like an angel, but how one wishes he wouldn't look like one), and a hyper trunk are crowded into a stateroom built for a young midget traveling light. Harpo, you will remember, is in a semi-comatose condition, trying, as Chico explains, to sleep off his insomnia. Into this stateroom, one after another, crowd a remarkable variety of people, including two chambermaids, a manicurist, a carpenter, a man to fix the pipes, a girl who would like to use the phone, and so on. The climax is capped, or madcapped, when the door is suddenly opened, and the entire population flies out exactly as if shot from a cannon.

As presented, this seems an air-tight comic situation: it is perhaps the funniest five minutes ever depicted on the screen. I went to see Harpo about one thing and another, and he told me that in its original form, the sequence, while comical, was not comical enough. It seemed to go a bit flat. Then one day, when they were on tour trying out the stage version of *A Night at the Opera* and checking the laughs to make the picture absolutely gravity-proof, Chico had an idea. In the first part of the sequence, Groucho is outside giving a breakfast order to the steward. As he finished the order, Chico thought of adding, in stentorian tones, "And two hardboiled eggs"—and Harpo, not to be outdone, blew his horn. For some reason or other, this gag, properly worked up, of course, made the whole scene jell. It turned something merely funny into something almost pitilessly hilarious. Harpo doesn't know why, exactly, but that's the way it happened.

The other great scene of exaggeration is in the last part of the opera house sequence, with the Marx Brothers swinging about unconcernedly on backstage pulleys and ropes, swarms of policemen like apes out of hell clambering about after them, and, on stage, as a result, standard painted backdrops, depicting battleships and fruit-stands, rising and falling in a knowing and animated manner, cutting off the singers from each other and in general transforming *Il Trovatore* into something more nearly resembling Bedlam rearranged by Mr. Thurber. This is the old Keystone Cop comic chase blown up into gigantic, almost nightmare proportions. Yet it never loses touch with that realistic satiric core imbedded in the Marxes' most fantastic japeries, for at the same time that a world of lunacy is being created, a conventional world in this case, that of grand opera, is being destroyed, more mercilessly and completely than ever Tolstoy thought of doing it in *What Is Art?* What with the unpredictable backdrops, the three conductors, the fluid passage from overture into "Take Me Out To the Ball Game," what with Harpo batting out flies, Chico catching them, and Groucho commenting on the entire performance like somebody out of Eugene O'Neill and in the loony-bin at one and the same time—what (long breath) with all this, you can take what's left of grand opera, put it in a collapsed top hat, and send it to the directors of the Metropolitan, with the compliments of the season.

Harpo told me that the backdrop business (an old-time vaudeville stunt, but here developed into something approaching a miracle) was a last-minute change. The original script called for a grand finale consisting of a fire. The opera house is set aflame by the earnest but misguided efforts of the fire department itself, and the Marx Brothers emerge as the heroes of the occasion. This looked pretty funny in rehearsal but Al Boasberg, an MGM man who, rumor has it, had much to do with making the picture as good as it is, kept on saying, gloomily but firmly, "You'll never film it." And they never did, partly because it was felt that audiences watching it might become just the least bit uneasy and run, not walk, to the nearest exit. At any rate, the backdrops *molto agitando* were rushed in as a substitute, and made the touchdown.

It is when you make a careful comparison of *A Night at the Opera* with its predecessors that you see how great a step forward has been made. It is true that there are isolated scenes in the other pictures that rival the stateroom and opera house sequences. The letter to Hungerdinger, Hungerdinger, Hungerdinger, and McCormack ("You left out one of the Hungerdingers—the most important one. Well, never mind, one of them will probably be out of town when the letter arrives") from *Animal Crackers* is a better job of satire than the contract dialogue in *A Night at the Opera.* The business with the mirrors (remember the trio of nightgowned Grouchos in *Duck Soup?*) is as ingenious as any in the current release. The house that Chico and Harpo didn't quite build, the left-handed moth that stole the Chandler painting, Groucho's *Strange Interlude* interlude (all from

Animal Crackers) the mustached chamber-pot on Groucho's head (in *Duck Soup*)—nothing the matter with them, either, my friends, nothing the matter with them.

But it is not the situations in themselves that give *A Night at the Opera* its superiority. It is the fact that these situations flow into each other so smoothly, are all climaxed so successfully, and mount up so surely with increasing waves of laughter. In *Duck Soup* or *Horse Feathers,* for example, a given sequence might end feebly with a conventional black-out gag; or, even if it ended well, there would be a lull or let-down before the next sequence attained momentum. This is not the case with *A Night at the Opera.* Just when you think the stateroom scene could not possibly be any funnier, you get the jack-in-the-box exit, inevitable yet startling, and completely satisfying.

An old weakness of the Marx Brothers was their inability to know when to stop. They would never let funny enough alone—the hat-and-peanut-stand business in *Duck Soup* is a case in point. In the new picture this defect has been overcome. Take the disappearing beds, for example, where reality is hoodwinked, insulted, transformed, and thrown out the window. Here the slightest error in tempo, the tiniest overdevelopment, would have meant ruin. It is perfectly done, even though, as Harpo told me, it is still funnier when presented on a three-dimensional stage than on the screen.

Their calculation has been shrewd even to the point of foregoing sure laughs when necessary. In one of its earlier forms, the film was prefaced by the usual MGM trademark—except that instead of the lion's head, Harpo (not so much with a grin on his face, as with a face on his grin) was substituted. It was funny. Too funny. The audience laughed so hard and so long that they were cast almost into gloom by the comparatively quiet opening scene (everybody singing) of the picture itself. So they threw Harpo out and enticed Leo back. However, if you *will* demand Harpo's head, it may be seen in the trailer.

Another improvement is evident along the lines of what might be called personal editing. Certain mannerisms have been dropped, as too familiar or as having exhausted their comic value. Groucho no longer makes great play with his cigar; Chico does not indulge in a spate of schoolboy puns; he and Harpo omit their mock fist-fight; Harpo does not drop stolen silverware out of his pockets, or crook his knee to the discomfiture of his neighbor.

Then, there is the progress, if you want to call it that, toward sanitation. There is no question that, as compared with *Horse Feathers,* for example, *A Night at the Opera* is good, clean fun. Apparently the provinces did not take kindly to Harpo's satyriasis, to Groucho's innuendos, or, more simply, to such single-*entendre* lines as his all-inclusive invitation to Mrs. Rittenhouse: "Won't you come in and lie down?" in *Animal Crackers*. In *A Night at the Opera* Groucho is as beautifully cynical as ever and he still shows no inclination to make those eyes behave, but whatever his heart may be his lines are pure. I shouldn't be surprised if commercial considerations had entered here the weeniest bit, but, to my mind, whatever the motives, the picture is all the better for having its atmosphere one of gaiety rather than the Gaiety. After all, the game wasn't worth the scandal.

But, even when an old tag is retained, it is vastly improved. Harpo's Harpeggios, I must admit, are still there (Harpo told me, his face all innocent candor, that the music-lovers of America demand it), but Chico's piano playing is given new life by a carefully worked-out special treatment. In the first place, it occurs naturally and as part of the picture. In the second place, somebody with a real feeling for poetic fantasy has replaced Chico's usual grown-up audience with a ring of awed children, their quick, delighted eyes following every tiny acrobatic of Chico's whimsical fingers. This scene has a tenderness and purity which are absolutely genuine and yet do not jar with the hilarious spirit of the picture itself. And—this is the third part of the handling—the transition back to straight comedy is accomplished by having Chico followed by Harpo's parody of him. It is this sort of thoughtful reorganizing of familiar Marx-material that lifts *A Night at the Opera* into a new dimension. One could find a dozen similar instances to match it.

On the plus side of the ledger, also, is the vastly improved handling of the story, which of course, has to stumble in from time to time in order to interrupt the picture. Actually there is a little more plot here than in previous Marx films, but it is less mechanically handled, less intrusive, better balanced. The substitution of a conventional juvenile for Zeppo is all to the good, for Zeppo's face and gestures were far too intelligent to harmonize with the imbecile requirements of the juvenile role, and, on the other hand—though in private life he is said to be as funny as you please—he had never been able to elaborate a specific comic character for himself. He fell between two stools, being neither a first-class fool like his brothers nor a first-class ass like the "hero."

Chico is as good as ever, particularly in the contract scene. Groucho is a little better, he has cleverer lines, and they are poignantly characteristic. "You big bully, why are you hitting that little bully?" in addition to being witty, is supremely Grouchesque, expressing in ten words his misanthropy, his self-satisfaction, his mock pugnacity, his cynicism, and his paradoxy. And he has done few things more engaging than his ride through the boat's passageways, proudly perched, like Halliburton on his elephant, atop his enormous steamer trunk.

But Harpo seems to me to have established a really new high in comic artistry. In the steerage-carnival scene, when, half-starved, he watches the free food inexhaustibly heaped upon his plate, the range and change of his expression go far beyond the comedy of mere grimace. His growing bewilderment and incredulity under which lies a joy that dare not speak its name, create a complex effect of combined pathos and humor, for which there is only one word and that a great one—Chaplinesque. I had the feeling all through *A Night at the Opera* that Harpo, were he not shrewd enough to realize that everything depends on a proper balance among the three brothers, could develop into one of the greatest clowns in the entire history of entertainment. And even if he stamps his foot and refuses to develop, he has my vote.

A Night at the Opera, to relapse for a moment into the judicial, has its weak moments. But, like the weak moments of a lovely lady, they relieve the strain and really seem to make things pleasanter than ever. Still, I could have spared Harpo's playing about with the food in the breakfast scene. (Harpo told me, his face all innocent candor again, that the kids of America demand it.) The songs are mediocre—and why isn't there a comic song for Groucho as good as "Whatever It Is I'm Against It" from *Horse Feathers* or "I Must Be Going" from *Animal Crackers?* The new songwriters' price may be, in the Bible's phrase, above Green, Kalmar, and Ruby's, but they don't give as good value. And I didn't like the curious sadist-masochist appeal in two scenes—one where Harpo is beaten and whipped by his master, Lassparri; the other in which Groucho is kicked down three flights of stairs. They seemed unnecessarily violent and out of key. But these are minor carpings.

The title of these stray notes isn't really fair, for it seems to me, that with all its extravagance, and complete lack of "seriousness," there is as much wisdom in *A Night at the Opera* as there is in the polite anemias of drawing-room *petit-maîtres* like Mr. Philip Barry and Mr. John van Druten—and a darned sight more wit. I like a high-brow better than the next man, but a great deal of intelligence seems to me hidden—and not too remotely either—behind the rapid fire gags of Messrs. Kaufman and Ryskind, and the horse-play of the Brothers Marx.

Sam Wood, too, has done a superb job with the megaphone, but it would be interesting to see what a director with an entirely fresh and radical viewpoint could extract from the riches of the Marx repertoire. What would happen if René Clair, for instance, directed their next picture? I am, by the way, reliably informed that the successor to *A Night at the Opera* will have for background a circus, a World's Fair grounds, or a department store, almost certainly not all three. Please, Messrs. MGM, make it the department store. I want to see Harpo on an escalator.

Stage, January 1936

Robert Forsythe was the pen name used by Kyle Crichton
when writing for Communist journals such as *The New Masses*.
Under his own name Crichton was an editor of *Scribner's* and
Collier's magazines and published numerous books including
one about the Marx Brothers.

MODERN TIMES

ROBERT FORSYTHE

If you have had fears, prepare to shed them; Charlie Chaplin is on the side
of the angels. After years of rumors, charges and counter-charges, reports of
censorship and hints of disaster, his new film, *Modern Times,* had its world
premiere (gala) last week, with the riot squad outside quelling the curious
mob and with the usual fabulous first-night Broadway audience gazing
with some doubt at a figure which didn't seem to be quite the old Charlie.
For the first time an American film was daring to challenge the superiority
of an industrial civilization based upon the creed of men who sit at flat-
topped desks and press buttons demanding more speed from tortured
employees. There were cops beating demonstrators and shooting down
the unemployed (specifically the father of the waif who is later picked up
by Chaplin), there is a belt line which operates at such a pace that men
go insane, there is a heart-breaking scene of the helpless couple trying to
squeeze out happiness in a little home of their own (a shack in a Hooverville colony). It is the story of a pathetic little man bravely trying to hold
up his end in this mad world.

Chaplin's methods are too kindly for great satire, but by the very implication of the facts with which he deals he has made high humor out of
material which is fundamentally tragic. If it were used for bad purposes, if
it were made to cover up the hideousness of life and to excuse it, it would
be the usual Hollywood project. But the hilarity is never an opiate.
When the little man picks up a red flag which has dropped from the rear
of a truck and finds himself at the head of a workers' demonstration, it is
an uproarious moment, but it is followed by the truth—the cops doing
their daily dozen on the heads of the marchers. In the entire film, there is
only one moment where he seems to slip. After he meets the girl and gets
out of jail for the third time, he hears that the factory is starting up again.
What he wants most in the world is a home, where he and his girl can

settle down and be happy. It is the same factory where he has previously gone berserk on the assembly line. From the radical point of view, the classic ending would have been Chaplin once again on the belt line, eager to do his best and finding anew that what a man had to look forward to in that hell-hole was servitude and final collapse. Instead of this there is a very funny scene where Charlie and Chester Conklin get mixed up in the machinery in attempting to get it ready for production. Just when they have it ready, a man comes along and orders them out on strike. At this point I was worried. "Uh-huh," I said to myself. "Here it comes. The usual stuff about the irresponsible workers, the bums who won't work when they have a chance." But what follows is a scene of the strikers being beaten up by the police and Charlie back again at his life of struggle. Except for that one sequence the film is strictly honest and right. It is never for a moment twisted about to make a point which will negate everything that has gone before.

If I make it seem ponderous and social rather than hilarious, it is because I came away stunned at the thought that such a film had been made and was being distributed. It's what we have dreamed about and never really expected to see. What luck that the only man in the world able to do it should be doing it! Chaplin has done the entire thing himself, from the financing to the final artistic product. He wrote it, acted in it, directed it, wrote the music for it, and is seeing that it is sold to the distributors who have been frantic to get it. It is not a social document, it is not a revolutionary tract, it is one of the funniest of all Chaplin films, but it is certainly no comfort to the enemy. If they like it, it will be because they are content to overlook the significance of it for the sake of the humor.

And humorous it is. Chaplin has never had a more belly-shaking scene than the one where he is being fed by the automatic machine, with the corn-on-the-cob attachment going daft. The Hooverville hut is a miracle of ruin. When he opens the door, he is brained by a loose beam; when he leans against another door, he finds himself half-drowned in the creek; when he takes up a broom, the roof, which it has been supporting, falls in. He comes dashing out of the doghouse for his morning dip and alights in two inches of water in a ditch.

Religion comes off a trifle scorched in the scene where the minister's wife, suffering from gas on the stomach, comes to visit the prisoners in jail. There are hundreds of little characteristic bits which build up the picture of Mr. Common Man faced by life. To the gratification of the world, Chaplin brings back his old roller-skating act, teetering crazily on the edge of the rotunda in the department store where he is spending the night (one night only) as a watchman. He gives the waif (splendidly played by Paulette Goddard) her first good meal in months and a night's rest in a bed in the furniture department. His desire to get away from the cruel world is so strong that he deliberately gets himself arrested, stoking up with two full meals in a cafeteria and then rapping on the window for the attention of a policeman when he nears the cashier's desk.

From the standpoint of humor, however, the picture is not a steady roar. The reason for it is simple: You can't be jocular about such things as starvation and unemployment. Even the people who are least affected by the misery of others are not comfortable when they see it. They are not moved by it; they resent it. "What do you want to bring up a lot of things like that for?" That Chaplin has been able to present a comic statement of serious matters without perverting the problem into a joke is all the more to his credit. It is a triumph not only of his art but of his heart. What his political views are, I don't know and don't care. He has the feelings of an honest man and that is enough. There are plenty of people in Hollywood with honest feelings, but with the distributive machinery in the hands of the most reactionary forces in the country there is no possibility of honesty in films dealing with current ideas. It is this fact which makes *Modern Times* such an epoch-making event from our point of view. As I say, only Chaplin could have done it. Except for the one scene I have mentioned, he has never sacrificed the strict line of the story for a laugh. That is so rare as to be practically unknown in films. *Modern Times* itself is rare. To anyone who has studied the set-up, financial and ideological, of Hollywood, *Modern Times* is not so much a fine motion picture as an historical event.

The New Masses, February 18, 1936

Alexander Woollcott, referred to in the last sentence below, was a critic and a professional public figure whose writings were often tinged with waspishness but were more often drenched in syrup.

MODERN TIMES

OTIS FERGUSON

Modern Times is about the last thing they should have called the Chaplin picture, which has had one of the most amazing build-ups of interest and advance speculation on record. Its times were modern when the movies were younger and screen motion was a little faster and more jerky than life, and sequences came in forty-foot spurts, cut off by titles (two direct quotes here are "Alone and Hungry" and "Dawn"); when no one, least of all an officer of the law, could pass a day without getting a foot in the slack of his pants, when people walked into doorjambs on every dignified exit, stubbed toes everywhere on the straightway, and took most of their edibles full in the face; when tables and chairs were breakaways, comedy was whiskers and *vice versa,* and heroes maneuvered serenely for minutes on abysses that were only too visible to the audience. It is in short a silent film, with pantomime, printed dialogue, and such sound effects as were formerly supplied by the pit band and would now be done by dubbing, except for Chaplin's song at the end. And not only that: it is a feature picture made up of several one- or two-reel shorts, proposed titles being *The Shop, The Jailbird, The Watchman, The Singing Waiter.*

Part of this old-time atmosphere can be credited to the sets. The factory lay-out is elaborate and stylized, but not in the modern way or with the modern vividness of light and shadow; the department store might have been Wanamaker's in its heyday; the "dance" music is a cross between Vienna and a small-town brass band, twenty years old at least; the costumes are generally previous; and as to faces and types, Chaplin has kept a lot of old friends with him, types from days when a heavy was a heavy and Chester Conklin's moustache obscured his chin (still does). Above everything, of course, is the fact that the methods of silent days built up their tradition in group management and acting—in the first, a more formal explicitness, so that crowds gather jerkily from nowhere, emphasized players move stiffly front and center, the camera does less shifting; in the second, actors tend to underline their parts heavily and with copious motion (see the irate diner, see the hoitytoity wife of the parson, see Big Bill and the rest).

Modern Times has several new angles, principally those of the factory and the occasional offstage reports of strikes and misery (the girl's father was shot in a demonstration). But they are incidental. Even in taking René Clair's conveyor-belt idea, for example, you can almost hear Chaplin, where Clair directed a complex hubbub, saying to one of his old trusties: You drop the wrench, I kick you in the pants, you take it big, see, and we cut to chase, got it? It has the thread of a story, Chaplin's meeting up with the orphan girl, very wild and sweet, and their career together. For the rest it is disconnected comedy stuff: the embarrassing situation, the embroilment and chase, and the specialty number, *e.g.,* the roller skates, the completely wonderful song-and-dance bit, the Chaplin idyll of a cottage and an automatic cow, beautiful with humor and sentiment. These things and the minor business all along the way—in jails, cafeteria, with oil cans, trays, swinging doors, refractory machinery—are duplicates; they take you back.

But such matters would not call for discussion if all together they did set up a definite mood, a disturbing sense of the quaint. Chaplin himself is not dated, never will be; he is a reservoir of humor, master of an infinite array of dodges, agile in both mind and body; he is not only a character but a complex character, with the perfect ability to make evident all the shades of his odd and charming feelings; not only a touching character, but a first-class buffoon, and I guess the master of our time in dumb show. But this does not make him a first-class picture maker. He may personally surmount his period, but as director-producer he can't carry his whole show with him, and I'll take bets that if he keeps on refusing to learn any more than he learned when the movies themselves were just learning, each successive picture he makes will seem, on release, to fall short of what went before. The general reaction to this one anyway is the wonder that these primitive formulas can be so genuinely comic and endearing.

There has been a furor here and there in the press about the social content of *Modern Times,* and this could be skipped easily if Chaplin himself were not somehow confused (see his introduction to the film) over its worth as corrective comment. Well, the truth is that Chaplin is a comedian; he may start off with an idea, but almost directly he is back to type again, the happy hobo and blithe unregenerate, a little sad, a little droll. Whatever hapens to him happens by virtue of his own naïve bewilderment, prankishness, absurd ineptitude, and the constant support of very surprising coincidence. He couldn't keep a job or out of jail anywhere in the world, including the Soviet Union—that is, if he is to be true to the Chaplin character.

And Chaplin is still the same jaunty wistful figure, pinning his tatters about a queer dignity of person, perpetually embarked on an elaborate fraud, transparent to the world but never very much so to himself. He brings the rites and dignities of Park Avenue to the gutters of Avenue A, and he keeps it up unsmilingly until it is time to heave the pie, to kick the props out, to mock with gestures and scuttle off, more motion than headway, all shoes, hat, stick, and chase. With him it is all a continuous performance, played with the gravity, innocence, and wonder of childhood, but with ancient wisdom in the matters of sniping cigar butts and tripping coppers into the garbage pile. He is pathetic with the unhappiness of never succeeding, either in crossing a hotel lobby without at least one header into the spittoon or in eating the steaks, chops, and ham and eggs that are forever in his dreams; and yet he somehow cancels this or plays it down: when the ludicrous and debasing occurs, he picks himself up with serenity and self-respect, and when it is time for heartbreaks he has only a wry face, a shrug, some indication of that fall-to-rise-again philosophy that has made hoboing and destitution such harmless fun for his own special audience, the people of America. His life on the screen is material for tragedy, ordinarily. But on the screen he is only partly a citizen of this world: he lives mostly in that unreal happy land—you see the little figure walking off down the road toward it always into the fade-out—where kicks, thumps, injustice, and nowhere to sleep are no more than a teasing and a jolly dream (Oh, with a little pang perhaps, a gentle Woollcott tear) and the stuff a paying public's cherished happy endings are made of.

The New Republic, February 19, 1936

New Theatre has been called by historians both the "unofficial organ of the new insurgent movement in the theatre" [11] and "the official organ of left-wing theatre." [12] It began as *Workers' Theatre* in 1932, changed its name in 1933, and ended in 1937.[13]

Robert Stebbins was the pen-name of Sidney Meyers, at this time a musician, but who later became a distinguished maker of documentary films, including *The Quiet One.*

MR. DEEDS GOES TO TOWN

ROBERT STEBBINS

In the event that no one has mentioned it before, let us state, without fear of contradiction from our colleagues, that reviewing movies is a very dull business. There are few surprises. By the time you've read the advance production notes, the commercial publicity, and the preview notices, you know just what you're getting. Besides, to make it easier, a good quarter of the stories have already been produced as old silents and early talkies. But nothing we had read in advance prepared us for the amazing qualities of *Mr. Deeds Goes to Town.* According to all the rules, Frank Capra, director, and Robert Riskin, screen author, could only have been expected to go on turning out dilute imitations of their 1934 Academy winner, *It Happened One Night.* Their *Broadway Bill,* a pallid assemblage of whimsies about horses and followers of the sport, pointed the way to such a prediction.

For that matter, *It Happened One Night,* stripped of its pace and interest of incident, was a pretty indefensible affair. The film was based on a notion dear to the hearts of a people reared in the school of wish-fulfillment— that if you stepped up to a grumpy plutocrat, who, of course, had a heart of gold despite it all, bawled him out, told him his daughter was a spoiled brat, he'd at once grow enamored of you and you'd come into his millions. Produced in the fifth year of the crisis, *It Happened One Night* took place in a social and economic vacuum. People behaved lovably and for the most part went through recognizable actions, but the realities of 1934 were barred from the lot and integrity checked at the gate.

Now along comes *Mr. Deeds* to astound with its unexpected warmth and indubitable sincerity of purpose. The whimsies are still here, the wit of line and action still crackles as in few other films, but underlying all is the salutary implication, if not recognition, that the world is a place of sorrows where the great multitudes of men suffer for the excesses of the few.

As the story begins a Mr. Longfellow Deeds (Gary Cooper) comes into a fortune of twenty million dollars left him by an eccentric uncle who dies in an auto crash in Italy. Deeds, a young post-card poet, tuba player in the village band, and voluntary captain of the fire-squad, reluctantly leaves the only life he knows and goes to the big town to shepherd his fortune. At once his name is front-page news. Babe Bennet (Jean Arthur), star reporter on the *Gazette,* is put on the job of splitting Deeds wide open. She succeeds by palming herself off as a poor out-of-town steno looking for work. By dint of deliberately turning everything he does or says to ridicule she makes him the most derided man of the hour, but in the process she falls for him and viceversa. On the day Deeds is to propose marriage to Bennet, he's tipped off to her true identity. Thoroughly disheartened and sickened by the savagery of the big city, he prepares to leave for his home town—"Mandrake Falls, where the scenery enthralls, where no hardship e'er befalls, welcome to Mandrake Falls."

Up to this point in the narrative we've a brilliant, though characteristic, Boy meets Girl—Boy loses Girl situation, with Boy gets Girl not far in the offing. Then something unanticipated happens. As Deeds is about to descend the huge marble staircase of his Drive mansion he hears a commotion down below and sees a shabbily-dressed stranger struggling to get into the house. Deeds comes down and asks what he wants. The stranger, a dispossesed farmer, breaks out into tirade against Deeds for sitting on his millions and not reaching out a hand or penny for the relief of human suffering. Deeds, who has been betrayed by everyone in town, thinks he's in the presence of a new racket.

To quote from the script:

Deeds: "A farmer, eh? You're a moocher, that's what you are. I wouldn't believe you or anybody else on a stack of Bibles. You're a moocher like all the rest of them around here, so get out."

Farmer: "Sure. Everybody's a moocher to you. A mongrel dog eating out of a garbage pail is a moocher to you."

Suddenly the farmer pulls a gun on him.

Farmer: "You are about to get some more publicity, Mr. Deeds. You're about to get on the front page again. See how you're going to like it this time. See what good your money's going to do when you're six feet under ground."

At this stage, according to all the sanctified rules laid down by years of custom, Jean Arthur should have rushed in, kicked the gun up, and gotten prettily pinked in the process. Then, after the maniacal worker, now frothing at the mouth, is led away by the police, the film should have faded out in a clinical clinch. But Arthur somehow doesn't appear. Instead, the farmer continues.

Farmer: "You never thought of that, did you? No. All you ever thought of was pitching pennies. You money-grabbing hick. You never gave a thought to all those starving people standing in the bread lines, not knowing where their next meal was coming from; not able to feed their wife and kids; not able to. . . ."

He is unable to go on. Drops his gun, falls into a chair, weeping.

Farmer: "Oh, oh I'm glad I didn't hurt anybody. Excuse me. Crazy. You get all kinds of crazy ideas. Sorry, didn't know what I was doing. Losing your farm after twenty years' work, seeing your kids go hungry, a game little wife saying everything's going to be all right. Standing there in the bread lines. Killed me to take a hand-out. I ain't used to it. Go ahead and do what you want, mister. I guess I'm at the end of my rope. . . ."

Deeds sits down to eat with him and the scene is at an end.

Here we have not only a magnificently conceived and acted sequence (the part of the farmer is played by John Wray), but even something more significant—for the first time in the movies we have been given a sympathetic, credible portrait of a worker, speaking the language of workers, saying the things workers all over the country say. How far removed this is from the beery, rapacious radical of *Little Man, What Now?* the feebleminded ego-maniacs played by Paul Muni and Spencer Tracy in *Black Pit* and *Riff-Raff,* the howling foreman of *Men of Iron!*

Deeds decides to spend his entire fortune on farm lands for the unemployed. For his pains, he is taken into custody as insane. The trial scene during which Deeds establishes his sanity, gets the girl and the farmers get their land, is probably the most brilliant piece of screenwriting to come out of Hollywood.

Now, the captious will undoubtedly point out that *Mr. Deeds Goes to Town* is as flagrant a flaunting of reality as its predecessor, *It Happened One Night.* "Certainly Mr. Capra and Riskin don't think the world can be pulled up from the mire that way. In the long run, pictures like Mr. Capra's only serve to dull the militance of labor. Pure wish-fulfillment all over again." To which we can only reply by pointing out the difference between wish-fulfillment based on a sincere and understanding awareness of the world's ills and the pure soothing syrup that constitutes the staple export of Hollywood. For Hollywood, *Mr. Deeds* is a tremendous advance.

After commending the work of the cast, Gary Cooper, Jean Arthur, Lionel Stander, Walter Catlett, the greatest share of praise must be Capra's and Riskin's. If Mr. Capra could trick us once more and in some unaccountable way avoid the chauvinist, jingo pitfalls of his next picture, *Lost Horizons*—which places Ronald Colman among Chinese "bandits" —our pleasure in *Mr. Deeds* would be quite complete.

New Theatre, May 1936

Frank S. Nugent succeeded Andre Sennwald as film critic of *The New York Times* in early 1936 and remained there until 1940 when he became a screenwriter. He was especially noted for his work on the scripts of John Ford films, including *Wagonmaster, She Wore a Yellow Ribbon, The Quiet Man,* and *The Searchers.*

FURY

FRANK S. NUGENT

Let it be said at once: *Fury* is the finest original drama the screen has provided this year. Its theme is mob violence, its approach is coldly judicial, its treatment as relentless and unsparing as the lynching it portrays. A mature, sober, and penetrating investigation of a national blight, it has been brilliantly directed by the Viennese Fritz Lang, bitingly written by Norman Krasna and Bartlett Cormack, and splendidly performed by Spencer Tracy, Sylvia Sidney, Walter Abel, Edward Ellis, and many others. It should appeal mightily to those of you who look to Hollywood —forlornly most of the time—for something better than superficial, dream-world romance.

Mr. Krasna's story, elemental in its simplicity, is yet an encyclopedia of lynch law. It permits us to study this great American institution from every angle and from points of vantage provided by Mr. Lang's unquestionable camera genius. We see it as the victim sees it, as the mob sees it, as the community sees it, as the law sees it, as the public sees it. We see a lynching, its prelude and its aftermath, in all its cold horror, its hypocrisy, and its cruel stupidity; and it disgusts us and fills us with shame for what has been done, and is being done, in our constitutional republic.

The case of Joe Wilson is fictitious and it is laid in a nonexistent Midwestern city; yet the case of Joe Wilson is typical of all lynch outrages, wherever committed. The Joe Wilson of *Fury* is a gasoline station owner, driving happily down a byroad to meet the girl he plans to marry. It is a day they have awaited for years. The world is bright, men are good, justice prevails. Then a deputy sheriff, with leveled shotgun, stops the car. "Weren't letting grass grow under yer tires, were ye? Illinois license plates, too!" The tragedy has begun.

There had been a kidnapping. A few shreds of evidence are enough to lodge Wilson in the county jail at Strand, held for further investigation. Rumors spread through the town. The knaves and the righteous, the loafers and the businessmen, convert Wilson from suspect to swaggering criminal. The mob storms the jail, beats down the sheriff and his deputies, and, unable to reach the prisoner, sets the building afire. Wilson's sweetheart arrives in time to see him burned alive as men gape, as a woman holds her child aloft to get a better view, as an ogling youth pauses between bites of a frankfurter and roll. Call this the prelude.

Fury has been objective so far; now it goes beneath the surface of the news reports and considers a lynching in terms of community reaction and the law. Strand returns to righteousness. The responsible businessmen agree that it was a "community, not an individual thing"; they pledge themselves to cover up. The women quote the minister: "Some things are better forgiven and forgotten." But the law, handicapped by hypocrisy and perjury, moves to punish the mob leaders; twenty-two citizens of Strand go on trial for their lives; and Joe Wilson, who had miraculously escaped, sits by his radio and hears them perjure themselves. His enjoyment is keen and his course of action clear to him: he is legally dead, legally murdered; he will let his legal killers stand a legal trial, get a legal sentence and a legal death.

The trial proceeds, and its outcome will not be divulged here; but you will see in it a reenactment of hundreds of lynch trials that have been held, of thousands that might have been held to determine the guilt of the men and women responsible for the 6,000-odd lynchings in this country during the last forty-nine years. And it is a trial scene written in acid, a searing commentary upon a national disregard for the due processes of law and order that finds flower in such organizations as Detroit's Black Legion and kindred "100 percent American" societies.

This has been a completely enthusiastic report, and such was our intention. Hollywood rarely bothers with themes bearing any relation to significant aspects of contemporary life. When it does, in most cases, its approach is timid, uncertain, or misdirected. *Fury* is direct, forthright, and vehement. That it is brilliantly executed as well makes it all the more notable.

Cinematically it is almost flawless. Mr. Lang, director of *Metropolis* and *M,* had been in Hollywood almost two years before Metro-Goldwyn-Mayer permitted him to make this picture. It was worth waiting for. Nor can we fail to salute its cast for their sincere and utterly convincing performances. Mr. Tracy's bitter portrait of Joe Wilson, Miss Sidney's moving portrayal of the sweetheart, Walter Abel's district attorney, Edward Ellis as the sheriff, Bruce Cabot as the town bully, Frank Albertson and George Walcott as Wilson's brothers, Walter Brennan's loose-mouthed rustic deputy— all of these, and others, have a share in the glory of *Fury.*

The New York Times, June 6, 1936

Kenneth Fearing was best known as a poet but also wrote novels. One of his murder stories, *The Big Clock,* was filmed in 1948.

FURY

KENNETH FEARING

All of you movie hopheads taking the cure under Prof. Fearing, how many of you can remember as far back as *Fugitive from a Chain Gang?* It's not likely that many can. The cinema addict who can come out of his coma in front of the theater and remember how he got there, let alone recall the title and plot of the film that has been enthralling him for the last sixty minutes, really belongs in some other, less-serious ward, possibly the revolutionary dance. But if you do have a dim and confused recollection of *Fugitive from a Chain Gang,* MGM's current *Fury* is just like it, only better and it's a pretty good picture.

To be accurate, it's one top-notch picture with two or three mediocre ones tossed in on top of it just to make sure the basic story doesn't make too much sense. Nobody knows what we moviegoers would do if confronted with a film that took a substantial theme and follcwed it through to its logical end. Maybe we wouldn't know the difference. Or we might explode. There might even, as some say, be a revolution.

Lynching is the subject of *Fury,* and the first half of it is so realistic that when flames leap up the old courthouse and encircle the caged victim, you actually smell the burning flesh. It's really as savage and convincing and as good as that. If you think of the story as ending there, where it always does end in fact, and if you also imagine the victim to be Negro, as he usually is and not white, then this is a film that will haunt your dreams for many a night and make the ordinary Hollywood thing seem tamer than a vacation postcard.

But there are a lot of "ifs" barring *Fury* from being the great picture that it might have been, and not even Spencer Tracy's fine electrically charged acting convinced me that a man so starkly burned to death could manage, by a simple miracle in the scenario, to come back to life. Saint Metro-Goldwyn-Mayer, be with me in my hour of need! You can avert famine, war, and pestilence by a close-up of Garbo singing a presidential proclamation; you might even, I imagine, pass a liberal law that wouldn't be declared unconstitutional.

Considered strictly as melodrama, however, *Fury* is still an exceptional film. Some day in the future some great master of the cinema art, possibly myself, will write a serious treatise called "Evasion and Exposition: The Essential Methods of Each, with an Analysis of Their Relative Values, Purposes, Habits, and Habitat." It will run to at least six volumes and undoubtedly be the opus your son works his way through college on. The principles advanced in the first three of them will be that evasion is the essential element of any art in a society based upon exploitation, that evasion's inner secret is the business of building improbability upon improbability whereas the process of exposition is the opposite, building probability upon probability, and lastly, that although evasion predicates a stagnant art, it also forces increasingly brilliant technical innovations.

Fury has this technical ingenuity, this time simply in the field of plotting. After the realism of the lynch scene has built up the picture's tension, the remaining half of it is kept going by a series of surprises—the victim's survival, his self-concealment that leads on to a trial of the lynchers, the seeming collapse of the case against the lynchers until the dramatic introduction of motion picture evidence, and so on—each improbable, but not impossible, event skillfully connected to the next. Nothing but good acting could put the latter half of the film across, and the cast was extremely good. It's amazing, seeing how much technical perfection alone can do for a picture.

But the real story lies wrapped up in the first part of it, and it's fine anti-lynch stuff, though not as pointed as it could have been—remember, we have to sell these pictures in the South. See the film, and imagine what might have been done with it.

The New Masses, June 16, 1936

SECRET AGENT

OTIS FERGUSON

Secret Agent is a Gaumont-British film on the old formula of love and spies and wartime. But it is the work of Alfred Hitchcock—which makes all the difference. The rapid development of this genius in the form—his eternal inventive sense, wit and good taste and flair for swift, open movement—is already making some big names look rather lower-case. Mainly against him so far is his material (easier to concentrate on good effects if you don't have to make your story come out even). In *The Man Who Knew Too Much* the story about the people shown was so unlikely and maudlin as to spoil the picture for me—even if there hadn't been an amateurishness about much of the direction that can only be explained now by crediting Hitchcock with the rare quality of developing his strong points to the exclusion of all else. *The Thirty-nine Steps* went far beyond this: it was a delightful film, really a miracle of speed and light. But its story was hokum, you had to accept that at the start and keep on accepting.

And now in *Secret Agent* there are still a lot of holes—the hero's squeamishness, unlikely in wartime; the general reluctance of deadly enemies to kill anybody who would interfere with plot development; the British War Office's cueing in feminine interest by sending some silly society girl out to ball up deadly missions and practically lose the War. But in general there is a lot of sounder stuff—still on the surface, but present at least and with motivations. Madeleine Carroll makes fine capital of her first breakdown and subsequent near-hysteria. And John Gielgud is right for the character of one of those backbones of empire, brave and decent enough to get into a horrible spot of conflicting loyalties (Dash it, man, and all that).

Best of all is Peter Lorre's study of the assassin as artist. As satyr, humorist, and lethal snake, he shows, here as always, a complete feeling for the real juice of situations and the best way of distilling this through voice, carriage, motion. He is one of the true characters of the theater, having mastered loose oddities and disfigurements until the total is a style, childlike, beautiful, unfathomably wicked, always hinting at things it would not be good to know.

His style is most happily luminous in the intense focus and supple motion of movie cameras, for the keynote of any scene can be made visual through him. In close-ups, it is through the subtle shifts of eyes, scalp, mouth lines, the intricate relations of head to shoulders and shoulders to body. In medium-shots of groups, it is through his entire motion as a sort of supreme punctuation mark and underlineation. A harmless statement is thrown off in a low voice, and it is felt like the cut of a razor in Lorre, immediately in motion—the eyes in his head and the head on his shoulders and that breathless caged walk raising a period to double exclamation points. Or the wrong question is asked, and the whole figure freezes, dead stop, and then the eventful flowering of false warmth, the ice within it.

And Alfred Hitchcock is the kind of director who can make the finest use of such character effects, neither exploiting nor restricting. The vital imagination behind almost every detail shows in the fleet economy of the opening sequence: the false funeral, the Chief, the mission. It seems hardly three minutes before everything is known, and the scene gathers itself into premonition merely through the wide, dark flight of stairs being seen from that angle, with the men at the top. Then the scream, the horrified servant girl running up, then back to the door and Secret Agent Peter Lorre in hot and sly pursuit—a perfect entrance.

All the usual expository sediment of a play, that is, runs off in solution like brook water here; and presently we are in Switzerland, spy meets girl-spy with some fetching and varnished by-play, and here is Lorre again, barking like a spaniel, breathless with the devastation brought about in him by sight of anything wearing pants that don't show, and already established as a major and mysterious force. And then the absolutely stunning sequence in the church. The organist being their agent, they come in, light the candle signal, wait and wait, and there is no answer but the sustained organ chord of minor thirds, which swells and becomes tremendous as they creep up on the organist, to find him strangled across his keys. There follows the flight to the belfry and that beautiful shot looking down from there—the space and dwarfed perspective, the twisted form sprawled on the stones, and the pulling of the bell rope.

After this comes one of the finest suspense foundations I know of: their singling out the wrong man and hoaxing him up the mountain to his certain death. The hard intention is set off against the humor on the surface, the act against the result. The mountain, Gielgud's revulsion and quitting of the expedition to watch through a telescope, the house back home with the wife complacent in her German conversation class but anxious over the husband's dog, who worries the door and whines—and the visual bridge between these in Madeleine Carroll. And finally the three scenes merge in one as the act is framed in the telescope, a terrible moment of space and falling and cloud-shadows over the snow, the dog's howl rising over the picture above and bringing the camera back to the quiet, terrified home scene below.

There is no space for going into the manner in which superimposed images, throwbacks in character, blended contrasts and camera positions and well paced cutting, constantly heighten effects. Or for any analysis of just how Hitchcock and his cameraman can load the simple entry of a building with suspense and terror. But something should be said of the use of sound, which is not equaled anywhere else: the music in the church, the howl of the dog, the disembodied voice in the rhythm of the train wheels (he mustn't, he mustn't, he mustn't, he mustn't), the deafening factory and steeple-bell noises, etc. Then there is the growing discord of the peasant-dance scene, after the murder, where the voices go from sweet to wild and the accompaniment becomes the metallic scream of coins whirling in bowls.

In all matters of treatment, the director of this film hardly has a rival. And whatever may be said for the boys who start out with a conviction and philosophical goodwill large enough to cancel out all the unimaginative heaviness of their execution, I still think Hitchcock should be rated among the best if only for what he can teach them. In a latter-day fashion, he is a pioneer of the movie, increasing the range of its plasticity and power; he can take something that is practically nothing and make it seem like music and give it wings.

The New Republic, June 24, 1936

Welford Beaton's *Film Spectator* had become *The Hollywood Spectator* in June 1931.

MY MAN GODFREY

WELFORD BEATON

One of the smartest, most amusing comedies of the season. If we may accept it as a sample of what we may expect from Universal's new management, we can look forward to getting some superlative entertainment when Charlie Rogers really gets under way. The picture is mounted handsomely and in his selection of the cast to support the stars the producer showed no disposition to squeeze pennies.

Gregory La Cava makes his director-producer debut with *My Man*

Godfrey. I do not see how Greg has kept hidden so long his flair for the smartest kind of comedy. If he displayed it before it must have been in pictures I missed. Anyway, his direction is nothing less than brilliant. It is not obvious and reveals no striving to achieve results. He is not afraid to allow his characters to whisper when they should whisper and shout only when they should shout. Although he has a set of the most amusingly crazy characters ever assembled in a sophisticated comedy, he keeps them well in hand, blends the performances nicely and never resorts to farce.

The script sparkles with witty speeches, and the only weakness of the picture is its failure to space laughs, many lines being lost to the audience. We enjoyed such comedies as *It Happened One Night* and *The Thin Man* because we could finish our laughs before anything else was said, a privilege too few pictures accord us.

William Powell and Carole Lombard seldom appeared to better advantage, their roles being tailored to fit them like gloves. Powell's part is a straight one, but Carole's is a hilarious one which permits the garnering of a steady flow of laughs. Others who give superlative performances are Alan Mowbray, Mischa Auer, Gail Patrick, Gene Pallette, and Jean Dixon. Each of them seems to be just a little bit better than ever before, particularly Miss Patrick, who makes impressive a rather catty characterization. Auer reveals a fine flair for comedy.

All in all, *My Man Godfrey* is a thoroughly enjoyable picture which safely can be put on your list of those you must see.

The Hollywood Spectator, August 15, 1936

Jessie Matthews was a star of British musical films, probably most widely seen in the United States in *Evergreen.*

SWING TIME

WELFORD BEATON

Fred Astaire's pleasing personality, his rhythmic grace as a dancer, charm and intelligence as an actor, and proficiency as a singer make *Swing Time* a highly entertaining picture. He is teamed again with Ginger Rogers, who continues to make progress, but still has some distance to go before her contribution to one of their joint appearances measures up to that of her partner. I confess that when the two dance, I keep my eyes on Astaire, but nevertheless I got the impression this time that Ginger was dancing better than ever. Her chief failing still is her inability to make full use of her hands. A great deal of the charm of the dancing of Jessie Matthews is the artistic manner in which she brings her hands into play. From her hips down, Ginger displays grace and rhythm, but she still is somewhat awkward from there up.

However, there is one thing about Ginger which I admire greatly—she is ambitious, determined, and works like a Trojan to acquire what was not born in her. When we consider that in her appearances with Astaire she is pitted against perhaps the world's greatest dancer and by no means shames the combination, we must praise her for what she has done and not criticize her too sharply for what still is lacking. I do not know any girl who can both act and dance up to Astaire's dual standard, which suggests the thought that RKO might get two girls to do the chores. I see no reason why Astaire always should have to love the girl he dances with.

George Stevens was given a mass of material to work with—two established stars, a capable cast, gorgeous scenic effects, and big ensembles, and succeeds admirably in pleasantly befuddling our senses until we are indifferent to the weaknesses of the story. Pan Berman no doubt would get in bad with the other fellows who produce musicals if he supplied one of his with a coherent story having some appeal to an intelligent audience, but I think he should have a go at it. The innovation might provoke the box-office into hearty response. I know of no law that would be broken if a picture like *Swing Time* were made to appeal to the intellect as well as to the eye.

But the eye appeal of *Swing Time* is quite sufficient to make it worth your while. In Fred Astaire you will see an extraordinary artist brilliantly revealing his versatility. And there are Helen Broderick and Victor Moore in comedy roles which will delight you. Georges Metaxa—I believe it is his screen debut—contributes a worthy performance, and Betty Furness adds a charming feminine note.

Jerome Kern has provided the production with some notable music which Nathaniel Shilkret brings to the screen in a manner that does full justice to the score. Shilkret is a valuable addition to the music masters whom the screen is attracting. Van Polglase and Carroll Clark provided magnificent settings for some of the sequences, and David Abel's expert photography brings out all their pictorial values. Hermes Pan, dance director, and Bernard Newman, designer of the gowns, also deserve praise for the artistic quality of their contributions.

The Hollywood Spectator, August 29, 1936

For many years a distinguished professor at Columbia University, Mark Van Doren is also celebrated as a poet. He wrote film criticism for *The Nation* following William Troy's tenure there. The Fielding quotation is from *Jonathan Wild*.

CARNIVAL IN FLANDERS
(La Kermesse Héroïque)

MARK VAN DOREN

A new theater has been opened in New York with the design of proving to interested persons that the studios of Europe are once more, after several years of faltering and eclipse, a challenge to Hollywood. The inaugural program of this theater, named rather unpleasantly the Filmarte, offers "a haven from all that is philistinism in the movie-at-large" and "a rendezvous for the cinema devotee to whom films are something more than an innocuous diversion." The Battle of the Films, with all of Europe on one side and all of Hollywood on the other, is to my mind something of a bore; but this does not prevent my being glad that the facilities for seeing foreign films have been increased, and it certainly does not discourage me from saying that the Filmarte's first picture, *La Kermesse Héroïque,* is one of the most diverting I have ever watched, innocuous or noxious as the case may be.

It comes with a grand prize from France, and its director, Jacques Feyder, may well be the successor to René Clair for whom we have been looking. The scene is a Flemish village and the date is 1616; and the theme, while generally reminiscent of *Lysistrata,* is better stated in the immortal sentence of Henry Fielding concerning Letitia Snap, who would have been ravished by Mr. Fireblood "if she had not, by a timely compliance, prevented him." While the trembling burghers of Boom are busy with a foolish piece of strategy against the approaching soldiers of Philip II, their women prepare to meet the Spaniards considerably more than halfway—with wine at the gates and with a key to the village which unlocks everything from the Town Hall down to the smallest bedroom there is. The result is peaceful and blissful occupation for a night, with the troops moving off the next morning wreathed in flowers and smiles, and with the burghers blindly congratulating themselves upon the success of their strategy. The film as a whole is deliciously high-spirited, and its many details are directed with fine care toward a comic end which leaves everything in Boom exactly as it was before, only more so. The acting of Françoise Rosay as the mayor's wife is alone worth going miles to see. But perhaps it is more to the point to speak of the way the entire cast wears its clothes. I have seldom seen a more convincing costume piece, and the reason seems to be that nobody is aware that he has stepped out of a seventeenth-century Low Country painting; or if he is, then the fact amuses him somewhat as Hals's people are amused—if that is what they are laughing at—by their ridiculous rig. The clothes are worn, in other words, both naturally and with art. And thus *La Kermesse Héroïque* becomes a satire no less upon the stilted costume picture than upon the male vanity which is ostensibly its target. It becomes in addition, because it is good comedy, a commentary upon all of life which experience permits us to know. But if nothing else it will be remembered by those who see it as an extraordinarily finished film.

The Nation, October 10, 1936

DANCING IN FILMS

LINCOLN KIRSTEIN

The films have frequently employed dancing for one reason or another, and even increasingly in the last two years. But from any objective point of view it cannot be said Hollywood has enhanced either the vocabulary of dancing in general or created an idiom for its particular use. While theatrical dancing in all forms has created great interest in the legitimate areas, Hollywood has done its best to capitalize on this rise in prestige without involving itself in any danger of creative pioneering. The more one investigates Hollywood possibilities for dancing, the more hopeless they seem. The treatment of dancing in films is just another piece of testimony corroborating an almost complete impasse.

There are, however, some special considerations to be investigated in the problem of adapting dancing to camera. There is a curious change effected in the carryover of human movement from the stage to the screen. In the theater we see directly whatever image the proscenium focuses. In a film our eye is controlled by the range of the camera's eye. In this transposition something vital is often lost. It is lost even in acting, but in dancing, which is so much more the electric essence of physicality, the loss seems proportionately greater.

In film, as in the theater, the problem of a dance-director is to project soloists against a choral or mass background. There is usually one soloist, and the chorus is further complicated by elaborate scenic "presentation" wherein the ingenuity of the studio engineers ekes out the poverty of the dance-director's imagination. The human scale is, of course, wholly lost.

The movies have developed a few simple tricks to cover transitions from an intimate or naturalistic scale to a cinematic or gigantic one. For example, in the Astaire film *Follow the Fleet* there was a "Riviera" sequence in an impromptu revue set on an old schooner. The scene opened as it might have on any Hudson River show boat, but almost before one could realize it, another enormously amplified set was being used to accommodate the necessary regiment of dancers. Similarly in "opera" sequences, an "opera-house" set of an Italian square will suddenly give place to the square itself. But with music dominating such a scene the visual shift is less of a wrench than in sequences where physical movement is foremost.

Dancing must appeal to movie audiences or it would not be added to production costs. What kind of dancing has the greatest appeal? Largely, the kind that exploits a personality pleasing for reasons quite apart from dancing. It would hardly help Garbo to dance well (through on several occasions she has), but it is very hard for even first-rate dancers to be effective from the Hollywood standpoint if they haven't sex appeal. Virtuosity is of course compulsory, but many virtuosi exist who can never face a camera. Virtuosity, for film audiences, usually means excessive capability in any one field, as for example, the feet in tap-dancing. It's hard to see how a precision troupe like the Rockettes would have film value except as background since they are so anonymous. And one can even imagine, from the opposite point of view, Fred Astaire being almost as valuable without his taps since he has so much practical charm and so good a vocal delivery. He is surely the best that dancing has to say for itself in our films. Plus his natural elegance and musical instinct, he seems to use more than one part of his body and he makes his camera follow him, seemingly for miles, so that in more inspired moments a very dramatic tension is built up over a large terrain. He is lucky in having such an able partner as Ginger Rogers, and in his dance-director, whoever Hermes Pan may be. But even in such a well-studied genre as the musical, Hollywood is only beginning to make use of dancing as inherent part of dramatic action instead of as interpolated "relief" as in most of the Eddie Cantor works.

There are other good music-hall dancers who have done films. Ray Bolger, a distinguished tap-dancer who, judging from "Slaughter on Tenth Avenue" in *On Your Toes,* would seem to be able to give to his medium a tragic quality it has never enjoyed, was seen briefly in *The Great Ziegfeld.* Paul Draper to a large extent redeemed *Colleen,* in spite of Ruby Keeler, and he also contributed a very imaginative "wedding" sequence which survived the cutters. Eleanor Powell has some box office draw. She is accomplished, monotonous, and comforts many nice people inasmuch as she is so patently a "nice" girl. "Isn't it nice that such a nice girl dances so nicely." Bill Robinson, appearing with Shirley Temple in *The Littlest Rebel,* was superbly himself, the old master. His brilliant style, clear in its unostentatious but transparent theatricality, showed the best that a personal manner in taps can give. Tap-dancing in the films, as on the stage, is a very limited, undramatic form of dancing. It appeals chiefly to the ear, not to the eye, and if a drummer beat out the same rhythms with his hands it would cause little comment. Taps are often badly synchronized. On the stage there is a sharp but delicate sonority to the beats. Frequently on the screen a dancer's feet detonate like a machine gun. Chaplin may be said to use his whole body better than any other dancer in Hollywood, but this usage would probably fall strictly under the category of pantomime. His movements, highly stylized for the sake of instantaneous legibility, are frequently a parody of the five classic ballet positions, which speaks well for his apprenticeship as an English music-hall comedian schooled in the tradition of the old Alhambra. As for ballet-dancers in the classic genre, few have left any imprint. Harriet Hoctor can be counted on for her pastiche of a ballerina, and Gambarelli is less than a mediocrity. Tap has fared comparatively well at the hands of the film in spite of its inexpressive silhouette and its repetitious noise. Audiences like it because, for the most part, it's all they've been given, and since the only dance-directors of influence in Hollywood have been brought over directly from the musical-comedy stage.

Although it has little enough to do with dancing proper, Hollywood has created a type of spectacular diversion employing dancers which has not been seen previously, at least on the same scale. This is the Babylonian vision sponsored by Busby Berkeley and culminating in *The Great Ziegfeld.* He may use forty crystal pianos, seven intercircular ramps, a baby Niagara, and the U. S. Marines, but the result is, more often than not, too big for camera lens, too much to see, and only awe inspiring for its multiplicity of effects. But such evidence that a picture costs money to produce does something mysterious in selling it. Berkeley used to employ overhead symmetrical shots which reduced eighty dancers to an opening eight-petal bud or an American flag. Hermes Pan is far more clever with his trucking shots because he is not interested in making his girls look like flags or flowers but merely like girls dancing in various places on various levels threaded together by the continuity of music and plot. Bobby Connolly does average work-a-day musical-comedy stuff transferred more or less modestly to the screen. Albertina Rasch is distinguished for an operetta-style, in contradistinction to the revue-style of the above. Her dance arrangements for *The Merry Widow* were really imaginative with waltzers floating in doors and out of doors with corresponding pretty shifts in the color values of the costumes. Her sequences seem impersonal and well rehearsed, but she is not free from the general Hollywood elephantiasis and if she can get two more dozen girls in a frame, she'll do it. Chester Hale staged a good pastiche of a ballroom mazurka for *Anna Karenina* in which Garbo's dance-steps coincided with her dialogue. It was not an original achievement, but in its good taste, a model for a kind of choreographic underscoring which is perhaps the most that can be hoped for dancing in our films. In *David Copperfield* there was a quaintly executed ballet sequence of mid-nineteenth century London with the dancers hauled up to heaven on wires. In *Operator 13* there was a similar decorative old-Southern ball with flashes of square-dance figures that had genuine charm and usefully contributed to the atmosphere of a silly story. Margarete Wallman, the ballet-mistress of the Vienna *Staatsoper* did a ridiculous and inappropriate ballet of Russian peasants for *Anna Karenina*. She is without talent, and fondly imagines that she has solved all cinematic problems by photographing everything from two angles directly above her stage. But she is the stype of European reputation which represents "Art" and "Class" to the spenders of million-dollar budgets. Agnes de Mille did some splendid work for MGM's *Romeo and Juliet*. Her scholarly research in Renaissance music and dancing produced some touching and vivid backgrounds, particularly the lovely masque in the spirit of Botticelli, framing Juliet at the Ball. It is difficult to say how much will survive in the cutting, since the scenes were shot simultaneously from numerous angles with little intelligence. Benjamin Zemach's dances for *She* in the modern idiom made a ridiculous production funnier. The naïve and calisthenic quality of contemporary concert-dance is eminently unsuitable to the vast technical possibilities of films.

The ballet has much to give to the films, and were the directors wiser they would study classical dancing for its spectacular richness with which a well-handled camera could work wonders. Eisenstein has written well on film technique as applied to dancing, and he had in mind certain choreographic conditionings which must be respected parallel to, but not necessarily overlapping, cinematic conditioning. The ballet is an encyclopedic tradition and it can be pilfered with reward if any Hollywood director has the patience and sense to spend a week on it. Diaghilev had a superstition about films, and he would never permit his ballet to come before a camera, although as early as 1910 a French company was eager to shoot *Scheherezade.* Perhaps he was aware of the limited technical facilities that the epoch offered. *Prince Igor,* or some version of it, has been filmed, however. It appears, weirdly enough, as the ballet given to entertain the Congress of

Vienna in *Congress Dances*. When Nijinsky was in Hollywood in 1916, Chaplin took him through his studios, and he was very much interested in the medium, although he said at the time that it would be unwise to film ballets head-on, the way one sees them in the theater. He knew a separate technique would have to be worked out. Douglas Fairbanks and Mary Pickford lent Pavlova a studio, and there are extant records of some of her more famous divertissements such as *The Swan* and *The California Poppy,* but these are documents and not examples of dance made expressly for film. Every classic choreographer of our time has had a little to do with films. Adolf Bolm's *Mechanical Ballet* for Barrymore's *Mad Genius,* based vaguely on Diaghilev, was a great waste. Massine created dances for an unreleased French film, *Le Roi Pausole,* in which his work alone was impressive. Nijinska's sequences in *A Midsummer Night's Dream* have been universally condemned. But, nevertheless, they possessed ideas of film and dance interplay that were not wholly negligible. Reinhardt, as usual, crippled one more collaborator, even had it not been difficult to master an unfamiliar medium as well as create a major work in six weeks. As is frequently the case, a director thought it might be a good idea to have ballets somewhere in the picture, but just where and how he could not be sure. Surely the last thing to be done was to consult the choreographer. When a good choreographer designs, mounts, and rehearses dances for films that is usually considered enough. It is inconceivable that they should also have a hand in pointing the camera-eye at the express angle needed for their preconceived pattern. Frderick Ashton did an agreeable ballet for Bergner's *Escape Me Never,* and in general the English dance sequences in serious films have been far better than the American. Anthony Asquith has an extremely stimulating technical article on "Ballet and the Film" in *Footnotes on the Ballet* (Lovat Dickson, 1936) in which he projects a very free treatment of combined theatrical dancing and atmospheric landscape. Many of René Clair's earlier films had excellently woven dance sequences, notably the scenes in the opera house of *Le Million* where the insanity of backstage life in a superannuated theater floated madly in and out on some fine dancing. Aside from documents of national dances, the Russians have not been lucky in filming dancing. In *Moscow Laughs,* Alexandroff followed super-Hollywood to an unfortunate degree. But perhaps the greatest dance sequence ever filmed was the Xandunga of the Tehuantepec Indians shot by Eisenstein and Tissé and never recovered from the wreck of *Que Viva Mejico!* It is Eisenstein above all others who understands the moving human body in its stylized lyricism, even when he uses skeletons or puppets as in the "Days of the Dead" from the same heroic and disastrous picture.

Jean Cocteau, from his association with Diaghilev and the Russians, achieved an almost perfect synthesis of pantomimic-plastic gesture which was almost dancing in his *Sang d'un poète.* As in the *Cabinet of Dr. Caligari,* the camera was at all times the mind's eye, not the eye of a second-hand audience. His film with Chaplin, if ever achieved, will be of the greatest interest.

Is the idiom of classic theatrical dancing suited to films? In its most extended uses it most surely is. However, there is little to be gained by photographing the Basil Ballet in *Scheherezade* in Technicolor, or *Sylphides* with a group of Chester Hale girls. Aside from a good musician, or at least good music, a choreographer educated not only in ballet but in all the fullest possibilities of the film is needed. By the fullest possibilities one means a treatment of human bodies comparable to the way Disney treats his puppets. *Cock o' the Walk* was an inspired satire on a Busby Berkeley super-super, but its color and fantasy were incidentally beautiful in themselves. The camera can diminish and enlarge, accentuate and subdue, not only tone-values but actual shapes. The retarded camera can be studied for slow-motion emphasis. In Mrs. Frank Tuttle's short film *Spring Night,* two of the dancers from the Monte Carlo Ballet were used. Their plastic pantomime was less rewarding than the use made of certain ballet gestures emphasized by the camera. A leap, for example, was indefinitely prolonged in space, almost an idealization of the mythical leap of Nijinsky in *Spectre de la Rose* in which no one any longer believes. Ballet plus camera would be something not seen before, but a valid something.

What has already been done with the dance in films has been, all things considered, very little. The camera as an eye for dancing is as yet more unstudied than misunderstood. The dance sections of travelogues or news reels are generally carelessly shot and stupidly edited with no sense of climax and with music far from authentic dubbed in. Dancing in feature-length films has little or nothing to do with dramatic continuity, and is introduced as incidental divertissement similar to ballet in nineteenth-century opera. Even in revues or "Parade" pictures the sequences have little interest except as build-ups for stars. This is not always the fault of the dance directors. A sequence involving many well-trained and long-rehearsed dancers and much ingenuity must be shot in about one hour and a half of actual camera clicking. Hollywood insists on a shiny dancing surface, a floor of composition board covered with layers of baked enamel. This gives the effect of a super varnish or halation, a glow of richness that reflects the dancers. But this softens with only a little use. The sequences are cut by editors who have no more idea than their stop-watches and no more policy than to accommodate a pre-indicated direction from on top: "We gotta have eight minutes of dancing." The use of the dance bears intense technical research, but this is never considered as rewarding as the investigation of some new commercial gadget like sound-allocation, the three-dimensional screen, or a super Technicolor. It is difficult to see why a dancer of intelligence would hope much from the present set-up in Hollywood. Much could be done, but from the point of cash there is slight impulse to do it.

New Theatre, September 1936

CAMILLE

HOWARD BARNES

The incomparable Greta Garbo has returned to the screen in a breathtakingly beautiful and superbly modulated portrayal of *Camille*. As the tragic Dumas heroine, she floods a romantic museum piece with glamor and artistry, making it a haunting and moving photoplay by the sheer magic of her acting. It was not my good fortune to witness the great Eleanora Duse in the play, but I have seen many other illustrious actresses in French and English versions, and none have remotely matched Miss Garbo. Infinite care has gone into the production. It has been adroitly staged by George Cukor, and it has a brilliant supporting company, but it would have proved a musty and slightly ridiculous dramatic resurrection without the participation of the First Actress of our day. She dignifies this latest of many presentations of *Camille* with a magnificent and unforgettable performance.

There has been no diminution of Miss Garbo's flaming genius during her recent absence from motion picture acting. Her command of the subtleties of an impersonation is even greater than it was in the past, and her voice has taken on a new range of inflection. The Marguerite she brings to the screen is not only the errant and self-sacrificial nymph conceived by the younger Dumas nearly a hundred years ago, but one of the timeless figures of all great art. With fine intelligence and unerring instinct she has made her characterization completely credible, while giving it an aching poignancy that, to me, is utterly irresistible. She achieves a consummate balance between the conflicting qualities that made up the nineteenth-century demimondaine, and she plays the big flamboyant scenes of the piece with a versatile intensity that unshackles them from all their creaking artificiality and fills them with brooding emotional power and ineffable splendor.

While *Camille* is essentially an acting triumph, it is also something of a tour-de-force on the part of the screen. The most exacting and painstaking of the film companies has endowed the production with a veritable largesse of talent. Zoe Akins, Frances Marion, and James Hilton, in their script, have distilled all the romantic fervor and cunning juxtaposition of character that may have once distinguished the Dumas drama. They have adhered to the structure of the original, while breathing new vitality into many of its absurd situations. Mr. Cukor, who may be remembered for his splendid realization of *Romeo and Juliet* on the screen, has done a sensitive and visually absorbing job of staging, and Miss Garbo's assistants out-do themselves.

Although one of the newest notables in Hollywood, Robert Taylor, has the important role of Armand, it is Henry Daniell's fine characterization of the Baron de Varville which most perfectly supplements Miss Garbo's interpretation. As the cynical but enamored nobleman who pays handsomely for a courtesan's favors, he is a perfect foil for her exquisite realization of an enormously difficult role. The scene which finds them in her house, drowning the insistent bell-ringing of Armand by playing the piano, both perfectly aware of all that it portends and hating each other desperately, is likely to echo in your memory for some time. Mr. Taylor, considering his inexperience, is surprisingly good. His Armand is dashing, while tempered, and his love scenes are certain to make most pulses beat more quickly. In no sense of disparagement, I should say that Miss Garbo has made him play far beyond the talent he has previously shown.

The others in the cast have been selected knowingly. Lionel Barrymore tends to overdo the part of Armand's father, who successfully persuades Marguerite to give up his son, but Laura Hope Crews is viciously amusing in the part of the beldame, Prudence; Rex O'Malley plays Gaston with genuine tenderness, and their colleagues collaborate with them in a strikingly effective revival of an outmoded work. With scarcely an exception, they follow the mood and tempo that Miss Garbo establishes, giving *Camille* a far more reverent and sure performance than it deserves. It is likely that Miss Garbo still has her greatest role to play, but she has made the Lady of the Camellias, for this reviewer, hers for all time.

The New York Herald Tribune, January 23, 1937

CAMILLE

WELFORD BEATON

For one thing, we have Garbo's finest performance. Then there is a refreshingly young, talented, and handsome Armand in the person of Robert Taylor. We have an investiture that never has been surpassed for artistic conception and sympathetic execution, a brilliantly written screenplay based on the Dumas classic, a cast of outstanding merit dressed in superb creations, and brilliant direction which not only reveals the soul of the story, but which composes beautiful pictures from the material at hand for the camera to bring to us as a series of gorgeous creations in shades from white to black. We have had quite a number of outstanding productions this season, but none which outranks *Camille* for visual beauty and expert storytelling. It had progressed so far under his guidance that we may accept it as another tribute to the genius of the late Irving Thalberg, something to crowd in among the memories of the other great things he did while with us.

Camille has served opera, the stage, and previously the screen, but never before was presented so imposingly as Metro offers it to us now. Garbo's poor health during its making gives her a spiritual, delicate quality which admirably matches the mood of her role. She is captivating in her lighter scenes and appealingly tender in the romantic ones she shares with Taylor. And Taylor adds to his stature as a motion picture actor, bringing a refreshing quality to his Armand, an ingenuousness which gets its strength from its lack of suggestion of stage experience.

The even excellence of the performances is a tribute to the superlative quality of George Cukor's direction. He makes his people human by the simple expedient of having them talk like human beings addressing one another and making no effort to reach an audience. Jessie Ralph, Lenore Ulric, Lionel Barrymore, Laura Hope Crews, and Henry Daniel, have the most important roles and each gives an impressive performance. The emotional values of the story material are admirably developed by Cukor and sustained throughout with an evenness which gripped the friendly audience invited to the preview, but which presented no dramatic climaxes to stir it into applauding. The very absence of physical manifestations of its appreciation was indicative of the audience's complete absorption in the drama.

The visual beauty of the production is compelling. Cedric Gibbons and his talented associates have accomplished great things before, but I can recall no other picture which surpassed *Camille* in production so completely in sympathy with the mood of story. William Daniels and Karl Freund, master craftsmen both, provided gorgeous photography, being particularly effective in bringing out the beauty of the gowns designed by Adrian and the delicacy of the materials used in their creation. Cukor's eye for composition gave the cameramen opportunities to bring to the screen a series of arresting scenes rich in pictorial value and right nobly did they realize them. Douglas Shearer's contribution to *Camille* is a big one. This young sound genius has completely mastered the microphone until it brings to our ears even the subdued sighs of *Camille* in her love scenes with Armand.

The Hollywood Spectator, December 19, 1936

A WOMAN ALONE
(Sabotage)

MARK VAN DOREN

Alfred Hitchcock . . . in *"A Woman Alone"* seems to me to prove once again that he is the best film director now flourishing.

The maker of *The Thirty-nine Steps* and *The Man Who Knew Too Much* keeps, as always, perfectly within his bounds. His story (from Conrad's *Secret Agent*) is a melodrama; his scene is a theater—this time a small London cinema; the streets through which his people occasionally pass are beautiful in their meanness and their truth; he does not spare us several painful deaths; he is merciless with his suspense. But what is more important than all that, Mr. Hitchcock keeps perfectly within the bounds of the movie art. He knows exactly what a movie should be and do; so exactly, in fact, that a live wire seems to run backward from any of his films to all the best films one can remember, connecting them with it in a conspiracy to shock us into a special state of consciousness with respect to the art. There is something old-fashioned about his pictures, as there is about the best things of any kind; and not the only sign of this in *A Woman Alone* is the circumstance that its dialogue is unnecessary without being precisely superfluous. He has told his story with the camera. And how he has told it! The beginning is possibly no more brilliant than the beginning of *Lost Horizon;* but it is only the beginning of something that moves with an actually increasing smoothness and speed to the very end. An analysis of the film would reveal not merely that there were many good details but that there was nothing but detail, and all of it good. Sylvia Sidney in the ticket booth, the boy in the bus, Oscar Homolka at the aquarium and in the turnstile, the episode of the knife and fork—these are only a few among the hundreds. The whole thing is irreducibly concrete, as if a master had decided to show us how much of a virtuoso he could be. And yet the final effect is not a virtuoso effect. It is merely the most interesting story that any film has told this year—the most interesting because Mr. Hitchcock has told it with the simplest, the deepest, and the most accurate imagination at work anywhere.

The Nation, March 13, 1937

Laurel and Hardy began making features in 1931. This was their ninth. The critical attention they got, though almost always friendly and appreciative, was still generally jocular.

WAY OUT WEST

FRANK S. NUGENT

Too many books are being written on the anatomy of humor and none on the humor of anatomy. If we ever get around to it, we intend to do a special chapter on the Messrs. Laurel and Hardy, who scampered into the Rialto yesterday in an irresponsible little slapstick called *Way Out West.* In it we should mention that they would not be funny if both were fat or both skinny; or if the cherubic Mr. Hardy could not arrange his dimples into a perfect pattern of pained resignation; or if the long-jawed Mr. Laurel was not, by the very cut of his jib, the model of a complete dolt.

Nature meant them to be anatomical funny men, and there's nothing much any one can do about nature, not even a scriptwriter. *Way Out West* tries to go against it by withholding all but the merest hint of a plot, but anatomy overcomes that. We still chuckle when Ollie falls off a roof, or has a bucket thrust over his head or a lighted candle applied to his trousers-seat. We still sputter when Stan, who is expected to eat a derby hat on a bet, takes a tentative bite, smiles, and reaches for the salt and pepper. It is not subtle or witty or clever. It's anatomical humor, as agelessly and irresistibly comic as a little man with oversize pants or a big man wearing a baby's bonnet.

One thing more: the picture reveals that Mr. H. and Mr. L. are song-and-dance men. They run through a brief routine in front of Jimmy Finlayson's frontier-town saloon just before turning over the deed to a gold mine to the wrong young woman. (Shucks: there we've gone and told the plot!)

The New York Times, May 4, 1937

DEAD END

GILBERT SELDES

Another sockeroo now current is *Dead End.* When it was shown on the stage, I considered it a production in search of a play, and oddly enough, the movies found a play in it and have completely bogged down on what must have been the simplest and easiest of all problems, which was the production. After I had seen the name of Samuel Goldwyn, like Abou Ben Adhem's, leading all the rest and occupying no less that three hundred square feet of space, everything else I saw was a fairly good reproduction of the original stage setting with real water added and real moving picture value totally destroyed. Back in the 1890s the players of the

Comédie Française were directly photographed for the movies in a stage setting; since that time, with infinite reluctance and considerable prodding from the critics, the movies have learned that the cinematic reproduction of a stage play definitely does not make a movie. The movie version of *Dead End* tries vainly to turn back the clock. To be sure, the camera does at times move away from the theater setting. It is, in fact, notable that the two most effective scenes in the picture are the interior of a slum and the running gunfight in the neighborhood. The interior scene, which, as I recall, was not even suggested by the original text, shows the mistress of a rich man appalled by the filth and degradation of the tenement home of the young architect whom she really loves. The whole thing was done by the camera: the fastidious girl picking her way, the stricken lover watching her unseen, understanding her emotions, and slipping away so that she does not even have to explain to him. That was motion picture work of high order whereas the reproduction of most of the play was ordinary illustration.

An interesting point was mentioned to me by a professional observer. In the play and in the movie also, a yacht is supposed to be ready to steam down the Bay; obviously it could not be shown in the theater; obviously it could be shown in the movie. Because it was not shown, one did not believe it was there: or, to put it another way, you missed it; you felt that somebody was faking. And this very simple difference indicates that the makers of *Dead End* were so bemused by the success of the play on the stage that they forgot the basic requirements of the motion picture.

Scribner's, November 1937

Archer Winsten has been film critic of *The New York Post* since 1935. *Mayerling,* a point of reference he uses, was one of the more successful imported pictures of the thirties; it starred Charles Boyer and Danielle Darrieux and was directed by Anatole Litvak, all of whom spent at least some time thereafter in Hollywood.

GRAND ILLUSION

ARCHER WINSTEN

The Filmarte Theatre, which started the season of 1936 with *La Kermesse Héroïque* and 1937 with *Mayerling,* last night brought in *Grand Illusion,* the French film concerning which enthusiastic reports have been heard for almost a year. It lives up to the high Filmarte precedent, justifies the reports and, in addition, has the virtue of shocking timeliness with respect to current war threats.

It is the story of a group of Frenchmen in German prison camps during the World War.

Jean Renoir, director and coauthor with Charles Spaak, has enriched his film not only with masterly direction throughout but has also been able to create three separate planes of reality.

First, the prisoners are seen as men living under the modifying conditions of wartime imprisonment. Their one automatic response is the attempt to escape. It is inevitable and natural as breathing. It also provides the framework for the plot and its suspense.

Second, the prisoners become distinguishable as individuals by reason of their class backgrounds and loyalties. De Boeldieu, played by Pierre Fresnay, is an aristocrat. Maréchal, played by Jean Gabin, is a man who could not have been an officer before the French Revolution, nor could Rosenthal, the Jew, played by Dalio. Their loyalties as fellow prisoners and fellow Frenchmen are contrasted with the feeling that springs up between the two aristocrats, De Boeldieu and his jailer, Von Rauffenstein, played by Erich von Stroheim. These relationships are handled with assurance and truth, giving rare depth to the picture's insight.

The third plane is the simply human. A man is not always a prisoner. He is not always bound by ties of class and nation. He is a man who, when he sees others digging a tunnel for escape, remarks that the war will be over before they finish it. Another replies, "What an illusion." Or he falls in love with a German woman who gives him food and shelter while he is trying to escape. And she, husband and brothers dead in the trenches, loves him. He will hope that some day, "when this accursed war is over," he can come back and marry her, that this will be the last war.

The answer comes, "What an illusion."

Instead of attacking war by picturing its physical horrors, *Grand Illusion* cuts underneath to the fundamentals of human beings. The conflicts are shown, captor and captured both caught. Conflict is repeated between two French comrades when they have escaped. The minor fight between the comrades is easily resolved through understanding and sympathy. No such settlement is possible in the greater world, and the picture does not make the foolishly optimistic mistake of creating one. Its tragedy was the world's tragedy then, just as it is today. It does not preach; it shows.

The film's performances are flawless, Jean Gabin, Pierre Fresnay, Erich von Stroheim, Marcel Dalio, and Dita Parlo as the German woman put the seal of absolute authority on their characterizations. Their admirable restraint is matched by abilities to give full meaning to their roles.

In this picture, then, you have a happy conjunction of significant subject matter, a director equal to his task, and actors equal to theirs. A masterpiece is the inevitable result.

English subtitles of satisfactory quality but too few in number give the gist of some of the many conversations that occur in French and German. Fortunately, the work of director and actors possesses a clarity that often renders words unnecessary, and the general plot development is obvious without any translation. My only objection is that, in a picture of such absorbing interest, it is annoying to miss a single word.

The New York Post, September 13, 1938

Richard Griffith was well-known as a critic before he became curator of films at the Museum of Modern Art in New York, where he served from 1951 to 1965. He was the author of several film books, including *The World of Robert Flaherty* and, with Arthur Mayer, *The Movies.*

GRAND ILLUSION

RICHARD GRIFFITH

It is unkind of Erich von Stroheim to debunk war's illusions in this graceless year. Only two decades ago it was this same von Stroheim, "the man you love to hate," who sketched for us the aspect of the hideous Hun in Hollywood's anti-German films. Now he returns in what is outwardly his familiar character—the same white gloves, polished boots, and dextrous cigarette, the same steely stride, and that extraordinary face, glazed and immobile as its ingrown monocle, yet far more eloquent than "acting" ever is. Seeing him thus solidifies old memories, the fine moments in *Blind Husbands* and *Foolish Wives,* that made him an image of evil fascination. But though the form of his work is the same, its meaning has changed. In *Grand Illusion* the aristocratic Hun is a pathetic figure from which the menace has gone out. His epicurean elegance is preserved now merely to keep up appearances. Even his strength, his immense vitality, are no longer frightening, because they are atrophying through want of use. It is the same character, yes, but deepened by events, adapted to new conditions. And this development from caricature toward dimension is the measure of von Stroheim's growth since the florid cynicism of his early days. In the man's long struggle against box-officialdom, the actor has been humanized.

Like most of Jean Renoir's films, *Grand Illusion* is an example of what Harry Alan Potamkin used to call "intensive cinema." Sketching quite simply the outlines of life in a German prison camp during the World War, Renoir develops the significant incidents one by one, dwelling upon them until they deepen into a motif, an idea, an opinion. What, asks Renoir, is the experience of a man in modern war? On the battlefield it is obvious enough: kill when you must, escape death when you can. But here in the prison camp, removed from the fact and fear of death, men still try to influence an event which is so much larger than their lives. The two who struggle hardest are aristocrats, survivals of a day when individual effort had military value. Von Rauffenstein (click), officer in the imperial Germany army (bow), has been ruined physically in an airplane crash, but he accepts the tedious post of camp commandant in order to continue serving the state. That is the function to which he was bred, without which he does not exist. His French counterpart, Captain de Boeldieu, dies that two fellow-prisoners may escape. He knows that he shivers his painted lance in vain, that this last gift to France is almost theatrical in its futility. But, *noblesse oblige!* For a gentleman, even death must be a gesture to the world passed away. The men for whom he dies have no such sense of personal obligation. Maréchal the mechanic and Rosenthal the Jew are democrats. To them war is no profession but a duty, as meaningless as it is unpleasant. Why escape, then? Why not make captivity a refuge until the thing is over and life's familiar outlines reappear? But prison camps are made to escape from; one must do something to feel one's weight in affairs, to seem to affect the issue. So Maréchal and Rosenthal start their miserable journey, hardly knowing why they go on. Is it good luck, or bad, or merely another experience, that they fall in with a lonely German woman, widowed by the war, who welcomes them because she wants to hear a man's tread on the floor again? This is their haven, and in it Maréchal finds all a man needs, but even here they are still prisoners of circumstance. There is danger in finding peace in the midst of war, danger even in loving a girl who speaks another language. So they go back to France, to help push the war through or to wait for it to wear itself out. After it is over, will Maréchal come back to the happiness he has found? But yes, naturally. If he is alive.

The picture, especially this last sequence, is played in muted undertones. Even von Stroheim's powerful presence is subdued to the quiet level of French acting, and Pierre Fresnay, Jean Gabin, and Dita Parlo are people so easy to know that one thinks of them as contemporaries. For though the picture is a period study, its minor and major illusions still prevail in the divided world of 1938. In the Fascist countries men turn back to the Rauffenstein ideal, asserting themselves by becoming a unit in the state, making its corporate quarrels their own. To the democracies war is repugnant, but in recent weeks they have seemed to think that in the end it is a necessity. Their illusion, grand only because it is shared by so many people, is that good intentions produce good results. They have forgotten Versailles; they have forgotten that war is now a human enterprise beyond the scope of single human beings. Though it may force them into action, their efforts for good or ill have no weight in its vast, incalculable total. *Grand Illusion* reminds us that this is so, but that is all it does. Renoir, who invokes so skillfully these terrifying images of distintegration, offers in contrast only the old ideal of man's brotherhood, and his film does not tell us whether it is illusion or reality. Maréchal and Rosenthal, plebeians that they are, feel kinship with their captors. But their affectionate gestures across the barriers of class and race come too late. Peace is the time for mutual understanding. Once the war mills start grinding, they do not stop until there is nothing left to feed them.

The Nation, October 22, 1938

Franz Hoellering was born in Vienna, directed in the European theater, wrote novels, and arrived in the United States in 1934. He was film critic for *The Nation* in the late thirties.

The Citadel was made from a British novel with British actors in Britain but was directed by an American, King Vidor.

PYGMALION

FRANZ HOELLERING

A quarter of a century ago George Bernard Shaw wrote the satirical play *Pygmalion,* which still sparkles as it did on its first night—which cannot be said about many plays of such great stage age. Mr. Higgins, professor of phonetics and, for purposes of the last act, not only a fanatical scientist but a confirmed bachelor, wagers that he can, within six months, transform a Cockney girl into a lady who will stand the high test of a royal reception. He wins his bet by teaching her correct English and superficial manners. The course is pretty strenuous for the victim. He treats her like a guinea pig and does not see—though otherwise he is intelligent and sophisticated

—that she is falling in love with him, or, for that matter, that he is falling in love with her.

I could never detect more than an artificial analogy to the Greek myth which the title of the play suggests. The sculptor Pygmalion formed Galatea from a piece of clay, whereas Professor Higgins (Leslie Howard) attempts the opposite—to change a most lively and unspoiled piece of nature, the wild, dirty guttersnipe Eliza Doolittle (Wendy Hiller), into a piece of soap. But the movie edition of Shaw's play informs me again in an introduction that Pygmalion is the modern version of the Galatea theme. I suspect that this claim, which takes a device for the real story, is partly responsible for what is wrong with an excellent, witty, and always entertaining picture. To confess it right away, nothing is wrong if one compares it with the average picture; but if one considers it as literature, which is permissible in this case, criticism is in order.

The fault seems to lie with the script. It not only follows the play too closely, repeating its errors, but even more than the play it stresses the situations of the transformation process at the expense of more important values. Miss Doolittle is washed, learns to spell, to speak words and sentences. At a tea party—a most delightful scene in itself—she passes her first examination. Finally she triumphs by duping the nobility in a long sequence outstanding in every respect but especially in restraint and taste. But the lessons, her scenes alone with Professor Higgins, remain less convincing for the reason mentioned. We see the pupil suffering under the untiring fanaticism of the teacher, but we do not see her falling in love with him. This development is neglected to make way for cheaper effects, until it is needed for the end. Then the newly created lady throws the professor's slippers in his face, and we are allowed to guess what must have been going on all the time. Could we have followed it, the unfolding of a character and a soul would have counterbalanced the gags, subtle though they are, and the whole picture, without losing its lightness, could have achieved depth. Instead of three dimensions it might have had four, and it is with the fourth, the irrational, that art begins.

If the shortcomings of the script are not felt as long as one looks at the screen, we have to thank Wendy Hiller, who steals the show. Miss Hiller's performance on Broadway two years ago in *Love on the Dole,* where she had occasion to exploit the wide range of her personality, was a great experience. She must win the hearts of all moviegoers, and surely not with cuteness and pretense. She is the type the great industry needs badly—a full-blooded person who creates a role out of the abundance of her nature. She makes one forget the tricksters who turn their defects into virtues or, at least, salaries.

Leslie Howard does very intelligently everything a Professor Higgins may do, but one cannot quite believe him. He is too conscious, too slick. He plays with skill a thought-out conception. In lesser parts Wilfred Lawson, Esme Percy, and David Tree give excellent performances. They breathe contemporary English atmosphere. The direction (Anthony Asquith and Leslie Howard) and the production (Gabriel Pascal, who must have the credit for conquering Shaw's antagonism to the movies) compete successfully with Hollywood's best works of this kind. More pictures like *The Citadel* and *Pygmalion* from London, and there will be story conferences in California.

The Nation, December 24, 1938

THE LADY VANISHES

FRANK S. NUGENT

Just in under the wire to challenge for a place on the year's best ten is *The Lady Vanishes,* latest of the melodramatic classics made by England's greatest director, Alfred Hitchcock. If it were not so brilliant a melodrama, we should class it as a brilliant comedy. Seeing it imposes a double, a blessedly double, strain: when your sides are not aching from laughter your brain is throbbing in its attempts to outguess the director. Hitch occasionally relents with his rib-tickling, but his professional honor would not brook your catching up with his plot.

A lady vanishes on a train. One moment she was sitting there, plump, matronly, reading a needlework magazine, answering to the name and description of Miss Froy, governess, London-bound from the Tyrol. The next, she was gone. And the young woman in the compartment, awakening from her doze, was solemnly assured by her neighbors that they had seen no Miss Froy. A brain specialist aboard suggests that Miss Froy was a hallucination induced by the blow she had received when a flower box fell on her head at the station.

The young man, who had been one of the avalanche-bound guests at the inn was skeptical, too, but offered to help. The two Englishmen aboard didn't want to be involved; they were eager to reach England in time for the cricket finals. The pacifist was afraid his reputation might suffer; he obviously was traveling with a woman not his wife.

Still, there was something about Miss Froy. When we first saw her she was being serenaded (odd for a woman her age) by an elderly porter in the Tyrolean inn. And then, although she didn't know it, a pair of shadowy hands knotted about the porter's neck and he died. Besides, she was standing beside the young woman at the station when some one pushed the flower pot off the roof. Could that have been meant for Miss Froy? Yet it doesn't seem quite credible for every one in the train to enter a conspiracy about her—conductors, dining room stewards, a countess, a noted surgeon, a music hall performer, a nun, two cricket-mad Englishmen, a woman in tweeds. (Mr. Hitchcock, a very old Nick of a St. Nick, is laughing fit to kill.)

Well, there's the puzzle, and we cannot conceal our admiration over the manner in which Mr. Hichcock and his staff have pieced it together. There isn't an incident, be it as trivial as an old woman's chatter about her favorite brand of tea, that hasn't a pertinent bearing on the plot. Everything that happens is a clue. And, having given you fair warning, we still defy you to outguess that rotund spider, Hitch. The man is diabolical; his film is devilishly clever.

His casts are always neglected by reviewers, which isn't fair, especially since he has so perfect a one here. Honors belong, of course, to his priceless cricketers, Caldicott and Charters—or Naunton Wayne and Basil Radford—whose running temperature about "how England is doing" makes the most hilarious running gag of the year. Margaret Lockwood and Michael Redgrave as the puzzled young woman and her ally are just the sort of pleasant, intelligent young people we should expect to find going through a casual Hitchcock gesture to boy-meets-girl.

The others are equally right—Dame May Whitty as the surprising Miss Froy, Paul Lukas as the specialist, Cecil Parker, Linden Travers—in fact, all the others. Did we say *The Lady Vanishes* was challenging the best ten? Let's amend it: the bid has been accepted.

The New York Times, December 26, 1938

STAGECOACH

FRANK S. NUGENT

In one superbly expansive gesture, which we (and the Music Hall) can call *Stagecoach,* John Ford has swept aside ten years of artifice and talkie compromise and has made a motion picture that sings a song of camera. It moves, and how beautifully it moves, across the plains of Arizona, skirting the skyreaching mesas of Monument Valley, beneath the piled-up cloud banks which every photographer dreams about, and through all the old-fashioned, but never really outdated, periods of prairie travel in the scalp-raising seventies, when Geronimo's Apaches were on the warpath. Here, in a sentence, is a movie of the grand old school, a genuine rib-thumper and a beautiful sight to see.

Mr. Ford is not one of your subtle directors, suspending sequences on the wink of an eye or the precisely calculated gleam of a candle in a mirror. He prefers the broadest canvas, the brightest colors, the widest brush, and the boldest possible strokes. He hews to the straight narrative line with the well-reasoned confidence of a man who has seen that narrative succeed before. He takes no shadings from his characters: either they play it straight or they don't play at all. He likes his language simple, and he doesn't want too much of it. When his Redskins bite the dust, he expects to hear the thud and see the dirt spurt up. Above all, he likes to have things happen out in the open, where his camera can keep them in view.

He has had his way in *Stagecoach* with Walter Wanger's benison, the writing assistance of Dudley Nichols, and the complete cooperation of a cast which had the sense to appreciate the protection of being stereotyped. You should know, almost without being told, the station in life (and in frontier melodrama) of the eight passengers on the Overland stage from Tonto to Lordsburg.

To save time, though, here they are: "Doc" Boone, a tipsy man of medicine; Major Hatfield, professional gambler, once a Southern gentleman and a gentleman still; Dallas, a lady of such transparently dubious virtue that she was leaving Tonto by popular request; Mrs. Mallory, who, considering her condition, had every reason to be hastening to her army husband's side; Mr. Gatewood, an absconding banker and windbag; Mr. Peacock, a small and timid whisky salesman destined by Bacchus to be Doc Boone's traveling companion; Sheriff Wilcox and his prisoner, the Ringo Kid. The driver, according to the rules, had to be Slim Summerville or Andy Devine; Mr. Devine got the call.

So onward rolls the stage, nobly sped by its six stout-hearted bays, and out there, somewhere behind the buttes and crags, Geronimo is lurking with his savage band, the United States Cavalry is biding its time to charge to the rescue, and the Ringo Kid is impatiently awaiting his cue to stalk down the frontier-town street and blast it out with the three Plummer boys. But foreknowledge doesn't cheat Mr. Ford of his thrills. His attitude, if it spoke its mind, would be: "All right, you know what's coming, but have you ever seen it done like this?" And once you've swallowed your heart again, you'll have to say: "No, sir! Not like this!"

His players have taken easily to their chores, all the way down the list from Claire Trevor's Dallas to Tom Tyler's Hank Plummer. But the cutest coach-rider in the wagon, to our mind, was little Donald Meek as Mr. Peacock, the whisky-drummer. That, of course, is not meant as a slight to Thomas Mitchell as the toping Dr. Boone, to Louise Platt as the wan Mrs. Mallory, George Bancroft as the sheriff, or John Wayne as the Ringo Kid. They've all done nobly by a noble horse opera, but none so nobly as its director. This is one stagecoach that's powered by a Ford.

The New York Times, March 3, 1939

STAGECOACH

WELFORD BEATON

One of the greatest of all Westerns. And one of the most interesting Hollywood possibly could have for study. It is superb entertainment, but take it apart and we discover all the story it has could be told comfortably between the two ends of one reel of film. That interests me because one of the beliefs the *Spectator* has expressed at intervals during the past decade is that the story is not the thing of most importance to screen entertainment, that what really matters is the manner of telling what story there is—that it is the medium that entertains. Film producers as a whole know too little about their medium to give them confidence to test a theory. Walter Wanger apparently is an exception. *Stagecoach* is evidence of his willingness to put to a test the theory that the medium, not the story, is the thing. He takes us with a stagecoach on a trip across a stretch of Western territory at a time when prowling Indians made it perilous. After one brush with the Redskins, the coach gets through; at the destination one of the passengers kills the three desperadoes who had killed his father and brother. There you have all the story there is. And for one hour and thirty-three minutes it is gripping entertainment. It is a *Grand Hotel* on wheels.

Only great screen craftsmanship could elongate so slim a story without stretching it too thin in spots. In Dudley Nichols, writer, and John Ford, director, Wanger had a team with many notable screen achievements to its credit, but no other I can recall matches *Stagecoach* as an example of cinematic skill. Quite extraordinary is the manner in which Dudley has strung together a series of little incidents, snatches of dialogue, gems of humor, to enlist our interest in a strangely assorted group of people—a young woman of commercial virtue, the refined young wife of an army officer, a drunken doctor, a timid whiskey peddler, an escaped prisoner on his way back to jail, a pompous banker who is absconding, a stagecoach reinsman who is not brave but bravely carries on, a United States marshall, resolute, fearless, sentimental. They are the people whom the stagecoach carries into and out of danger. Another, a professional gambler with a gallant side, falls victim to an Indian bullet. Each of these people has his or her individual problem, and all of them are worked into the script with a literary version of the skill a juggler displays when he keeps an equal number of balls in the air simultaneously, each ball being a separate unit, but it is as a group they hold our interest.

When John Ford was given the Nichols script he must have seen it as a series of pictures, he could not have read it as a story in words. Its literal translation in screen terms would have achieved poor results. It essentially was a script we had to *see,* one containing only one chase and a triple killing. And Ford makes us see it, and makes the seeing continuously thrilling. It is a production of tremendous physical sweep of pictorial grandeur, of superb beauty which the preview audience greeted with rounds of applause. Photography has the velvety warmth of masterly graded light and shade, not the gaudiness of Technicolor which cheapens so many screen productions. To the cameras of Bert Glennon and Ray Binger we are indebted for some of the most imposing pictures that ever adorned a screen. Through all the feast for our eyes to feed on, Director Ford weaves strongly the thread of human values. He gives us no hero, no heroine—just the people I have mentioned, each to himself being the most important, but to you and me being only one of the group. The forward progression of the story is one of the most brilliant exhibitions of sustained filmic motion the screen has given us in recent years of the talkie era. We have the feeling all the time that we are pressing onward with the characters, going with them on their perilous journey, hoping with them that they will reach their destination in safety. And for that, we have John Ford to thank.

As for the individual mention of cast members, no more evenly balanced set of characterizations ever has been presented, the prominence of the individual plays being dependent entirely on the length of his or her role. Hundreds appear in the picture, and all of them are merely human beings whom we are permitted to see as they live their lives. Claire Trevor, as the prostitute, earns our instant sympathy and retains it throughout, her performance being the most penetrating she has to her credit. John Wayne seemed born for the part he plays, but the same might be said of the others in the most prominent roles, Andy Devine, John Carradine, Thomas Mitchell, George Bancroft, Louise Platt, Donald Meek, Berton Churchill. In all its technical aspects the production maintains the high level of the writing, direction, and acting. Cutting the film presented some nice problems, particularly in a sequence in which a few score mounted Indians attack the stagecoach, and which, incidentally, is an intensely thrilling sequence. Otho Lovering, editorial supervisor, and Dorothy Spencer and Walter Reynolds, editors, deserve praise for their skillful assembling of the film. The excellent results achieved with the sound recorded by Frank Mayer have much to do with the success of the production.

The Hollywood Spectator, February 18, 1939

ALEXANDER NEVSKY

FRANZ HOELLERING

In his newest picture, *Alexander Nevsky* Sergei Eisentenstein, the famous director of *Potemkin* and the fragmentary but unforgettable film about

Mexico, appears to be limited to his excellent abilities as a movie technician. After a preview of *Alexander Nevsky,* Stalin slapped Eisenstein on the back and called him a "good Bolshevik." The events which led up to this cordial Kremlin scene, as reported by the professional apologists of the Russian Thermidor, reveal that Eisenstein has been *gleichgeschaltet,* subordinated to the orders of the monolithic state.

On March 17, 1937, when the liquidation of the Old Bolsheviks was in full swing, the Central Administration of the Photo-Cinema Industry of the U.S.S.R. stopped the production of the picture *Bezhin Meadow,* on which Eisenstein was at work. The film had a contemporary and highly controversial theme—collectivization and the opposition met by this tour de force. But Eisenstein, so argued his administrative superiors and artistic inferiors, was not up to date in dealing with this vital problem. "His conception of the social forces involved was fundamentally fallacious, he resorted, instead of learning from life, to far-fetched symbolism, didacticism, schematization, scholastic profundities, and harmful formalistic exercises"—whatever all this may mean. Eisenstein, of course, "agreed with many criticisms" and confessed to "having been possessed by the intellectual's illusion that revolutionary work could be done individually in segregation from the collective"—forgetting that much revolutionary work has been done, especially in art, in exactly this forbidden manner. After this he received profound advice: "Only by starting with man, for man. and in the name of man is it possible to work in our art." He swallowed the hollow phrase, which sounds like Silone's Professor Pickup, and "went to the country to rest and reexamine his past." After his return he "immediately" started to work and produced, it seems immediately, a masterpiece—so the Soviet critics say unanimously. He received in Moscow the Order of Lenin and in New York the four stars of the *Daily News.*

The story of *Alexander Nevsky* is a vision of a future war between Russia and Germany in the costumes of the thirteenth century. German Templars—white coats, red crosses—invade Russia from the west; Mongols from the east. The rich merchants of Novgorod plot surrender. The common people want to resist but are unable to do so without a leader. They find him in the person of Prince Nevsky, who promptly beats the Germans in a terrific battle on a frozen lake. To this political-military action some byplay is added. Two subordinate leaders, the one blond and jolly, the other a dark-haired, rather melancholy expert with the battle-ax, fall in love with the same girl. She likes them both and escapes the pains of choice by deciding to marry the braver. A draw threatens to complicate the situation, but a superficial happy ending is easily reached.

This framework contains two long mass sequences: first, the helpless common people shouting for a leader, a scene any dictator would enjoy;

second, the battle—first-class Hollywood with touches of von Sternberg and von Stroheim. Though we are not left in doubt about the outcome, suspense is achieved through the machine-like advance of the German army. The constructed historical parallel—Templars=Nazis, Nevsky=Stalin—is labored but effectively driven home. Nevsky has a very winning and simple personality: he is a patriotic hero and nothing else. The German members of the nobility class, if it is proper to use in this connection a Marxist term, are on the other hand cruel villains and nothing else. The style of characterization throughout is operatic. One expects Nevsky to sing his unfailing orders.

Alexander Nevsky is primitive, patriotic propaganda—we are good, the enemy is bad. With a simple change in costume and locale—instead of the Templars, Roman legionaries, instead of the frozen lake near Novgorod, the swamps of the Teutoburg forest—it would be a perfect Nazi picture. It has nothing whatever to do with "revolutionary art." It is not proof of Eisenstein's resurgence but of his suppression.

The Nation, April 8, 1939

GONE WITH THE WIND

FRANZ HOELLERING

As you may have heard, *Gone with the Wind,* the $3,900,000 super-picture in Technicolor—playing time: three hours and thirty-seven minutes—has arrived. During years of preparation and twelve months of actual shooting, hundreds of people under David O. Selznick's supervision were at work to produce the epoch-making picture of our time. The result is a film which is a major event in the history of the industry but only a minor achievement in motion picture art. There are moments when the two categories meet on good terms, but the long stretches between are filled with mere spectacular efficiency. One admires an excellent cast and a hundred technical details, but one's heart seldom beats faster. While one waits to be carried away, critical thoughts have time to develop. The feeling grows that one is sitting in a Hollywood Duesenberg with nowhere to go.

The picture consists of two parts punctuated by a brief intermission. The first starts with the Civil War and ends with its close; Scarlett O'Hara is back in Tara. The second is essentially the story of her marriage with Rhett Butler. In the first part the Civil War is the driving force, not the characters. In the second the characters dominate. The hospital scenes and the evacuation and burning of Atlanta are dramas in themselves, and their cinematographic reproduction is unforgettable; at the same time they reveal the principal weakness of the picture as a whole: the characters alone do not suffice. This would be no fault if not they but the times were the focus. As it is, a Strindbergian theme is attacked without Strindberg's power, hate, and insight. In spite of many excellent scenes the drama is not convincing. With the camera turning from high spot to high spot the psychological development is neglected. One understands less and less why things happen and thinks easily of more plausible alternatives. This also explains why in the end Rhett Butler's "I don't give a damn" comes as a surprise and shock to the audience.

These are critical remarks dictated by absolute standards. Relatively the picture represents progress in many respects. The courage of its producer deserves sincere acknowledgment. He proves that films of more than three hours' playing time are possible, opening the way to movie epics. He sets a new technical standard: the era of the sixties is reproduced in architecture, costumes, and make-up as never before. The Technicolor photography is so superb that the normal preference for black-and-white pictures is forgotten. And the cast, in the main scenes as in the episodes, is excellent.

Vivien Leigh in appearance and movements is perfect as Scarlett. Her acting is best when she is allowed to accentuate the contrasts of the split personality she portrays. Why she loves Ashley Wilkes (Leslie Howard, who is convincing in his specialty as noble sap) remains a riddle, but that is not the actress's fault. She is particularly effective in such moments of characterization as on the morning after Rhett has carried her up to her room against her will. Clark Gable as Rhett Butler is best in the second part, where he can show the heart of the tough guy though he cannot bridge the gap between his love and his final disgust—but again, it is not his fault. Of the other characters I have only space to mention Hattie McDaniel as Mammy and Butterfly McQueen as Prissy. Victor Fleming's direction is expert and always tasteful with one exception: when he lets Scarlett stand like the Statue of Liberty on the barren fields of Tara after she has vomited (a scene which is hidden in shadows).

Of course one can easily conceive of a less polished and more exciting production of *Gone with the Wind*—for example, as an independent Erich von Stroheim would have done it. On the other hand, the fact that the hero and heroine of a super-picture are no longer merely noble and glamorous indicates a development which deserves high praise.

The Nation, December 30, 1939

Films was a quarterly published only from 1939 to 1940. Its editors were Lincoln Kirstein, Jay Leyda, Mary Losey, Robert Stebbins (Sidney Meyers), and Lee Strasberg.

History in American Films
(GONE WITH THE WIND)

LINCOLN KIRSTEIN

Anyone reading the news reports of the Atlanta opening of *Gone With the Wind* will not deny the historical significance of this film. History itself, though, the history of the Civil War period, serves no more than a decorative purpose, a background painted with a distorted set of values and an even falser Technicolor. But history has rarely been told with even an approximation of truth in Hollywood, because the few men in control there have no interest in the real forces behind historical movements and the new forces that every new epoch sets into motion. *Gone With the Wind* deserves our attention because it is an overinflated example of the usual, the false movie approach to history. Selznick's four-hour feature represents all Hollywood might do, and, unfortunately, most of what it usually does. In every foot of it is inscribed the tragic gap between possibility and achievement.

Margaret Mitchell's novel is a cheap work, but it has the distinction of its reported facts. She was raised in Atlanta, and heard first-hand most of the stories she tells. Her details are, at least, full and indicative. The coarseness of the writing, its superficial retailing of the social background, its slipshod handling, can be ignored because the narrative is so readable and the characters so plausible. When the book was transferred to the screen with a capricious reverence that was as uncalled for as it was dramatically disastrous, only the chronological sequence of its original superficialities was retained. Perhaps Sidney Howard and Selznick assumed that everyone who saw the picture must already have read the book. Hence, they accelerated toward the end to batter down the tired audience with a series of violent personal incidents isolated from a social background, which, if one only took the testimony of what is seen on the screen as opposed to what may have been remembered from reading, are arbitrary, unmotivated, and largely unexplained.

In the introduction to his mother's play in blank verse on the life of Savonarola, T. S. Eliot writes that historical dramas frequently tell us more about the times in which they are written than about the times of which they treat. Yet historical novels and plays continue to interest us by presenting the seeming persistence of human behavior with a difference in social background. In America, the contemporary formula for producing historical films and novels consists, generally speaking, of simple debunking. That is, those people in odd hats and hoopskirts were not a bit different from you and me, except that they wore odd hats and hoopskirts. Whether or not they were essentially different or humanly identical has little to do with their clothes. It has everything to do with how much money they had, where they had been brought up, and where they lived. The main weakness with such pictures as *Gone With the Wind* is that no trace of essential social background is evoked. To be sure, we see antebellum belles in their pantaloons, laced into their corsets, we see a few dancing parties, a couple of house servants, and there is a single reference to the Grecian symmetry of Georgia planter society, but one is never genuinely made to feel it. Consequently, when the War comes to wipe out this life, the break between the old and the new society is not fully comprehended, because no opposite or contrast has ever been suggested.

The genre of the historical film or novel attempts to revive a past epoch. An epoch which is more or less recently familiar to the public, such as 1850-60 in the Old South, offers a different problem to an epoch which is more remote. The recent epoch must be *reconstructed* according to the best available sources, to coincide with traces of eye-witness accounts. The remote epoch, whose documents are more obscure, must be *recreated,* as, for example, in *Alexander Nevsky,* or the Babylonian sequences in *Intolerance.* The last three centuries, presented in the films, usually seem stuffed. The people look and act as if they were embalmed. Adrian, Cedric Gibbons, and their colleagues have delivered history to the interior decorators and dressmakers. Instead of reading history critically, the directors and producers employ "research" experts who correct unimportant details, invisible to anyone but an auction-room expert, thereby absolving themselves from the necessity of photographing anything which might genuinely illuminate the course of recorded events.

The best historical films, either from Europe or Hollywood, have been those which employ a preponderance of out-of-door shots. The interior decorator is no match for nature, particularly in good Technicolor, which was so expertly used in John Ford's *Drums Along the Mohawk.* It is significant that the phoniest scenes in *Gone With the Wind* were those taken in the studio, to imitate exteriors. The ruined wall against which Leslie Howard and Vivien Leigh meet after the war, reads exactly as if it were made of wallboard and paint, which it was. The interior decorator and his accomplice, the set-dresser also conquered every house, hospital, ballroom, annihilating the actor. A heavy shine of luxurious unreality oils all the motion (even that of Max Steiner's syrupy score). The clothes have never been worn before the camera saw them. We read how food in films is sprayed to look more edible. A similar varnish surfaces the rich textures of even Joseph Platt's most homely sets. Worse than this is the shift in scale and style from realistic to mildly expressionist. The staircase at

"Twelve Oaks" is conceived in a thrilling double curve, up and down which pass girls in their billowy crinolines, as easily as on a high-road. It is not a country house, however spacious. It is an hotel foyer in Southern Colonial style. The stairs down which Scarlett tumbles in Rhett's mansion have the proportions of the Doge's staircase. The figure of the woman is dwarfed meaninglessly. The house in the novel was large and nouveau riche; on the screen it is merely inhuman. In Marcel l'Herbier's *La Citadelle du Silence,* the Polish prison is frankly based on Piranesi's "Carceri"—but the gigantism enhances the human atmosphere; it does not suffocate it. The crowd of wounded in the Atlanta street is enormous—but the impression is not of a suffering army, but only of a lot of extras who must have cost a lot of money—bleached out in the flat perspective of an "uncorrected" Technicolor long-shot. In black and white its faults of realization might have been less obvious. Some day someone, possibly John Ford, will make a good Civil War picture, and base his camera-eye on the clear, airless wartime photographs of Matthew Brady.

As for the dramatic implications inherent in the passing of the Old South and its planter, "darkey"-owning aristocracy in general, in the siege and suicide of Atlanta in particular, there is little impact. In the film, the city never seems to have been threatened, is not defended, is scarcely evacuated, and is surely not occupied by conquerors. The burning of Atlanta, potentially a powerful symbolic sequence, became a super-production background for two figures, who from this point on (and on) lost all identification with the audience. I have not met anyone who was moved by the travels, diversions, and duels of Vivien Leigh and Clark Gable after the intermission curtain—and there was nothing besides that pretended to claim one's interest, certainly not the sop to the modern North in the philosophy of Ashley Wilkes.

There have recently been a few interesting Hollywood pictures, which, far less pretentious than *Gone With the Wind,* have aroused some genuine interest in their historical sources. John Ford's *Young Mr. Lincoln, Stagecoach,* and *Drums Along the Mohawk* share an excellence of evocative background, an employment of poetic detail with illuminating pictorial composition, as expert as they are amusing. These details and tableaux, to be sure, are more purely decorative, in an emotional sense, more stylized and formularized than the striking symbolic yet human details in good Eisenstein or Pudovkin films, when the Russian directors, who were more efficient historians than the Americans, could catch whole epochs in a brief sequence of static shots of architectural sculpture, or in masks of a Mongol or a Mexican. But we are forced to recognize that, generally speaking, American films are not *about* much of anything, as *The End of St. Petersburg* was about the end of Imperial Russia, or *Potemkin* was about the nature of fraternity. American films are about boys and girls with love troubles, unless they are about character actors disguised as famous men. In either case, in American films, if an historical frame is for one purpose or another accidentally involved, it is only a frame, or at best, a background. It must *never* compete with Paul Muni, it must never (consciously or unconsciously) omit the obvious impress of its Hollywood set-dresser, producer, star. Ford's *Drums Along the Mohawk,* in so many ways a fine effort, was let down every time Claudette Colbert and Henry Fonda were shown expressing whatever their relationship was to each other. All the careful work of constructing and indicating frontier-life was wiped out whenever Colbert was seen, true to the Claudette Colbert expectations her previous pictures had aroused in her present fans. The corroboration of the Colbert they already had seen is a financial necessity, reaffirmed every time a "star" is cast in a "character" rôle. Clark Gable as Rhett Butler made no attempt to be anything but Clark Gable, since the fans reading the book had made it easy for him by immediately deciding Rhett Butler *was* Clark Gable. In certain Class B or C pictures like *Allegheny Uprising,* or *The Sheriff of Mesa City,* the stars involved are not so exalted as to rip the texture of historical reality. In spite of the fact that they are not "epics," they are pictures which you can look at without looking at your watch. In Westerns, to be sure, the formula for action and diction is as set as a declamation of Racine by an actor in the *Académie Française.*

It is extremely disconcerting to see how Hollywood affects the European historical film via its directors. Anatole Litvak's *Mayerling* has become a kind of standard for the romantic film in an historical setting. His comprehension of psychological nuance, his tactful and judicious recreation of the strict Hapsburg etiquette contrasted with free *Alt Wien,* sincerely indicated the course of liberal and conservative political conflicts which preceded the Triple Alliance. He was never afraid to use a range of emotion which to Hollywood might have seemed "unpopular." He contrived incidents full of petulance, adolescent shyness, boredom, hurt feelings, and family misunderstandings, in a scale which was as adult as it was intense. In Hollywood, Litvak has done *The Sisters* and *Confessions of a Nazi Spy.* In the first, Errol Flynn and Bette Davis were seduced from their normal pretentiousness into giving simple performances, although their script was uninteresting. The background of Western America ca. 1910 was tastefully revived, but where the Hofburg had seemed domestic in its magnificence, and hence, real—a political rally in a northwestern town now became inflated, and hence only decorative. Hollywood insists on such a change of scale and makes reality, or at least essential naturalism, commit suicide. *Confessions* was a kind of historical picture—only it happened to be our own period. It was unburdened by too much stardom, and the background, which we could think of as "documentary" rather than as "historical," read well.

Another picture of the American past, *Destry Rides Again,* was a very superior Western, with remarkable evocations of its period—the synthetic super-serial-wild-west-thriller period, a period real enough to fans, but invented within film history. This was scarcely an historical picture. Rather, it was a starring vehicle for Stewart and Dietrich in a colorful setting, in which the appealing fragrance of nostalgia was skillfully whipped around to preach a contemporary fable of nonviolence (up to the point where a man can't take it). *Destry* survived its stars because it was slight in concept. *Gone With the Wind* failed because its stars even increased the transparently artificial treatment of a tremendous theme, unsupported by background or idea.

A sense of the past, our own or our country's or another country's, as parallel to our times, or as escape from them, is something that will always be explored. The exploration can be made to pay, but it has its dangers. Costume pictures cost money, and the costumes and the famous characters they clothe do not of themselves attract customers, as Hollywood seems too often to expect. For there are two historical sources to be investigated—the superficial, literary, and fictitious realm, diluted from Walter Scott, Victor Hugo, Dumas, or their imitators, which at best result in fast adventure films (a genre forever identified with Fairbanks' memory), at worst in bores—or the documents composed of incident and accident which, because they are widely known to have actually happened at a certain juncture in the historical process, illumine their epoch like a great image in a line of verse, to become quotable, to have valid reference, as representative and explanatory of their time and place.

Dieterle's *Hunchback of Notre Dame* is the most flagrant example of irrelevant waste, with Charles Laughton a gutta percha gargoyle, and the whole proceedings weakly devised, and without tension. *The Hunchback* obviously cost more than either *The Private Lives of Elizabeth and Essex* or *The Tower of London,* but they are of an equal tepid pretense. Max Beerbohm once had a friend who wanted to write a tragedy on the subject of Sardanapalus, but the Encyclopedia Britannica (his only source) opened to "Savonarola" instead. The ensuing masterpiece was larded with such stage directions as *Enter Guelphs and Ghibellines, fighting* and *Pippa passes.* It could serve as the next vehicle for Boris Karloff's benevolent mania without change.

On the other hand, in Max Glass' *Entente Cordiale,* there are half-a-dozen curiously effective scenes that, whether they may be independently true or not, read with the ring of truth. For example, when the German ambassador, trying to understand the exact nature of the new alliance, and fumbling for the correct diplomatic terminology, hitting on—*"Bien, une espèce d'entente cordiale"*—sees the smug security on the faces of the Brit-

ish and French envoys, we know how each of them felt. Edward VII at
Marienbad, in the hostile lobby of the French theater, at the café concert,
is not merely a well-known character actor in a beard, like Paul Muni or
Bette Davis in whatever their architectural make-up. Victor Francen has
digested Edward, his epoch as well as his symbolic mannerism. Bette Davis
had only glanced at portraits of Elizabeth as a springboard for an effective
Bette Davis gutsy performance. No one pretended to imagine Paul Muni
was the novelist Zola. Everybody merely pooled their homage, to say how
life-like his simulacrum was, and that his beard was his own, not crêpe-hair
—as one might say of waxwork, "It's almost real enough to be alive."
Almost, but never quite.

Hollywood attempts to corroborate its audience, although it can never
be sure exactly what its audience expects. Hollywood knows Abraham Lincoln looked like Frank McGlynn, Walter Huston, and Raymond Massey.
Henry the Eighth looked like Jannings and Charles Laughton; Stephen
Foster looked like Don Ameche, and young Thomas A. Edison looked
like Mickey Rooney. Oddly enough, as in *The Story of Alexander Graham
Bell,* such a palpable lay-figure as Don Ameche becomes real and touching,
partly because his story of deafness and patent rights is in itself moving, and
hardly anybody had any preconceived ideas about what Bell actually did
look like. Yet every time a star is presented as a familar statue, the barriers
of incredulity bang down, the only interest is in the resemblance to the
bronze or marble. In acting, it's translated into wood. The combination of
predominantly decorative values in background, and of star-casting for
heroes, makes the historical film one of Hollywood's fanciest failures.

Films, Spring 1940

"Patterson Murphy" was the pen name that the editors of
Esquire imposed on Meyer Levin without even notifying him,
because his own name sounded too Jewish.[14] This for a review
that celebrates "one of the great triumphs of the democratic
method!"

MR. SMITH GOES TO WASHINGTON

PATTERSON MURPHY

For the first time, this critic applauded a picture at a preview. The picture
was Mr. Capra's *Mr. Smith Goes to Washington,* and the applause was
spontaneous.

It happened that as we were on the way to the show the visitor from Amarillo made the usual remark about didn't I get tired of going to pictures and I grunted the usual response. But as a matter of fact, critics enjoy pictures more than most folks because there are more points of interest for the critic. Even if a picture is entirely flat and boresome, the critic can get some interest out of the evening by counting the ways and the whys of the failure, whereas the pure spectator can only sit there feeling bored.

But can a critic ever sit back and simply relax and enjoy a picture, without thinking about what he is going to say about it? A few times a year that happens, and that happened with Mr. Capra's *Mr. Smith Goes to Washington.* This critic has plenty to say about the film, on afterthought, and may even find shortcomings, but he wishes first of all to attest to the fact that as entertainment the picture was carried out with such sweeping confidence that it is irresistible. Not that anyone should want to resist.

A few more bows should be made before we start talking turkey. Bow, very deep: This is the best film I have ever seen about American democracy. Bow to the middle: This is Mr. Capra's best film to date, far excelling such pish as *Lost Horizon* and such tosh as *You Can't Take It With You.* A worthy forerunner was *Mr. Deeds Goes to Town,* but the relation of Smith to Deeds is as the relationship of Washington to a county seat.

Mr. Capra never departs from the basic legends and parables in his choice of stories, he only freshens them in retelling, and this is as it should be, for it affirms the universalism of his art. Mr. Smith, therefore, is the story of Christ and the money-changers: he drives them out of the Temple. This story has been done in American political terms many times; the most notable theatrical treatment of recent times, and the one which is closest to Mr. Smith, is Maxwell Anderson's play called *Both Your Houses,* also about a young and naïve but Lincolnesque soul who comes to Congress and gradually becomes aware of the graft and corruption that really goes on in the national capitol, finally finds that even the men he admired know and share in this looting, but nevertheless retains enough faith and energy for a struggle against the windmills.

What makes Mr. Capra's treatment of this standard story valid and original is his use of the story to expose in detail the operations by which democracy is perverted, by which the freedom of the press is destroyed, by which the air is polluted with propaganda, by which votes are annulled. His sharp mounting of Sidney Buchman's outspoken script reveals not only this apparatus of corruption, but smashes home the meaning of corruption; Mr. Smith is not merely a story of how a few million dollars may be stolen through the construction of a needless dam; it is a revelation of the vulnerability of the democratic method.

It falls short because it fails to suggest and develop thoughts of safeguards and remedies.

The democratic system is a system of balance. Of all the political systems
that have been invented by man it is the most difficult to follow because
we have not yet found a way of providing liberty and justice for the vast
majority, who are good, without permitting the same liberties to the rapacious and unscrupulous elements of the population who use their privileges
to enslave others. This weakness can sometimes prove fatal, as it proved
to the European democracies whose liberties coddled fascism. But the
greatest problem of our time is the question of whether such defeat is inherent in the democratic system, or whether it is the fault of the way in
which the system is used.

Obviously, in a perfect democracy, all citizens would be so conscious
and so jealous of their equalitarian powers that they would never relax
their vigilance to the point where political machines could be built within
the voting system. We in the United States have as a mass been sloppy and
careless and stupid and criminally negligent of our duties as voters; it is
only occasionally that a scandal of fantastic proportions, or a protracted
misrule of the Jersey City variety awakens us to the factual loss of the
power in our votes.

A picture like *Mr. Smith Goes to Washington* may be listed in that category of awakener. But it does not tell us what to do when awake; much
less does it tell us how to keep from falling asleep.

For what is the resolution of the problem, in *Mr. Smith?*

A situation of high individual drama is evolved, in which Mr. Smith,
framed by the political machine controlled by his state's super-tycoon,
finds himself on the point of being ousted from the Senate. He determines
to expose the machine before he is kicked out. He manages to get the floor,
and announces that he will keep the floor, and keep on talking until the
people of his state hear him and in some way make truth prevail.

There ensues a titanic struggle between young, slender Mr. Smith fili-
bustering on the floor of the Senate, and fat tycoon Taylor, boss of the
state, owner of newspapers and radio stations, nested in his den of telephones and teletypes, hurling orders for the suppression of Mr. Smith's
truth. The tycoon is able to control every newspaper in the state, and every
radio station in the state, he keeps the truth from the public, and instead
deluges them with lies and propaganda, smearing Smith as a swindler and
a proven thief, as a disgrace to the Senate; the tycoon sends out rabble-
rousers who hold meetings and parades against Smith, and finally he
arouses the public to the pitch where thousands of telegrams and letters
are sent to the Senate demanding that Smith be stopped, that he be thrown
out.

This becomes the "reply from the people" for which Smith has been waiting. Even the little four-page boy rangers' newspaper which Smith's kid-clubs print and try to distribute, in order to get the truth to the people, is ruthlessly squashed; the tycoon sends out truckloads of gangsters who run down the kids with their scooters full of newspapers.

And Smith, exhausted after nearly twenty-four hours of talking on the floor of the Senate, is confronted by the Silver Knight, his senior senator (who, unbeknownst to him is of course a tool of the tycoon), with the people's perverted answer: lack of faith.

Now here is the end of the film, as far as its value as a social document goes. Up to this point Messrs. Capra and Buchman have shown the operation of the spoilers of democracy; they have demonstrated the complete ruthlessness by which the Taylors stay in power, and, most important of all, they have shown how the public can become utterly unconscious of the vast fraud in which they themselves are used to pervert their own liberties. Freedom of the press is gone, freedom of speech is gone: except to that one lad clinging to the cliff: using the Senate's filibuster.

That little device is apparently all that Messrs. Capra and Buchman can suggest as a safeguard of democracy. If a man can talk long enough on the Senate floor, truth will somehow prevail, they suggest. Unfortunately, human endurance is limited.

Take away, then, the conventional bowknot tied at the end of *Mr. Smith:* the plot device requiring Claude Rains as the Silver Knight to have a stroke of conscience when his junior senator collapses on the floor, requiring Claude Rains to rush out into the hallway to shoot himself, and being prevented in this act, to rush back into the Senate and confess all, accusing the tycoons, exposing their frameup of the boy senator, winning the girl for the boy, making everybody happy: take away this conventional climax which fools nobody, and there remains a profoundly pessimistic photoplay. For, aside from the miraculous intervention of a remorseful boodler, the film suggests there is no way to break the throttling hold of the tycoons upon the throat of democracy, Mr. Taylor is completely successful in strangling the press and the radio, in strong-arming the feeble resistance of a few kids and a few reformers.

Now, this critic would be the last American to minimize the achievements of the Taylors. In most instances they are apparently successful. At this moment political and tycoon machines of one sort or another probably have more than a 50 percent control of all others in this country. It is a fact which the public stodgily and lazily accepts as a concomitant of democracy.

But I would ask that a film about democracy do more than state our dilemma. It must remind us of some of the ways to regain control, to re-establish the full meaning of our citizen government.

To do this, the solution of the dramatic crisis in the film would have had to be through a people's, rather than an individual's action. Young senators fainting on the floor will never prove or solve such dilemma. We cannot expect a Silver Knight to go out into the halls and try to commit suicide every time a chain of newspapers perverts the truth.

Have we no true remedies against such powers?

It may be that Mr. Capra felt it a necessity, in a photoplay, to find resolution in terms of a single Galahad's heroism. But on afterthought, and the supreme virtue of this photoplay is in its stimulation of afterthought, it appears that he muffs or throws away a very simple opportunity for an effective, affirmative solution of the play's crisis.

Mr. Smith's tycoon controls a state—but what of the nation? Capra shows us Mr. Kaltenborn (in person), at the microphone, broadcasting the news of the thrilling filibuster to a presumably nationwide audience, only a small proportion of which has been shut off by Mr. Taylor and his friends; we are shown how the press gallery becomes convinced of Mr. Smith's truth, and how the tone of the news despatches changes, until, we presume, newspapers all over the country, except in his own state, are headlining the news of his Galahad attack upon the malefactors of great wealth.

Now, a hole in a story often covers a lapse in logic; it seems to me that this is such a case: we must assume that Mr. Smith's appeal to the public for backing would arouse great response, outside of his own state, response sufficient enough to expose and overcome the manipulated localized public opinion as delivered by Mr. Taylor and the (tarnished) Silver Knight.

This factor is entirely omitted in the film; and by its omission Mr. Capra slights one of the safeguards of American democracy: the spread and largeness of America. It is not easy to fool all of the people even some of the time.

Let me hasten to affirm that I realize Mr. Capra's intention of statement through example, and that I am familiar with the literary and dramatic device which may be called the example in miniature. I know well enough that the entire national press is, in a major sense, controlled by and for tycoons, in the way that this photoplay shows the press of one state to be controlled. But I repeat that if Mr. Capra means to say that much, and only that much, by his picture, then he is a bitter and hopeless messenger.

For I think his picture could show that the resources of democracy are so great that it cannot be entirely suppressed. His picture could reveal the safeguard in our balancing of power between local governments and larger bodies of government, he could show how the state stands watch over the municipality, and the federal government stands watch over the state; which is essentially to show how all of the people of the entire United States stand behind the citizens of the smallest community, to help them retain their liberties if—and that is the great if—if they care enough about them.

Unfortunately, this wonderful power is but rarely exercised in pure manner. But the function of art as propaganda is twofold: to expose the flaws and abuses in our social system, and to remind us of what weapons there still remain to us, to correct such wrongs. *Mr. Smith Goes to Washington* does an admirable job on the first of these functions. In spite of itself, unless the makers are much more subtle than I give them credit for being, it performs some part of the second function; for the film cannot help making citizens question the situation in their own locality, and even question problems of national control, it cannot help arousing citizens to awareness and use of their citizenship. All that true democracy requires is watchfulness and participation from all the people. This point could have been more powerfully emphasized.

As to the technique of the production, it may be said that Mr. Capra presents in this film what amounts to the complete flowering of a style; and that the players, many of whom have now been associated with Capra in several films, perform not only with individual brilliance but with that element so rare in films: company cohesion. This is the best example to date of what may be called a genre in cinema, Capra being the largest contributor to the invention of this genre, and its best expositor; the style involves goodheartedness and heartiness; also, the ability to refrain from taking ourselves too seriously. Almost a symbol of this method of approach is Capra and Harry Carey's treatment of the Vice-President through all of the Senate sequences, including the crucial filibuster. Carey, without diminishing the gravity of any situation, is nevertheless constantly chuckling to himself, with a confidence of wisdom and experience, in the resources of the American system, for turning out an acceptable solution to any dilemma. We have not always done so; we have made tragic mistakes, and the total state of the people during the crisis years is not at all amusing; but we are less desperate than almost any other people on earth, and at least we can still kid ourselves. We still feel we have strength to waste, and that in an emergency we can buckle down and straighten things out.

That is the essential good humor in the Capra films. A few of the Capra tricks are somewhat overdone in *Mr. Smith;* they may be toned down by the time the film is generally released. James Stewart makes such a gosh-awful awkward oaf of Mr. Smith, in the scene with the elder senator's glamorous daughter, that we feel Mr. Capra is descending to slapstick for his laughs. Having the girl-flustered young senator back into a table, knocking over the lamp and knickknacks, is too cheap a stunt. Another gag which might be eliminated, but for a different reason, is the carrier-pigeon sequence; when Mr. Smith arrives in Washington he brings with him a crateful of his fliers. Obviously there must have been an intention to utilize the pigeons later in the script, perhaps to have pigeon flocks carry messages over the state when the radio and press were blocked. Fortunately we were spared this trick, but as it is, the entrance of the pigeons, while good for a laugh, is pointless, and could be dispensed with.

Perfect Capra touches abound; the best is the shot of the fat man getting out of a telephone booth.

Best-played scene in the film is Jean Arthur's rendition of the don't-give-up-the-fight speech to James Stewart as he sits on his suitcase at the foot of the Lincoln Memorial, ready to go home. Most forced scene is her drunken sequence. Most impressive performances are those of Harry Carey and Claude Rains, though Thomas Mitchell as a newspaperman nearly equals his mighty performance in last season's *Only Angels Have Wings.*

It is always annoying to have to wind up a review with the pointing out of minor flaws, minor excellencies, with the crediting of all who deserve credit, and such chores. A picture of this sort, it should be repeated, goes beyond entertainment. It is a pure lesson in civics. And it is one of the great triumphs of the democratic method that such a film of self-criticism can be made, and universally shown, in our land.

Esquire, January 1940

THE GRAPES OF WRATH

HOWARD BARNES

A great film has come out of Hollywood called *The Grapes of Wrath.* Based on John Steinbeck's account of the "Okie" hegira from the dust bowl to California, it is an honest, eloquent, and challenging screen masterpiece. Great artistry has gone into its making and greater courage, for this screen tribute to the dispossessed not only has dramatized the large theme of Mr. Steinbeck's novel in enduring visual terms—it has demonstrated beyond any question that the cinema can take the raw stuff of contemporary living and mold it to a provocative photoplay pattern. For once in a long, long time the screen has made electric contact with the abiding verities of existence in *The Grapes of Wrath,* and the result is a heart-shaking and engrossing motion picture.

When it was first announced for production many of us had grave doubts as to the book's eventual materialization as a film. The former was a tough, authentic account of the plight of sharecroppers and homesteaders run off their barren Southwest acres by tractor farming and ganged up on when they became migratory laborers in the rich valleys of southern California.

It was the very antithesis of the fairy tales and the romantic and melo-dramatic stereotypes which Hollywood fancies. It is all the more to the credit, then, of Twentieth Century-Fox and the craftsmen in that organization who made the current offering that it is even more tough and authentic than Mr. Steinbeck's original. Here is a film which speaks straight and passionately of things close to the hearts of the people.

As is always the case when the screen is flooded with beauty and deep feeling, *The Grapes of Wrath* is the product of consummate collaboration. Nunnally Johnson, who has run the scrivening gamut in Hollywood from the thoughtful and memorable *The House of Rothschild* to the synthetic and preposterously successful *Jesse James,* has adapted the novel so superbly that it would be difficult to give him too much credit for a triumph of artistry and showmanship. John Ford, who has few peers among the directors, has staged the work with extraordinary skill, understanding, and feeling. The players, from Henry Fonda's embittered Tom Joad to Dorris Bowdon's bewildered Rosasharn, act their parts like figures in the mainstream of history rather than puppets in a shallow bit of make-believe. For my part I would give Gregg Toland, the cameraman, special commendation for the way he has photographed scenes of this modern Odyssey in the stark terms of the documentary film.

In any case, *The Grapes of Wrath* is a film which should mean, for nearly everyone, an exciting and enriching emotional experience. Mr. Johnson has lopped off the embarrassing and lurid ending of the Steinbeck novel, in which Rosasharn feeds a starving migrant, and has knit the whole tale into a stunning screen unity. The tale starts with Tom pounding a state road in prison boots; it documents the Joad flight from dust storms and eviction to the supposed land of milk and honey in California in magnificent fashion, and it ends on a note of tremendous conviction as it has Tom going off to be "wherever there's a fight so hungry people can eat" and Ma voicing that challenge to the whole of present-day existence with: "We're the people that live. Can't nobody wipe us out."

While Mr. Johnson has turned out a script which is close to perfect in its appreciation of an original and sure sense of screen values, Mr. Ford has used all of his great talent to give it the overt and subtle statement which a director alone can achieve. He has launched the production slowly, but it builds to a terrifying crescendo as the Joads are beaten down by the self-constituted law officers of a hostile California and find a grim recipe for modern living. Meanwhile, he has directed a large company with brilliant knowledge of their capabilities.

Mr. Fonda, for example, has never been better on the screen than he is as the surly but reasonable Tom. John Carradine, in the role of the preacher who loses the call but becomes a martyr to the cause of the dispossessed, is extremely good; Miss Bowdon is fine as Rosasharn, and Charley Grapewin, Russell Simpson, O. Z. Whitehead and Zeffie Tilbury make various members of the Joad clan take on memorable contours. Jane Darwell, as Ma, misses some of the desperate courage which the part had in the book. On the whole, though, the acting is first rate. *The Grapes of Wrath* is a collaboration, as all fine photoplays must be. It has flaws, as any extensive collaboration would predicate. But, taken by and large, it is a genuinely great motion picture which makes one proud to have even a small share in the affairs of the cinema.

The New York Herald Tribune, January 25, 1940

Edwin Locke was in charge of photographic research for the U.S. Film Service and worked on such productions as *The Fight for Life* and *Ecce Homo.*

Martin Quigley, the publisher of *The Motion Picture Herald* and other trade journals, was coauthor of the restrictive Production Code drawn up in 1930. Martin Dies (D., Texas) was the first chairman of the House Committee on Un-American Activities.

THE GRAPES OF WRATH

EDWIN LOCKE

Mr. Martin Quigley and various other spokesmen of the *movie business* will continue to demand that the commercial screen be reserved exclusively for the presentation of elegant untruths, gilded dreams, and badly refracted memories. Mr. Quigley has proved many times that social, religious, political, or economic problems are not fit subjects for the motion picture. He insists that American audiences, for whom he presumingly speaks, want nothing for their money but entertainment, undefined. But he is not fooling the men who put *The Grapes of Wrath* on the screen. He is not fooling the producers and working people of the industry, nor Twentieth Century-Fox, nor the Chase National Bank. He is not fooling anybody, because audiences who have never heard of Mr. Quigley are crowding the box offices and breaking into spontaneous applause after each screening of the picture.

Hollywood knows that a good deal of box office turnout can be bought with heavy investment in stars, publicity, and production, as in *Gone*

With the Wind; but it also knows that no investment can purchase the little restless movements of an audience building up a static charge of excitement and appreciation which finally breaks out in crackles and little thunder of applause. The reactionaries of the *movie business* who have fastened themselves to the production of motion pictures, like shark suckers to their host, would seem to be in the position of having to revise their concept of the audience or to enlarge their definition of what constitutes entertainment. They may prefer to believe that those who remained in their seats to applaud *The Grapes of Wrath* were Leftists of one sort or another. Unfortunately, that belief leads to the unpleasant conclusion that the American audience is lefter than they think. The critics too would seem to be bidding for honorable mention by Mr. Dies.

A great picture has been produced and the verbal flares and bombshells of the critics have not been touched off altogether without occasion. The realization that motion picture history has been made is calling forth audible appreciation from the usually silent tiers of watchful darkness. The crowds—typical crowds of clerks, homebodies, casuals, and intellectuals—are deeply impressed by the outcome of what looks like singular intrepidity on the part of Mr. Darryl Zanuck.

The motives compelling Mr. Zanuck to buy *The Grapes of Wrath* and to produce from it a motion picture that loses none of the sincerity and power of the book have been widely speculated upon. Those who have been wondering forget that he is still a good businessman. Although *The Grapes of Wrath* is his finest, it is not his first venture into sociological themes. He has been quick in perceiving and exploiting the current interest of the public, whether it be directed toward gangsters, chain gangs, or Oklahoma migrants. He may be also possessed of information which leads him to believe that audiences are a little tired of the usual vast and stupid antics of Hollywood. But whatever his motives, he cannot be denied courage and vision for his part in bringing John Steinbeck's novel, artistically intact, to the screen.

The filming of *The Grapes of Wrath* took more than a decision to be faithful to the book. Producer, director, cameraman, actors, all were confronted by new material which demanded that they discard some of the comfortable certainties of the average Hollywood production and learn how to bring something of the quality of real people to the screen. Meanwhile, the watchful and belligerent gaze of Steinbeck was upon them.

Nunnally Johnson has used his disposition and ability to think in terms of people to make an excellent script from the novel. He has articulated the main episodes of the book into a straight line of action so that the gain in power and simplicity offsets a good deal of the loss in perspective. In his handling of the dialogue he has used the same discriminating selection, almost always going to the book for his lines, but not hesitating to transpose lines among the characters where the purposes of the film seem better served by the changes. For the most part the dialogue has the ring of the people's language, and he has made John Ford's task a little easier by holding long speeches to a minimum. After wondering why Johnson's script treated hardly at all of the destruction of the land, which was so effective and necessary a prelude to the book and regretting that the woolly lines about how the people go on and on are handed to Ma to end the picture, there is nothing to cavil with.

None of the gains made by Johnson have been lost in John Ford's direction. There is no hesitation, no milling around on film. That the master of dark milieu and driven men has a powerful way of putting people on film is a matter of record in *The Informer, Lost Patrol,* and *Stagecoach.* Ford's work in *Grapes of Wrath* is outstanding again in terms of people. His sense of the value of a face, of a voice, of a posture, of clothing, has served him well in his excellent casting of the supporting players: the truckdrivers, migrants, deputies, and vigilantes. And Ford has done more than to choose good examples of real people. He has come upon something that could never have been discovered in the studios: a realization of the highly developed awareness which the common people of the world have of one another. He has used the knowledge in the memorable scenes of the picture: in the lunchroom where Pa Joad buys a loaf of bread; in the first migrant camp entered by the Joads, where we get a full and immediate understanding of their plight, not only from the wretched tents and pasteboard hovels and the litter, but also from the apathetic curiosity of the miserable squatters as silent notice of the new arrival runs intuitively through the camp; in the very first part of the scene where the kids of the same camp, attracted by Ma's stew, gather to beg silently, realizing the needlessness of words; in the masterful scene of the dance in the government camp where the direction measures up to Steinbeck's full meaning by a brilliant handling of mass and detail that would have been impossible if Ford had not understood the innate decency and joy of life and goodness which bloom in the lowliest people with the slightest encouragement. It is a pity that Ford's sense of environment has not come through as well as his sense of people. The opening of the picture is greatly weakened because he has given us no feeling of the country or of the people's background. Where are the vast stretches of the dust bowl and the tiny houses as lonely as ships at sea? Where is the dust? It is hard to believe that Ford has ever seen *The Plow That Broke the Plains.* It is baffling to hear that a camera crew was sent into Oklahoma along Route 66; certainly but a few feet of their film was used. It is regrettable that the Joads were snatched across the beautiful and terrifying expanses of the country in a few pans and process shots; we could justly have expected more. We could have expected more of what it is like to be tractored off the land, more than the knocking over of a prop house by a Caterpillar roaming at large, more than a hackneyed montage of clanking monsters in abstract maneuvers. We might have had all these things, and a richer picture, if Ford had followed a little further the documentary technique that is now being talked about in connection with his work.

Like Ford, Gregg Toland, director of photography, has a long record of fine work. The excellence of his photography in *Grapes of Wrath* cannot be appreciated fully without realizing what it means to a Hollywood cameraman to be denied the use of most of his cozy little studio tricks: backlighting, baby spots, gauzes, and diffusion: and to be called upon as well to shoot players without make-up. Toland has worked the hard way and has distinguished himself by the naturalness of lighting throughout most of the film. His work is beautiful, once or twice too beautiful, too reminiscent of *Wuthering Heights*. There are beautiful skies in Oklahoma and westward, but they are not the skies Toland has given us.

The work of director, writer, and cameraman could have been considerably enhanced by a good musical score. Alfred Newman has provided little more than a fitful accompaniment by dragging two undistinguished come-all-ye's thinly through the picture. Oscar Levant has written that for some reason or other two government pictures he has seen have been unique in their intelligent use of music. Mr. Newman, as well as Mr. Levant, might look more closely into that reason.

The casting of *The Grapes of Wrath* strikes a good average somewhere between the fine choice of Henry Fonda as Tom Joad and the unhappy selection of Charley Grapewin as Grampa. Fonda, in playing Tom, knows what the story is about and what he is about in relation to it. He gives a fine performance throughout, and one of his finest bits is the scene in which he chases the hungry kids from the stewpot, using an apologetic gruffness to cover his sympathy and the unpleasant logic of his common sense. Jane Darwell, as Ma Joad, seems a less fortunate choice. Although she plays intelligently, no amount of experience or artistry could make her look like a woman of the Oklahoma people. A lean, stringy rawhide woman would have been excellent for the part, or a woman heavy with unhealthy flesh, but never a firm, plump, shiny woman like Darwell's Ma, who defies wearing down even after a catastrophe and the long trek from Sallisaw County to Fresno. John Carradine makes a good Casy except for several times in the opening scenes where he looks like a Zombie. Dorris Bowdon makes of Rosasharn a shy, sweet girl, entirely passive in character and not very convincingly pregnant despite help from the family in pointing out her condition. John Qualen's Muley is excellently fey. Russell Simpson's bewildered and ineffectual Pa is adequate. Grampa and Granma are a silly pair of japes. The superb casting of the supporting players has already been remarked.

Hollywood has given us in the past a fine series of frontier epics: the great American romance of a people hacking its way westward through forests and redskins, the quiet courage of pioneers in wagon trains lurching along the Santa Fe trail surrounded by a big still rim of hostile eyes that might close in at any moment in a grotesque carrousel dealing death by gunshot and arrow. But not before *The Grapes of Wrath* has it given us a picture that totalled, in human values, some of the results of our drive to the frontier. The cost of making a grabbag of our country, while it has provided stirring subject matter for the art of Pare Lorentz in *The Plow That Broke the Plains* and *The River,* has never before been reckoned by Hollywood. Now, in one brave leap, the industry has caught up with at least one phase of our current economic history. By touching on some of the results of land speculation, submarginal farming, agricultural mechanization, and the California latifundia, *The Grapes of Wrath* has set a precedent for contemporary and historical honesty in movie-making. It has dramatized and memorialized one wretched section of the victims of American history. No succeeding picture can alter or erase the gaunt, hungry image of the tractored-out farmer menaced in his struggle to keep alive no longer by Indians, but by starvation.

> *The big fellows is workin' their farms with tractors an'*
> *   day labor . . .*
> *The peoples is walking the road, looking for places.*

That is one of our twentieth-century psalms, the words of an Oklahoman, recorded in the field by the photographer Dorothea Lange, the wisest and most compassionate observer at work in our country, whose book, *An American Exodus,* is the result of her study of migratory workers up and down the country since 1934. Those words are a simple summary of *The Grapes of Wrath,* and the proof of the picture's greatness lies in the fact that it is as simple, as dignified, and as moving as the statement of one of the people.

Mr. Quigley, referred to at the outset of this review, has been brooding forebodingly over the consequences to the screen of the production of *The Grapes of Wrath.* What they may be he does not state, but it is unlikely that they will be unpleasant to any but members of the Old Guard of the *movie business.* How much longer audiences will continue to gape at the usual run of vapid and distant dreams when they can have, if they support them, beautiful and stirring accounts of reality like *The Grapes of Wrath* is still a matter for speculation. The public reaction toward *The Grapes of Wrath* will give the answer. The steady decline in attendance at the movies, traceable mainly to boredom with the average Hollywood product, offers some encouragement. If Hollywood persists in squandering most of its energies of talent and wealth in making pictures considered good enough for the audience by the *movie business,* it will sooner or later run up against the fact that there are not enough Shirley Temple devotees left in this country to go around. If *The Grapes of Wrath* achieves the success it deserves, perhaps some elementary calculations will be made by the producers of bad pictures. Perhaps Mr. Quigley will permit the audience to enlarge the scope of its desires.

Those who expect that the major result of *The Grapes of Wrath* will be some sort of change in Hollywood's attitude toward what it does would seem to be more realistic than those who expect something in the way of a social upheaval close upon the run of the picture. Most people already feel that something should be done about the migratory workers. The picture will undoubtedly make more converts to the idea of government-owned and -operated camps for the dispossessed. Few will derive from the picture—and it is the picture's fault, not theirs—that the plight of the people they pity is the result of a land tragedy, a terrible blunder of our civilization for which all of us will eventually suffer if more strenuous and rational efforts of correction are not quickly made. The picture may stir up bad blood in the more backward parts of the country among those who fear its message, but it is unlikely that the reaction will be violent or widespread. There is no chance, as some people seem to think, that those who consider themselves as badly off as the Joads will arise with clenched fists after seeing *The Grapes of Wrath*. After all, the picture has two endings. The spirit of burning revolt in Tom Joad is overlaid by the final smugness of the incredible Ma. Her ultimate realization that *we* are the people, that *we* will go on even if *they* bash in *our* heads with sawed-off bats and cuesticks, that *we,* the meek, shall inherit the earth, may put comforting and proud thoughts into the heads of the wretched, but like many other middle-class philosophies, hers are not the words which move men, except in the endless and overgrown paths of acceptance.

Films, Spring 1940

This brief review notes that an era of French film was being ended by war.

DAYBREAK
(Le Jour Se Lève)

Daybreak is built on a dramatic foundation often tried and usually untrue: the device of discovering a character in a narrow corner, where he sits obligingly remembering his story for the camera. The story that passes before the blank eyes of François (Jean Gabin) in his garret room, as the police stand waiting for him on the street beneath, is strange and more worth remembering than most. François is a happy workman on a sanding machine when he meets Françoise (Jacqueline Laurent) on their saint's day. Pursuing elusive young Françoise, he meets worldly-wise Clara (Arletty). Over both women has been cast the dark and fascinating spell of Valentin (Jules Berry), an aging dog trainer who loves to tell lies and make simple people unhappy. When François climbs to his garret for the last time, Valentin has accomplished his masterpiece.

Not up to *Grand Illusion* or *La Kermesse Héroïque, Daybreak,* perhaps the last major product of a cinema industry that was as long on brains as it was short on budget, is a worthy swan song. It has the same distinguishing Gallic qualities of artistic shrewdness and spiritual disenchantment that make most Hollywood pictures by comparison seem, for better or for worse, not quite grown-up.

Time, August 19, 1940

FANTASIA

FRANZ HOELLERING

Fantasia, the newest Walt Disney production, is a promising monstrosity and an experiment containing many lessons. There is enough in it to make up for the shocks one suffers. And to be shocked in these times of blood and tears by the handling of a problem of art is in itself an experience of temporary relief.

The essentially new and essentially problematic in *Fantasia* is the use of great music as accompaniment for Walt Disney cartoons. To be sure we are told that it is the other way around, and no doubt the intent was the opposite one, but the effects achieved are nevertheless Walt Disney plus Bach or Beethoven. And the audience applauded exactly where it would have applauded if the score had been composed by a Hollywood musician. Specific pictorial innovations of characteristic Walt Disney charm delighted most. Yet to have the *Pastoral Symphony* interrupted by applause for sugar-sweet centaurettes is painful.

The program tells us that Walt Disney and his staff, "faced with the tremendous problem of translating the music of *Fantasia* (Bach, Beethoven, Dukas, Stravinsky, Ponchielli, Moussorgsky, Schubert) into pictures, simply listened and tried to capture the moods, movements, situations, colors, and characters which the music painted on the canvas of their imaginations." The result is, the program continues, "that kind of entertainment which has been described as 'seeing music and hearing pictures.' "

I belong to those who had no need of that kind of entertainment, being content with seeing pictures and hearing music. And I was never particularly concerned whether I had to hear, see (read), or smell in order to have a great experience. In *Fantasia* the paintings on the canvas of Walt Disney's and his staff's imaginations did not help but most of the time disturbed my appreciation of the music they tried to make me "see." One of two reasons, or both of them, may be chiefly responsible: either these imaginations did not live up to Bach and Beethoven and Schubert, or the whole idea of adding pictures to music composed to be appreciated best with the eyes closed is fundamentally wrong. I am sure of the first reason, not so sure of the second. There is a short moment in *Fantasia* when picture and music fit admirably together, and the experience is heightened by the combination; this is the moment in *Night on Bald Mountain* when the Black God reaches down into the village (art direction by Key Nielsen). But generally the discrepancy between pictures and music is deplorable, especially between the *Pastoral* and the sweet Olympus of the scene, or between the *Rite of Spring* and its popular-science illustrations, or between the *Ave Maria* and the *Kitsch* landscapes. And no wonder! There just does not exist—not even in Hollywood and not even in Walt Disney's admirable company—a staff of geniuses. One would need a Michelangelo or a Breughel to "picture" the music of Beethoven.

Where the music itself deals with a more or less conventional story, like Dukas's *The Sorcerer's Apprentice* (Goethe's *Zauberlehrling*), there is of course no problem, and one can enjoy Disney at his known best. Mickey Mouse as apprentice is a natural, and more delightful than ever. The same holds for the picturing of such ballet music as Ponchielli's *Dance of the Hours.* Disney uses this score for an unforgettable parody, his dancers being elephants, rhinoceroses, and ostriches. Profoundly sound, too, is the visualization of the *Nutcracker Suite,* music also written around a story. It does not matter that Disney's fantasy is different from that of the original *Nutcracker* tale. In certain details he achieves here the best effects he has ever achieved. The mushroom dancers will be loved all over the world—may the whole world soon be able to see them!

In technical respects the picture is of unsurpassed quality. New methods and tricks of all kinds had to be invented to produce the hundreds of new effects never seen before. In the color photography, in the lighting—everywhere one notices great progress.

Fantasia, in spite of shortcomings partly due to the exploring character of the whole, partly to fundamental errors, is a work of promise. One day, one feels, Walt Disney and his people may produce a film which will truly combine all the different branches of art.

Leopold Stokowski, with the Philadelphia Orchestra, and Deems Taylor, functioning also as the film's commentator, are responsible for the musical aspects of the picture, with which Mr. Haggin will concern himself. I leave to him also discussion of the new technique, "Fantasound," especially designed for the recording and reproduction of Fantasia.

The Nation, November 23, 1940

B. H. Haggin has been writing music criticism, exceptional and exceptionally iconoclastic, since 1923 for many serious journals. Among his books are *Conversations with Toscanini* and *Music Observed.*

Deems Taylor, a composer of limited merit, achieved popularity as a radio commentator on music. Walter Damrosch, composer and conductor, spent many of his last years on music popularization. Karl Muck, a German conductor of high reputation, was the leader of the Boston Symphony from 1906 until the United States entered the First War.

FANTASIA

B. H. HAGGIN

If *Fantasia* were being shown in the way anything else of Disney's is shown —that is, just the sequences of images and music with no verbal introductions in the program or from the screen—one would take it as one takes anything else of Disney's: as something primarily and chiefly for the eye. One takes a Disney film in this way despite its occasional use of music; and one would take *Fantasia* in this way even though the music was by important composers and was used in the film sequences as it is in a ballet. And taking it in this way one would not be too upset when the music was misused.

One would, that is, note that in certain instances—the Chinese Dance and Russian Dance of Tschaikovsky's *Nutcracker Suite,* and Dukas's *L'ap-*

prenti sorcier—the pictorial sequences had the feeling for the quality of the music that is revealed in the "Hand of Fate" pas de deux which Balanchine devised for Chabrier's music in *Cotillon*. One would note in other instances the use of music without such feeling for its essential quality, and without regard even for specified programmatic meaning and for organic structure. Disney's Water Ballet may be charming, but Tschaikovsky's music is an Arabian Dance. The first and second movements of Beethoven's *Pastoral Symphony* have programmatic meaning, but only of a generalized sort—only as much as is embodied in the "pastoral" idiom of the first, the murmuring strings of the second, not Disney's charming pictures of flying horses in the first, nor his monkeyshines of centaurettes in the second; moreover, the music establishes an emotional level for any imagery associated with it—a level which some of the centaur-centaurette details fall far below; and finally, with the country indicated by the "pastoral" idiom of the first movement, the emotions aroused by the country are embodied in a purely formal design which is not indicated in the pictures of *Fantasia* and is destroyed even in the music—the exposition of material being used without the development and recapitulation that make out of his material the organic sequence which *is* the first movement of Beethoven's *Pastoral Symphony*. One would note the similar inadequacy of the pictures to the content and quality of Stravinsky's *Sacre du printemps,* and the fact that the work was not only chopped up but rearranged. One would note that Disney failed equally when he set out to be faithful to large-scale musical content and structure—when for the purely formal design of sounds in combination and motion in Bach's *Toccata and Fugue* he created a purely formal design of line, mass, and color in motion, a literal sight-for-sound translation (like Massine's of the final passacaglia movement of Brahms's *Fourth*) which did not even remotely represent the substance and organic development and structural complexity of Bach's music or exert anything remotely comparable with the power of the music's formal eloquence. But in the situation I have assumed, in which *Fantasia* would be offered as something for the eye, these things would not be anything to get upset about, as they are in the actual situation, in which *Fantasia* is offered as a presentation of the music—in the combined form of the sound itself and a pictorial representation of its meaning, quality, structure.

Actually, that is, one is handed a program which opens to a statement by Stokowski that "the beauty and inspiration of music must not be restricted to a privileged few but made available to every man, woman, and child. That is why great music associated with motion pictures is so important, because motion pictures reach millions all over our country and all over the world." This act of Stokowski's, in which he brings to the many what has been jealously withheld from them by the privileged few, was phony even ten years ago when with four one-hour broadcasts spread over months he first brought the beauty and inspiration of music to those who had been hearing Toscanini's two-hour broadcasts with the New York Philharmonic every Sunday. But even if one accepts Stokowski's assumption that the millions who will see *Fantasia* have never heard a broadcast of a symphony or an opera, then it is a matter of great concern that what is offered to them as the first movement of Beethoven's *Pastoral*—to consider only the music itself—is the exposition of material without the development and recapitulation which continue and complete the organic sequence; that they are offered Stravinsky's *Sacre* chopped up and rearranged, its essential quality falsified by things like the perfumed phrasing of the stark opening woodwind passages, the lush sonorities elsewhere; that Bach's *Toccata and Fugue,* played complete, is falsified by a performance which imparts to it the feverish excitement that Stokowski imparts to any music he conducts, and which makes of it the mere succession of dazzling effects of orchestral virtuosity and sonority that music is for him.

But *Fantasia* does not offer the music by itself; and a couple of pages further one reads that the "movements, situations, colors, and characters which the music painted on the canvas of [the Disney artists'] imaginations" should make the average listener "much less humble about his ability to understand good music." Images of movements, situations, colors and characters are properly the effect of program music; but not any and all such images; and it is a matter of some concern that millions of people should be given the idea that images like Disney's represent understanding of some of the program music in *Fantasia.* Moreover, it is questionable whether from music with generalized programmatic significance like the first movement of the *Pastoral Symphony* one should derive anything more specific than the impression of "country" from the "pastoral" idiom, and whether, for the rest, the effect of the movement should not be that of its formal design. Of this formal design, obviously, representational images of characters and situations are not properly the effect; but neither are nonrepresentational images, such as Disney offers with Bach's purely formal *Toccata and Fugue.* Speaking from the screen, Deems Taylor introduces this sequence with the statement that "what you will see . . . is a picture of the various abstract images that might pass through your mind if you sat in a concert hall listening to this music." The fish swims, the woodpecker pecks, and Mr. Taylor—called on to speak about music—exercises his extraordinary capacity for subtly, and in effect treacherously, obfuscatory statement that gives error the appearance of reasonableness and truth themselves. I once cited an example worth recalling now—his statement that Walter Damrosch "never was a Karl Muck, and I don't believe he ever wanted to be one. He seems curiously impatient of ultra-subtle readings of the classics"—which converted the difference between Damrosch and Muck into a difference between simplicity and ultrasubtlety, and Damrosch's inadequacy into a defect in Muck. And in the present instance there are implicit in Taylor's statement, as though they were true, certain ideas that are false: the idea that the images which accompany Bach's *Toccata and Fugue*—images contrived by long and hard imaginative effort—are the kind that would pass through anyone's mind at a concert, or the ones that did pass through the Disney artists' minds in this casual way; the idea that these images can be taken as the proper effect of Bach's *Toccata and Fugue;* the idea, in general, that images are the proper effect of such music. It is cause for great concern that millions of people are to be given these ideas about music; and on this point there is more to say, but it will have to wait.

The Nation, January 11, 1941

THE GREAT DICTATOR

PAUL GOODMAN

1. If this singular film were not by Chaplin and with Chaplin, it would be both more satisfying on first view and less integral and comprehensible on reflection. More satisfying because we'd take the laughs without expecting the perfect comic continuity, which is not here, and without disgust at the poor timing. We'd never give a second thought to the calamitous music (Meredith Willson) nor the feeble dialogue. The persistent lapses in style —in the color of the photography, unity of the sets, formality of the acting of the secondary roles—would even be in the usual order of things. And the democratic Message, direct address to the audience and all, would belong only to the political bias of the spectator to judge: he would call it collective security or Aid to Britain depending on the date he likes to project himself and the film into; he might wonder a bit at the words "gentleness," "unnatural men," etc.; in any case it would all seem out of place, "out of character" as the critics have agreed to call it. But it's Charlie Chaplin! and what have these remarks to do with him? For instance, what possibly is the meaning of "lapses in style" when applied to Charlie Chaplin? Therefore I have had to turn to the following *genetic* considerations to explain the puzzle; and perhaps to find that this is something different, and something better, than the "grandiose failure" of the worried reviewers.

2. From the earliest two-reelers, the Chaplin hero was, of course, the square peg in the round hole; but this genus was specified by several con-

siderations: (a) the environment to which the hero could not quite adjust was realistic, not fantastic; (b) it was in principle *approved,* so that the hero had to try to make an adjustment—this was the pathetic humor of "good intentions" and "try, try again";.(c) the comic difficulty of the hero was not common to others, all were not in the same boat—this was the "isolated and lonely Charlie," the "one black sheep"; (d) yet the courageous little hero was not excluded because he was a freak, but somehow because he had a power and duty *freer* than the reality. This last point is capital; because by it the comedy became absolute, distinct from that kind of comedy which turns on some original disproportion in the hero or situation which is ultimately reconciled, as, e.g., in Buster Keaton. By it, too, a strong irony is cast over the attempts of the hero himself (point b) to make an adjustment; so that not only the indifferent in the environment is comically criticized, but the good as the hero sees it is comic in the same way. Along these lines, I think, we can explain the remarkable comic continuity of such long films as *The Kid, The Gold Rush,* and *Modern Times;* for the set-up in them is such that there is no distinction in kind between the slapstick of jarring with mechanical nature and the humor of the jarring characters and desires. Put otherwise: the audience need not change its attitude from sequence to sequence. It is within this master conception that the development among the films, from 1915 to 1935, takes place: it consists of the enlargement of the comic environment from, say, the Murphy-bed of *One A. M.* to the assembly-line of *Modern Times;* and with this, naturally, a corresponding intellectualizing and refining of the thoughts and desires of the Little Man (as Chaplin calls him). Now there is no reason why this development could not have proceeded also into the political environment, even the environment of international politics; and finally, I suppose, into the divine order of the worlds so we could have had the Comic Angel in the celestial choir. (Let us hope we are to have him still!)

3. This is not the development in *The Great Dictator.* Rather we suddenly find that the environment is in principle *not approved;* the poet finds, suddenly, that it is wicked to try to make an adjustment to the Nazi order. Then note: (a) A completely different kind of comedy appears, comic Invective, directive satire, which turns not on the relation between an approved situation and an amiable individual, but on the immediate assault, in a multitude of debasing parodies, on the situation itself, as against a possible approved situation. We here see the introduction of the remarkable contraries "Unnatural" and "Natural." (b) But in the second place, contrasted with the Unnatural object of the Invective, we find the Natural amiable situation becoming a noncomic object of desire, for which we try try again; therefore, *all irony is withdrawn from these efforts*—the life in the Ghetto—and the relevant comedy, far from absolute, turns on the fact

that these people have human frailties, mainly inveterate hopefulness and pacifism, which can be altered, and in the resolution of the film are altered. Then, instead of a single comic conception, continuous from slapstick to the most probing comedy of life, we have at least the following three kinds of comedy: (a) Invective against the unnatural Nazi regime; (b) Sentimental handling of the natural life in the Ghetto; (c) Slapstick in the two environments: 1. Amongst themselves the unnatural men are natural men, and we can return to the older unitary conception, as in the slapstick relation of Herring and Hynkel, or pre-eminently in the relation of Hynkel and Napaloni, where Hynkel is the Little Man!—a slapstick which passes over without break into the most tear-moving burlesque, as the Balloon Dance. 2. Slapstick in the Ghetto, for the natural men are only men—so, Charlie with the derby and the cane, or the puddings with the coins. It is clear in several places that Chaplin toyed with the immensely elaborate idea of having the Barber be transformed from the older role of the hopeless hoper to the new role of resident in an evil order.

An analysis such as this explains well enough the construction of the film in parallel plot-strands, related indirectly through thoughts and causes rather than directly through will and action.

4. (a) The invective against Hynkel is to my taste all-powerful: disgust expressed by the basest tricks of low vaudeville, gibberish, belching, dirty words, and radio static. You will not find the like outside of Juvenal. It is so successful that even many of the slapstick errors do not fail to create the impression "Good! hit 'im again!" On the other hand, the personal Hynkel is not the political Hitler, a point to which I must return. (b) The sentimental comedy is catastrophic. Concerning Maurice Moscovich and Paulette Goddard I don't know what to say, but the pain in the neck is with me as I write. But the coup de grace is the sunlit agriculture of Osterlich-Tel Aviv-Pasadena. Nevertheless! paradoxically I shall almost argue that it is just these horrors which lead to a kind of triumph, the major triumph, of the film as a whole. (c) The slapstick and burlesque, it cannot be denied, badly weaken the force of the invective. It's no doubt a kind of invective to show that a dictator is all too human, but slapstick in general involves at least neutrality toward the victim, and Chaplin slapstick almost always turns out with the victim made amiable; it is a kind of pat of approval. In itself, however, the Hynkel-Napaloni business is a first-rate example of the ordinary; and the burlesque character-exploration of the soulful Hynkel is often great. I must speak of the Ballon Dance again: this is almost the only dance in the movies so far (the others are in Chaplin's other films); he fills the screen and the whole screen dances, so the processions of Eisenstein dance; and the strains of *Lohengrin* are pat as can be.

5. Hynkel is not Hitler. It is clear from the foregoing that this Hitler can be only the natural and unnatural man to whom Chaplin's old little

man can entertain personal feelings. There is absolutely no political comedy in the film. Propaganda, in the person of Herr Garbitsch, is treated with solemnity. Where, for instance, is the comedy of the atrocities that would exhaust the Phooey's patience and be the prelude to invasion? English mustard lays the dictators low, but where is the comedy of non-intervention, etc., etc.? Certainly the real Hitler and his real world are, in their dry way, funnier than Chaplin's Adenoid Hynkel. But if Chaplin had in fact engaged in a more objective satire, it seems to me that the most precious effect of the entire film would have been lost. This brings me to my last point.

6. Except for a few documentaries, like Joris Ivens' *Spanish Earth, The Great Dictator* strikes me—obviously I cannot speak for any one else on this point—as the only earnest propaganda film. How is this amazing effect achieved? Most, perhaps, by the ring of autobiography never absent from Chaplin's art, the ring which made the song at the end of *Modern Times* seem the pathetic return of the great silent mime to the singing variety performer. In this film, for instance, what is the significance of the curious amnesia after the memory of *Shoulder Arms?* It is achieved, again, by the very restriction of the invective to what the Chaplin we really know and are sure of can express by the means or the genre of means, and the kind of feelings, that belong to *him*. Again, by the unashamed representation, once he has withdrawn the irony from them, of the *very same sentimental ideals* which are tearful *and* funny in *The Vagabond, The Kid, Modern Times*. To say this rather wickedly, many a spectator might think that the ecstatic last close-ups of Miss Goddard aren't so pretty as all that, but there is not the least doubt that Charlie thinks she is just beautiful. So, to return to the celebrated Message-speech at the end of the film: it does not seem to me, as it did to most others, that he here steps "out of character"; on the contrary, this speech is just the character of the Jewish Barber (who was at no moment made unrestrainedly funny). The speech is too long, it is not even well spoken throughout; but when he says, "We think too much and feel too little" and "Now we must fight!" —we know that the context for the truth or falsity of these propositions has been fairly given to us by the speaker; if this isn't meant from the heart, we have been deceived for twenty-five years.

Partisan Review, November/December 1940

Rudolf Arnheim was born in Germany and published his first film book there. He came to the United States in 1940 and taught at various institutions. He is now professor of Psychology of Art at Harvard University. He has written *Film as Art, Art and Visual Perception,* and *Visual Thinking.*

Sir Nevile Henderson was British ambassador to Germany at the outbreak of World War II and wrote *Failure of a Mission.*

THE GREAT DICTATOR

RUDOLF ARNHEIM

In my opinion there are two men able to make a great film on Hitler and fascism. One of them is Erich von Stroheim, whose film probably never will be made because it would push the cruel truth too far beyond anything a film producer can accept. The other man is Charles Chaplin, and he has already offered his film. Chaplin saw the great theme of our day and did not shrink from grappling with it, despite its considerable risks, artistic as well as personal. *The Great Dictator* emerges as a film full of the authentic Chaplin genius, a work far above anything the pleasure industry is able to turn out. And still there are many of us who feel that in it Chaplin did not fully realize his intentions.

Here is the most striking subject our epoch has to offer to an artist. Here is an enemy of mankind, a Goliath, who can be met not only on the battlefield of bombs and castor oil, but also with the weapons of the spirit, a brute who can be partially disarmed, at any rate, by ridicule. And Chaplin seemed the David who could do it.

For what is the comic essence of the screen character created by Chaplin some twenty-five years ago? He is a poor man, not conscious and certainly not proud of his state, pathetically eager to imitate the smart elegance of the rich that he admires as his superiors. His vain attempts to pass for a dandy, with a swagger cane and a fop's mustache—the sharp contrast between a vain intention and a miserable effect—this is the essence of Chaplin's comedy. And in his creation he embodies the mentality of that lower-middle-class from which sprang Adolf Hitler. Clearly, the similarity between Charlie and the Führer is no accident—nor that Chaplin should be able to play Hynkel to such perfection. The giddy perplexity of the autocrat, his pathologic restlessness, the haunted dwarf in the huge palace halls with his megalomaniac fantasies, his Blitz-patronage of the arts, his hissing convulsive attack on the woman—this is a true, an illuminating piece of art. This is without question the real perfection in *The Great Dictator*.

However, what are we left with after we have seen this film? A ridiculous man, mad and cruel, who takes his delight in persecuting the poor and the weak, a man who regales himself by invading neighboring territory. Why?

Simply because he is mad and cruel. An individual, one concludes, whose elimination would restore peace and order to this pain-racked world. This is a view expressed at this very hour by many misguided people. It must surely be apparent now that much more is involved than the fight against a few criminals. This is a fight against a system, against fascism. Anyone who wants to make effective his fight against Hitler has to know this, and to show this.

Could such a subject actually be incorporated into a film? a work of art? a comedy? Is it possible to show in visual action abstract political theory, diplomatic chess games, economic intrigues? Is oppression and sadistic torture a source of laughter? Well, I think fascism is not only a possible subject for a film, but that it positively demands filming. And I am not at all sure but that satire is actually the best approach to it. Anyone who has seen fascism in action on the spot must have marveled at the divine justice that places its every villainy in the light of the sun: its meanness of spirit, the hollowness of its boasting, the coexistence of enormously contrasting social elements—they are all on the surface, openly exposed for all to see. There are unmistakable symbols in the streets, in the shops, in the offices—wherever people go in vain to seek their human rights. Just think of the May Day "celebrations" for the exploited and oppressed workingmen; the *Volksgemeinschaft*—that mole-maze of spying, informing, bribing, blackmailing, and robbing; the "cultivation" of science for creating devilish methods of destruction; the "cultivation" of the arts to the taste of a Goering! The Father of the People rushing through blocked-off streets in his bullet-proof car, mingling cordially with secret police disguised as joyous peasants and workers. Cheerless party members ordered to shout hate slogans aganist foreign governments. The inhuman mechanization of man by supermilitarism. These are the ingredients of a Chaplin film that anyone can see uncensored everywhere in day-to-day life under fascism. Fascism seeks to attain its evil aims through simulated virtue and hollow schemes for "public welfare." Is there any better subject for satire than the false front? Chaplin has always taught us that profound laughter reveals tragedy. Unfortunately, there is much more Chaplin in fascist reality than in *The Great Dictator*. In his attempt to brand fascism, Chaplin adopted many exterior aspects of the Nazi milieu, but I remember at least a dozen wisecracks invented by the victims of fascism themselves that convey a deeper insight and a more essential interpretation than anything in *The Great Dictator*.

Anti-Nazi films stress particularly the features of horror, violence, and cruelty. They have become a new kind of gangster film. For all their emotional effectiveness, I wonder if there is not a better method of political illumination. After all, the Nazis will tell you that a surgeon's work also looks rather gruesome. There are knives, there is blood. When you ask a Nazi about concentration camps and tortures and purges, his answer is that this is the only way of operating on a deadly cancer of corruption, of moral and physical decay, and destructive mentality. The searchingly anti-Nazi film would show rather how little this never-ending series of "operations" actually accomplishes. In treating the Jews, Chaplin stresses the sadness of their inhuman persecution, while the real approach of satire would seem to be to throw in relief the pointlessness of these proud Nazi victories over the few scared, helpless shopkeepers their speeches and illustrated papers have set up as a satanic and mysteriously strong enemy. There was an opportunity to present much more effectively the connection between the Nazi charge against the Jews of "race shaming" and the shameless Nazi pillage of Jewish money and property. It would even have been possible to explain, as Konrad Heiden did in his masterly book, how Hitler's anti-Semitism sprang from his early experiences with some clever Viennese Jews whom he was unable to manage; to show the psychopathology of a man too weak to live with his fellow-men on equal terms and whose solution was therefore to dominate them.

But Chaplin wanted to show the pitiful aspects of this persecution, choosing to create pity rather than understanding. To do this he had to paint his Jews like the funny but sad curly-bearded man whom he calls, I think, Mr. Mann, instead of like the white-haired Old Testament patriarch who plays the dignified martyr. The club strokes of the storm troopers had to be as abstract and harmless as the slapsticks of the old Keystone Kops. How far are Chaplin's "realistic" pogroms from giving an idea of the horrors really happening in Germany!

Chaplin succeeded in making tragedy arise out of the figure of his comic dictator. On the other hand, too much of his film wavers between the crude comedy tradition of throwing dishes into people's faces and the pathetic sermon on a brave, indignant girl. It has been suggested that the film's lack of homogeneity may be explained by the fact that when work started, as early as three years ago, it still seemed possible to make fun about Hitler, but that in the meantime the gigantic destruction spreading over Europe has made the subject more and more serious in Chaplin's mind. I find it difficult to understand how after five years of Hitler terror (and in the year XV of Mussolini's regime) the sensitive creator of *The Gold Rush* and *Modern Times* could still have considered fascists and fascism as something just funny. At any rate, the fact remains that in the last phase of his production Chaplin failed to translate Nazi violence and persecution into satire. Perhaps he felt himself too immediately touched by the events; it may be that he found himself unable to keep up the stylized manner against the ever-increasing naturalism of the materials with which he was working. Look at his Herring and Garbitsch. In them is nothing of the mythological sublimity of those swarthy, eye-rolling monsters that Charlie used to fight and to defeat in his earlier films. Rather there is a painful resemblance between this Garbitch and the Goebbels of *Confessions of a Nazi Spy*. Nothing of "Wotan's Mickey Mouse," as the people call Goebbels after a very Chaplinesque formula, nothing of the wretched little intellectual in the uniform of the smart warrior, the poor herald of a strong blond race, the actress-hunter. The real Goering's imposing façade becomes irresistibly comic only when he poses, as he does in reality, as the steel-hard air hero. Remember him breeding prehistoric aurochs on his estate near Berlin and hunting them with ancient spears; remember this official patron of the arts and his pornographic fresco gallery as described by Nevile Henderson and realize what chances for satire the film has missed.

And what about Mussolini? There are, of course, psychological differences between the German and the Italian dictator; and once Chaplin decided to show both of them it was necessary to create, for dramaturgic reasons, a contrast between these two personages. As a consequence, Mussolini appears as a good-natured, chubby fool—an interpretation that tends to support the dangerous belief that Italian fascism is not much more than a harmless Neapolitan puppet-show and that stresses unessential individual differences between the two dictators instead of showing that they are in reality two branches of the same tree.

One may also cite the first reel of *The Great Dictator* to show how Chaplin used marvelous raw material without drawing from it its full significance. In the World War sequence, Chaplin makes the little Jewish barber the hero. The whole sequence actually has very little inner connection with the film that it introduces, serving as a gag situation and an explanation, but little more. The World War sequence could have become a very essential introduction had the future dictator been its protagonist. For here too real life was the better director. Just imagine the Chaplinesque quixotism of the fanatic little corporal in the trenches, his strategic fantasies and foolhardy enterprises, his violent harangues on heroism to his skeptically smiling, tired comrades. It would have been possible to show where the man came from and how life molded him.

When Chaplin at last put the finishing touches to his film he must have realized by how much he had fallen short of his main purpose. And so, after nearly two hours of exposition, the puppet-master found it necessary to put his own head upon the stage and say directly what he had failed to convey artistically. A desperate attempt, moving because it is the open manifestation of an artist forsaken by his medium and, too, because it is the sincere expression of an honest, warm-hearted man; still this curtain speech proves once more that artistic unity and homogeneity are esthetic demands not simply for the sake of a pleasing order or harmony, but because without them no desired effect can ever be obtained. At the first sentences of that final speech, people were still laughing as they had been laughing at the little barber for the past two hours. Dictator Hynkel had preached, in the purest Chaplin style, the gospel of hate. Now, on the same platform, the little barber, dropping that style, failed to confute him.

Many years before, Charlie had told from a pulpit and in pantomime the tale of David and Goliath. *The Pilgrim* indicated that there is a Chaplin way of expressing David's challenge to violence, oppression, mechanization, and hypocrisy. If Chaplin had been able to perform this difficult task, the similarity between the little Jewish barber and Dictator Hynkel would perhaps have ceased to be merely accidental, as claimed in the opening subtitle.

Charles Chaplin is the only artist who holds the secret weapon of mortal laughter. Not the laughter of superficial gibing that self-complacently underrates the enemy and ignores the danger, but rather the profound laughter of the sage who despises physical violence, even the threat of death, because behind it he has discovered the spiritual weakness, stupidity, and falseness of his antagonist. Chaplin could have opened the eyes of a world enchanted by the spell of force and material success. But instead of unmasking the common enemy, fascism, Chaplin unmasked a single man, "The Great Dictator." And that is why I feel that this good film should have been better.

Films, Winter 1940

THE PHILADELPHIA STORY

OTIS FERGUSON

To judge whether *The Philadelphia Story* is more effective on the screen than it was on Broadway would be to raise a lot of useless issues, and cloud others. I think the thing to say is that it was originally constructed for the strict tightness of a few sets, and that in remaining faithful to it, the picture's producer (Joe Mankiewicz) had to make some of his successes the hollow victory of just overcoming obstacles. Two things have resulted from this: (1) the play has been opened out into natural shifting scenes, if not actually broadened in effect; (2) the story seems to slow up toward the end, where everything was talk anyway.

A great deal depends, for sense and meaning, on Katharine Hepburn as the central character; and there are things in the range of her personality too delicate and subtle for anything but the close, pliant observation of cameras. Here she is, as I did not find her coming through so clearly before, the high-strung but overpetted thoroughbred who must be broken to be released into the good stride of her nature; and here the breaking is a gradual and visible process at once painful, touching, and funny. You know the story and Philadelphia too, and there is little new to say about the work of Miss Hepburn, whose peculiar dry radiance and intelligence, whose metallic and even-mannered voice finding its special beauty, are known if not defined, easily imitated but never reproduced in their final style.

But the story is no mere vehicle; it was not written, picturized, or directed as such. Donald Ogden Stewart is credited with an exceptionally bright job of screenplay writing; George Cukor seems to sit with more authority in his director's chair than he has on many another such occasion of reverential transfer; and to have Cary Grant, James Stewart, Roland Young, Ruth Hussey, and John Halliday posted all about in key positions was a happy thing for all. Grant is perfectly gracious to a thankless part, winning sympathy and belief. Stewart keeps to his level of near-perfection as the impulsive, wrong-moving, ordinary guy, and certainly adds another star to his honor chart for the whole sequence of moonlight and four roses. Young Virginia Weidler has a good part and time for herself.

Having expended so much care to such effect, they might have considered also that it is only brooks in poems that go on forever without somebody's beginning to yawn, scratch, and wonder seriously whether it is the suspense or just his underwear that is climbing. They might have cut out the boob move of the writer proposing at the wedding and right before his own fiancée. They could have gone back through the last third and clipped lines of dialogue all along in the interest of general motion. They could, I suppose, have extended the very funny business at the expense of *Timelife* and its prose-bearing oracular baby-talk—though I wonder whether even the keen edge that is present as it is cuts any of the dull butter that must be out there haw-hawing at the performance and trundling up with a ring in its nose to the same newsstand afterward. But there is nothing served in figuring how to do something after someone has very well proved that it's done already because he did it. Though films like *The Philadelphia Story* do little to advance the art of pictures, they may help convince some of the more discerning among cultural slugabeds that when the movies want to turn their hand to anything, they can turn it. Or, what's he got that I haven't got?

The New Republic, December 9, 1940

At the risk of heaviness about Ferguson's joke, perhaps it should be noted that W. C. Fields's given names were in fact William Claude.

THE BANK DICK

OTIS FERGUSON

Woolchester Cowperthwaite Fields is among the great one-man shows. He has been able to write his name in lights since before the incandescent bulb was invented, and within his own special province he is still the funniest fraud who ever pitched them into the aisles from laughter. He started with a line of chatter and some balls and cigar boxes, which he juggled with a snore of comment and defiance of the laws of gravity, which quickly established him as a character, which character he gradually filled out to the full limits of burlesque and vaudeville and Follies skits. Since then the movies were invented and a form for them gradually developed. But nobody told him about this new invention; nobody was able. He made movie shorts of course, and they were wonderful; he did skits in feature pictures and they were wonderful too. But movies as something different he never heard of. They grew up, and he never found out which shell the pea was under, because he couldn't be bothered: that was just a rival pitch. This way, folks, test your skill, etc.

Biographers of The Incomparable, the Marvel of the Aged in Wood, will, I am sure, find it in the record that he was not only a bad boy in school but they had to change the numbers on the rooms to get him from one grade to the other. And that when he was kidnaped from upper third at the age of fourteen by a passing minstrel show he was already very unruly and set in his ways. That learning was the other fellow's game, and being a born pitchman he would never be a sucker for it; but that when he played he played for keeps. That when movies came along he took a look at his first camera and said, Why I can lick that, easiest thing in the world, yes—did you note what I did to them at the Palace by any chance? (You did, eh. . . .) And that even after he had got himself blackballed in every producer's office on the Coast, his firm belief was that any wheeze routine could be extended by gags and names like Throttlebottom to what the rest of the world was beginning to know as a modern film comedy.

He still believes it. His new movie was written by him and mostly directed by him and then stolen by him in the principal part. It is called *The Bank Dick* and it shows Fields in the uniform of a detective and all-around door man for the local bank (he was given the job as a reward, under the severest misapprehension). He gets into trouble as nobody else can, and gets out the same way; he is the harried man of family and emperor of the world, his address and resource are infinite except when approaching a simple flight of steps, he is fastidious to the high point of using his chaser for a finger bowl, he is dignity with a red nose, and courtly, and he has never truckled to any man, which would naturally not include small boys and his own shadow—which if it ever moves back a step he will make like he is going to wring its neck. He is W. C. Fields, which is a considerable sort of thing to be, and purely a joy to watch. But that is all the movie is about.

When the man is funny he is terrific, but in between the high points— and they are as good in stage device as in line and in character conception —what is the audience doing? The story is makeshift, the other characters are stock types, the only pace discernible is in the distance between drinks or the rhythm of the fleeting seconds it takes Fields to size up trouble coming and duck to hell out. The audience is asleep because this was never made as a picture. It is stiff and static and holds no interest outside of W. C. Fields—you don't care what happens to anybody else, you don't care what the outcome; you forget immediately if there was any. Today there are no one-man shows in good pictures, unless the man is a director, and even then he must have a script and people to work with. Today we ask that even such a genius of character act as W. C. Fields be built-in, and that the structure as a whole amount to something, however light or little.

I hoped once that he would some day be content not to run the whole show in his own way, and let someone write him into and direct him through a story infinitely more absorbing than anything he has ever done. It would be the story of one of the world's deathless fools, a snide and bulbous sort of man who knew the top from the bottom, having been on both; a man who could make a comeback and throw it away and make another, a man getting old and very sick, and still coming back to damn all and do it his way, with his legs weak and his face changed to puffy, still talking through his nose like a bugle and still touching here and there the springs of human laughter. In this dream story you could even call the character Throttlebottom, though we would know who he is; and though we don't know the end, you could make one that would bring home not only what a joy he has been, to the hearts of his countrymen, but how dear. The end would be that he made a picture called *The Bank Dick* in which he was a good part of his old and indomitable self, and which he was fully himself in writing, directing, acting, and atmosphering in the face of almost everything that ever happened in the movies. He was W. C. Fields in it, the trouper of all troupers once again. And the picture opened in Brooklyn.

The New Republic, December 30, 1940

THE GREAT MC GINTY

GILBERT SELDES

The best picture I've seen in many months is another tough one which stays longer but wobbles internally. It's *The Great McGinty,* and you can roll all the credits into one bundle and deliver it to the address of Preston Sturges. I seem to recall a lot of ballyhoo some five years ago about Mr. Sturges and his development of a new technique, as important to sound pictures as montage *à la russe* was to silents. (Probably it was *The Power and the Glory.*) Well, it didn't work then, and now without ballyhoo, Mr. Sturges has really worked out a new technique, which has passed unnoticed because the other things in the picture are so fresh and good. It does wobble amidships; it's uneven; but man and boy I've seen thousands of pictures, and highly praised ones at that, which weren't a patch on this one.

The toughness and the charm are all given to Brian Donlevy, the Great McGinty, who begins as a tramp voting thirty-seven times or so in an election and rises to being governor—at which point he reforms. And that isn't too incredible because he has married; there are some good ideas about sex and marriage implied in the simple and attractive conversations between Donlevy and Muriel Angelus (wife in name alone because she was his secretary and he married her only to win the election but finally he discovers her!). One of the most comic and at the same time most enchanting scenes in recent movies is the one in which McGinty reads a Peter Rabbit sort of story to his stepchildren; the mother signals to him that he can stop as the children have fallen asleep; but McGinty brushes her aside because *he* wants to know who it was that was coming down the road. Sometimes it is encouraging to see how effective simplicity can be.

The Great McGinty obviously started out to be two other pictures. I'd bet that a complete six-reeler lies on the cutting room floor. The opening— I hope I'm telling you something you already know—showed two men in a tropical bar; one had been honest all his life except for a single moment of temptation; the other had been a crook all his life until he turned honest

—and his crook-pals rounded on him so he fled the country. Of course the original intention was to tell both stories; perhaps to intercross them. Thank Heaven this didn't happen. The picture runs away with the theme; it just tells the story of a reasonably attractive scoundrel who becomes not too unreasonably honest. There's a trick O. Henry payoff, by the way. Don't give it a thought.

But you might give a thought to the fresh way Sturges has produced the picture. The tough dialogue is matched by short, snappy scenes; the picture seems to have wasted no time, no money. It flashes from small scene to small scene, with an occasional spread for variety; the incidents are brief; the story skips years when it wants to, making bridges by technical devices; it snaps along, never bogging down; it has real pace, the pace that its harsh and comic story requires.

Esquire, March 1941

CITIZEN KANE

JOHN MOSHER

The noise and the nonsense that have attended the release of *Citizen Kane* may for the time being befog the merit of this extraordinary film. Too many people may have too ready an inclination to seek out some fancied key in it, after the silly flurry in our press, and to read into the biography of its leading character extraneous resemblances to persons in actual life. There is a special kind of pleasure to be found in such research, and the success of the most commonplace movie often lies in the simple fact that it suggests one's neighbors, or the scandalous people who took the house on the corner one year, or the handsome bootlegger who used to call every week. *Citizen Kane* can hardly suggest the ways and habits of neighbors, at least to most householders, but it may remind some of revelations in Sunday supplements. To others, I suppose it will all seem more like Mars —just Mr. Orson Welles and his Mars again.

Since movies hitherto have commenced with a cast list and a vast directory of credits, we are promptly jolted out of our seats when *Citizen Kane* ignores this convention and slides at once into its story. For introduction, there is only a stylized and atmospheric hint of background, of shut high gates and formidable fencing, and this formal difference seems revolutionary enough to establish Mr. Welles's independence of the conventions. This independence, like fresh air, sweeps on and on throughout the movie, and in spite of bringing to mind, by elaborately fashioned decoration, a picture as old in movie history as *Caligari,* the irregularity of the opening sets a seal of original craftsmanship on what follows. Something new has come to the movie world at last.

Mr. Welles is not merely being smart, clever, or different. By the elliptical method he employs, he can trace a man's life from childhood to death, presenting essential details in such brief flashes that we follow a complex narrative simply and clearly and find an involved and specialized character fully depicted, an important man revealed to us. With a few breakfast scenes, the progress of a marriage is shown as specifically as though we had read the wife's diary. By a look and a gesture, electricians high above a stage describe the sad squawks an opera singer is giving below them. The use of an imaginary March of Time provides an outline which allows us to escape long exposition. Scenes in the great man's Xanadu never drag, never oppress one with useless trimmings, yet we get an immediate comprehension of the unique, absurd establishment, with its echoes and its art collection, and the one gag allowed ("Don't talk so loud. We're not at home") becomes just a reasonable statement.

Sometimes I thought there was too much shadow, that the film seemed to be performed in the dark. Mr. Welles likes a gloom. He blots out the faces of speakers, and voices come from a limbo when it is what is being said and not how people look that is important. Only once or twice, at times like these, does the film seem mannered. For the most part we are too absorbed in the story and its characters to observe any tricks, too swiftly carried on by its intense, athletic scenes.

Dorothy Comingore, George Coulouris, and Joseph Cotten are on the list of the fine players, but clearly it is Orson Welles himself, as Mr. Kane, the great millionaire publisher, the owner of Xanadu, the frustrated politician, the bejowled autocrat, the colossus of an earlier American era, who is the center and focus of all the interest of the film. By a novelist's device, we learn of this man through the comments of the few who have been close to him, the second wife's being the most sensational—that second wife whom he drives into the grotesque mortification of an operatic career for which she has no talent. The total impression, though, is not of something entirely monstrous. Mr. Kane does not come out of all this a melodrama villain. I think it is a triumph of the film, and proof of its solid value and of the sense of its director and all concerned, that a human touch is not lost. Sympathy for the preposterous Mr. Kane survives. Indeed, there is something about him which seems admirable. I can imagine that various rich gentlemen who own newspapers may find the characterization only right and proper, and claim that their sensitivity, like Mr. Kane's, has been misunderstood by their intimates, and others may recognize many a Mr. Kane among their competitors.

The New Yorker, May 3, 1941

Joy Davidman, a poet, had her first book, *Letter to a Comrade,* published in the Yale Series of Younger Poets in 1938. She published subsequent collections and edited anthologies of poetry.

CITIZEN KANE

JOY DAVIDMAN

Citizen Kane is a magnificent if unfinished portrait. Orson Welles went to Hollywood to break conventions, and he has succeeded in finding new and splendid ways of casting, writing, directing, photographing, and cutting motion pictures. He has united an admirable group of actors with a vigorous script and a startling technique. The result makes most experienced Hollywood directors look sick. There is only one fly in the oinment; Welles has not escaped one Hollywood convention, the smirking thesis that the important thing about a public figure is not how he treats his country but how he treats his women.

In consequence *Citizen Kane* is content to achieve a murderous study of the private life of a public egoist. Alleged (we take no chances) to concern a newspaper publisher whom we will not name, the film is calculated to stab its prototype in all his softest spots. Kane's character, built up in what one of the actors calls a jigsaw puzzle method, is presented by sending a reporter, after Kane's death, to interview those who knew him. We see first, a brilliantly handled March of Time sequence of Kane's life as it appears to the general public; then we see him through the eyes of, successively, his banker, his manager, his best friend, his mistress-wife, and his butler. The last piece drops into place, and Kane is summed up as a man who loved only himself, but demanded the love of the whole world as his birthright. His egoism destroys his marriages, alienates his friends, wrecks his political career, and brings him with iron inexorability to his death, a wretched, apoplectic old man alone in a dream castle crammed with meaningless possessions.

The portrait is beautifully done; if Kane were a private citizen, the film would be complete. But Kane is a publisher of enormous influence, an aspiring politician, a captain of industry, a friend of dictators; in short, what Mr. Roosevelt before his apostasy used to label a malefactor of great wealth. This, in real life, is his more important aspect; yet in the film it is given only occasional and casual mention. In two hours there is not one shot of Kane performing any significant political action. He makes love, he makes meaningless speeches; he goes to Europe and the opera; he rushes in and out of newspaper offices. We are told that he exerts great influence on the people of America. But we never see him doing it. True, there are references to his instigation of the Spanish-American War, his hobnobbing with Hitler, his insincere pretense of speaking for the common man. But how does he instigate the war? what is behind his appearance with Hitler on a balcony? how does he betray the common man? There is not even a hint. His only visible violation of journalistic ethics is an insistence upon favorable reviews of his blonde wife's appalling opera singing, and his only political activity seems to be getting caught in a love nest during a campaign. Not one glimpse of the actual content of his newspapers is afforded us. One or two advertised scenes of political relevance, indeed, appear to have been cut out of the picture. As a result the audience is left with a vast confusion as to what Kane really stands for in public life. This grotesque inadequacy in the midst of plenty keeps *Citizen Kane* from fulfilling its promises. In place of an analysis of Kane's true significance, the picture resorts to the trick of giving him a mysterious dying speech, supposed to be "the real clue to Kane," the sentimental explanation of which is coyly delayed until the fadeout.

Considered for its technique alone, however, *Citizen Kane* is worth a couple of visits. Sometimes splendid, sometimes merely showy, it is always interesting. The device of telling Kane's history no less than five times is ingeniously managed to supplement and intensify rather than to repeat. Welles has achieved the miracle of making photography "unphotographic"; instead of the usual unimaginative reproduction of scenes and faces, *Citizen Kane's* camera seizes on a significant detail, emphasizes it in a flash, and swoops on to the next point. Like painting, it stresses the important; like poetry, it suggests far more than it says. Needless to say, this new technique is far from perfect. The staccato brevity of the earlier sequences is painfully confusing, and at times the story seems to be told entirely in a series of montages. There are far too many trick camera angles, too many fantastic combinations of light and shadow, indicating an incomplete translation of Welles's famous stage technique into screen terms. Frequently he lets his showmanship run away with him, preferring to astound rather than to convince. The construction of the film, otherwise magnificent, is weakened by the introduction of irrelevant suspense about the meaning of Kane's dying murmur, "Rosebud." Yet *Citizen Kane,* technically, may well serve to inspire a new school of filmmaking.

It is hardly necessary to add that the picture is brilliantly acted. Welles himself makes the overpowering and violent personality of Kane believable. The Mercury Actors are what Hollywood has needed for years; George

Coulouris as the pompous banker, and Joseph Cotten as Leland, the honest friend who serves as a contrast to Kane, are superlative where all are good. And Welles's Hollywood discovery, Dorothy Comingore, is the most astonishing young actress since Garbo was a pup. To emotional power and versatility she unites an exquisite beauty as yet unremodeled by makeup artists. Bernard Herrmann's musical score is not the least of the film's distinctions, and Gregg Toland deserves as much praise as Welles for the camera work. The final word on *Citizen Kane,* in spite of its limitations, is that this reviewer is going to see it again—even if she has to pay to get in.

The New Masses, May 13, 1941

Anthony Bower contributed frequently to *The Nation* in the early 1940s.

CITIZEN KANE

ANTHONY BOWER

Citizen Kane has probably had more advance publicity of one kind or another than any other picture yet produced. Practically everybody connected with the production has been reported on the verge of a lawsuit. Some have said that all this uproar was nothing but exceptionally well-handled publicity, while others have sworn that William Randolph Hearst was determined to prevent the picture's release. Finally it was announced that the picture would definitely be released in the near future, and the press assembled at last week's preview in a state of great expectancy.

Many would probably have rejoiced to find producer, director, actor, and part-author Orson Welles's ambitious first effort in Hollywood not an unqualified success: after all, the man had no previous cinema experience, and if reports were true he had walked into the studio and produced on a very low budget a film which was a masterpiece.

It must be stated here that no amount of advance publicity or ballyhoo could possibly ruin the effect of this remarkable picture. It is probably the most original, exciting, and entertaining picture that has yet been produced in this country, and although it may lack their subtlety it can certainly be placed in the same bracket as the very best prewar French productions.

The film may not have been inspired by the life of William Randolph

Hearst, but the story of Charles Foster Kane, as unfolded in the picture, certainly bears a remarkable resemblance to Hearst's career. The incident concerning the Spanish-American War, the vast collection of useless antiques acquired by Kane, and certain details such as the picnic, with the guests compelled to spend the night under canvas, are familiar parts of the Hearst legend; and the castle of Xanadu, Kane's retreat from the world, with its endless acres and private zoo, is more than reminiscent of San Simeon. If Mr. Hearst decides, as many others undoubtedly will, that the film is only the most thinly disguised version of his life story, he will perhaps be favorably impressed with the sympathy and understanding with which the subject has been treated, and may even be delighted to have provided material for a drama of almost classical proportions.

The film opens with the death of Kane, a very old man, alone in the colossal, ugly monument to his wealth and power—Xanadu. A sort of March of Time dealing with Kane's life is then presented. The producers of this short are dissatisfied, finding it too superficial and impersonal, and are determined to obtain more intimate details of the man's personal history. The remainder of the picture deals with the information on Kane's life and character obtained respectively from his guardian, his chief assistant, a dramatic critic who was once his best friend, his second wife, and his butler. This technique of unfolding the story necessitates five separate flashbacks and creates a certain amount of confusion which is more than compensated for by the powerful effect obtained by the gradual illumination of character, until with the click of the final switch he is fully revealed—empty, lonely, and unhappy, a victim of his own personal power.

This excellent cinematic material Welles has embellished with brilliant directorial, pictorial, and dramatic touches. He breaks, with the greatest effect, practically every photographic rule in the business, employing very few close-ups, playing whole scenes with the faces of the performers in shadow, using lighting to enhance the dramatic value of the scene rather than the personal appearance of the actor. He is, in fact, one of the first Hollywood directors really to exploit the screen as a medium, and it is interesting to note that in doing this he has used an entire cast with no previous screen experience.

The acting both of Welles and of the rest of the Mercury Theater cast is excellent. Dorothy Comingore as Kane's second wife, whom he forces to sing in opera to gratify his ego, is particularly effective; so is Joseph Cotten as the dramatic critic. Welles himself gives an amazing performance as Kane, equally convincing in youth, middle age, and senility. The photographer, Gregg Toland, has achieved some wonderful effects, particularly the scene in the projection room of the newsreel company.

The picture has made a tremendous impression in Hollywood. Charlie

Chaplin is reported to be prepared to back any venture that Welles may have in mind. Perhaps when the uproar has died down it will be discovered that the film is not quite so good as it is considered now, but nevertheless Hollywood will for a long time be in debt to Mr. Welles.

The Nation, April 26, 1941

Native Son, a dramatization of Richard Wright's novel, was staged by Orson Welles in New York after he finished *Citizen Kane* but five weeks before the picture opened.[15] "Mr. Nathan" was George Jean Nathan (see p. 294), at this time writing for *Esquire.*

Radio Boy Makes Good
(CITIZEN KANE)

GILBERT SELDES

I do not call Orson Welles a radio boy to remind people either of his early terrorism or his later development as a first class producer of radio drama. On two successive days I listened to and looked at the works by which he is today being judged: his production of *Native Son* and his creation of *Citizen Kane;* and all through both, which were miles above anything in the theater or the movies of the year, I was aware of a skillful radio man, a man trained to know the value of sound, and even of the despised "sound effects." I do not mean that the overwhelming effectiveness of Welles's methods derives entirely from his experiences in radio; they are a factor, and the circumstance that he has used his radio experience for stage and screen work proves him far more intelligent than most people in any of the three mediums.

My thank-god-not-too-often-too-amiable colleague Mr. Nathan has certainly conveyed to you some sense of the atmosphere in which *Native Son* plays; as I haven't even yet read the book, which the play is said to follow closely, I shan't go over the story again. Actually the production of the play reminded me a little of the American expressionists; they, too, were liberal in outlook, experimental in method; and some of the same characters occur: the rich girl, half tart, half earnest radical; the noble savage, in this case a simple, not intellectual Negro, with a vile temper and a tendency toward crime; the aggressive young man radical; and so on. Occasionally scenes were telescoped, condensed out of all nature, and these "imagist" scenes came between straight realistic passages, which was confusing. But Welles had brought several new technical tricks and a new kind of suspense to the theater. In fact, he used both the old and the new, and the combination makes the suspense of even a Hitchcock picture feel like nothing more than a slightly stretched rubber band.

He has used his own suspense in *Citizen Kane,* also, so it is worth examining a little. In *Native Son* you simply wait for something to happen; you wait for the central action to start. You begin with a group of poor Negroes in a one-room tenement, four of them sleeping, getting up, snarling at one another, the big boy furious at his mother's piety, angry at the welfare worker who offers a job. From that time on you wait for an event; and that is Welles's suspense, because you don't know what the event will be. You only feel that it will be violent, maybe tragic. And the dramatization of the story helps, because you are running into a holdup, but you detour, and you get the boy set in a job, still a bit surly, but on the right road; then you see the event beginning to take shape: the employer's idle daughter, the idle white half-patronizing, half-envying the Negro, egging him on to social revolt and sexual conquest. That leads to murder—not a crime of passion, merely the boy's attempt to prevent the girl from betraying his presence to her blind mother; merely that, at first, anyhow.

That scene is not suspense, but grim horror; in the pursuit, suspense begins again: the good Hitchcock suspense which depends on the accidental coming together of certain circumstances; the good suspense of the criminal cornered and shot at from all sides; there is even an expressionistic trial at the end, so you have the suspense of not knowing the answer till the end.

You can't do that in the theater; experts say you can't. You can't keep people waiting half the night before your main action is even hinted. Well, you can. You can if you can create characters and circumstances which will keep people interested; that's all. I've forgotten Welles's degree of familiarity with the daytime serial of radio; but he has heard of it; he knows that the moment people are concerned with a character they are content to wait; just as they are content to wait for the people they know to do or say something interesting. It is only when characters are not absorbing that we demand action at once.

Welles has connected the scenes of *Native Son* with musical bridges; he has invented reasons for bringing on music; you have heard the sounds of the city, full of outcries and motors, or dying down; the locomotives shunting in the railyards, in balance with the searchlights hunting for the hidden criminal. Sound has always been there, creating atmosphere.

One other man seems to know about the use of sound to create pictures. It is Robert Edmond Jones, who, in one way or another, gets to know everything about the theater, and most of it exactly right. Jones has written a book on The Dramatic Imagination; he speaks of radio's way of inducing the sense of place by means of "spoken descriptions and so-called 'sound effects.' These devices have caught the imagination of radio audiences . . . It is odd that our playwrights and stage designers have not yet sensed the limitless potentialities of this new enhancement of the spoken word. A magical new medium of scenic evocation is waiting to be pressed into service."

Mr. Welles has made a start.

In *Citizen Kane* he has gone further. He has created specific psychological effects by use of filters and other devices of the sound engineers. He has given you the effect of space—and of the feeling characters have for one another—by the artificial timber he has given their voices. He has played the tinkle of a glass, the climax of an orchestra, and the blacking out of a light in a window, in tremendous counterpoint. The whole picture has a web of sound, a pattern traced as surely as it has a pictorial pattern, and an intellectual one.

That, by the way, is its supreme virtue: it has sense, in every medium it uses; it has—so emphatically that you can't miss it—a single guiding intelligence, operating right through; the errors of judgment rise from the same intelligence, from a person knowing what he wants, going ahead and getting it—once in every forty minutes or so, that person wanted the wrong thing for about a minute—and you get a dull or a stupid spot. But you have to go back to the days of Griffith, and to the almost forgotten days of one or two Russian and German directors, to catch that feeling of a sure hand *directing* the course of the picture. Our directors generally tell an actor what to do; but the director who makes a picture go in a certain direction is exceedingly rare among us. Welles had it written into his contract that he should write, if he wished, direct, and act in his own pictures; that's the story and with the story came the cackles from Hollywood about this bearded boy who was going to come an awful cropper, because didn't even the great Thalberg put six men merely on writing; didn't Selznick have three directors in succession on this success—or that flop? Thalberg had his reasons, and Selznick, too, for all I know; Thalberg wasn't an effective writer, nor a good director; he was a producer of genius, who could combine the work of others. But not one picture bearing his name has the unity of *Citizen Kane*—the unity inside, which makes everything in it ten thousand times more effective than it would otherwise be—because each item multiplies the effectiveness of all the others.

You have heard it said that this is a travesty on the life of Mr. Hearst. Maybe. There are touches of the Thaw legend, touches of even earlier episodes among the rich and unruly. Welles apparently courted scandal when he threw together four or five of the most notable features of one man's life, and added others which hadn't happened, but easily could have, to the same person. Maybe it will serve Welles right if the newspaper stuff in the picture will prove so dull that people will walk out on it. The struggle between men—not over a woman—may be box office poison. Everything else in the picture is Broadway's gift to Hollywood. From recent reports, I gather Hollywood is grateful. For Welles has shown Hollywood how to make movies.

You wonder what good Hollywood directors mean when they say that after seeing *Citizen Kane,* they feel they've never made a real picture in their lives. And when you start looking at *Citizen Kane* you see the camera traveling up, up, up, an enormous fence, with a "no trespass" sign; and presently it's a cage of some obscene monkeys; and gradually a process-shot of a castle on a hillside—and soon you're through the casements and a man lies dying, and the light goes out as the object he holds in his hand falls to the ground; he utters a word . . . and almost at once you are seeing a March-of-Timish newsreel obituary of *Citizen Kane.* What is different? What is so new?

The intercutting of sound-and-picture, the beautiful counterpoint of movement and music—that is simply done better than most people do it. The slow suspense of the opening is pictorially better; the angles, here and later, of the camera, are the angles of the German cinematographers, brought to American uses, making sense. (Incidentally, about half of the picture must have been shot with a low camera, making Kane and several other figures loom over you, slightly distorted; a doubtful effect.) The cutting is the Russian montage system brought to American uses, making sense, as it made once for the Russians and was then translated into a trick.

You must remember Welles spent some time in Hollywood; the cacklers had their fun when nothing—absolutely not a foot of film—resulted for nearly a year; the flattest and most foolish of actors played practical jokes and told the gossip columnists about them, but Welles was working; he was studying pictures; he knew what he wanted a picture to look like, to sound like, and to feel like. That is the new thing. That is revolutionary. And the second revolution is that he made the picture sound and look and feel just that way. The third revolution, somewhat delayed, is in the public exhibition of the picture. If the scandal doesn't arouse excitement in the backwoods, the tremendous sense of actuality in the picture may offend the lotus eaters. It will be a pity, but only for a little while. Welles can't fail now in making pictures.

It's a long picture and the Wellesian suspense keeps Kane out of it for a long time; you see him shrouded in gloom on a deathbed; you catch a glimpse of him in a marvelously faked old-fashioned newsreel with Teddy Roosevelt, as part of the Time on the March reel; you see him as a bad little boy; but you hear of him for an interminable time before he appears as a young man. (I had by that time become so engrossed in the picture that I didn't even recognize Welles as the actor in the part; it's a good job, but the picture towers over it.)

Again, Welles has created your interest in a person by keeping the main action of his life away from you, so that you're almost breathless when he arrives upon the scene.

You can say, with justice, that the story he told was obviously derived from the lives of some of the most colorful and exciting characters in America; so he had that to start with. That's true, and his handling of the stories is good, too; so he gets credit. There is a foolishness about "rosebud"—the dying man's last word and the silly idea, which would never, I hope, occur to an editor of *The March of Time,* that if one knew why he said that word, the meaning of his whole life would be revealed to us. That is the only bit of stale stuff in the picture; and incidentally it's a phony; because we do find out and nothing is any clearer than it was. Apart from that, and the necessity of interviewing half a dozen people, with flashbacks for their stories, the manipulation of the narrative is skillful: if there's too much talk, it's remarkably easy on the ear; the Hollywood clichés have been erased from the script.

They have also been erased from the acting. None of the principals are old troupers of Hollywood; many come from Welles's earlier theatrical work. And they hardly ever are allowed to fall into the postures, gestures, grimaces, and tonalities of Hollywood. They are as fresh-seeming as the faces of peasants were when we first glimpsed them in Russian films. They talk and look like human beings; they are.

In the past six months I've seen a lot of regular studio pictures which I have liked; and there is always John Ford who, with not one-tenth of Welles's material, can do a great picture. But the Hollywood product has become remarkably slick and smooth and polished; and every studio turns out three pictures about someone who isn't married to the person with whom, for some reason, he or she must share a bedroom. Heaven knows these are wittier jobs than the movies of 1926; they are downright good entertainment; but there isn't any character to them, no stamina, no formative, energetic, pushing intelligence which takes a theme at the beginning, develops it, and brings it to a legitimate end.

Orson Welles hasn't shown Hollywood how to get these qualities; he has shown them that you can make a picture by using these qualities. Moreover, the next great picture will not necessarily be another semiscandalous biography—as of Warren Gamaliel Harding. It may be a romance. Will the next great picture be made by another newcomer, or by an old hand? I don't know. It will be made by someone who forgets a lot—forgets even a lot that Welles has taught—and gets down to the roots of his subject, as Welles has done. For you feel, at times, as if Welles had known everything there is to know of all the techniques of the motion picture, and had used them better than anyone else has used them in a generation; and at other times you feel that he has made such a moving picture as a man of genius would have made if he had never seen a picture before in his life—but was a genius in the monstrously difficult art of writing with images.

And just for a bit of mockery, Welles has made exactly the kind of picture that half-a-dozen writers have been describing and predicting for years. Some of the writers went to work in Hollywood, too, and forgot to make their picture. Welles never, to my knowledge, said a word about the movies one way or the other. But he has made the movies young again, by filling them with life.

Esquire, August 1941

NOTES

(After a book's first listing, it is referred to
only by the author's last name.)

Part One
THE BEGINNINGS

1. Lewis Jacobs, *The Rise of the American Film* (New York: Teachers College Press, 1968), p. 5.

2. Robert M. Henderson, *D. W. Griffith: The Years at Biograph* (New York: Farrar, Straus & Giroux, 1970), pp. 158, 193.

3. James L. Limbacher, *Four Aspects of the Film* (New York: Brussel & Brussel, Inc., 1969), p. 4.

4. Terry Ramsaye, *A Million and One Nights* (New York: Simon and Schuster, 1964), p. 511.

5. Mrs. D. W. Griffith, *When the Movies Were Young* (New York: Dover Publications, 1969), p. 246.

6. Benjamin B. Hampton, *History of the American Film Industry* (New York: Dover Publications, 1970), p. 128. Ramsaye, p. 819.

7. Jacobs, pp. 102, 134.

8. M. O. Lounsbury, *The Origins of American Film Criticism, 1909–1939* (New York: Arno Press, 1972), p. 28.

9. Jacobs, pp. 81–84.

10. Henderson, pp. 67, 199.

11. Arthur Knight, *The Liveliest Art* (New York: Macmillan, 1957), p. 21.

12. *The New York Times*, October 10, 1909.

13. A. Nicholas Vardac, *Stage to Screen* (New York: Benjamin Blom, 1968), p. 90. Vachel Lindsay, *The Art of the Moving Picture* (New York: Liveright, 1970), pp. 180–84.

14. Jacobs, p. 134.

15. Henderson, p. 101.

16. Edward Wagenknecht, *The Movies in the Age of Innocence* (Norman: University of Oklahoma Press, 1962), p. 58. (See also photographs, pls. 5–7.)

17. Brooks Atkinson, *Broadway* (New York: Macmillan, 1970), p. 88. Quoted from *The New York Dramatic Mirror*, n.d.

Part Two
THE FEATURE FILM

1. Henderson, pp. 153–57.
2. Jacobs, pp. 91–92.
3. Georges Sadoul, *Dictionnaire des Cinéastes* (Paris: Éditions du Seuil, 1965), p. 106.
4. Georges Sadoul, *Dictionnaire des Films* (Paris: Éditions du Seuil, 1965), p. 211.
5. Walt Whitman, *Democratic Vistas,* in *The Portable Walt Whitman* (New York: Viking, 1945), pp. 393–94. Also see Lindsay, passim, on the democratizing influence of film. In *The Moving Picture World,* April 9, 1910, Jane Elliott Snow writes of "The Workingman's Theater": "The reason why the motion picture show is the workingman's theater is because it comes within the limits of his time and means. The theater proper is held of late hours, unless it be the matinee, which comes when all working people are engaged in their legitimate occupations. It is rarely that a person who works from eight to ten hours a day feels like spending the evenings up to ten or twelve o'clock at a place of amusement. But at a picture show one can step in and spend an hour very delightfully, and in many cases very profitably. Then the cost of the thing appeals to people with limited incomes. Few men with such incomes would think they could afford to take their wives and children to a place of amusement, where the least expense would be from twenty-five to fifty cents each; but they could take them where they only had to pay five or ten cents each."
6. Theodore Huff, *Charlie Chaplin* (London: Cassell, 1952), p. 34. Davide Turconi, *Mack Sennett* (Rome: Edizioni dell'Ateneo, 1961), p. 108.
7. Kalton C. Lahue and Terry Brewer, *Kops and Custards* (Norman: University of Oklahoma Press, 1968), pp. 58, 74.
8. Kenneth Macgowan, *Behind the Screen* (New York: Delacorte, 1965), p. 198.
9. Lindsay, p. 85.
10. Lindsay, pp. 71–74.
11. Fred Silva, ed., *Focus on Birth of a Nation* (Englewood Cliffs, N.J.: Prentice-Hall, 1971), p. 26.
12. Lounsbury, pp. 43–50.
13. Macgowan, p. 180.
14. Donald W. McCaffrey, ed., *Focus on Chaplin* (Englewood Cliffs, N.J.: Prentice-Hall, 1971), pp. 69–70.
15. Macgowan, pp. 204–5.
16. Hugo Münsterberg, *The Film* (New York: Dover, 1970). Originally published as *The Photoplay* (New York: Appleton, 1916).
17. Penelope Gilliatt, "Le Meneur de Jeu," in *The New Yorker,* August 23, 1969, p. 52.
18. Iris Barry, *D. W. Griffith* (New York: Museum of Modern Art, 1965).

This information comes from the annotated film list added to the book by Eileen Bowser.

19. Gilbert Seldes, *The Seven Lively Arts* (New York: A. S. Barnes, 1962), p. 27.

20. Arthur Calder-Marshall, *The Innocent Eye* (New York: Harcourt, Brace & World, 1963), passim. Lewis Jacobs, ed., *The Documentary Tradition* (New York: Hopkinson & Blake, 1971), p. 7.

21. Lounsbury, p. 134.

22. Harold Lloyd, *An American Comedy* (New York: Dover, 1971), p. 124.

23. Charles Chaplin, *My Autobiography* (New York: Simon and Schuster, 1964), p. 300.

24. Kenneth W. Munden, ed., *The American Film Institute Catalog: Feature Films 1921–1930* (New York: Bowker, 1971), p. 412.

25. Hans Pensel, *Seastrom and Stiller in Hollywood* (New York: Vantage, 1969), pp. 55–64. Norman Zierold, *Garbo* (New York: Popular Library, n.d.), pp. 26–27.

26. Lounsbury, p. 159.

27. Lounsbury, pp. 188–89.

28. Josef von Sternberg, *Fun in a Chinese Laundry* (New York: Macmillan, 1965), pp. 138–39.

29. Jacobs, p. 307.

Part Three
SOUND

1. Limbacher, p. 207.

2. Zierold, p. 44.

3. Munden, p. 20.

4. John McCabe, *Mr. Laurel and Mr. Hardy* (New York: Doubleday, 1961), p. 182.

5. Jay Leyda, *Kino* (New York: Macmillan, 1960), p. 272. Leyda writes: "A microcosm of the political world hurtling through the night on rails towards a certain geographical point and an uncertain destiny is such a dramatic idea that it is no wonder that it has been often repeated in film history, almost as effectively in Sternberg's *Shanghai Express*."

6. Herman G. Weinberg, *Josef von Sternberg* (New York: Dutton, 1967), pp. 54, 236.

7. This review was unsigned, but it is credited to Barrett by *The Film Index* (New York: H. W. Wilson, 1941), p. 337.

8. Sternberg, p. 151.

9. This review was unsigned, but it is credited to Hamilton by *The Film Index,* p. 399.

10. This review, signed with the initials W. A. B., is credited to Barrett by *The Film Index,* p. 520.

11. Harold Clurman, *The Fervent Years* (New York: Hill and Wang, 1957), p. 138.

12. Gerald Rabkin, *Drama and Commitment* (Bloomington: Indiana University Press, 1964), p. 154.

13. Rabkin, pp. 47–48, 66.

14. Meyer Levin, *In Search* (Paris: Author's Press, 1950), p. 128. *The New York Times Book Review,* December 12, 1971, p. 27.

15. For details about the production of *Native Son* and the writing of *Citizen Kane* see *Run-through* by John Houseman (New York: Simon and Schuster, 1972), who was intimately involved in both.

BIBLIOGRAPHY

(An alphabetical list of books and articles
cited in the notes preceding.)

ATKINSON, BROOKS. *Broadway*. New York: Macmillan, 1970.

BARRY, IRIS. *D. W. Griffith*. New York: Museum of Modern Art, 1965.

CALDER-MARSHALL, ARTHUR. *The Innocent Eye*. New York: Harcourt, Brace & World, 1963.

CHAPLIN, CHARLES. *My Autobiography*. New York: Simon and Schuster, 1964.

CLURMAN, HAROLD. *The Fervent Years*. New York: Hill and Wang, 1957.

Film Index, The. New York: H. W. Wilson, 1941.

GILLIAT, PENELOPE. "Le Meneur de Jeu" in *The New Yorker*, August 23, 1969.

GRIFFITH, MRS. D. W. *When the Movies Were Young*. New York: Dover, 1969.

HAMPTON, BENJAMIN B. *History of the American Film Industry*. New York: Dover, 1970.

HENDERSON, ROBERT M. *D. W. Griffith: The Years at Biograph*. New York: Farrar, Straus & Giroux, 1970.

HOUSEMAN, JOHN. *Run-through*. New York: Simon and Schuster, 1972.

HUFF, THEODORE. *Charlie Chaplin*. London: Cassell, 1952.

JACOBS, LEWIS, ed. *The Documentary Tradition*. New York: Hopkinson & Blake, 1971.

————. *The Rise of the American Film*. New York: Teachers College Press, 1968.

KNIGHT, ARTHUR. *The Liveliest Art*. New York: Macmillan, 1957.

LAHUE, KALTON C., and TERRY BREWER. *Kops and Custards*. Norman: University of Oklahoma Press, 1968.

LEVIN, MEYER. *In Search*. Paris: Author's Press, 1950.

LEYDA, JAY. *Kino*. New York: Macmillan, 1960.

LIMBACHER, JAMES L. *Four Aspects of the Film*. New York: Brussel & Brussel, Inc., 1969.

LINDSAY, VACHEL. *The Art of the Moving Picture*. New York: Liveright, 1970.

LLOYD, HAROLD. *An American Comedy*. New York: Dover, 1971.

LOUNSBURY, M. O. *The Origins of American Film Criticism, 1909–1939*. New York: Arno Press, 1972.

MACGOWAN, KENNETH. *Behind the Screen.* New York: Delacorte, 1965.

MC CABE, JOHN. *Mr. Laurel and Mr. Hardy.* New York: Doubleday, 1961.

MC CAFFREY, DONALD W., ed. *Focus on Chaplin.* Englewood Cliffs, N.J.: Prentice-Hall, 1971.

MUNDEN, KENNETH W., ed. *The American Film Institute Catalog: Feature Films 1921–1930.* New York: R. R. Bowker, 1971.

MÜNSTERBERG, HUGO. *The Film.* New York: Dover, 1970.

New York Times, The. October 10, 1909.

New York Times Book Review, The. December 12, 1971.

PENSEL, HANS. *Seastrom and Stiller in Hollywood.* New York: Vantage, 1969.

RABKIN, GERALD. *Drama and Commitment.* Bloomington: Indiana University Press, 1964.

RAMSAYE, TERRY. *A Million and One Nights.* New York: Simon and Schuster, 1964.

SADOUL, GEORGES. *Dictionnaire des Cinéastes.* Paris: Éditions du Seuil, 1965.

———. *Dictionnaire des Films.* Paris: Éditions du Seuil, 1965.

SELDES, GILBERT. *The Seven Lively Arts.* New York: A. S. Barnes, 1962.

SILVA, FRED, ed. *Focus on Birth of a Nation.* Englewood Cliffs, N.J.: Prentice-Hall, 1971.

SNOW, JANE ELLIOTT. "The Workingman's Theater," in *The Moving Picture World,* April 9, 1910.

STERNBERG, JOSEF VON. *Fun in a Chinese Laundry.* New York: Macmillan, 1965.

TURCONI, DAVIDE. *Mack Sennett.* Rome: Edizioni dell'Ateneo, 1961.

VARDAC, A. NICHOLAS. *Stage to Screen.* New York: Benjamin Blom, 1968.

WAGENKNECHT, EDWARD. *The Movies in the Age of Innocence.* Norman: University of Oklahoma Press, 1962.

WEINBERG, HERMAN G. *Josef von Sternberg.* New York: E. P. Dutton, 1967.

WHITMAN, WALT. *The Portable Walt Whitman.* New York: Viking, 1945.

ZIEROLD, NORMAN. *Garbo.* New York: Popular Library, n.d.

INDEX